Just Enough to Put Him Away Decent

Just Enough to Put Him Away Decent

Death Care, Life Extension, and the Making of a Healthier South, 1900–1955

KRISTINE M. MCCUSKER

UNIVERSITY OF ILLINOIS PRESS
Urbana, Chicago, and Springfield

1 2 3 4 5 C P 5 4 3 2 1
∞ This book is printed on acid-free paper.

Library of Congress Cataloging-in-Publication Data
Names: McCusker, Kristine M., author.
Title: Just enough to put him away decent : death care, life extension, and the making of a healthier South, 1900–1955 / Kristine M. McCusker.
Description: Urbana : University of Illinois Press, 2023. | Includes bibliographical references and index.
Identifiers: LCCN 2022054744 (print) | LCCN 2022054745 (ebook) | ISBN 9780252045080 (hardcover) | ISBN 9780252087219 (paperback) | ISBN 9780252054402 (ebook)
Subjects: LCSH: Death—Social aspects—Southern States—History—20th century. | Burial—Social aspects—Southern States—History—20th century. | Life expectancy—Southern States—History—20th century. | Medical care—Southern States—History—20th century. | Discrimination in medical care—Southern States—History—20th century. | Southern States—Race relations—History—20th century.
Classification: LCC HQ1073.5.U62 S686 2023 (print) | LCC HQ1073.5.U62 (ebook) | DDC 306.90973—dc23/eng/20230110
LC record available at https://lccn.loc.gov/2022054744
LC ebook record available at https://lccn.loc.gov/2022054745

For Katie Lou and Grace

and

in loving memory of Jo Wintker

Contents

Acknowledgments

It has taken a long time to finish this book and my list of thank-yous is extensive. I want to first thank Samantha Cantrell for helping me win a National Institutes of Health/National Library of Medicine (NIH) grant #1 G13 LM010074–01 in 2009. The grant paid for two years of research as well as time off from teaching so I could travel to southern archives. It also paid for a trip to the National Funeral Directors and Morticians Association's 2010 conference where I conducted oral interviews. I am grateful to the Association's former director, Sharon Seay, and the membership for welcoming me to their conference. Prior to 2009, I also received fellowships from the Virginia Museum of History and Culture (a Mellon grant), from Duke University (John Hope Franklin Fellowship) and a Non-Instructional Assignment from my home institution, Middle Tennessee State University (MTSU). These grants allowed me to do early research that eventually led to the NIH grant.

Helping me organize the material was a stellar group of student assistants and others who provided crucial information, including Jenny Epp, Samantha Jackson, Lauren Pate Lawson, Jillian Smith, and Steven Lamar Thomas. Robbie Roydsden took me to his family home in East Tennessee and showed me the proximity of his family's graveyard to the tumbledown shack they used to live in. Keneisha Mosely organized my archives so I could find my documents once again, Amy NeeSmith caught a ton of errors in my endnotes, and Michaela Wegman got me over the finish line. Faith Bagley held down the fort when I was busy. Many thanks to former students who said, "How are the dead people?" and my Just Love Coffee friends who kept asking, "Aren't you done with that book yet?" Ashley Carter reminded me why the dead continue to matter in the South; Mary Probert showed up and cared for me and my dogs; and David and Stacey, and their kids, Peyton, Andie, and Hayes, were examples of real grace in a brutal time. Cheers to my friends and family at St. Paul's Episcopal Church for their support.

I am especially grateful to my colleagues who reviewed successive drafts and told me to keep going. I am deeply grateful to my friend Antoinette van Zelm, who read the first draft. As it was an initial seven hundred pages, her reading it was quite a feat. Stacey Owen taught me about Freud, and David Rowe helped me with the section on Episcopalians. Steven M. Stowe wrote seven pages of comments (single spaced!) that made this a much better book. Mark McGarvie knows how to write a really good footnote. I am also deeply grateful to the University of Illinois Press reviewers who said that fourteen years of work had not gone to waste. In each of these cases, my reviewers boosted my confidence while helping me refine important parts. Any errors that remain are obviously my own. Finally, I am really, really happy that Laurie Matheson at the University of Illinois Press is a patient, supportive person, because it was a long time between books.

The NIH's money allowed me to travel to archives across the South. I spent my first year or so of research at the Tennessee State Library and Archives, and I am grateful for the archivists' help as I confronted the large number of death documents in their holdings that showed the promise of this work. I also thank Patrick County (Virginia) Historical Society's Greg Arens who provided me information on Mabel Clark, and Joe Smith from the Campbell County (Tennessee) Historical Society who took me to Bakers Forge Cemetery. DeLisa Harris provided me with last-minute documents from Fisk University's William Faulkner Sr. papers. I visited a lot of archives over the last decade, and I am grateful for all of the help.

Friends and colleagues heard about my topic and searched through family papers for documents that might help. I especially want to thank Collier Andress Smith and Bob and Roberta Jones. I am deeply grateful that I could talk to Roberta's mom, Ruth Clark Blevins, before she passed away. My MTSU Department of History colleagues and chairs have been a source of steady support, and the librarians at James E. Walker Library helped me chase down lost citations. Tara White helped me secure permissions and was a good friend; Kevin Kiyoi helped me with JPEG conversions; and Martha Ann and Vinnie Cantrell took photos of Olin Dorn's Clemson memorial for me. I am sure that I have forgotten someone because it took a long time to finish this, so thanks to those whose help was crucial. I did not intend to forget you.

I am profoundly grateful to the friends I made through my volunteer work with Alive Hospice. I especially thank and remember Sara, Kendall, Loretta, and my dear friend Marjorie Jones for reminding me that I write about sacred moments that should always be taken seriously, even those that might seem superficial or superfluous. I wish my dad, Bob McCusker, and my aunts, Marie Kiyoi and Mary Peter McCusker, could have seen this book published.

I am grateful to my husband, Larry Puzzo, and our daughters, Katie Lou and Grace, for not groaning (too much) when we stopped at yet another cemetery. The cats and dogs kept me company while I wrote at our kitchen table, except for Rudy the cat who insisted on sitting on my notes and had to be banished.

Finally, my dear friend Jo Helton Wintker died just before I turned the manuscript over to the press in 2021. "Miss Jo" was a Hollywood actress in the 1950s and 1960s before becoming a social worker. She later adopted my daughters as her pseudo-grandkids and came to my classes to tell my students about working in Hollywood during the Cold War. We knew she considered us part of her family when she took us to Chester County, Tennessee, to visit her family graveyard. We love and miss you, Miss Jo.

Just Enough to Put Him Away Decent

Introduction

Death and the South

It was one of the more charming rituals I encountered when I moved to Tennessee in 2000: when a hearse-led funeral procession drives down the road, everyone moves over, no matter which side of the road you are on, and stops until the procession has passed. To be on the receiving end of this ritual is remarkable because pedestrians will also stop and hold their hands over their hearts as you pass by, acknowledging the grief and sadness of the entourage. It is also an ironic ritual because no self-respecting southerner, intent on practicing for his or her qualifying round at NASCAR, will let a speeding ambulance go by. One must be dead, not dying, for cars to pull over and stop. But newcomers learn quickly to pull over for a funeral procession (the police escorts are an easy reminder) because it is in good taste to stop and pay your respects.[1]

Pulling over for a funeral cortege is a poignant reminder of a time when death was a common, though miserable, experience in the South, when the region, its people, and its landscapes were intimately connected with dying young.[2] Rituals like these were fashioned to account for its commonness, a twentieth-century form of death care that linked the dead to the region's cultural, economic, racial, and political systems. Yet this ritual is now a remnant, made so as death care—the burial of the dead, the mourning of the loss, and the comfort extended to the living—evolved to include a fourth ritual, life extension, fostered by an emerging death commercial industry and institutionalized by the federal government. The region became both a lab experiment and a national example as a diverse group of actors changed not just death care, but ideas about health and wellness in general. Death did not die, as some scholars have argued, but became commercialized and privatized as a group of professionals took over the physical care of the dead and as southerners retrained their focus on other components of death care.

This book, then, purports to be about the dead, but really is a book about the living, more than clichés might suggest. How southerners (and Americans in general) changed their ideas about when one should die, how that death should occur, and what being buried decently meant in the first half of the twentieth century is really the focus. The cementing of these practices into federal policy was crucial as living longer became an implied right of citizenship on rural landscapes, on battlefields, during the Roaring Twenties, and in the Great Depression. By the time the final deceased World War II soldiers were escorted home in 1955, Black and white southerners had a different sense of death care, indeed, of themselves as American citizens, more akin to national practice than regional whim.[3]

This relatively narrow focus on the South means this book must be about race, in particular the ways that Black and white southerners redefined, in conjunction and in opposition, what good death care was. Black and white southerners agreed that family should play a central part in burials, especially in rural areas where death care duties were shared cross-racially. They also agreed on shifts in religious justification for life extension. But they disagreed when poverty or white violence resulted in Black death. Thus, the evolution to more national assumptions came slowly to the South because of its potential to upset a rigid racial caste system and weak governmental systems. When good healthcare came, it evolved to be a kind of "deluxe" Jim Crow that provided segregated, but still meaningful, care for Black southerners.[4] Moreover, if being put away decent conferred dignity on the dead, Black death commercial actors (insurance agents, burial societies, and funeral directors) were key players in restoring that dignity, as scholars Karla F. C. Holloway and Suzanne Smith have noted, to dead bodies and to the broader community. In this book, then, when I identify someone by race, I am describing that racially specific death care. Otherwise, the rituals I describe are shared ones, fostered by a miserable climate where dying young was common.[5]

Viewing death as common and ordinary means we will ignore some topics that are extraordinary. For example, while the Civil War's carnage was horrific, death care in 1900 reflected the sharecropping system that emerged after the war rather than the war itself. Nor does this book examine the memorials to soldiers who served. In the early twentieth century, the Daughters of the Confederacy put up hundreds of soldier statues on public squares in homage to their fathers and grandfathers who fought for the Confederacy. They seemed to memorialize the dead, but in fact were attempting to vindicate their service. This discussion also avoids discussing mourning clothes, the typical fare of museum exhibits, because they focus on Victorian-era mourning among the elite. In the rural South where this history starts, there was neither the time nor the money to mourn the dead with special clothes. We do not discuss New Orleans' famed jazz funerals, remarkable events that do not occur elsewhere in the South; my focus is a broader one that accounts for both rural and urban ritual. The book will also only focus on the three most common Protestant religions: Southern Baptists, Methodists, and Episcopalians. Space keeps me from examining Catholics, Pentecostals, the Church of God in Christ, and other religions that are the foundation of the South's religious diversity. Finally, we will not discuss Elizabeth Kubler-Ross's stages of grief, those five discrete phases the dying go through, namely, denial, anger, bargaining, depression, and acceptance. Those five stages were likely not possible until the end of World War II when dying young became less common and when Americans believed they had a reasonable chance to live to their three score and ten. In the end, the goal of *Just Enough to Put Him Away Decent* is to see common, ordinary rituals surrounding death rather than the extraordinary, and to see how dying (meaning how people died and were buried) provided a context for *understanding* death (meaning what happens to us once we stop breathing and how regional identities intersect with those shifting beliefs).[6]

Some of the death care I describe may not be as southern as I think, however. Raised in the San Francisco Bay Area, my own experience of death and graveyards is formed by Colma, California, the so-called city of the dead where many from the Peninsula, including my aunt, Sister Mary Peter McCusker, are buried. Encountering different practices in Murfreesboro, Tennessee, I assumed I was seeing regional diversity. Space and time do not allow me to examine how wide-ranging (for example) pulling over for a funeral cortege in fact is, and I invite my readers to suss out the regional breadth of these rituals.

This book sits at the nexus of two groups of scholarly writing: scholars of death rituals and social demographers examining the distinct decline in death rates during the twentieth century. When scholars write about death rituals, they tend to look at "ways," so-called after Jessica Mitford's muckraking book, *The American Way of Death*, appeared in 1963.[7] "Ways" of death suggest closed systems, relatively separate from other cultural or practical rituals, and seem prone to stasis. There is also a laser-like focus on the funeral profession rather than a broader examination of death care. The etiquette of pulling over for a funeral tells us that rituals, causes, even beliefs about death, do indeed morph over time. Locals now move over for a motorized hearse that is carrying a (most likely) embalmed body to a cemetery situated on the outskirts of town for burial in a park-like setting where death seems more like a picnic than what it really is. We also expect the deceased to be relatively elderly. By this description, southern burial rituals are now similar to the rest of the nation. But in 1900, death care was fundamentally different, as the region was sicker and its inhabitants more likely to die young than in the rest of the country.

Moreover, the solemn procession seems to hide a body that is whispered about. Death died, according to scholars such as Philippe Aries, meaning it became as scandalous to speak of as suicide or sex as funeral professionals took over the care of the body. But the argument here is that death did not "die." As funeral professionals came to care for the body itself, southerners (and Americans) came to think about death in new ways, especially when it was linked to other cultural systems like consumerism, psychoanalysis, etiquette, civil rights, and health rights. Dying instead became an entirely new system that a focused look on the South allows us to examine, one that privatized rather than denied death.[8]

Social demographers, on the other hand, argue that death did indeed "die"—literally—meaning that death rates declined steeply over the course of the twentieth century. Recent writings tend to fall into two classes. Social demographers are sounding the alarm over newly rising mortality rates that had seen a steady decline during the twentieth century. Now, those rates are rising again among Midwesterners especially, particularly among white working-class Americans, ages 46–59, with only a high school degree. This has been the crux of Princeton demographers Anne Case and Angus Deaton's work. Gerontologists like Louise Aronson, on the other hand, examine the consequences of extending life. The elderly, who now can live to one hundred years old, tend to live in poverty and difficulty, treated by doctors who really do not understand how to care for an aged body. Medical care, in Aronson's view, has not evolved to account for this vast decline in mortality rates, and therefore has caused significant suffering for those who now can expect to live much longer than their nineteenth- and twentieth-century counterparts.[9]

Thus, this book examines the evolution of southern death rituals from 1900 to the last soldier reburials of World War II, peeling away the layers of what southerners meant when they "put someone away decent," slang that acknowledged local practices that evolved as ritual met national trend, and mingled together into a meaningful modern set of practices about the dead, dying young, and living longer. That this occurred in a region rooted in a political hierarchy based on racialized power structures is critical because new ideas about life extension and death rituals, incipient and incomplete, had the potential to empower the poorest of southerners, both Black and white. Lowering high mortality rates and investing in good health practices thus became imagined as a civic responsibility and a civil right. Shifts in language accompanied shifts in ritual and thinking about the dead, initially emphasizing life extension and life conservation; then life-saving; and finally, vitality as the new watch word of both a healthier South and a vibrant nation.

The truism that everybody dies requires an addition, however. Everybody dies—they were not that successful in the twentieth century—but now, everybody requires paperwork at their death, creating a vast number of primary sources. Moreover, death was so ordinary, so integrated into the everyday life of a deadly, rural South in 1900 that this book has had to rely upon a vast number of primary sources that differ from state to state. To provide a consistent foundation, the discussion uses two core sets of documents that transcend state boundaries: the Federal Writers' Projects (FWP) "life histories" from the 1930s and funeral ledgers. Interviewers crossed much of the South from 1936 to 1940, funded by the Second New Deal, and interviewed hundreds of ordinary southerners who described the illnesses and deaths they suffered. These documents are difficult to read at times because interviewers, mostly white and middle class, tended to record what they heard in terms of tone and language rather than what the interviewee actually said. This means many of the quotes in this book will be written in dialects that interviewers used to define their subjects as Black, working, or middle class.

The second set of documents, funeral ledgers, made their general appearance in the 1910s and evolved over the next forty years. Life extension advocates used the demographic data funeral directors collected to count causes of death and to mitigate some of the more egregious problems, even as the ledgers document significant changes in death commerce. Funeral ledgers from both Black and white funeral professionals, from small towns and large cities, provide a consistency across the region where the daily care of the dead by professionals required a notation in a book, becoming extraordinary enough to separate out and write down as a unique business transaction. As a data set, they provide an order to a chaotic moment in describing the mundane details of commercialized death, the names and demographic data of the dead, and the purchase of death goods.

This book is laid out in five parts. Part one begins with a typical, rural funeral around the year 1900, rooting it in the South's deadly landscape and examining the death care provided by families and the rural South's most ubiquitous healthcare workers, Black midwives. Fights over cemeteries were common because they rooted a community's identity on that deadly landscape. More importantly, this section describes the theological shifts, especially in Southern Baptist and Methodist churches (the two most common Christian denominations) where an early death became an evangelical failure. Initially coached to think death was God's plan and therefore not to be questioned, evangelicals took comfort in the family reunion promised by John 14:2 KJV[10] ("In my Father's house are many mansions"). An emerging industrial economy and scientific advancements suggested, however, that an early death could be avoided and in fact, a longer life had biblical sanction. This vested Progressive reformers with an evangelical zeal to attack high mortality rates. A death commercial industry that included burial societies, funeral professionals, and insurance agencies formed and professionalized when there was a lot of business. But the industry came to see early death as expensive for its business, writ large, and began to invest in "life extension" practices, aimed at making people live longer.

Part two examines two simultaneous catastrophic death events: World War I and the Spanish Influenza epidemic. The war began the first substantial federal incursion into the South's poor health, with an expansive immunization and health program aimed at making soldiers fit for the battlefield. But the flu's incubation in the very processes used to mobilize for war exposed the limits of that healthcare, providing conflicting poles as southerners struggled to claim war deaths as honorable, even as flu deaths exposed the failures and incomplete medical breakthroughs of the previous generation. Some southerners also encountered new ways to bury the dead as the military's Quartermaster Corps imposed its perception of an honorable ritual on the war dead, which included all deceased bodies, Black or white. Struggling to honor the dead, southerners were faced with ambiguous deaths, as some bodies were left overseas in newly created American cemeteries or could not be found. In either case, the military tried to avoid leaving coffins with deceased soldiers alone on train platforms where they were visual displays of the war's actual costs.

Part three examines the aftermath of World War I as the military industrial apparatus shifted its focus from munitions production to domestic commercial goods production. This vested death-related commercial actors with greater authority and power as consumers imagined the silk dresses and purple coffins they would have at their funerals. New influencers—Sigmund Freud, etiquette gurus like Emily Post, religious authorities who changed centuries-old documents—gave grief a more prominent place as those funeral professionals attended to practical details. That southerners did this even as federal public health officials expanded their sphere of influence to areas around military training camps demonstrates the continued influence of the war well after it ended in making life extension practices more common.

Part four examines the Great Depression as a new death event. As deteriorating economic conditions exacerbated the incomplete and even stalled activities of public health workers, the First New Deal provided the opportunity to systematically sever the links among the region's landscape of death by literally removing bodies from hundreds of small graveyards in order to build the Tennessee Valley Authority's dam projects. The Civilian Conservation Corps (CCC) followed, with significant environmental work conducted (for example, planting trees and eliminating malarial swamps) and the young men who conducted that work cared for as well. The Second and Third New Deals then used their expansive programs to build hospitals and septic systems, all the while redefining what a modern funeral was and what looked old-fashioned and passé and while simultaneously institutionalizing good health into new legislation like the Social Security Act of 1935.

Part five argues that World War II capitalized on the New Deal's promises of good health by requiring young men to serve in a war that killed more than four hundred thousand Americans. World War II expanded the New Deal's work, even as American men died in naval ships in the South Pacific and in plane crashes over Europe. After the war, memorial activities once again challenged families to transform rituals, as they worked together without regard for region to search for their dead. Military escorts who accompanied the repatriated dead home bore witness to the evolution of death care in profound ways as Mississippi families insisted on viewing their soldiers' bodies. Finally, an epilogue describes a supposedly healthier suburban South as new landscapes of death in the upper Midwest (Ohio, West Virginia, and other states in the old Northwest) have caused new alarm among twenty-first-century statisticians. The coronavirus, obviously, has also exposed some of the limits of twentieth-century changes as well.

In 1939, FWP author Sadie Hornsby interviewed Mrs. Omie Williams Epps, a white woman whose husband was one of the first pilots flying near Augusta, Georgia, as well as one of the first killed in a plane accident in the area. When her husband's plane crashed, he had two burial policies that left "just enough to put him away decent."[11] "Decent," in southern vernacular, was a term understood to mean something in common by both Black and white southerners as a set of death rituals that evolved over the course of the twentieth century, sometimes in concert with national objectives, at other times in response to regional whims. The evolution of what decent meant, of death care in general, gives us a new way to view the twentieth century's vast changes, seeing urbanization, consumerism, global war, and other events through the lens of dying and death. These changes had significant implications not just for the South, but for Americans in general, as a new health citizenship emerged, eclipsing older expectations of dying young.

PART ONE

Death and the New South

At the turn of the twentieth century, burying the dead was not just a commonly enacted ritual, but critical to local political practice. Many southerners did not live to their three score and ten, as promised by Psalm 90:10 (KJV), and the ubiquity of infants, children, and young adults dying long before their seventieth year marked the turn-of-the-century southern countryside, literally in small family graveyards, and figuratively in the religious and social practices that sustained political and racial hierarchies. That ubiquity solidified a community's identity, helped rank locals on its hierarchy, and—with many graveyards well within sight of a family's front porch—fostered a feeling of unity, reminding all who had deep roots in the region and who did not. The commonness of death also made the handling of the deceased body an interracial community act. The perception of tradition, of an unchanging death practice, was underpinned, however, by a rapidly changing rural landscape that would welcome (at times) new reform movements and a new death commerce.

Indeed, as the Progressive Movement spread across the region, some questioned whether high death rates should be the norm and whether the family reunions promised by John 14:2 ("In my house are many mansions" [KJV]) was enough recompense for those high rates. Many thus began to see an early death as one that defied God's law. Religious bodies like the Southern Baptist and Northern Baptist Conventions willingly contributed time and resources to lowering mortality rates as national charities like the Rockefeller Foundation provided funds to identify and attack some main causes of early death.

Pressure also came from an emergent death commercial industry, namely, insurance companies, burial societies, and funeral directors who found an early death was an expensive one. Crucial to their emergent professionalization was the claiming of younger bodies as expensive problems. It was not necessarily a matter of going against God's promise of three score and ten, but an economic problem that had the potential of undermining a New South. Insurance companies and eugenicists crafted a new phrase, "life extension," or "life conservation," to account, literally, for the costs of dying young.

But in 1900, the South still seemed predominantly rural, and death was commonplace. Funerals occurred often and grief was ignored because, after all, there was only so much time and energy that one could expend, in light of a hardscrabble rural homestead. The Civil War's death practices, fostered by its unbearable carnage so poignantly described by Drew Gilpin Faust and recalled though the ubiquitous dedication of Confederate war memorials, had in fact evolved to better reflect the crop lien system. Many saw funeral rites as tradition, even as they were already changing to better reflect the region's industrialization and urbanization, that southerners took time out from their labors to bury the dead and then go back to work. But grief did show up in unexpected ways. Perhaps the best place to start is with a fight over an old cemetery.[1]

1 Selling Our Dead

Evolving Rural Burial Practice

Cades Cove residents became "wonderfully alarmed" when New Dealers tried to buy their land to build the Smoky Mountain National Park (Tennessee). One resident accused them of asking residents to "sell our dead," the cemeteries that anchored rural southerners to their land, and with them, locals' sense of place and community identity. "Our dead are so close to our hearts, we cannot and do not want to give them up," that resident argued.[1] Carefully tended family graveyards oft times were built within sight of front porches, reminding families of the ancestors who ranked them in the South's social order and with whom they would be reunited at their own deaths. In turn, deceased family members consecrated the land, linking the living to a complicated and expansive landscape of death that was common and normalized.[2]

What seemed to be an old tradition of burying the dead to Cades Cove residents was really an evolving landscape that had changed since the Civil War. Familiarity, in particular the emphasis on the natal family and community as the key actors in burial rituals, provided cover for what was rapidly changing, in particular the requirement that family and community join together to bury the dead. Deceased family members, ritually cared for in an attentive, prescribed manner, were included as key characters in the family's rank and rooted them to the South's power structure. The burial ground was the physical manifestation and a reminder of a future where all would be reunited in Heaven.

But the dead came to have a practical purpose, too. Land was a tangible manifestation of power in 1900, and those buried on it linked the living, whether Black or white, to the land in ways no deed nor flimsy wooden house could. High death rates made graveyards a solid, rooting force around which southerners arranged their mental landscapes, evidenced as late as the 1930s when the New Deal tried to untangle the links between the landscape and death. The dead were evidence, too, of ritual practices that southerners used to define "decent," as people who buried their dead with a basic minimum of care—a casket, a grave dug and then covered with dirt, with words spoken over the body—were good people. The common, ordinary funeral in 1900 thus emphasized tangibility and visibility, a laying on of hands and eyes on the body, buried by kin and neighbors.

A Deadly Landscape

While the Bible taught that God allowed believers to live to three score and ten, according to Psalm 90:10 (KJV), few southerners seemed to live that long. Exact numbers have been difficult to find because death registration areas in the South were not fully established until 1933, when Texas was finally added. However, death seemed to be a part of its geography, its ecology, even its weather patterns. Living in the South was a constant struggle against natural and godly forces that seemed to batter its residents and take many before their biblically decreed time. Mississippian David Cohn believed that "since we were few under the pitiless dome of heaven and we huddled together for warmth against the chilling winds of the cosmos," the death of one man "seemed a blow to the collective strength of our tribe—the drowning of the man next to you on the levee as you furiously fought together to keep the flooding river out of the town."[3]

That deadly distinctiveness came first from the environment. "Let us begin by discussing the weather," southerner and Yale University historian Ulrich Bonnell Phillips wrote in 1929, arguing it was the semitropical weather that formed the core of the South's deadliness.[4] Heat was the prime culprit, sapping the strength of those laboring in the fields. By the "killing months" of August and September, Charleston morticians knew they could count on a brisk business, a kind of death boom as heat and humidity exacerbated other fragile health conditions.[5]

Rain, hurricanes, and tornadoes also made the South's landscape deadly, especially the regular flooding of large rivers. The Mississippi River, for example, flooded eleven times between 1858 and 1927 after rainstorms. When rivers overflowed their banks, the danger was more than the drowning of residents unable to swim or the catastrophic loss of property. Animals died and were left to rot, human waste spread throughout the flooded area, and mud clung to every place, creating an environment ripe for epidemic disease. Torrents of rain and wind from hurricanes and tornadoes also marked the South as a dangerous place.[6] At eighty-two years old in 1939, Julia LaRoche remembered well the 1893 and 1911 hurricanes on Edisto Island, South Carolina. "I suppose you know that there has been no hurricane on the island since 1911," she said in 1939, "Oh yes, minor blows—gentle little breezes that knocked over a few pine trees several summers ago, but nothing that could hold a candle to the 1911 storm or the famous one of 1893."[7]

Equally deadly was the labor required to control the vegetation spawned by hot, wet summers. Hot, humid air allowed native plants to thrive, requiring intensive, year-round labor to clear land for crops. Sharecroppers, Black and white alike, believed their families worked themselves to death, literally, while clearing land for white landowners. South Carolina sharecropper Emaline (no last name) described her husband Abel's death from what she thought was overwork (more likely, heat stroke). Emaline recalled:

> My Abel jes' kill hese'f wuckin' fer Mr. Carrington what is daid now, may de good Lawd rest he sinful soul. I warn Abel bout killin' hese'f in de hot broilin' sun. He tell me he got to keep goin' sun er no sun. He comed in fer dinner one day at lay-by time, jes' naturally burning up, an' most pantin' to death. He stretch out cross de bed, and teck de baby wid 'im whilst I gits he dinner fix. When I went to git him up, he never answer when I calls, so I calls 'im again, and sez: "What ail you, honey, come on, yo' dinner gwine git col" . . . I walked oer an' shuck him, an' den I seed he eyes wuz wide open, an' so big an' glassy dat hit nearly scairt me clean to death. I knowed Abel daid.[8]

White landowners' belief that sharecroppers were keen on avoiding work caused them to laugh off these deaths. The death of a sharecropper from labor thus seemed a kind of anachronism since, according to white landowner stereotype, sharecroppers rarely worked. Emaline bitterly noted the profound harm caused by the infamous Carrington who laughed off Abel's death:

> When Mister Carrington come out an' seed me standin' dere crying . . . he look kinda funny an sez: "What ail you, Emmy?" "You done kill my Abel," I sez. Mister Carrington jes' laff, an' sez: "Onliest way to kill a [n———] is to hit him on de heel, he haid too hard to hurt him!" "Eiffen you doan believe hit, go see," I sez. He did, an' comed back an' sez: "Hafta git somebody to finish Abel's crop. Dat darkey done up an' daid sho' nuff!" Dat's all he sez! He ain' kere nothin' bout po' Abel, jes' de crop![9]

Not only was the countryside deadly, but southern cities such as Memphis, New Orleans, and Charleston were synonymous with high death rates well before the Civil War. The massing together of large groups with little regard for infrastructure was an example of an "incomplete" urbanization process that elicited large slums, a lack of sanitation, and a constant battle with bugs, rats, and high mortality rates.[10] Disease-carrying insects like mosquitoes flourished in the wet, warm, and long summers in unsanitary cities which, in turn, fostered deadly epidemics. In New Orleans, the high death rates earned it the nickname "the graveyard of the [old] Southwest."[11] Epidemic diseases like cholera, malaria, yellow fever, and dysentery killed many southerners. When Mary G. Jones, the labor activist known as "Mother Jones," lost her husband and four children in the infamous Memphis Yellow Fever epidemic of 1867, for example, it became a catalyst for her labor organizing. With many dead from epidemics and few left to bury them according to custom, cities quickly created cemeteries where the dead lay forgotten, a sinful act for a culture that incorporated the dead into its social worlds. In David Cohn's Greenville, Mississippi, a long-forgotten yellow fever cemetery was within the town's borders, but was an anathema in a place where the dead were supposed to be remembered with clarity and precision.[12]

A deadly environment elicited both a sense of contingency and a certain resignation to imminent death as well as "the realization that there was little or nothing they could do to prevent it," historian Sylvia Hoffert argued.[13] Children were especially aware of death because of its constancy in their lives and their high death rates. Georgian Lillian Smith recalled that:

> No wonder we children feared Death as if he lived next door! For always he was slyly reaching out to snag our lives on his bony fingers if we once passed him carelessly. Graveyards full of baby dreams planted themselves in our past and stayed there, mouldering greenly. Tombstones stiffened in our minds, carving their inscriptions restlessly at night when we could not sleep. Born . . . died . . . born . . . died. We sometimes did not know how we were born but we knew how we would die.[14]

Pauli Murray remembered feeling that the cemetery behind her house in Durham, North Carolina, made it seem as if "death was always waiting just outside our back door to grasp me."[15] In many cases, it was.

Visiting and Informing

David Cohn claimed death in the "sensual South" was different from death in the "Gothic North," where it was "shrouded in anonymity. A private affair, it affects principally the dead man's family and his friends—an enclave within enclaves, as Oriental boxes are 'nested' one within the other."[16] The implication was, of course, that southerners did not consider death care to be a private matter, but a community rite. If you were a good Christian, then your family, with help from local family and friends, claimed you and buried you, ensuring your trip to heaven. The worst kind of death was one where there was no family, no community, no one to ensure your trip. No family literally meant no Heaven, and people like Georgian Molly Kensey worried that she was "all alone wid nobody, no relatives. No one ter do for me" when she died.[17]

Kin and neighbors were thus essential to enacting prescribed rituals, beginning when a death seemed imminent. Using a key southern courtesy—the visit—locals came to sit with the dying, providing comfort to both the family and the ill person. Visiting was a leisure activity that carried practical, political, and social implications. Some people with time and leisure visited each other and reinforced their collective solidarity, a typically elite crowd. But visits were common more generally, especially on Sundays, as friends and family hoped their kin and friends would recuperate, even though they knew the South's geography of death made sudden turns for the worse common. The "death watch" or a "sitting up," all names for a death visit, sometimes went on for hours, days, or months.[18] The careful visitor wanted to watch the transition from an ill person to a dying person, searching eyes for the "look of death," a sign that death was imminent.[19] To die suddenly meant no one was able to see that look, to view the transition to the next, holier world. Many a friend hurried to a bedside to hear last words, to say goodbye, or to gaze one last time on a dear one's face and watch this transition. The dying seem to have participated willingly. Lillian Smith's father quoted portions from the apostle Paul's second letter to Timothy 4:7 (KJV) to his witnesses as he lay dying, "I have fought the good fight; I have kept the faith," as evidence that he was assessing his Christian life for his bedside audience.[20] Elite Black southerners published final words in newspapers, for example, AME Zion Church's Bishop Charles Pettey's when yellow fever killed him in 1900: "I will lay down here and put up my tools, believing that God doeth all things for the best. God bless my wife. God bless my dear wife and children."[21]

Final visits were also a way to discern if someone died a good or bad death. Maulsey Stoney was always, for example,

> pressing closely around the death bed, wait[ing] with bated breath to hear the last words to be spoken. Much depends upon those words. If the dying one prays or reports a heavenly vision, the souldwill [*sic*] be lifted up to heaven, they say. But if the vision does not come and there is no prayer offered, the person had "died bad" and his soul will descend to hell. [Maulsey] is frightened when somebody she known [*sic*] dies bad, for she says that the person's ghost will return to earth to haunt the living, "I 'fraid to walk the road now," she will proclaim. "Josie Smith die yesterday and he spirit going to roam 'round. I sure, God ain't want for meet um."[22]

Other final acts became part of a family's lore. Louisianan Treeby Chaffe Miller's father lifted her up to kiss her dying mother goodbye when Miller was two years old. That kiss was supposed to root an image of her mother in her memory that would sustain her through a motherless life. But it did not work. "Father," she said, "tried to help me remember kissing her goodby, but there is no picture of her left to me."[23]

In the intimacy of these final goodbyes, visitors provided real comfort to the dying while ensuring racial hierarchies remained firm. If the dying person was Black, a white person sitting up with them was an act of benevolence, one that acknowledged the white person's altruism and, therefore, higher class and racial status. To sit by someone as a racial equal simply was not done. James Weldon Johnson, future Executive Secretary of the National Association for the Advancement of Colored People (NAACP), noted that:

> The proudest and fairest lady in the South could with propriety—and it is what she would most likely do—go to the cabin of Aunt Mary, her cook, if Aunt Mary was sick, and minister to her comfort with her own hands, but if Mary's daughter, Eliza, a girl who used to run round my lady's kitchen, but who has received an education and married a prosperous young coloured man, were at death's door, my lady would no more think of crossing the threshold of Eliza's cottage than she would of going into a bar-room for a drink.[24]

Once death occurred, notifying the community was an essential first step. Telling the news in rural areas sometimes meant tolling a church or farm bell, one peal for each year of age, to signify who had died. More typically, families were notified personally. Alabaman Ann Pointer recalled:

> See, they'd get somebody and run them through and tell the news. Wasn't no telephone or anything. [Sam Kelly, a local man] said, "Miss Clare [Pointer's grandmother], Miss Bees just died a while ago. She stuck a nail on her foot and [it] give her lockjaw." [My grandmother] said, "Well, I heard the bell. We should come right on and down there." If you got sick, they'd come and sit at your house all night long and help you, wait on you and everything. All of that was loving.[25]

Elite white families used their servants to inform neighbors of a death. The use of Black men, dressed in livery, to deliver the news of a death reminded everyone of their place, even as death potentially disrupted it (for example, in the death of a breadwinner). South Carolina Federal Writers' Project (FWP) writers described one Black male servant sent to inform the white community of an elite white man's or woman's death:

> Upon a sheet of writing paper was written the following: "Relatives, friends, and acquaintances of _____ are requested to attend _____ funeral at _____ church on _____." At the top, mid-way the sheet of paper, two slits were made crosswise, and a piece of black grosgrain ribbon, about one-inch in width, varying in length, was pulled thru the slits-extending downward over the written notice. A white or Negro man, riding or walking, took this death notice to all the homes in the community. As quickly as a member of the family read the notice, the messenger would continue from one home to another until every home had been visited.[26]

Treeby Miller recalled that families placed a death announcement on a silver tray and surrounded it with violets. The tray was offered to other elite whites, a way to confirm who deserved the news and who did not.[27]

Preparing the Body

Informing was a call to enact a carefully orchestrated set of responsibilities that reflected and affirmed social hierarchies. Acquiescence to local elites in quotidian ways, for example, gifted Blacks and lower-ranked whites with patronage at death as the crop lien system required landowners to cover basic medical and death services. At settlement time when the costs accrued throughout the year were paid from that year's crop, sharecroppers most likely repaid the burial costs or went into debt which was carried over to the next year. One man recalled his repayment after burying his "step-mammy," a former slave:

> She died too a few months atter I started workin' for Mr. Bascum. I had to borrow forty-five dollars from Mr. Bascum to bury her wid. It kept me in the hole all the rest of the year payin' for that casket . . . Hit were a lot of work jest to put away a woman. But I never minded it nary bit. She was a mighty good woman.[28]

Coffins were the most obvious act of patronage, descended from plantation owners who furnished the boards during slave times; local Black carpenters like Alabaman Onnie Lee Logan's father then constructed them to fit the dead. Later, when manufactured coffins became available, funeral ledgers were littered with references to probable landowners buying caskets for their sharecroppers. Smyrna undertaker Walter King Harris sold an eight-dollar coffin and box for Smyrna, Tennessee, resident Ed Gregory on January 7, 1917, who purchased it for the "Pitts baby" [*sic*] (the Potts family rented land from Gregory).[29] One North Carolina landowner remembered a sharecropper whose family included three children sick with colitis. "The baby died," he recalled, "and I had to furnish the plot for its grave and its burial expenses."[30] Some landowners required their sharecroppers to stay current with their burial insurance, once it became available, as Georgian Minnie Stonestreet did when she hired "her farmer Lee." She recalled, "I did have sense enough to see that he kept up his insurance so there was enough from that to pay the doctor and the burial expenses [when he died]."[31]

Death care itself centered on the family's preparation of the body, emphasizing the sacred while minding the need for haste. Families readied the body for its trip to heaven, with its sins washed clean and the body posed as if asleep on a bed, an almost domestic scene that assumed that death was just a different kind of sleep. Preparing the body for burial displayed a rural domesticity and gendered labor divisions, with women, especially local Black midwives, caring for the body, and men building the coffin and digging the grave. Burials occurred within a day (and in some cases, the same day if the death was expected) since very few deceased bodies outside of larger cities were embalmed. Heat made this a practical necessity.

Local women prepared the body as part of a community's reciprocal responsibilities where one gave help when needed, in order to receive help when required. When called to care for the deceased, these midwives were called "shrouding women," both a biblical reference and a practical justification. Bible verses from Luke 7:37–38 (KJV) describe a sinful woman anointing Jesus with her tears of repentance, her hair, and ointment, a verse used to justify women's expert work with the dead. In the South, those midwives were typically, but not always, Black women, with their skills passed down from one generation to the next. Onnie Lee Logan, for example, learned her trade from both her grandmother and mother. In some cases, families included three generations of midwives who provided general medical care, delivered babies, and when necessary, prepared the dead. Their work could also require them to sew shrouds for the dead, another reason for calling midwives shrouding women. The biblical seal of approval caused many evangelical women to consider their work a calling from God. Mary Johnson, eighty-two years old from Mississippi, told an interviewer in 1977 that:

> I had a working mother, a great mother . . . When the people got sick she went to visit the sick. Also when they died, she shrouded many, many souls. You know back in those days they didn't have undertakers to come to the people's houses. They would send around to the friends, and they would go and wash them and shroud them and fix them up.[32]

The care of the white dead by Black midwives was common. Less common was the care of the Black dead by white people. As with the visit, Black women were cared for by wealthy white women because of white women's patronage. Moreover, the work did not cross gender boundaries because the care of a Black man by a white woman could upset a racial system that declared that relationship off limits. In many ways, this kind of care was a paternalism, leftover from the slave South, where white plantation mistresses tended to the needs of the enslaved. Patronage carried on after slavery. Black friends secured the help of Laura Green's white employer, Ina Dillard Russell, in preparing Green's body for burial. Russell's description depicts her caring for the body while directing others to do her bidding:

> We sent word around and Laura's colored friends came in to fix her for burial. When Laura died her clothes and her bedding were so nice and clean. You know how neat she always went. We had her best under clothes [*sic*] put on her—some I had made—and we put white on her—white stockings and white gloves, and Ina [another Russell daughter] made a little white cap, of lace that Laura had washed for me. It was nice and Ina put it on her. I 'phoned papa at once and he notified her son and sister who live in Atlanta. Papa bought a nice coffin for Laura and a colored friend paid for the grave and two buggies from the livery stable. Ina made

a beautiful cross of evergreen and jonquils and several other designs were sent in by colored friends.[33]

The language used to describe the scene is telling. "We had her best under clothes put on" meant that Russell directed Green's Black friends, as she expected to do as a white woman married to a powerful man (her husband, Richard B. Russell Sr., was Chief Justice of Georgia's State Supreme Court and a former state legislator). The description is also a mix of good deeds done for a good friend: a hat made for her head; placed there by Russell's daughter; and flowers carefully designed to adorn the grave by that same daughter. "Colored" friends purchased a cemetery plot and two buggies to move the coffin.

Midwives and others began a decent burial by, first, washing the body, since water, reminiscent of baptism, washed clean the body's sins and purified it for the trip to heaven. Octagon soap, an all-purpose soap that could be purchased at the local store, provided the disinfectant; when one used a sweet-smelling soap, uncommon for a people used to practicality, Georgian Willie Mae Wright recalled, "That would be the talk for all the next week."[34] Once washed, women laid the body on a cooling board, straightening arms and legs to prevent rigor mortis from bending the body into odd shapes. Coins were laid on the eyes to ensure they stayed closed until burial, to mark the age of the deceased, or to become sacred mementos. Twentieth-century excavators discovered a nineteenth-century Black burial ground in Charleston, South Carolina, that included a young boy's body, perhaps a twelve-year-old, who had coins on his eyes that were dated 1870 and 1882. Some families retained the coins as reminders of the body. Mississippian Eudora Welty did not know she had an older sibling until she found two polished buffalo nickels hidden in a cardboard box that held her mother's calling cards, coins that had been placed over her older brother's eyes when he died. When she asked her mother, Mrs. Welty replied, "He was a fine little baby, my first baby, and he shouldn't have died. But he did." More importantly, Welty learned her mother had told her "the wrong secret—not how babies could come, but how they could die, how they could be forgotten about."[35]

Death furniture reinforced the domestic image of a body decently prepared. Local carpenters kept a store of wood in order to build custom-made coffins for the dead, fitting them for specific bodies, sometimes for pay, sometimes not, and constructed so that it would quickly disintegrate once it was interred, leaving only rusted nails as evidence that a body once rested there. South Carolinian sharecropper Emaline remembered when her beloved husband, Abel, died, "I got Brother Wilson what wuz a good carpenter to meck Abel a coffin outen white pine. He done hit, an' never charge me a cent."[36] Women lined the coffin with white sheets before bodies were laid in the casket with arms to their side. Burying the whole, complete body was critical as one had to face God as a complete person since eternity required all body parts.[37]

Committing the Body

Ritual firmly prescribed the next steps of burying the body, again rooted in practical considerations as well as religious belief. Services began with a wake, or "a sitting up," to ensure the body remained whole while out of the ground; those who sat up kept a good eye on the coffin's open lid as they sang hymns or reminisced. In this era before screened windows, cats and other predators, drawn by the smell of a decomposing body, were a special concern. Some southerners required whiskey or coffee and food be served as they kept watch, refusing to show up without the promised refreshments. Trumpeter Louis Armstrong, who led the singing at multiple New Orleans funerals, remembered:

> The family of the deceased usually serves a lot of coffee, cheese and crackers all night long so that the people who come to sing hymns over the corpse can eat and drink to their heart's delight. I used to go to a lot of wakes and lead off with a hymn. After everybody had joined in the chorus I would tiptoe on into the kitchen and load up on crackers, cheese and coffee. That meal always tasted specially good.[38]

Mourners brought food to the visitation, knowing that the family expected visitors. It was a strong enough ritual that even when the circumstances were awkward—in the case of murder or suicide, for example—food was still required.[39]

Once the body was properly waked, burial tended to be immediate for white families, but Black southerners held their services later. This was a nod toward the past when white masters did not allow the Black enslaved to hold funerals when it conflicted with plantation work. In pre–Civil War days, Sundays were set aside as a day for funerals.

The rural funeral followed certain traditions that comforted the family with their familiarity. Family and friends placed chairs inside the deceased's house during inclement weather or outside on a clear day, forming a half circle with the top of the circle being the open casket with the deceased's body. Strong-smelling plants—sprigs of rosemary, for example—were used, not necessarily for their aesthetic value, but for the strong smell that hid the odor of decay. Men preached a sermon or read from the Bible and then other men heaved the coffin onto their shoulders and walked to the cemetery. Kentucky folk singer Jean Ritchie described the walk from funeral to grave when her grandfather died:

> Finally the preachers said they'd finish up at the grave, with prayer and song, and so the men gathered around and bore Grandpa's coffin on their shoulders up through Uncle Lee's pasture, and all the people followed behind, winding around

> the narrow gravelly path, by the haw tree and across the gullies and among the pawpaw bushes, up the steep pasture hill to the graveyard.[40]

At times, a funeral dirge such as "Hark from the Tomb" accompanied the walk to the cemetery.[41]

Perhaps the most poignant cross-racial ritual performed at the graveside was one a Georgia preacher called "refreshing the grief," which operated as a kind of emotional release valve for grieving families. After pallbearers bore the coffin to the grave, the coffin was reopened, and family and friends passed by the body one last time. It was an emotionally intense moment where women cried and screamed their grief at the sight. To Jean Ritchie, refreshing the grief "looked to me like they were going crazy," as mourners screamed, cried, and waved their arms around.[42] Then, with the coffin lid now closed, the final shovels of dirt were thrown and the community went back to work.

Black and white southerners imagined the trip to Heaven in similar ways. The body might have ceased its physical functions, but going to Heaven did not occur until the body was buried, existing in a kind of liminal state until the final shovel of dirt was thrown. Then, it was as if a trap door opened under the coffin and the body slid its way to Heaven after the last shovelful of dirt. Many southerners, Black and white, thus believed they would be at their own funerals because that trip did not come until the ritual was complete.

Cemeteries

For all southerners, too, death was "intertwined so tightly with life as to be inseparable. They converse with the dead and leave favorite foods for the departed to consume. Life, death, and afterlife merge in the folk culture of the burial ground."[43] Thus, the land chosen for burial had profound meaning in the South because dead bodies, decently buried, consecrated it. There was no intention nor need to buy a grave marker, save for the wealthiest people. The bodies themselves were markers, since families knew where they buried their kin, and the knowledge was passed down sometimes from generation to generation. Vegetation decorated and beautified graves—typically trees or flowering bushes like peonies—making them blend into the rural landscape. Communities clung to the memory of the dead, as Durwood Dunn argued for Cades Cove:

> If the community claimed a person at the moment of death, they did not readily abandon his memory after the last shovel of dirt filled the grave. The folk memory clung tenaciously to much of the deceased's personality, habits, and even manner of speaking long after his death. This cataloging of innumerable individuals, living and dead, was an astonishing feat, given the sheer numbers of people involved. As long as the community existed, its members were thereby assured a kind of

immortality. Reflecting their concern for absent, but still full members of this community, cove people tended cemeteries with great care and decorated graves with flowers in an annual ceremony.[44]

The deadly landscape required southerners to find practical uses for the multiple bodies interred in family graveyards. The land was deadly, yes, but it was also a tangible asset that rooted families to its place, literally and figuratively, in the South.[45] In the post–Civil War era, land was in many cases the only tangible wealth left for white southerners after formerly enslaved, free Black people—no longer property—walked away. The graveyard situated on a family's acreage rooted constituent members to that land, meaningful in an era when the threat of losing that land was ever present. Moreover, the land was sacred because dead bodies made it theirs in ways that a home, vulnerable to fire, tornadoes, and other destructive forces could never do. A home was for a while; a cemetery existed in perpetuity. Tennessee native Jerry Gaither recalled:

> But then there were little cemeteries everywhere, and family cemeteries . . . Families were very strong. And they just buried them on their own land . . . there's lots of cemeteries around everywhere. It was more of a tradition of family and burying them and in the sense of taking care of them.[46]

Figure 1.1. Flimsy houses meant the family graveyard's permanence linked the land more firmly to the family. This is one of the few cemeteries where the house is still standing. Note the close proximity to the house's front porch.

For Black men and women, the burial of the dead on their land became a way to claim freedom in tangible ways. Some purchased it once they had control over their own wages. For example, the Reverend M. A. and Susan B. Jones bought a 67-acre farm near Charleston, South Carolina, in the early 1900s. They immediately set aside a portion of that land for a cemetery, burying all who needed space. Black wives and "free issue" children, meaning the children of white fathers and Black (sometimes free) mothers, were given land, sometimes at the end of slavery, sometimes at the death of the father. One white South Carolinian left his farm in Lincolnville, South Carolina, to his Black wife. Murfreesboro funeral director Revonda Rucker's family land in Middle Tennessee came from a white father at the end of the Civil War. Black landowners then buried bodies on that land in cemeteries that were opened to all. Thus, immediate burials on Black-owned land (and white-owned, too, in an era of economic uncertainty) secured it when unembalmed dead bodies, moldering to ashes and dust in a handmade wooden coffin, mixed with the soil and literally melded the land to the living family.[47]

Black landowners believed there was room for all and made room when necessary for others. The Ross Hill Cemetery in Chickasaw County, Mississippi, is an example, with multiple bodies buried and no clear idea of relationship between the original landowner and the deceased. For those who did not own land, finding space to be buried was problematic. According to some Black southerners, "not much respect was given to [B]lack folks who didn't own their own homes," in part because of the lack of a family graveyard. Moreover, when a white family sold its land, some believed that the new landowner also purchased the sharecroppers who worked the land and "he'd bury them [sharecroppers] out in the back somewhere."[48] For others, old arrangements between white landed families continued to guide cemetery use. Old plantation cemeteries became a continuum of burials, where the newly freed chose burials close to their ancestors.[49] Finally, local churches would bury the dead when there was no family land.

Cemetery burials in the South were far different from the North's garden cemeteries, where green grass and elegant benches made visitors think they were visiting a park rather than the dead. Southern family cemeteries evinced a number of different practices in creating an appropriate physical space and visual environment. Cemeteries were physical evidence that the dead continued to be a meaningful part of a family's social life in positive ways. Knowing that that effect could be negative unless a proper funeral and burial was conducted, one Georgia woman testified that, "I don't guess you be bothered much [*sic*] by the spirits if you give 'em a good funeral and put the things what belong to 'em on top of the grave."[50]

Cemetery space was typically marginal land that was useless to farm, but still meaningful to the family. Whether it was a mountain top in Appalachian

Tennessee like the Burris's family cemetery near Briceville, Tennessee, or a swampy area near Charleston, South Carolina, good farmland remained in cultivation, and eroded or rocky places became the family cemetery. The cemetery might also be within sight of the family's front porch so the dead could be seen with relative ease. Many of the more than six hundred cemeteries in Rutherford County, Tennessee, probably were well within sight of the front door or porch where the living could easily commune with the dead. They served as a reminder of who your ancestors were. In the case of Black families, they were also reminders of local white violence. North Carolinian Charlie Holcomb buried his son, Willie, near his house after Willie was most likely murdered by whites. Holcomb recalled, "We buried him at de foot o' dat big pine at de left o' de well, and made some grass to grow on de grave. Dat's de mound you was lookin' at as you come up to de house . . . I would go out at night and set under de pine by Willie's grave, and listen to de win' swishin' in de needles, and I'd do a lot o' thinkin.'"[51]

Once the land had been chosen, bodies could be buried in a variety of positions, but typically with an east-to-west orientation, with the head facing east and the feet facing west. While we now expect to be able to walk between neat and tidy rows, disorder reigned as much as anything in a rural family cemetery. White families were buried together, but not necessarily within nuclear family (mother, father, children) groups. Whites included aunts, uncles, cousins, or anyone with whom a blood kinship could be claimed. Many Black cemeteries had a more expansive vision of family. Anyone who lived in a given community was allowed to be buried in a Black-owned cemetery because "There was always room for one more."[52]

Park-like settings that dominated northern burials did not work in the South until the invention of motorized lawn equipment. Grass simply grew faster in the region's warmer, wetter climes. Mounded graves, used by Black and white alike, stood in place of the serene, tranquil graveyard disguised as a park, and visually signaled that someone was buried there. The rampant growth of grass gave the bareness of some mounds a clean, "scraped" look, suggesting the family cared for it constantly, keeping it free from weeds. As a Texan recalled, "Grandpaw killed himself keeping the weeds out of his cotton, and we're not about to let them grow on his grave now."[53]

Families then marked the grave with vegetation planted at the head of a grave: palmettos in South Carolina, or cedars and flowering bushes in Tennessee, for example. Rocks and stones covered still others, with the stonework protecting the body from desecration by free-ranging animals. Across the South, Black families typically, but sometimes white families, too, put broken cups, vases, pots, clocks, empty Colgate tooth powder cans, and other trinkets owned by the deceased on top of the grave in order to give the soul rest, a tradition carried over by the Black enslaved from West and Central Africa. Water was used symbolically, either represented by seashells, cups which held water, or in mirrors that reflected the world as water did, in reference to the belief among the former enslaved that water transited one to another place after death. Others assumed a spirit would not return to visit or haunt a family if its possessions were readily available to accompany the deceased to Heaven.[54]

Only the most elite southerners had granite markers, a physical reminder of a white family's power embedded into the landscape. These families had enough money to afford something as expensive as a stone marker in an era when memory and a cedar tree sufficed for common folk. The etching of names on those stones named the powerful and his family for all to see. For families who later visited graves, like Mississippian William Alexander Percy, cemeteries were among the "pleasantest places" because they were refuges with a "feel of home."[55] Arkansan Margaret Bolsterli noted that her family's tie to the land was an emotional one, one that was reinforced by her family graveyard. "The only oaks on our place now," she wrote, "are in the graveyard, where four generations of my family are buried and where I have picked my spot."[56]

Remembering and Mourning the Dead

Southerners distinguished among remembering, mourning, and grieving. Remembering the dead tended to be lessons to the living, a reminder that early deaths occurred because of human whim and frailty. Bolsterli thought she knew her cousin Frierson intimately because he was a constant reminder of how not to behave. Dead from acute indigestion after eating unripe pecans twenty-five years previously, "he was talked about as if he had just stepped into the wings (it was impatience that killed him; he could have waited for those pecans to get ripe)," she recalled.[57] Pauli Murray's grandmother said that when "people died their spirits hovered about their pictures, and I believed her. When I'd go into the parlor to dust or practice my music lessons, living and dead Fitzgeralds of all ages stared down upon me from every wall. No matter where I moved in the room their penetrating eyes followed me."[58]

While the dead could be ghosts who haunted a parlor, their entrance into Heaven was a sacred notation in a family Bible where important dates were listed. When a family recorded a death is unclear, but long before Progressives began counting the living and the dead, family Bibles acted as birth, marriage, and death records. Each date then was imbued with a meaning beyond simple demographic data, sacred because of a family's commitment to a Christian life. Nashvillian Laura Blalock invoked that sacredness when she wrote Mannie Howell after Howell's aunt passed away in 1913, saying, "I have placed April 19th in my Bible among my sacred days to be kept for her and devoted to her beautiful memory."[59]

Remembering was more than recording death; continuous visitation to graves during ubiquitous Decoration Days helped families reaffirm their commitment to their dead. Decoration Days, initially begun in the immediate post–Civil War era, kept the dead as part of the family. Floridian Eliza Kelly Brady recalled, "I have every week to visit the old Bosquobello Cemetery, this is Wednesday, my day to visit the graves of my family who are gone and my friends of earlier days, whom I have outlived. I have spent most of the afternoon there."[60] Church records documented Decoration Days as part of its liturgy, a way to build communion and community among those who lived while remembering those who had died. Midway Baptist Church (Alabama) recorded its decoration days in its minutes: "We served dinner then decorated the graves with flowers and after a very timely address and prayer by broth[er] J. L. Hudson we adjourned."[61]

Memory and commemoration were socially approved; mourning was not because it seemed, if not wasted energy, an act that questioned God's plan. Euphemistically referred to as "loneliness," southerners mourned in private, in letters or diaries, or carried on quietly with little acknowledgment. Ina Russell's grief at the loss of her cook and friend, Laura Green, caused her to write, "I know I have suffered a terrible loss, but I try to make the best of it. I expected to go to Knoxville Tenn. with papa, but I just couldn't go after Laura died."[62] Grief and paternalism mixed in the private setting of a diary or a letter where the grief between whites and Blacks could be acknowledged. Magnolia Le Guin, a white woman, grieved over the death of "Aunt" Mary, an old Black servant who left Le Guin's house to die. Mary was mentioned and mourned three different times in Le Guin's diary, including two notations of her burial. An entry dated December 22, 1905, reads, "Old Aunt Mary the negro woman who lived 2 or 3 years here, and who moved away from here a week ago, was buried yesterday. Poor old negro—how pitiful she did look when she left." Later, Le Guin wrote, "Old Aunt Mary (the negro who lived with us 3 yrs and moved severel [*sic*] days ago) was burried [*sic*] yesterday. Lived a week after moving there." Mary's appropriate death bed was one among her family and friends. Too, Le Guin's paternalism—that a dying Black woman should be let go from her employment—is evident in the passage.[63]

For others, external signs of sadness questioned God's plan or impeded a family's daily living. Grover Cleveland Goodwin consoled his mother in Durham, North Carolina, after the loss of "dear little Hattie," most likely a younger sister, in 1916. "Well, she has gone to a better place and for a permanent visit—that's our consolation," he wrote his mother. But he wrote, too, of a "strange loneliness as if one is gradually becoming alone, being left behind by those who have been dear to them so long."[64] Mountain southerners were adept at distancing themselves, acknowledging grief, but remaining focused on the practical. In a society where labor determined whether one could eat, there was little time to waste on mourning. One grieved for a moment and then moved on. Author Grace Lumpkin fictionalized mountain southerners' response to high infant mortality rates in *To Make My Bread* (1932):

> The church, a small log building, was up a short trail at the left. Across the road, on a slope, was the burying ground. Emma's husband and the three children who had come between Kirk and Bonnie were laid away there. There were not flowers in the burying ground. The graves lay flat and plain on the slope. The dead were dead and there was enough to do caring for the living. There was not a woman around that country who did not have one child or more in the ground. When a woman was ripe she gave birth, and if the child died, it did not help much, after the first days of sorrow, to weep. What was done was done.[65]

A Practical Approach to Infant Deaths

Mourning infants and children was seen as especially wasteful, given the high infant mortality rates in the South. Charleston funeral director Edwin G. Harleston Sr. and his wife, Louisa Moultrie Harleston, had ten children, five of whom died in infancy. Alabama soil pipe fitter Bill Jones and his wife lost five of their eleven children. Louisianan Lorita Rocca's mother had twenty-two pregnancies; fifteen children survived to adulthood. All of Martha Joint's children died at birth. North Carolinian Lizzie Linberger told an FWP interviewer, "Yes, I have three children living and I got eight dead. That's enough to kill anybody without anything else."[66]

Rampant infant death became part of a southern vernacular in which families stated they had so many children grown to adulthood, implying there were children who died along the way. As one anonymous woman told an interviewer, "I raised seven to get grown."[67] Southerners also distanced themselves linguistically by referring to children by the nickname "baby," e.g., that baby is John's, that baby is dressed in yellow, that baby is dead. Using "baby" until age five meant some infants never received names. New Orleanian Clotille said:

> I've had four babies—two girls and a boy, in 1904, but they died right away, so I never got to name them. They'd be more than thirty-four years old now—think of it! In 1906 I had a little boy, and he was born dead, but I named him James, just the same. Then in 1907 I had a little girl, and she died right away, so I didn't give her a name . . . We hadn't had no luck with our babies and we never did have no more.[68]

Stoic acceptance of grief also guided Magnolia Le Guin's hand. She buried her first child in 1894, three days after its birth; memorialized the child infrequently throughout her twelve-year diary; and planted a magnolia bush on the child's grave in 1902. Her language when referring to her living children was casually contingent. In February 1906, for example, she wrote in her diary:

Figure 1.2. One of many graves that remain on southern landscapes: Toddler Dorothy Lowe probably shares a grave with a sibling, simply called "Baby."

> We have a new baby—little over 3 weeks old—born on Jan. 25th—1906. Ghu [husband] named her Maggie Wynn. She is rite [*sic*] large for her age. Wasn't weighed at birth—tho' larger than Mary [her other daughter] was. She is rite long and will make a larger woman (if both live) than Mary will.[69]

To our modern eyes, the distancing of parent from child, in the phrase, "if both live," appears callous, but it was a protective mechanism that responded genuinely to a common, lived experience.

Letters exchanged between other families had the same distancing language. The Purvis family of Louisiana described to a distant sister named Carrie the death of a child in December 1901 in letters that lack an emotional involvement in the child's death. In one letter, a correspondent known only as "Sister," describes the death of her sister, Betty Purvis's child, referred to as "the baby":

> I wrote to you last Friday, but Mama has not written so I'll scribble you another note. You will see by this that I'm at Bettie's. I've been down since Saturday. Bettie 'phoned me to come right down. She thought the baby was dying. I got ready and before we got to Alto they phoned us she was dead. We buried her Sunday morning at cousin Nelson's . . . Bettie was right sad too but she had prepared herself for it. Mama had been with them a week. So I have been here several days. Will go home tomorrow. We have not made our fruit cakes, will make them this week and your white cake too. I have a dress to finish for myself and a percale to make for Rosa.[70]

Purvis's mother also wrote, describing in greater detail the child's death, now identified as "Little Bettie," and the greater depth of the letter allows the reader to hear the child's final words, a case of the "good death" expected among families and reported to others:

> As I have just finished cleaning up I'll try to write to you. I came home Monday from Bettie. I went down the Monday before to help nurse little Bettie who was very sick. Poor little child died Saturday between two and three oclock [sic] in the evening. The girls could not realize that she would die until just about three hours before she did, said all the time she was better. Bettie said she could not last much longer and was so anxious for you to go to Harriette's Thursday before she left to see her for she knew it would be the last time you would ever see her, she said just ten minutes before she died . . . "I is so tired" then held up her little arms to hug Bettie. Mary and I dressed her.[71]

Keeping the mix of mundane with death, which made it seem like a household issue, both writers reminded Carrie to approach "Aunt Hariette" because Bettie, the mother who had just lost her child, had left her bonnet and parasol at the aunt's house and wanted them back.

The practical eye cast on an infant's death was part of a common southern death experience, one so accepted, so mundane, that one must tease out descriptions of the process from a diverse array of primary sources. Even more difficult to find is the theology that was foundational to these rituals. That theology was also the bridge that southerners had to cross to reform their ideas about death, to loosen the strong ties between death and the southern landscape.

2 Heavenly Reunions and Progressive Reform

Stoicism and submissiveness to God's plan required southerners to distance themselves from their grief. Traumatic instances still stayed with them for years. For South Carolinian Alice Nashburn, it was a diphtheria epidemic in the 1880s that killed five girls in one family:

> [The girls] went down like nine pins, one after the other. They were buried in the little Episcopalian cemetery nearby . . . I went there with them to the cemetery to pick out a spot for the little graves. It was pitiful. I took the youngest girl to our cabin in hope she might escape the disease, but I heard her choke in the night and ran for the doctor. She followed her sisters to the cemetery.

Nashburn rued the theological assumptions that had underpinned real issues of life and death when she recalled them in 1939:

> Such scourges were then regarded as the dispensation of an inscrutable Providence, and they were borne with what resignation people could summon . . . Preachers sometimes exhorted their congregations to give up their sins in order to escape the wrath of an angry God. Fifty years ago not much was known about germs and sanitation and nothing at all about serums. So the five little girls choked to death and were laid side by side in a row.[1]

This shift in belief—from God the inscrutable punisher to death being caused by a knowable or discoverable entity in the physical world—came late to the South. But when it did, evangelical southerners grasped the possibilities with passion and fervor. In other words, by accepting that diseases had causes, they could transform landscapes of death into what historian Samuel Kelton Roberts called a "landscape of health."[2] That separation of death required evangelical Christian southerners to rethink who God was and what they were called to do. Because so many southerners did not live to their allotted three score and ten, according to Psalm 90:10 (KJV), evangelical Christians believed that, by lowering mortality rates, they could realize biblical prophecy. Indeed, with more time to save the sinful, Christians could ensure a sinner's trip to Heaven where he or she would be reunited with deceased family members. And the family reunion was key: Protestant theology promised that, according to John 14:2 (KJV), all family members who had been saved would be reunited in heaven. Want to know who those people were? Simply look outside your window to your family's cemetery, decently buried and well-remembered.

Protestant congregations firmly linked Christian ideas of life and death to the Progressive Reform Movement as it spread throughout the United States before World War I. Church-funded hospitals, tuberculosis sanitaria, and emergent healthcare movements (e.g., anti-hookworm campaigns) became a good Christian's new evangelical work, providing Southern Baptists and Methodists, the two most common Christian denominations (but other Protestant denominations, too), new spaces to evangelize the sinful. But this work had broader implications because it prompted new definitions of who and how one was sinful. Rather than a personal failing, sin became defined as a problem of environment that, if mitigated, could clear a path for a sinless and, potentially, healthier life. When reformers transformed the environment, evangelicals came to believe lowering mortality rates was both a new theology and death care ritual.[3]

Black and white southerners defined life extension differently, however, because their paths to the family reunion were substantially different, a product of a rigid racial system animated by violence and youthful deaths. As older mass epidemics like diphtheria, yellow fever, and malaria waned, white southerners focused on new epidemics, particularly tuberculosis (TB), working-class diseases like hookworm, and infant and maternal mortality. White Progressives, however, perceived TB to be a racial threat, too, in that contagious Black women who toiled as maids and laundresses in white houses might "infect" a white family. Tuberculosis, then, was simultaneously a theological problem, a potentially deadly illness, and a new social context that required new rules and regulations to manage the racial dangers associated with it.[4]

Black southerners also wanted to lower mortality rates because death was more common among them, given that living conditions, especially in burgeoning segregated industrial cities like Baltimore and Atlanta, provided a ripe environment for epidemics. Disease was rampant, to be sure, but so, too, were violent deaths visited on Black southerners by whites, particularly by lynching. If dying at an older age was the ultimate goal, then racial violence had to end. As they proposed anti-lynching laws, reformers simultaneously challenged the racial and political foundation of a white South that used legalized and legitimated violence. Lower mortality rates thus became a site through which Black and white southerners clashed over the potential of ending the South's high death rates, reinforcing or challenging the region's existing racial and social systems.

Give Me that (New) Old Time Religion

Progressive-era historians have long made the link between theological shifts in southern Protestant churches and new reform movements. Where those historians have erred, however, is in not seeing that older assumptions about death had to change before any real reform could occur. If religion was a cultural system, rather than simply a set of beliefs about the end of life, then that system as a whole had to change for Progressive reform to be meaningful. Making new Christians no longer could be the exclusive reason for denominations to exist; now Christian principles had to be applied to broader social contexts—like inadequate healthcare—for one to be a true follower.[5]

Evangelical Christianity spread across the South after the Great Revival of 1801, affecting Black and white alike. The ensuing shift in theology was a significant one. Unlike Puritans and other Calvinists who believed only a few "elect" could achieve salvation, evangelical Christians claimed anyone who accepted Jesus Christ as their Savior was eligible for Heaven, an everlasting life that mitigated the earthly death that awaited all mortal flesh. Evangelicals then incorporated the region's deadly landscape into sermons whereby preachers exhorted their parishioners to give up their sinful ways and accept Jesus. We die easily here, they said, so you had better prepare yourself by turning to Jesus sooner rather than later. If not, then you were doomed to Hell, to spend eternity away from your family.[6]

Heaven was, in real terms, a place for all saved family members to gather forever; a real death was an eternity spent away from the family because one had not been saved. Individual choice was crucial and the reward awesome. The willingness to be saved meant an afterlife in paradise where the deceased reunited with other family members. Southerners commonly referenced John 14:2 to describe that heavenly reunion: "In my Father's house are many mansions. If it were not so, I would have told you. I go to prepare a place for you" (KJV). Here, the gospel writer promised a celestial palace where a deceased family's reunion occurred under the watchful eye of their Lord, and as historian Ted Ownby wrote, southerners "viewed heaven as the setting for an eternally satisfying family life."[7] Mourning her mother's death in March 1904, Magnolia Le Guin wrote that her mother:

> [W]as homesick for her loved ones gone on before her. Just before taking her bed she spoke of her mother, her twin-brother, her first-born (Sunny he was called)

> and her last born, Splint. She told Papa . . . that she had friends (loved ones she meant) in a better world and it would not be long before she would be with them.[8]

"My heart ain't set on the comforts of this earth. Heaven, sweet heaven, is my home and—oh—I'm beginning to git homesick," Tennessean Parson Bill told a Federal Writers' Project (FWP) interviewer.[9]

It was during Sunday services and Wednesday night sermons that evangelical Christians learned these principles. Working from a Bible verse, preachers typically spoke as the spirit (or God) moved them, giving congregations the sense that God was speaking directly to them via the minister. Literacy was not a requirement for a man (and it was typically only men) to speak the Word; a "call" to preach and the Holy Spirit were. When sermons were recorded, it was outsiders like Fisk University sociologist Charles S. Johnson who wrote them down. Johnson recorded one minister at Mount Pizgah Church in Johnston County, North Carolina, in the 1930s, a minister who recognized he belonged to a pre-Progressive South. Telling his listeners, "I'm a lot old times. I'm one of them that don't go in for new fangled things," the minister preached on the Bible verses, "If a man die shall he live again?" (Job 14:14 KJV) and "I am the resurrection and the life" (John 11:25 KJV). He noted the deaths since his last visit to the congregation, saying:

> Since thirty days ago when we last met many things have been done. Some have gone to their judgment since that time. Gone to meet their Maker and stand in judgment before that stern judge. I'm glad God has spared me to be here. There're some who are sick today who desire this privilege we are enjoying [Audience responded Amen]. Since we met last, death has reigned right here in our neighborhood. As sure as you see a man living, you see a man who is going to die.[10]

Imminent death thus required an immediate repentance of sin and acceptance of Jesus.

The conversion experience where one claimed one's rightful place as a Christian redeemed sinners from a metaphorical death. So did membership in a specific church. New believers were quickly voted in as active church members; churches sometimes spent entire nights after a revival voting the converted into church. Kentuckian Maggie Dulin recalled, "Whatever they had to do, they had to do it all that night because in case you died that night, you'd be already in the church. You wouldn't die a sinner out of the church."[11] The communities forged in these churches then became the hands that were laid on the sick and dying.

Given the belief that the unconverted spent eternity in Hell, a family member who was not saved was a matter of significant anxiety because, without conversion, the heavenly family could not be complete. Evangelical Christianity imagined an either/or scenario. Either one was saved and upon death went to Heaven or one was sinful and went to Hell. Maggie Dulin told her father, "Daddy, if you should die a sinner and we have to go up and look down on you and you haven't give [*sic*] your life to God, it would kill every one of us . . . It would just kill us."[12] In other cases, the living were certain that unrepentant sinners went to Hell and mourned their presumed punishment. Neille Wesenger, an "inmate" at the Richmond County (Georgia) poor folks' home, was appalled to hear that a fellow inmate had died without repenting. She said, "I'm so sorry to know that he died without a moment to repent. If he had been a good man it wouldn't worry me."[13] As others lay dying, doctors reminded them of the potential exclusion, "It's no use . . . If you're not a Christian, you've still got time to make peace with your God. You're not going to die right away, but I've given you something to ease your suffering, and you're going to sleep soon, and—you won't wake up."[14]

The family reunion was imagined broadly and included more members than simply those related by blood. Because of high rates of death and remarriage, stepparents could be included in these reunions. Alabaman Dera Davis's stepdaughter, Rachel, whose mother had died, told Davis one day that she wanted to die first. Davis responded, "'What in the world are you thinking about, Rachel?' . . . 'Oh,' she said, 'I want to get to Heaven first so I can be there to get my mother's hand and put it in yours and tell her how good you always were to her children.'"[15] Reunions could also be between servants and their employers where white southerners imagined servants in eternal service to them. North Carolinian Lettice Boyer told an interviewer, "I knows I's gwine to heb'n and see Mistis and all my folks when I dies."[16]

Preaching the family reunion were Southern Baptists and Methodists, the two main southern denominations, although other denominations—Episcopal, Catholic, the Church of Christ, Presbyterian, and the Pentecostal churches—shared similar beliefs, albeit in segregated congregations. The Southern Baptist Convention (SBC), white, was founded in 1845 when doctrinal disagreements as well as slavery caused white southern Baptist churches to break from their northern counterparts and reunify as the SBC. By the 1930s, the convention could lay claim to some twenty-six thousand exclusively white churches in the South and Southwest. The vast majority of SBC churches, fully two-thirds, each had fewer than one hundred members. Loosely organized into "conventions," or groupings of individual churches, the SBC recognized that power lay within the local churches rather than in the church hierarchy. The organization required a doctrinal rigorousness that focused on making disciples of all humankind; in other words, one could not go to Heaven unless a Baptist and that Baptists had an exclusive path to Heaven, a practice called "landmarkism."[17]

The National Baptist Convention (NBC) represented Black southern Baptists in this era of segregated churches. White owners had worked to convert their enslaved before the Civil War; after the war, the newly freed established their own churches, and then formally convened as a group in 1895, with headquarters located just blocks away from the SBC in Nashville, Tennessee. In time, the

NBC published a newspaper, provided Sunday School pedagogy, maintained a book-publishing arm, and sponsored a Foreign Missions Board that sent missionaries out to make disciples out of the unconverted. But the NBC and its Women's Missions invested heavily in promoting a dynamic race consciousness and racial self-help. Powerful in number—nearly 2.2 million members belonged to the NBC in 1906—the convention foregrounded racial self-determination as it protested loudly against lynching, using its financial power and its press to proclaim a "[B]lack oppositional discourse," according to historian Evelyn Brooks Higginbotham.[18]

Methodists, who formed the second-largest denomination in the South, had a broader presence internationally with thirty million adherents worldwide by the end of the nineteenth century. Southern Methodist churches could have been considered an evangelical version of the Church of England (Anglican, known as the Episcopal Church in America) in their fidelity to a more liturgical structure. White southern Methodist churches shared a history similar to the SBC. They broke from their northern brethren over slavery in 1844, becoming the Methodist Episcopal Church, South. The southern church struggled with that break, given its willing adherence to external authoritarian structures, namely to Methodist bishops who established practice and doctrine. White Methodists reunited with the larger Methodist body in 1939 and renamed themselves the United Methodist Church.[19] Black Methodists, on the other hand, remained with northern Methodists after slavery ended, with two Methodist-derived denominations, the African Methodist Episcopal church and the Colored Methodist Episcopal (now Christian Methodist Episcopal) church.

Southern Baptists and Methodists both believed that, as their society modernized, their religious practices had to modernize so that they might mitigate the modern world's sinfulness. A modern civilization needed a modern theology rooted in institutions beyond the church building proper, for example, in new physical spaces like church-sponsored hospitals and tuberculosis sanitaria that simultaneously cured and rescued the sinful. With this shift, churches emphasized action rather than a specific theology, a southern interracial version of the Social Gospel that emphasized acts over Bible quotes and that could cater to a rapidly modernizing world. National Baptist Convention newspapers exhorted their readers to give up their "antiquated ideals" so that the church would seem modern to its constituencies.[20] One of the early shifts reconsidered disease causation itself. Whereas illness or an early death had once been seen as the evidence of a sinful nature punished by God, scientific advancements like the microscope meant the cause of illnesses could literally be viewed on a slide. Thus, instead of expecting death and preparing each parishioner to die sooner rather than later, some southern churches came to realize that investing in this new science meant living a longer life, giving them more time to transform the sinner into a saint.[21]

This required a firm focus on Psalm 90:10, which decreed, "The days of our years are threescore and ten; and if by reason of strength they be fourscore years, yet is their strength labour and sorrow; for it is soon cut off, and we fly away" (KJV). Far too many southerners died well before seventy years of age, not living up to their fully godly potential. The Bible provided examples that motivated this change. If Jesus performed healing miracles and God was the Great Physician, then healthy, long-lived Christians were living examples of God's favor. While no one expected evangelicals to raise their friends from the dead as Jesus did with Lazarus in John 11:1–46 (KJV), many considered good health and wellness an important part of a sinless Christian life. As an ailing Elsie Wall told an interviewer, "The Bible says send for a physician," once she found her "little home remedies" had failed to cure her.[22]

In a world with few doctors and even fewer hospitals, churches provided the physical space, giving emergent Progressive practices a sacred caste. But other factors provided more practical benefits. The system of tithing established a stable financial basis for that evolving care and foot soldiers from evangelical churches came to see public health as a new mission and early death a failure of not just good health practice, but of good religious practice. The SBC's convention proceedings for 1919 noted that Southern Baptists "go at this task of caring for all of our sick in a way that will meet to the utmost the every demand upon us as the followers of our Master, who healed the sick in His busy round of going about doing good."[23] The work of nurses in carrying out this biblical duty was so sacred that the SBC suggested a new order of deaconesses be created to make the link between lowering mortality rates and biblical justification more obvious.

More conservative theologians like Amzi C. Dixon—whose brother, Thomas Dixon, wrote *The Leopard's Spots*—argued otherwise. A prominent fundamentalist theologian, Dixon claimed an evangelical Christian's only job was to convert the sinful, not minister to their physical needs. A pastor known to him, he argued, said "he could not recall a single person who had been made a Christian through receiving material assistance." A Christian's only job was proselytizing, not seeing to welfare. This thread of fundamentalist evangelism would form a crucial roadblock to expanding healthcare, especially when those fundamentalist Christians were elected officials.[24]

Evangelizing Public Health in the South

The Progressive Movement thus found a reasonably warm welcome from churchgoing reformers, motivating a shift from preparing one for death to preparing that same person for a longer-lived, (hopefully) sinless life. The reform movement had been founded alongside the vast expansion of manufacturing and the ensuing influx of millions of immigrants who came to the United States from Southern and Eastern Europe in the 1880s and 1890s. Recoiling in horror at the awful conditions new immigrants lived in, middle-class reformers tried to mitigate poor living and working spaces, while science, with its promise of rational solutions to health and industrial problems, became the Progressives' most powerful tool. Definitions of poverty also shifted. No longer was poverty an example of a moral failing and an ungodly character, but an outcome of an environment that fostered poor health. Clean up the environment, Progressives argued, and poverty and illness would end.[25]

If science identified the causes behind disease, it also fostered new ways of interpreting high death rates, particularly from eugenicists who claimed it was the poor's genetic inferiority that caused them to live in squalor and die young. In the North, eugenicists focused on immigrants; in the South, some claimed high mortality rates among Black southerners were due to their genetic and evolutionary inferiority. Poor living conditions, in eugenicists' eyes, did not provide ripe environments for contagious disease; genetic inferiority did. The sheltering (read: ownership by white people) of the enslaved had supposedly kept them healthy; the end of slavery meant that freedmen and women were no longer "protected" by the slave system and their true biological destiny could emerge. Eugenicists claimed a significant uptick in death rates, or a "killing time," emerged in the immediate post–Civil War era, proof of Black supposed genetic inferiority and foreshadowing an eventual end of Black people as a "species."[26]

Black religious workers challenged eugenicists' arguments, latching onto environmental definitions of poverty. Their main focus was Black homes, which, they argued, simply needed to be uplifted to a healthier standard for death rates to fall. With that uplift, Margaret Murray Washington, Tuskegee University president Booker T. Washington's wife, argued, there would be "less disease, less sickness, less death, and less danger to others."[27] The Women's Missionary Union, formed just a few years after the NBC was founded, promoted healthy homes at its yearly Women's Conventions, believing a woman's place was to comfort the sick, advocate for temperance, and maintain a good home. Those conventions became a place to share information and plan policy that would trickle down to the local community.[28]

Even though they shared core Protestant and Progressive beliefs, it was eugenicists' arguments and white women's adherence to the South's racial system that created problems when Black and white Progressives worked together. Good health could not be achieved without a focus on both communities. White Progressives who worked with Black southerners thus had to rebut eugenics arguments, at least implicitly, that Blacks were slated to die out. Why help them otherwise? Moreover, white women had to account for the multiple ways that white southerners' neglect had in fact caused high mortality rates, requiring them to consider an environmental definition of poverty. Otherwise, their labor in promoting good health was a waste of time.[29]

Resolving—or avoiding—this conflict allowed white southerners to define specific working-class stereotypes as particularly deadly: the tuberculosis-infected Black maid who cleaned white homes or cared for white children, for example. This promoted a moral panic that forced white folks to attend to sick Black southerners. Black educators like the Tuskegee Institute's Robert Russa Moton and Booker T. Washington recognized this panic, using it to their advantage to draw white financial help to Tuskegee. But it was Black middle-class women who became ambassadors to the white community as Jim Crow boundaries hardened, building relationships with white women, even as those white women refused to see their Black counterparts as anything but junior partners. At the same time, that burgeoning relationship allowed Black Progressives to advocate for alternative causes of death. Illness and disease needed to be combatted, but economic segregation that relegated Black southerners to menial work and white violence against Blacks had to be addressed. Lowering mortality rates thus became a way to challenge a segregationist system built on violence and poor living conditions.[30]

Southern Diseases and Southern Healthcare

The loosening of strict fundamentalism from its biblical concrete allowed evangelical Christians to embrace science and modernism as mechanisms for knowing Jesus better. Baptist newspapers thus could claim that providing sanitary privies, decent housing for the poor, or safer working conditions was Christian work. Some Baptist churches took the reasoning a step further, turning their pulpits over to state health officers, hiring social workers as church employees, and paying for hospital beds for the indigent. The Nineteenth Street Baptist Church in Washington, DC, had, on its premises, a free dispensary with a dozen doctors, pharmacists, nurses, and dentists to cater to locals. The Alabama State Baptist Convention began financing its own hospitals for Black and white patients, segregating its medical care from the first.[31]

But the focus quickly turned to those epidemics that seemed uniquely associated with the South: tuberculosis, hookworm, and pellagra, albeit more so in the 1920s than before World War I. Initially called consumption for its ability to physically consume the body, tuberculosis was identified as an infectious disease when scientist Robert Koch discovered the tubercle bacillus in 1882; knowing the cause made new therapies such as quarantines available for a disease once thought to be inherited. That discovery also exposed the mechanisms by which TB spread (through the air via air droplets spread through sneezes, coughs, and speaking), transforming it into a great white plague. Tuberculosis killed

38-year-old author Thomas Wolfe; President Andrew Johnson's wife, Eliza, and probably several grandchildren; and 35-year-old country singing star Jimmie Rodgers, as well as thousands of ordinary southerners. Rodgers, who died in 1933, decried the epidemic in his song "TB Blues," singing with a fatalism that acknowledged his ultimate fate, a graveyard:

> I've been fightin' like a lion, looks like I'm going to lose
> I've been fightin' like a lion, looks like I'm going to lose
> 'Cause there ain't nobody ever whipped the TB blues
> I've got the TB blues.
>
> Gee but the graveyard is a lonesome place
> Lord but that ole graveyard is a lonesome place
> They put you on your back, throw that mud down in your face
> I've got the TB blues.[32]

Tuberculosis became both a medical problem to solve and a social context that required new rules and regulations. Nineteenth-century consumptive patients typically stayed home among family, infecting those around them, or traveled west to conquer the illness, infecting people on trains. Twentieth-century TB sufferers were isolated in or banished to the hundreds of new sanitaria that segregated the ill, mimicking the racial lines that were segregating Black southerners from white ones. Twenty-five health "resorts," mostly private, appeared in Asheville, North Carolina, alone. Moreover, southerners now wanted to see TB as a disease of the poor or of Black southerners, or both. Wealthy and middle-class people, Black and white, were stigmatized if they caught the disease because supposedly only the lower classes caught TB.[33]

Emergent urban spaces became cesspools that fostered TB as segregated housing and social space linked TB to the South's racial and class structure. Blacks lived here and caught TB; poor whites there and caught TB; and middle-class and elite whites lived somewhere else, trying to avoid being infected. In emergent urban spaces, new Black institutions like barbershops came to be known as breeding places for TB. "I was scared of barbering," Leroy Beavers Sr. recalled, "because they said all barbers died of TB. I know some barbers in my hometown that died with it. That scared me out of the barbershop."[34] Black parents and students also blamed Black colleges when their family members died from TB. York Garrett's mother held Shaw University (Raleigh, North Carolina) responsible for Garrett's brother's death from TB. Spelman Seminary (now Spelman College) administrators anxiously searched student applications for any sign of tuberculosis among their applicants in order to weed out potential problems.[35]

White working-class spaces, especially textile mills, also became linked to TB. Sisters Belle and Lottie Walter were put to work in a textile mill in Concord,

North Carolina, around 1910 because, "In two years we had to pay for five funerals, and you know how they cost," Lottie said. But Belle caught TB in the mill, and after spending time in a sanitarium, could no longer work.[36] Another mill worker, Martha Belk, recalled:

> That woman down the street had the toobercalosis. Ever'body else was scairt to go 'round her, but I figgered . . . I wouldn't ketch this. They wasn't anybody to look out for her whilst her husband was at the mill so I been goin' there. She died 'bout three weeks ago. It sure was pitiful. She was the purtiest woman I b'lieve I ever seen . . . She had a face jus' like a baby's. I sure hated to see her die."[37]

Evangelical Christian southerners claimed TB to be "the plague of all plagues which lays waste to the lives, the health, the homes, and the happiness of the people of the South," a symbolic description based on a close reading of biblical plagues.[38] But many came to see TB as the effect of an industrializing, modern South. "The South is predestined to be thoroughly industrialized—to become more and more the mill and shop center of the United States," the SBC's E. P. Alldredge wrote in a report entitled "Scope and Need of a Tuberculosis Sanitarium," arguing the organization would be "forced to take more active and strenuous measures against the encroachments of the great white plague."[39] The SBC's numbers, garnered from the federal government, seemed to support its argument that TB was specifically a southern plague that needed a Southern Baptist response. According to those numbers, more than 57,000 southerners died from TB each year and another 288,000 suffered from the disease, even as the rest of the nation had seen a steady decline in TB mortality. The South's rate remained a stubborn 169 per 100,000, with higher rates in North Carolina (378 per 100,000), Kentucky (201), and Florida (189). Alldredge claimed that the South's TB death rate was 14.2 percent higher than the rest of the United States and higher than most countries save China. This, he suggested to his Baptist readers, was the new field for missionary work since disease was evidence of a society's moral decline rather than an individual's.[40] Southern Baptists focused on Black men, claiming the "shadow of the Black Men" was a deadly spreader of TB, an easy jump given their already symbolic link to lynching. The SBC's convention records noted:

> The people of the South as a whole have failed to see the largest, darkest and most ominous cloud which overshadows the lives of those who live alongside of the Black Man—I speak of the negro's amazing susceptibility to tuberculosis, the sad lack of hospital or other form of care or restraint over those infected with the plague, the thousand and one ways in which they can and do spread the disease among themselves and the whites around them, the terrible fatality of the disease among the negroes when once it has infected them and, finally the problem of mitigating, if not eliminating, the plague from them.[41]

This "real" shadow scattered death and disease wherever he went. The solution was not for the SBC to build TB sanitaria for Black TB sufferers, however; instead, the SBC believed that Black leaders needed to build hospitals to segregate Black TB sufferers away from the white populace.

In framing Black southerners as TB disease vectors, the SBC used white moral panic to plant hospitals and TB sanitaria exclusively for whites. Tithing provided the stable financial basis; now the hospital bed could do the same evangelical work, and in a much more poignant moment, as the patient was sick and potentially dying (it also affirmed its racial work). In fact, the SBC erased the line between saving souls and healing bodies because the shifts in theology that made Progressivism logical to evangelical southerners also made ludicrous any division between healthcare and evangelism. SBC writers said:

> The lost man snatched back from the grave in a Christian hospital, where Christian physicians and Christian nurses attend him, where ministers of the gospel see and counsel him and where a faithful Bible woman comes with her tactful, tender messages of hope and ministry of good cheer, will almost invariably mean the conversion of that patient, the consecration of his life to the service of the Master, and often the consecration of his talents and his possessions. To the unsaved patient another lease on life means another chance for life eternal[.]

It was therefore a "divinely appointed mission" to build hospitals, and by 1918 eleven SBC hospitals had been built, mostly in the South, with three more hospitals and a TB sanitarium in El Paso, Texas, planned. Many of the state Baptist Conventions also had their own hospitals, whose solvency was viewed as evidence of God's favor. The first state Baptist hospital in Alabama was built in Selma, for example; another quickly appeared in Birmingham. Both were supported by Southern Baptist churches.[42] One should not underestimate the impact of these church-affiliated hospitals that provided care. Jackson, Mississippi's state capital and most populous city, boasted only four hospitals in 1913. Two were state institutions (a charity hospital and an insane asylum), one was a private sanitarium, and the fourth was the Mississippi Baptist Hospital.[43]

The Black Baptists' tithing system was not sufficient to build new hospitals, even with the NBC leading the way. They did build one hospital in Memphis, the Jane Terrell Baptist Hospital in 1909, which grew to 100 beds by the 1920s. But their money and church newspapers supported medical institutions like Meharry Medical College, which gladly accepted the donations generated by the *National Baptist Union-Review's* regular column, "Meharry News." Indeed, the medical college was a point of race pride for Black southerners, and the column reinforced that pride with announcements of important advances taken by the college and its faculty.[44]

What the NBC could not do in terms of institution building, it could in promoting good Progressive health practices on its newspaper's pages. In other words, it used its publications to link theological shifts to its Progressive work. In a February 1919 column entitled "Health Notes," for example, the *National Baptist Union-Review* decried the "primitive" nature of health remedies. The newspaper advised,

> No one would think of employing a blacksmith to repair and put in order a valuable watch. Yet many of us take a neighbor's advice to use a remedy he thinks would be good for an aliment [*sic*] we know nothing about. Thus we tamper with our bodies which are more *wonderfully* and delicately constructed than the finest time piece that was ever made. When your machine is in need of repair, try to get an expert to examine it and put it in running order again.[45]

The word "wonderfully" was a nod to Psalm 139:14, which claimed humankind was "fearfully and wonderfully made" (KJV). Investing in healthier bodies was thus sacred work. Ads for different health products, though they also supported the newspaper financially, reinforced the links between good health and theology. Ads promising to treat pellagra and promoting "health belts" that touted curative properties appeared on newspaper pages alongside Home Missionary Society news and obituaries for famed preachers.[46]

Other Black institutions joined the NBC in promoting good health. Tuskegee Institute, which was not church-affiliated, designed the National Negro Health Week to "enthrone health and long life."[47] From 1915 to 1951, this truly national week challenged both Blacks and whites to work together to create a healthier South. "Because if we die," Tuskegee President Robert Russa Moton argued, "they die," meaning that germs did not know a color line, even as white southerners attempted to establish one. Good Black health thus meant good white health.[48] Multiple organizations from the American Red Cross and the National Tuberculosis Association provided information for these mainly educational weeks which small Black Baptist and Methodist churches hosted and where religious space encouraged healthier living.[49]

High death rates were never solely caused by disease. In a sharp diversion from white Progressives and responding to the work that muckrakers like Ida B. Wells were already pursuing, Black Baptists pushed for an end to racial violence. Diseases like TB were "natural deaths," according to some, meaning there was a randomness that could attack anyone. Unnatural deaths were those perpetrated by others. Ida B. Wells found that, of the 292 lynchings she investigated in 1892, the victims were mostly Black men who had challenged the South's economic system. They were cast as rapists, however, who supposedly "defiled" white women, using what historians call the Southern Rape Myth. Many times, once a so-called rape charge had been levied, crowds stormed (or were handed the keys to) jail cells and the accused prisoner was lynched.[50]

The NBC promoted anti-lynching laws to counter those unnatural deaths on the *National Baptist Union-Review's* pages. "What was once excused as an extraordinary proceeding to prevent the commission of a peculiarly heinous offense has become a convenient medium for the gratification of savage revengefulness and barbarous impulse," columnists noted as they reported on the 62 known lynchings that occurred in 1918.[51] If whites believed eugenicists' descriptions of Black health and wellness, Black theologians countered that whites' own savagery had the potential to send them down the ladder of civilization, there to wallow with other "barbarous" sorts, and by implication, die out as well.

Private Charities

From the beginning of their work, however, a lack of financial reserves hampered Progressive work in the first decades of the 1900s. Thus, they willingly accepted the support of extra-regional charitable organizations who tended to isolate and attack specific illnesses rather than address death rates in a holistic fashion. Probably the most successful private charitable health program was the Rockefeller Foundation's campaign against hookworm. Considered a quintessentially southern illness, hookworm was linked inextricably to stereotypes of a lazy, indolent populace. The parasite grew especially well in the warm climes of the South, entering the skin of rural southerners, typically children who ran around barefoot in areas where someone, infected with the parasite, had defecated. Eventually, hookworms wrapped themselves around the small intestine of the host, causing anemia, lethargy, stunted physical and cognitive growth, and eventually death. Inadequate rural sewer systems failed to separate away fecal matter, hence the sanitary "privy" movement that sought to contain the problem.[52] If southern landscapes were deadly, then hookworms were one bullet that connected the deadly landscape to humans.

Under the auspices of the Rockefeller Sanitary Commission for the Eradication of Hookworm Disease, the Foundation invested one million dollars to eliminate hookworms and was so successful that the worms were virtually eradicated by World War II. Mobile medical clinics promoted the commission's work in rural areas as Sanitary Commission "health trains" were sent from one state to another, espousing the news of good health and good sanitation. Demonstration clinics, where good health practices were on display, were another mechanism, and thousands showed up for treatment in North Carolina, Alabama, and Texas. In Sampson County, Alabama, a doctor treated 136 cases of hookworm in one day. Those who were treated later wrote they recognized God's hand in this work. One woman, whose children had been treated for hookworm, wrote that God had "sent you within my reach when I look over them now."[53]

The promised family reunion did not cease being a southerner's goal as the potential of good health emerged. Evangelical Christians saw lowering mortality rates as a new form of evangelism because more sinners could be saved before dying, ensuring a complete familial circle. This theological shift did not come all at once, but continued to grow and evolve as the twentieth century unfolded. An emergent death commercial system was a powerful, albeit ironic, partner. A lower mortality rate might mean fewer customers for morticians, but insurance companies and burial societies, who formed the financial basis for funeral goods, made clear that dying young was not just a theological issue, but an economic one as well.

3 Life Extension and the Emergence of a Death Commerce System

A. D. Pool, an Elizabeth City, North Carolina, "pea" (soybean) farmer, considered himself a lucky man at settlement time[1] when there was enough money to pay for his grandchildren's industrial life policies at five cents per week. He told a Federal Writers' Project (FWP) interviewer in 1938, "I don't want de county to have to bury 'em if dey dies . . . about de biggest thing poor cullud folks get out of dis life is a funeral at de end of it, and when de county has to foot de funeral bill it aint much of a funeral I'm tellin you."[2] But Pool's response would have infuriated Booker T. Washington, long dead by the time Pool spoke to the interviewer (Washington died in 1915). Washington believed Black southerners focused too much on their deaths, saying,

> The trouble with us is that we are always preparing to die. You meet a white man early Monday morning and ask him what he is preparing to do . . . he is preparing to start business. You ask a colored man . . . he is preparing to die.[3]

But Washington's statement missed something important. Death was a new economic system that attracted funeral professionals, insurance agents, and burial societies who saw the South's high death rates as a good business opportunity. Emerging as evangelical Christians reimagined when one should die, customers like Pool recognized that professional morticians, especially Black ones, endowed southerners with a dignity in death that was not available in life. Even a small amount of money invested over time in insurance policies or a burial society gave them access to those professionals. With that new commercial system came new assumptions that dovetailed with Progressive-era healthcare. Early deaths became expensive deaths with financial implications for the emergent commercial system. If one extended life, then the insured could fully pay for their funerals.

This commercial system of death created new conflicts within southern racial hierarchies, however. Death commerce, with its elaborate rituals and consumer goods, promised a dignity in death even as some components reaffirmed segregationist practices with Black morticians burying Black customers while white morticians could bury anyone. Segregation, ironically, provided Black professionals with an economic security that allowed them to advocate for Black southerners in general, free from any white challenges. Death care thus became a new economic and political concern, not just a social and cultural one.[4]

The mediators between these interests were local, county, state, and, to some extent, federal governmental agencies, who began seeing the potential of life extension, although they remained stubbornly opposed to spending money. Whether by creating Death Registration Areas at the federal level, licensing new death care professionals at the state level, or assuming the care of the impoverished dead at the city or county level (badly, according to Pool), some government officials bowed to Progressives who saw reshaping government to be more interventionist crucial to their work. Local and county governments, especially, may not have wanted to pursue good health, but to be considered decent under the new rules laid out by Progressive evangelicals; governments (many of them staffed by those same evangelicals) had to make sure the indigent were buried, the causes of death identified, and a death certificate issued. Once the certificates were collected and causes of death counted, Progressives then targeted the diseases that created the highest death tolls. Good care in death thus became intrinsically linked to good care in life.

The Emergence of Death Professionals

The funeral profession's emergence is a story that has been well told by historians who have noted the rise of death professionals in the post–Civil War era, especially in large cities. But the now-widespread availability of funeral ledgers, which charted day-to-day operations as well as consumer choice, provides an intimate look at how daily transactions formed this new commercial system. That earlier work typically begins with how Black and white southerners came to the funeral profession. In the South, some used their skills as casket makers to start their funeral business. Others, typically Black, came to professional death care via livery services which could carry a casket a long distance. Mrs. Alfred P. Boyer, a New Orleans native, and Charleston, South Carolina's Edwin Harleston were both well-known stable owners who became undertakers. Their "rolling stock," buggies and horses, were available for rental, moving living bodies around their cities; it was an easy next step to move dead bodies from home to graveyard (funeral home services were still relatively rare). Rolling stock identified an undertaker as a respectable man or woman who could bury the dead decently with an elegance unmatched in the rural South, so much so that the Scales Funeral Home's first horse-drawn hearse is still on display in Murfreesboro, Tennessee, to honor that memory.[5]

Funeral directors provided another new service, embalming, especially in cities. But facing competition from itinerant "satchel" embalmers, many of them Black who brought vernacular embalming practices to the body, white undertakers organized state-level organizations such as the Georgia Funeral Directors' Association (founded 1886) to pass legislation that required a license to embalm, thus protecting their nearly exclusive right to legally embalm a body. These organizations were not open to Black embalmers, who organized their own associations, for example, the Independent National Funeral Directors Association in Georgia (founded 1924) and South Carolina Colored Morticians Association (founded 1925).[6]

For southern states that required voters to pay poll taxes, it made sense to pass laws that imposed high costs on professional licenses, hoping licensing fees would exclude all but the wealthiest white undertakers. State legislators in Tennessee, for example, passed two laws in 1909 that helped secure white undertakers' place as death professionals. The first stated that embalming licenses could only be acquired by attending an embalming college or by being examined by a local licensed undertaker. They priced licenses at $10 for the initial year and then $2 every year after, giving the State Board of Embalmers, also established by the 1909 law, the power to remove those who did not consistently keep up with licensing fees. The second law required that funeral professionals fill out a death certificate to be signed by a doctor. Death certificates were then sent to state officers who counted causes of death. The Tennessee laws were especially significant because the state borders eight other states, and many undertakers obtained Tennessee licenses, like Fletcher Fielder in Bowling Green, Kentucky, who purchased his Tennessee license in 1917.[7]

Even though government officials typically recognized white undertakers as death officers, evolving Jim Crow standards ironically provided a stable customer base for Black undertakers, particularly in large cities like Atlanta and Memphis. White undertakers were notorious for not bathing Black bodies nor styling hair appropriately, demeaning the body and, by extension, the family. Black undertakers, scholar Karla FC Holloway wrote, responded "not only to a business opportunity but also to a sense of cultural responsibility and community necessity."[8] "Black death," at the hands of a white mob or from impoverished circumstances, made Black undertakers crucial actors in racial dramas since their death care restored dignity to a family stripped of it. Additionally, as "race men" who followed Booker T. Washington's tenets of self-help and entrepreneurship, funeral home owners were self-made (typically) men who disproved white theories of their worth.[9]

White undertakers recognized the economic threat that Black undertakers posed and responded with violence. Clarie Collins Harvey's father opened an undertaking business in Hattiesburg, Mississippi, in 1916, threatening his white competition. White men passed out handbills on which, she recalled, "the white funeral home printed, 'Don't patronize those n———s, we can give you better service.' And there were threats, all kinds of threats. The KKK was menacing." Harvey's father and his partner traded nights sleeping at the business with shotguns ready. Implicitly, white undertakers understood that Black consumers sought a service from them but did not realize the use of colloquial language undermined their claims.[10]

The defining practice that affirmed one as a funeral professional, even more than an embalming license, was a funeral ledger that provided an order to the information the state required for a death certificate. The use of a ledger disengaged death from its secure place, woven as it was into the social fabric of daily rural life, and distinguished death as a unique business transaction rather than common and ordinary. Ledgers in general had a significant place in southern culture, since landowners relied on them to exploit sharecroppers or keep accounts of customers in rural southern grocery stores. While some ledger keepers were ethical, many were not, as the debits noted in a ledger could be used to prove a sharecropper or customer owed money, rather than the other way around. Ledgers were such a significant racial tool that landowners threatened violence if sharecroppers kept their own ledgers or demanded to see accounts. North Carolinians Aaron and Mary Matthews recalled the tantrum a white landowner threw when they asked to see his ledgers. "He said nobody should keep no dam' books on his place, and if we didn't like it, Goddam' it, git out. He charged us wid [*sic*] stuff we didn't know what 'twas for and wouldn't explain nothing," Mr. Matthews said.[11] Ledgers, then, carried with them the weight of decades of racial exploitation when used by white southerners.

The common, though not exclusive, use of a preprinted funeral ledger called the *American Funeral Record*, published in St. Louis, allowed national expectations of a "decent" funeral to guide an undertaker's hand and, perhaps, influence a consumer's choice. Other Progressive personality traits appeared here, too, for example, the desire to count causes of death, where the deceased died and other relevant family information. The ledger included a code of ethics that admonished funeral directors to "Be courteous and polite under any and all circumstances, however trying."[12] It also outlined appropriate funeral rituals, some at odds with southern practice, as when the ledger assumed a coffin would always be closed. Some larger funeral homes—the Memphis National Funeral Home and Atlanta's J. H. Hanley's Bell Street Funeral Home—printed their own forms, but Memphis's J. C. Oates Funeral Home, the Daniels Funeral Home (Rome, Georgia), and the Benson Funeral Home (Andalusia, Alabama) all used the *American Funeral Record*. Smaller funeral homes such as the Robertson County (Tennessee) Funeral Home used a truncated version.[13]

Because it was a data-driven document, the *American Funeral Ledger* required the undertaker to fill out a significant amount of demographic data. When was the deceased born? Who were the parents? Where were they born? And most importantly, how did the deceased die? Sam Stanley Rainey's ledger notation in 1904 by H. F. Hoover's book (Bedford County, Tennessee) was typical of an early twentieth-century ledger, a death noted with minimal information:

> Sam Stanley Rainey of Shelbyville, died Apr. 8, 1904 of consumption, buried Apr. 10, 1904. Benevolent Cemetery, age 19 years and 8 months. Ordered by S. V. Rainey. Coffin $30.00, Robe or Wrapper $3.00, hose 20 cents and gloves 15 cents.[14]

Dollie Hay's entry in 1930 when she also died from TB was more typical of several decades of Progressive influence and new Tennessee laws:

> Dollie Kate Hay, age 36 years and 29 months [*sic*], married, born in Bedford County, died June 11, 1930 at Camp White of tuberculosis, funeral at home, buried June 11, 1930 Willow Mount Cemetery. Husband Tom Hay. Father D. Helton who was born in Bedford County. Mother Donie McLaughlin who was born in Bedford County. Dr. Burdette and Ray [doctors who signed death certificate]. Ordered by Tom Hay. Clergy Rev. Sibley. Casket $115.00, metal box $6.00, robe $30.00, hose $1.50 and drayage on chairs $2.00.[15]

Ledger information was then reported to the state via death certificates and to statistical researchers at the federal level, and later became the basis for newspaper obituaries.

While ledgers assumed this level of demographic detail would be available, in many cases it was not since the clientele southern undertakers served did not necessarily think in Progressive ways. The Robertson County Funeral Home undertakers found this to be true in 1925 when they listed Mrs. Lizzie Chandler's age as "about 43" and Albert Henry as "about 98." When Jim Maxwell died in McKenzie, Tennessee, in March 1924 of pellagra, his wife did not know his mother's name nor her birthplace.[16] The same was true in big cities as well. Atlanta undertaker J. H. Hanley simply wrote "DK" for "Don't Know" when demographic information was not available.

But more than documenting family relationships—information that has since become a treasure trove for genealogists—ledgers also document the slow transformation of death practices from the rural, do-it-yourself affair to a commercial service. Ledgers suggest that customers, particularly rural ones, approached the purchase of new death wares warily, initially purchasing small consumer items that were difficult to produce at home, such as metal handles, name plates, and material to line a handmade coffin. Incipient purchases were recorded in ledgers into the 1930s. The Benson Funeral Home, in rural Andalusia, Alabama, for example, sold R. A. Kuloes's family $28 worth of hardware, most likely casket handles, when he died in July 1930.[17]

Metal name plates and handles indicate a significant, albeit incipient, shift in death rituals. In rural graveyards, trees, plants, and memories indicated where bodies had been laid, suggesting that the body's presence was an ephemeral one. Metal, however, did not waste away. The installation of metal handles was thus more than making coffins easier to hold and carry; it meant a relatively permanent presence in the ground. Name plates with names of the deceased engraved on them extended this. Not only was the body permanently marked in the ground, but the body was identified as a unique individual. The name plate ensured the person, named and known, was permanent in the grave, that is, if someone chose to dig up the grave. The Tennessee Valley Authority (TVA) found these early consumer habits when it moved more than five thousand graves in 1933 and 1934 to build the Norris Dam in east Tennessee. The TVA disinterred Bettie Hatmaker, who died in 1922, in October 1934, finding traces of her skull and large bones, a coffin with the top and bottom decayed, and four handles and a name plate.[18]

Purchasing an entire coffin, rather than just the handles, became more common by the mid-1910s. Memphis undertaker J. C. Oates, whose first record dates from 1916, sold coffins to rural Black southerners who lived miles outside of city limits. Multiple entries note sales of coffins, for example, to customers in Benjestown, Tennessee, some ten miles north of Memphis in what was then a rural part of Shelby County, for $13. Walter Harris King, a white Smyrna, Tennessee, undertaker, sold cheap caskets, too. In July 1917, for example, King sold a casket worth $20 to Marcus Wilson.[19] Initial purchases thus evinced a willingness to purchase some goods that eased the workload (a handmade coffin was, after all, a time-intensive task), but not a wholesale acceptance of new death care products.

As morticians documented purchases, the manner by which they recorded transactions displayed what historian Steven M. Stowe called "the local social order."[20] Using language cribbed from sharecropping and grocery store ledgers, funeral professionals structured purchases on a page so they fit (or not) within the South's racial and economic hierarchies. White undertakers handled this by reinforcing notions of race on their ledger books. The *American Funeral Ledger* had a separate line, for example, for the undertaker to note the race of the deceased. All of the white undertakers inscribed a "C" or "Col" (for colored) next to Black southerners' names as well as marking Black in that other space. Undertakers also distinguished men and women by race when using the honorific "Mr." or "Mrs." White people in southern society were referred to as Mrs. or Mr. while Black people were referred to by their first names or by "Aunt" or "Uncle." Even though the *American Funeral Ledger* provided a space to list a woman's marital status, Mrs. was typically noted next to white women's names, usually with little regard to their class status, and Black women were typically listed by first name and last name with no honorific listed. The Daniel Funeral Home (Rome, Georgia) recorded a typical instance in 1921, when it buried two women: Georgia Sparks (listed as Black) who died in July and Mrs. Francis Bryant (listed as white and 104 years old) who died in October.[21]

Black funeral ledgers fervently challenged that local social order as undertakers restored their living and dead clients the dignity and respect denied them in life. The restoration of titles seems to have mattered most. Atlanta undertaker J. H. Hanley buried Mrs. Rose D. Joseph's infant in 1924 as well as the "infant of Mr. Cornelus [*sic*] Benning," when that child died in February 1930.[22] It is unclear whether Mrs. Joseph or Mr. Benning saw their names written in the ledger. At the very least, written titles probably reflected a spoken conversation in which the undertaker used Mr. and Mrs. when both clients placed their orders. The services undertakers provided and the dignity they restored, however, cost money and the desire for these goods inserted a new worry into death care's prescribed rituals, how to pay for them. The evolving death commerce system provided clear solutions to that problem.

The Expansion of Burial Societies

Lacking money to put someone away decent could now provide humiliating moments. The most shameful scenario occurred when a family put a plate on the dead body, a silent request for funds. South Carolina mill worker Mattie Smith recalled that she would "hate to have a collection taken up for any of us, but then a body can't help getting down and out sometimes."[23] It was a public admission that the family was poor, becoming an insult to wield in fights. Pauli Murray's family members insulted each other in front of neighbors, saying, "You're so pore, they'd have to put a saucer on your corpse to get the money to bury you."[24]

Undertakers proved flexible in accepting payment, for example, when customers used commodities to pay for death goods. When Joe Chandler bought a casket, box, and a cedar plank for "baby," in January 1923 (the bill was $60), he used 22 heifers, corn, one goat valued at $1.50, and five other goats valued at $2.00 each to pay for the purchase. Sometimes, families left the undertaker's establishment with a note to pay back an undertaker or offered a mortgage, as Lee Robertson did when the bill for the casket and box to bury his son in 1917 came to $25. While this was a predominantly rural practice, Memphis undertaker Oates occasionally accepted commodities, such as a horse and wagon from Lamzy Scott in December 1918 to bury Scott's father.[25]

Shame was thus part of this emergent world of death commerce. To counter that, a new set of financial arrangements began to emerge, rooted in older practices where burial societies at first, and then later, insurance companies (both national and regional) promised a secure financial foundation to bury the dead. Along with those relatively secure finances, burial societies added ceremony to the funeral itself with intensive rituals intending to confer honor and dignity.

While there were multiple burial societies across the South for both Black and white southerners, the majority seemed to have been Black-run organizations. Some began with free Blacks who lived in urban areas, particularly Charleston and New Orleans, in the mid-seventeenth century. The Humane Brotherhood of Charleston was a burial society whose members were "respectable Free Dark Men," and who organized in 1843 because "Death, inevitable as it is, brings on its train numerous alarming and sensible privations."[26] Burial societies expanded in number between 1880 and 1930 as organized groups promised to care for each other in health, in sickness and in death. The emphasis on conferring solemn rites gave Black burial societies greater economic and social power. White burial societies did the same, with political groups such as the Association of Confederate Soldiers and the Sons of Confederate Veterans providing burial rites at a Confederate soldier's death, reinforcing the perception of heroism among Confederate soldiers and affirming the Lost Cause narrative.

Southerners joined multiple national burial societies, affiliating with organizations like the Maccabees, the Masons, or Eastern Star. The Stone Square Prince Hall Masons of Burnt Corn, Alabama, a local chapter of the Black Masons, charged its members anywhere from fifty cents to $1.25 in dues, and contributed $4.30 or $4.50 for burials. But there were plenty of local burial societies alongside the better-known societies. New Orleans undertaker Mrs. Albert P. Boyer's account books listed numerous local burial associations such as the Young True Friends, Les Dames St. Coeur, and the Lutheran Lodge.[27] At times, a burial society began locally and then spread across the region. The United Order of the Tents, for example, was a Virginia-based burial society organized by two Black women in 1867 that eventually spread nationally. North Carolinian Ruth Davis belonged to the Tents, and knew well its history, "It started out that these two slave ladies didn't like the way that the masters were burying the women whenever [they], you know, died. So they started this organization with the help of two white lawyers . . . so that the women that belonged to it could have a proper burial." When Davis joined, her monthly dues were thirty-five cents with a $100 burial guarantee. The pride she took in those two freedwomen starting the organization she now supported was priceless.[28]

The dues taken from constituent members created a set of responsibilities should illness or death occur. Leaders determined those rituals, gathered dues, vetted applicants, and kept minutes detailing the burial society's actions. The collected dues then became a relatively firm financial relationship with local undertakers, in some cases paying for an entire funeral, in others, just for the casket. Burial societies like Asylum Bersham Society contracted with Mrs. Boyer, who conducted thirteen funerals for the organization in 1897 and 1898 which paid between $2 and $13 for its members' coffins.[29]

Burial societies stood in as family and as a moral cudgel. New Orleanian Elizabeth Henry recognized her burial society would act as her family after her children had died. She told an FWP interviewer, "I pay fifty cents every month. Got to, I don't want no corporation [probably county burial] to bury me. I wants [*sic*] a respectable funeral. I'm goin' to scrap till I can't no mo."[30] But with the promise to bury well came strict rules about behavior that made death care both racial uplift and a staunch moral code. The Benevolent Aid and Burying Society of Glendora, Mississippi, organized in 1910, said its objectives were to "care for the sick, bury the dead and help the widows and orphans of deceased members and to generally uplift the colored race."[31] The Knights and Daughters of Tabor's (Mound Bayou, Mississippi) strong moral code included instilling Christian behavior in living members, pursuing an education, and being temperate. The implied threat was: Behave, or we will not bury you. The Mississippi Benevolent/Standard Fraternal Aid Society (Pickens and Lexington, Mississippi) levied fines on those who missed a funeral, for spitting on the floor or smoking, and for using vulgar language. If the inappropriate behavior was bad enough—if they were drunk in public, for example—a member could lose death benefits.[32]

Codes of conduct were essential, but precise, ceremonial rituals were required for the funerals themselves, with many Black burial societies simply bypassing white etiquette and creating their own. Formal titles, sometimes conceived by the organization, were used to create a hierarchy among the membership. Unique clothing such as special collars, badges, or sashes, as well as distinctive aprons, marked members as belonging. These self-created rituals motivated burial societies like the Christian Benevolent Society in South Carolina to march three times around an open grave and ring the society's death bell one time with each pass around it.[33]

Black burial societies were meaningful beyond the dignity the ritual conferred. In rural areas, it changed relationships between sharecroppers and white landowners. Once, white plantation owners provided the wood for coffins to be constructed by Black carpenters. The old system did not acknowledge the dead, only the compassion and generosity of the white person. Moreover, offering boards to make a functional, but plain, coffin reinforced assumptions that only certain types of burials were appropriate for Black sharecroppers. Burial societies now allowed sharecroppers to refuse the benevolent act. South Carolinian native Julia LaRoche, whose family owned a local plantation, said, "This was before burial policies came into style... We will give them boards now, but they don't want them. The old time funerals cost only a few dollars; now they pay 'em as high as two hundred [dollars]."[34] Burial societies had significant implications for relationships between Blacks and whites when burial societies simply ignored that older paternalism while forging a new set of death practices.

The Expansion of Burial Insurance and the Introduction of Life Extension

The line between a burial society and burial insurance was a fine one, to be sure. Really, the main difference was that a burial society provided a ritual as well as cash, while burial insurance simply conferred cash. Among white southerners, better access to Chicago and New York insurance companies and those companies' willingness to insure them meant a relatively secure financial basis to pay for a decent funeral, hence the tendency in funeral ledgers to note a white person's estate as responsible for funeral fees. Few national firms, however, insured Black southerners because of stereotypes about Black death. The Prudential Life Insurance Company, for example, did a study in 1875 on its Black insured, relying on eugenics arguments that so-called intrinsic traits would cause Black Americans to die out, costing insurance companies significant sums. According to historian William B. Weare, insurers believed "the Negro race was destined to die out within fifty years—and all for the good, because the [B]lack man was a parasitic weight on the progress of the republic."[35] Future North Carolina Mutual Insurance (NCM) president John Berry likened this perception of Black death to making Black Americans to be like "the Indians and the Buffalos, we were dying out and he [Black Americans] was a bad risk and so it was considered a hazardous thing to go into business of insuring people with the highest . . . mortality rate."[36] The 1875 report was so persuasive that most white-owned insurance companies, following Prudential's lead, discontinued insuring Black Americans or limited the insured amount to a $1000 policy for a middle-class person and $500 for a working-class one.

By the 1910s, life insurance companies modernized their eugenics arguments by claiming "life extension" or "life conservation" practices to be a sure way to making insurance policies more lucrative. While it is not clear when or how the language became common, in December 1913 E. E. Rittenhouse, the Conservation Commissioner of the Equitable Life Assurance Society, a New York–based insurance company, helped found the Life Extension Institution with a $1 million endowment and a famous board that included William H. Taft, Alexander Graham Bell, and William Gorgas, a southerner who is credited with curing yellow fever. The institute's work was rather vague at first, stating its job was to promote health and longevity through the dissemination of healthcare knowledge. But its work benefitted insurance companies who wanted better ways to assess risk, who wanted the insured to pay for a longer time period before cashing in their policies, and who subscribed to the institute in order to use its information.[37]

The institute also argued that a community could fix its own death rates, particularly through the control of epidemic disease. Epidemics were not the only cause of death that could be controlled, however. The institute's ideas were firmly rooted in a modern version of eugenicist ideas. Irving Fisher and Eugene Lyman Fisk's book, *How to Live: Rules for Healthy Living Based on Modern Science*, published by the Life Extension Institute and eventually having eight editions, argued that the "segregation" of "defectives" would isolate the genetically inferior from the more biologically fit. Once identified, those "defectives" should be sterilized so they could not procreate with better biological specimens whose potential for a longer life made them a better insurance risk.[38]

The implication, of course, is Black Americans were members of this "defective" pool; the use of the term "segregation" makes this interpretation possible and a reason for New York–based insurance companies to refuse insurance for Black Americans. Into this gap stepped Black entrepreneurs who successfully built an insurance market among Black southerners, with firms such as NCM; the Afro-American Life; and Atlanta Life insuring Black Americans. The most famous was NCM, which eventually became the twentieth largest insurance company in the country, as well as the largest Black-owned insurance company in America. Founded in 1898 by John Merrick, a bricklayer and barber, NCM was no mere "coffin club" (a.k.a. burial society). Merrick invited six men to charter the company in February 1899, and hired his cousin, C. C. Spaulding, to manage it. It was Spaulding, a master salesman, who made the company into a financial powerhouse, doubling its premiums by 1900 and becoming a vibrant counterpoint to tired eugenics arguments.[39] The original managers used the region's deadly landscape and the promise of the heavenly reunion to sell insurance. "Death is pursuing you at this moment," ads said while early marketing materials noted that "the man who dies expecting to go to heaven and leaves his sorrowing wife and hungry children to face the cold charities of the world . . . will deserve a seat away back behind the thief."[40]

Black-owned insurance companies promised more than money for a decent burial as they opened a "Door of Opportunity for the Race," Atlanta Mutual Insurance's stationary announced to its "85,000 Satisfied Policy Holders" in 1911.[41] Insurers hired Black agents and dues collectors, providing a new middle-class job for thousands. But companies like NCM were also vulnerable, especially at first, to high death rates. To make their businesses more financially viable, they countered those rates by pursuing new life extension projects. After all, the longer customers lived, the more money they paid into the system. Investments in incipient life extension practices, then, became good business practice when NCM sponsored Tuskegee Institute's Health Week and helped found a hospital for Black patrons only.[42]

Insurance companies found customers of all ages in the South, where many came to be insured by more than one policy by the 1920s. The numbers of policies one individual owned could be so extensive that the Mickey Funeral Home in Charleston, South Carolina, kept a separate ledger for customers' insurance policies. One customer, Amelia Chapman, had thirteen insurance policies totaling $431 when the funeral home buried her. The policies included burial services from the local Tents Society as well as five Liberty Insurance policies. Her daughter received two Liberty payments of $43 and $10; her son received two others for $20 and $18; and her grandson received the fifth Liberty Insurance policy for $20.[43]

Insurance Agents and Weekly Dues

Paid up insurance thus avoided the stigma of a county burial, to the point that some paid their insurance fees first before buying food. One woman named Ruth declared,

> I'll never be without it [burial insurance] long as I can drag and make a dollar. I seen what it meant to have somebody you loved dead and waitin' to be buried and not a penny to your name to bury 'em with. If I can help it the welfare won't have to bury me and the children. I may have to do without things I need to eat but I'll have money laid back in insurance for my folks to buy a coffin to bury me in when I'm dead.[44]

To collect the weekly fees owed by their customers, insurance companies inserted a new character into communities, Black and white: the insurance collector. Many future leaders began their work as insurance collectors. Mary McLeod Bethune, called Black America's "first lady," sold insurance for the Afro-American Life Insurance Company while she decided where to build the school that would become Bethune-Cookman University in Daytona Beach, for example.[45] Those who worked as insurance collectors used familiar rituals to sell policies, using religious symbolism and spaces. Author Richard Wright recalled helping an insurance man build his business when Wright was young:

> On Sundays Brother Mance would go to the nearest country church and give his sales talk, preaching it in the form of a sermon, clapping his hands as he did so, spitting on the floor to mark off his paragraphs, and stomping his feet in the spit to punctuate his sentences, all of which captivated the [B]lack sharecroppers. After

> the performance the wall-eyed yokels would flock to Brother Mance, and I would fill out applications until my fingers ached.[46]

Linking insurance to church attendance and biblical dogma thus gave the purchase of insurance a sacred quality.

Black and white insurance representatives collected money, making a mark in a book each customer held that signified a payment made. But sometimes, the insurance collector was white, exposing Black customers to a fraught racial system that intersected with the death commercial system. Heralded by a child who cried out, "In-surance man, In-surance man," to his neighbors, T. J. Marshall, a white man who collected dues from Black customers in St. Augustine, Florida, was professional, with his weekly visit a moment to exchange pleasantries. Marshall acknowledged the importance of insurance, stating, "These policies have been a blessing to many a family whose breadwinner has been laid up by an accident. You know that, due to the hazardous employment of many of the Negroes, sickness or accidents occur quite often."[47]

But others were not as congenial. "Installment collector" Homer Jordan (white), of Jacksonville, Florida, believed that "with a little time and sense ya can sell a [n——-] anything." Black consumerism put Jordan in an awkward place among his white peers because the ability to buy a policy required Jordan's acknowledgment of their financial ability. It also made him financially successful as he outsold his white peers who called him a "[n——-]-lover." His reply was "a dollar is a dollar, regardless of the color of its former owners." But Jordan was a powerful man in the Black community because he confirmed or denied that insurance had been paid, a power that he relished. It also gave him leverage when approaching Black women sexually. Black women, according to white men's racial ideas, were by nature licentious and supposedly willing (even when decidedly not) to be approached sexually. In one scene, for example, Jordan slapped one Black woman on the buttocks when he approached her for her weekly payment.[48]

A Statistical Assist

Not all white insurance men and women saw Black southerners in negative or exploitative terms. Metropolitan Insurance Company statistician Louis Dublin, who worked closely with Life Extension Institute personnel, saw insurance company statistics having the potential to create "socially useful insurance underwriting practices," especially when it came to counting Black death.[49] Dublin used census data, newly available data from death certificates, and his own insurance company's policyholders (the company insured more than two million southerners overall) to delve beneath eugenicist stereotypes.[50] In particular,

Dublin attacked what public health policy makers called "premature mortality," collecting data that proved a catalyst in addressing high tuberculosis and infant mortality rates.[51] In one study, Dublin attempted to nail down the exact mortality rates for the Black enslaved versus African Americans post-slavery, countering the rosy picture of health that white southern apologists used to justify slavery. Hampered by the lack of hard numbers especially before 1900, Dublin's census data still suggested a real killing time did occur in the immediate post–Civil War era, with a potential Black mortality rate of between 35–40 deaths per 1000. But his numbers also confirmed that, contrary to eugenicists's arguments, Black mortality quickly dropped to 17 deaths per 1000, and that Black Americans who reached the age of 50 had a nearly similar mortality rate as white Americans.[52] But Dublin's corporate numbers and census records did provide a grim picture of southern mortality rates in general as he and other insurance companies found that relatively few southerners were living to their three score and ten. NCM found that, in the 1920s, the average Black southerner died by age 40. White southerners were little better with their average deaths coming by age 50. What had been perception and stereotype was now a statistical nightmare that had to be resolved.[53]

Tuberculosis especially came under Dublin's and NCM's rigorous stare whereas other kinds of southern death like infant mortality did not. TB simply cost insurers more money. Each year, Dublin found, TB cost American businesses roughly $26.5 billion, mostly from lost wages. But his emphasis on cost suggested a second assumption, later stated explicitly to a group of Kentucky public health officials. A long life and good health were available for purchase, thanks to science which could help you avoid both an early end and an early insurance payout. Insurers began to make it good business to identify causes of poor health or mortality, ironically promoting good health. And by 1924, NCM created an office called "Life Extension" that promoted good health practices.[54]

The Federal Government and Death Registration Areas

Burial societies and insurance provided a solid financial basis for new death professionals to sell their wares. Federal officials, namely the new Children's Bureau, the United States Public Health Service (USPHS), and statisticians newly charged with counting the dead, added legitimacy to the system by counting causes of death. By counting cause, reformers believed they could then apply various scientific methodologies to curing high death rates. Funeral professionals' growing access to dead bodies meant that they, not doctors or midwives, could help with a more accurate count of the dead when they issued death certificates.

Thus, a Progressive early step was the establishment of Death Registration Areas, a national system whereby death certificates were collected, causes of death counted, and results published in federal pamphlets. Coming in the 1880s to Massachusetts and other New England states, expanding from there to other states in the North and West, and finally, in the 1910s to the South, Death Registration Areas were areas typically defined by state boundaries. Some large southern cities had already been gathering this data, for example, Memphis from 1848 and Nashville from 1874, but Tennessee and North Carolina passed statewide laws late, requiring death certificates in 1909. From there, federal public health officials added Mississippi (1912), North Carolina (1913), Tennessee (1914), and Georgia (1919) to the Death Registration Area. Because Alabama did not pass a law requiring death certificates until the late 1920s, it was not added until then and Texas was not added until 1933. These laws vested county clerks as the primary data collectors, but in practice, it was new death professionals who issued death certificates.[55]

Statisticians quickly found problems with funeral directors' data. Dublin, the Metropolitan Insurance statistician, found that descriptions of cause varied widely. How could Death Registration Areas work if doctors used disparate and sometimes archaic terms, local vernacular, or used symptoms to describe a cause of death? This required public health organizations and professional societies like the American Public Health Association to design an International List of Causes of Death. This list drew death professionals and doctors into an international network where local vernacular came to be supplanted by national and international terms for what actually killed southerners. Then, Dublin and his statisticians carefully examined death certificates that were submitted to see how death was described, contacting the doctor who signed the certificate using older language. A patient dead from dropsy? That was a symptom, not a cause. Did peritonitis kill someone? Was it peritonitis ensuing from typhoid? TB? Appendicitis? The change of descriptions immediately caused a substantial drop in some causes of death; for example, peritonitis deaths dropped by nearly 83 percent in Dublin's record set, clarifying the picture of how people died.[56]

The Federal Government and the Children's Bureau

Building on these new numbers, a dynamic group of women, a "female dominion," as historian Robyn Muncy called them, formed the first female-headed federal office, the Children's Bureau in the Department of Labor, catalyzing a shift in focus away from why adults died young to why infants and children died young. The Children's Bureau was founded after Chicago Progressives Lillian Wald and Florence Kelley realized they could not answer a basic question about infant mortality. Was the stereotype correct that more infants died in the summer than in any other season? They could not answer this question because there was no national requirement that certificates be issued at birth. They had to know how many babies were born before they could count how many died. To answer this, Wald and Kelley helped create the Children's Bureau in 1912. Their first task was the establishment of a Birth Registration Area that issued birth certificates and then gathered data regarding infant births. Once they knew how many babies had been born, they could assess how many died. Finally, the Bureau would provide educational materials and best practice information to decrease mortality rates once the causes were identified.[57]

Numbers gathered by the Bureau showed a bleak infant mortality picture with only Switzerland and Spain having higher infant mortality rates than the United States. To attack those high rates, the Bureau linked the health of the nation to infant mortality rates. Civilized nations had low rates; those countries on the decline posted higher rates as their civilization devolved. One author argued, "As civilization goes down the baby death rate goes up," since the most "sensitive index" of the nation's health was the relative health and wellness of its most fragile citizens.[58] Thus, as the United States became a world power in the 1910s, dying children gave lie to the claims that its power was sustainable and moral. After all, if the nation could not care for its most vulnerable citizens, how could it be a global leader?[59]

What made the Children's Bureau effective in the South (and nationally, too) was its ability to mobilize incipient Progressive organizations like women's clubs, some state and county boards of health, and academics. While the efforts were relatively piecemeal compared to the efforts after World War I, the same evangelical zeal that motivated the building of new hospitals motivated those who wanted to know when and how infants died. They recognized that the Children's Bureau provided an expertise that could be linked with their efforts, and they incorporated the Bureau's literature and practices into their work. Home Economics professor Lucius Moody Bristol promised Bureau head Julia Lathrop that West Virginia was "alive to the need" for practical social work.[60] Mary L. Railey wrote the Bureau, asking if it was acceptable work for her sorority's alumni to count deaths in New Orleans. Georgia Progressives gave their fellow Georgian, Children's Bureau doctor Frances Sage Bradley, an "ovation," an indication to Bradley that "Georgia is just awakening and needs all the encouragement possible. Their new Board of Health is very eager to do children's work."[61]

While some embraced the Children's Bureau, other southerners dismissed its work as intrusive, particularly those who profited from conditions that caused high death rates. In 1919, for example, the North Carolina Department of Health invited the Children's Bureau to study two counties that had large textile mill communities. The Bureau found living conditions abysmal, and blamed overcrowding for high rates of pellagra and other significant health problems. *The Southern Textile Bulletin*, the textile owners' newsletter, took great offense at the Bureau's conclusions, arguing that it made false statements based on faulty research. A *Wilmington Journal* (North Carolina) editorial, "As Others See Us," also charged the Bureau with making such false claims as, "North Carolina has the worst reputation of any State in the Union in the treatment of her children."[62] Mill owners' defensiveness came from the implications of life extension. Bureau reformers believed women should give birth, stay home, and raise their children, claiming that mothers who worked during pregnancy and went back to work within a year of the baby's birth had higher infant mortality rates. This was a direct attack on owners' use of the family wage system, which meant that the father was paid a low enough wage that other members of the family, including the mother, needed to work as well.[63] The specter of losing a substantial portion of its labor pool could force mill owners to raise wages or search for new workers. In this way, life extension threatened to undermine class systems in the South that provided cheap textile labor.

County and State Efforts at Life Extension

As the federal government began to look at individual groups (like infants) and their high rates of death, reformers hoped that local governments might do the same, but county and city governments believed their job was to bury the dead, not ensure death at an elderly age. Being put away decent did not mean luxurious or even mildly extravagant, and the most a poor person could count on was an inexpensive, but still manufactured, casket; a burial plot; and (perhaps) a few words spoken over the grave. H. F. Hoover's ledger illustrates the difference. Families who could afford a funeral paid $19, $30, and $85 for coffins in 1904; Bedford County (Tennessee) paid $2 for Willie Jones's funeral. Lizzie, a North Carolina millworker, recalled burying one of her boarders, relying on the county for burial services. She recalled:

> When he did die, I went to see the county and after I'd been to a sight of trouble they said they'd make the arrangements. I'll tell you it's a sad thing to see a person buried by the county. I thought of course they'd send out a [*sic*] awful cheap coffin but they never sent no coffin atall. They sent out a wooden box with a lid that screwed on. And to make it wusser they had it painted red. Sometimes yit when I'm here by myself it gits on my mind.[64]

White morticians typically received county contracts to bury both the Black and white indigent because county governments, all white, gave lucrative death care contracts to other white men. Dave C. Elder, the head of the Giles County

(Tennessee) Farm, a home for county indigent, acted as the "inmates'" parent when he purchased caskets from a local funeral home owned by a white man. Flora Hall (noted as "c" for colored on the funeral ledger) died in January 1924, and her final arrangements mimicked the paternalistic care taken of her in life. Poor, female, and Black, Hall was perceived to be helpless, hence the need to live in a county home where white men could make sure she did not starve. Then, they made sure she was buried.[65]

In large cities like Atlanta, local governments contracted with both Black and white morticians to bury the indigent dead, segregating bodies in death as in life. By claiming that only Black morticians could bury Black bodies and white morticians could bury white bodies, cities reinforced emergent segregationist practices. At the same time, county governments reinforced economic independence for Black morticians by vesting them as uniquely responsible for burying Black bodies. J. H. Hanley, the Atlanta funeral director, buried multiple bodies for the county, many of them unknown infants, but also some adults. In August, September, and October 1923, Hanley buried five infants, sold a cheap casket to the county for Amos Mosely, and buried Nancy Hugley, wife of Warren Hugley, by order of the county commissioners.[66]

The shift away from the family burying the dead to undertakers caring for them gave a new group of professionals a poignant responsibility in caring for the dead. However, if death was to be a commercial enterprise, it had to come after a long life that allowed one to fully pay for life insurance policies and burial society benefits. What catalyzed the death commercial system further were soldier deaths, the Spanish Influenza epidemic, and military rituals for burying the dead during World War I.

PART TWO

World War I and Challenging Southern Death Care

Southern Progressives had created a religious justification for extending life even as a burgeoning death commerce business decried the expensive early death. World War I was that first systematic external incursion into death care, in terms of how people died (overseas battlefield deaths and Spanish Influenza); where a body was buried (family graveyard or a military cemetery); and how the sites were marked, in subtle but still influential ways. But as the federal government tried to marshal an armed force fit and free from illness, it confronted the ill health of southerners in general. As the military set up a large number of training camps in the South's plentiful rural areas, it was exposed to the deadliness of the region. Moreover, it failed to realize how its own practices created the perfect mechanism to nurture a global pandemic: the Spanish Influenza epidemic that killed at least 675,000 Americans.

The ways the dead were memorialized also had to change, given the circumstances of an overseas war. The difference in death care between that done by the military's Quartermaster Corps and longtime southern practice caused some clashes. But perhaps one of the more poignant changes was accounting for what psychotherapist Pauline Boss calls "ambiguous loss." Particularly associated with both world wars, one of the larger transitions in twentieth-century death care has to be American encounters with unknown, uncertain deaths. Rather than dying in or near the family, service overseas on European (and later, South Pacific) battlefields introduced Americans to that broader uncertainty.[1] Like the Civil War some fifty years before, the war scattered those assumptions as chaotic battlefield situations made information about how and when a soldier died difficult to find. The flu simply added to the chaos. Perhaps the best way to begin this section, then, is by noticing a lonely military casket on a train platform.

4 Lonely Coffins

World War I and the Spanish Influenza Epidemic

It was the visual experience of servicemen's bodies coming home for burial that hinted at the changes soon to come. Margaret Mitchell, who later wrote *Gone with the Wind,* saw those changes from a train's window. Writing to a beau, she described the effect of seeing a lonely coffin on the train platform,

> with an American flag draped over it. The station was very still, there was only one light on the platform—directly over the box—no one was near. I sat here in the dark, hugging my knees, thinking of that boy, wondering if he had a sister or a mother or a sweetheart—wondering too, rather foolishly, if he wasn't just a little lonesome and hurt, that there was no one to meet him or care—after he had come all that long way and given everything. I felt that I knew him, some how and some thing in me began to ache . . . that chap coming home and no one there.[1]

The closed coffin meant that no one could see the body inside, and thus, in a region where whites were honorable and Blacks were not, anonymous soldiers resting unseen in their caskets became noble dead, no matter who they were. The military reinforced this notion with new rituals. Louisianan Albert Abraham, for example, was a member of the "colored" casket detail at Camp Beauregard, Louisiana, when he died from the Spanish Influenza epidemic. His body was promptly sent home to his mother, who was addressed as Mrs. Ruth Abraham, a breach of southern racial etiquette where Black women were never referred to by that honorific. Her son's death in military service conferred on her the dignity that white southerners might never have acknowledged, but that the federal government was willing to do, even in the midst of the military's own segregated facilities and structures.[2]

It is this collective experience of death—noble soldierly loss, lonely deaths, and the Spanish flu epidemic—that caused some changes in death care during

World War I. As it was the nation's first large-scale military effort since the Civil War as well as its first large-scale effort off continent, some southerners believed World War I was their best opportunity to live the same glory their ancestors had during the Civil War (if white). Others joined believing their willingness to die for their country would secure them a citizenship denied at home (if Black). No matter who you were and what you wished for, the military buried you, using precise, albeit evolving, rituals, desiring a more coherent and controlled response than occurred during the Civil War.[3]

If young men were going to die, however, southerners (and others) wanted the war to be about the noble dead, plucked in their prime in battles against dastardly Germans. What they got was a new epidemic catalyzed by the very systems that mustered and fielded armies. Mobilization required enlisting, drafting, outfitting, training, and shipping four million soldiers overseas. These very mechanisms—particularly, new training camps, trains that mingled citizens and soldiers together indiscriminately, and naval ships crossing the Atlantic Ocean that became floating coffins—catalyzed the Spanish Influenza epidemic. Appearing in September 1918, the epidemic eventually killed more than 675,000 Americans nationwide, many of them between the ages of 18 and 34. At a time when fielding healthy troops was paramount to a successful war effort, 50 percent of the 116,000 military dead died from illness while 43 percent were killed on the battlefield (the remaining 7 percent died from accidents). There were noble tales to be told of soldiers dead on a battlefield, but no one could quite fashion a narrative of nobility as the flu killed thousands of young men and women, precisely those deaths Progressives had tried to avoid.[4]

Preparing for War

Subtle challenges to southern death care began almost immediately after the United States entered World War I. The United States declared war on Germany on April 7, 1917, and naval destroyers quickly joined British convoys, escorting ships filled with American-made munitions and other war materiel across the Atlantic. It would take more than a year to field a substantial military force on European soil, a force that eventually numbered four million soldiers. Training camps had to be built (hastily and poorly, it turned out); men had to be drafted, trained, and supplied; and ships had to be constructed to ferry them to the front. The first substantial military force, nearly three quarters of a million strong, finally appeared at Chateau-Thierry, France, in June 1918, a boost to the low morale of British and French troops and a devastating blow to the Germans.[5]

Many of the new training camps were built in the South, where rural land was abundant. But even with Progressive efforts, the lack of local governmental investment in healthcare became quickly obvious, as those establishing training camps evaluated their surroundings for healthy infrastructure, for example, sewage systems. The American Red Cross (ARC), the War Department, the United States Public Health Service (USPHS), the Public Health Service's Malaria Force, and others found, to their dismay, that county health organizations were nearly nonexistent. Areas lacked basic health services, like clean water supplies in Augusta, Georgia, where a typhoid epidemic broke out during the war, or swampy Alexandria, Virginia, where soldiers had to clean up malarial swamps. Training camps and their surrounds thus became places where officials claimed good health was a military necessity. That wedge then allowed the ARC, relatively new to the region, to identify public spaces like department stores, boarding houses, hotels, and barber shops as potential health risks. Inspections soon followed, with units like the Spartanburg, South Carolina, ARC inspecting local milk and water supplies; visiting homes to make sure privies had been installed (in one month, it installed 560 sanitary privies); attempting to control the region's vast malarial problems; and examining local school children for potential health issues.[6]

The ARC's work, of course, was national in scope as the number of active units exploded from 107 to 3864 across the country, but many of the new units were in the South. Churches, already focused on life extension, added military preparedness to their work via the ARC, as it relied on local networks of church women to roll bandages and make other materials of war. Ensley Red Cross Unit #3 met weekly at the Ensley Baptist Church in Birmingham, Alabama, where women ate box lunches and rolled bandages. Church bulletins announced weekly ARC meetings next to lists of parishioners who were currently serving in the Armed Forces, and later, next to lists of soldier deaths. Those lists reminded parishioners as they made war goods that soldiers "gave their lives that others might have the freedom that rightfully belongs to all mankind."[7]

Gazing Out from the South

This war work, down to the intimacies of eating a sandwich while rolling a bandage, caused some whites to believe the South was reemerging from a self-imposed exile and reengaging once again with a world it had turned its back on during the Civil War. Southern writer Allen Tate noted, "With the war of 1914–1918, the South reentered the world—but gave a backward glance as it stepped over the border."[8] Historian Walter Edgar wrote that for the port of Charleston, South Carolina, "World War I began the waking of this sleeping beauty. The navy base located north of the city in 1901 became the headquarters of the Sixth Naval District. Thousands of service men and workers moved in."[9]

But conflict inevitably ensued as "outsiders" challenged local officials. Locals preferred to keep the status quo, for example, in Augusta, Georgia, where county commissioners were "antagonistic" to the ARC's good health efforts.[10]

The war also raised the specter of racial conflict as Black southerners claimed their right to serve their country, and, in turn, fought against their second-class citizenship in the South. Certainly, some hoped that the turn of gaze outward meant that the federal government might intervene on their behalf. Richard Wright, in his autobiographical novel, *Black Boy*, recalled his mother teaching him pride of uniform and country. While he interpreted uniformed Black soldiers marching with rifles at the ready as frightening, his mother taught him that those soldiers protected him from Germans who "want to kill you and take your country away from you."[11] It became a matter of pride for many Black southern families to say that their father or grandfather served during World War I. Emmett Emmanuel Cheri was never allowed to say his New Orleans family was poor because his father had served in the war, which raised the family's status above their class level.[12]

Black undertakers understood the political implications of serving and signed up early. Edwin "Teddy" Harleston Jr., a Charleston undertaker, a well-known Harlem Renaissance artist, and president of the local NAACP branch, rendered significant war service by helping set up an officers' training camp for Black soldiers in Des Moines, Iowa. The military recognized Harleston's service to his country, noting, one writer said, that he had

> rendered . . . very valuable service in compiling data in connection with the establishment of a Training Camp for colored citizens . . . the general impression that I gather from my association with him is that he is an exceedingly valuable man, and that he will be enabled to render to the Government valuable and efficient service . . . I believe he is a double "A" man.[13]

That early service fostered Black medical opinion that Black men were physiologically better fit for the military than white men, and their inclusion in the military would, by extension, lead to a stronger overall military effort. Tuskegee's Monroe Work's *Negro Year Book* for 1918–1919 noted that, "Conclusions drawn from military examinations and experience of the past few years appear to indicate that the Negro is constitutionally a better physiological machine than the white man." While some maladies (for example, respiratory ailments) affected Black men more than white men, Work argued that other maladies, for example, "nervous system" ailments (most likely a reference to post-traumatic stress disorder), were not as common in Black soldiers. That resulted in "fewer cases of instability than those of white men. Thus there is far less neurasthenia, there are fewer instances of psychopathic states, and there is only half as much alcoholism in colored troops as in white troops."[14] Perhaps, living in the South under its fraught racial conditions, not unlike a war, better readied Black men to withstand the emotional rigors of the battlefield.

Honoring the Confederacy

Southern white men, who believed that honor and chivalry were the core characteristics that made them masculine, believed the war was a noble effort where they would show their honorable selves. Perhaps, too, memories of Confederate losses could be wiped away on European battlefields by those who had been raised on their fathers' and grandfathers' tales of grand service. Katherine DuPre Lumpkin said, "It gave us no pause to put our men into uniform, and raise the Stars and Stripes, and sing *America* . . . Southerners of my kind were steeped in calls to duty, especially the call to war. We had already fought one war as a united nation [the Civil War]."[15] Indeed, white southerners learned faithfulness and duty to country from Confederate heroes who regaled young and old alike with tales of noble Confederate sacrifice. The Confederate statues on local courthouses may have caused them to hope, too, that a statue might honor them one day.

The desire for honor earned on the battlefield motivated some older white men, like Edward Wells, to seek commissions. His father was a member of the Charleston Light Dragoons during the Civil War, but Wells, at nearly 31 years old, was over the maximum draft age of 27 years old. He pleaded with the Secretary of War and his congressman to be given a commission. He was finally commissioned as a 2nd Lieutenant in August 1917 and later killed in France. Obituaries for Frederick "Fagg"[16] Malloy, who died from the flu in the Argonne Forest, recalled his great grandfather's service to the Confederacy, as if to say that this was another noble effort that conferred a similar honor onto its combatants.[17]

Not every white southerner believed that death in service to his country was noble, as middle-class parents kept their sons from serving. One economics professor, writing to his son's employer, said, "This boy is willing enough to give his life to his country, but he'll serve humanity better alive than dead, I think."[18] Others believed World War I was another rich man's war, but a poor man's fight, and dodged the draft. Rural white farmers, in particular, saw rich white men's sons gather up officer commissions or avoid the draft altogether while their own sons were hunted down by federal agents and forcibly drafted. Still others saw a double standard when their preachers exhorted male parishioners to volunteer and then avoided the draft themselves. H. L. Harper, a cotton mill worker, was one young man who joined the military effort because his pastor told him "what a glorious thing it was to die for one's country." But Harper, wounded and gassed at Chateau Thierry, recalled, "I noticed later that none of them [the pastors] ever shouldered a gun."[19]

Going to War—Preparing for Death

Soldiers going off to war prepared themselves and their families for their potential deaths, purchasing life insurance policies, settling financial matters, and dictating their burials. North Carolinian Carl Brindley signed insurance papers for three members of his family. For his mother, he secured $5000 in insurance; for each of his siblings, he bought $2500 in insurance. He survived the war.[20] Few were more attentive to final burial instructions than Edward Wells, who not only dictated his final wishes, but planned burial details for his recently deceased father and older brother. Fearing his mother, left anxious, depressed, and "nervous" from the two deaths, was incapable of fulfilling his wishes, he wrote his sister:

> I am insured in the U.S. Bureau of War Risk Insurance for the sum of $10,000 which goes to Mother in case of my death at the rate of $57.50 per month, during 20 years. Also either Arthur Huger or Henry Connor [family friends] have my policies for either $3,000.00 or $4500.00 in two or three life insurance policies of $1500.00 each. Also in case of my death in action, possibly in service, 6 months pay is due Mother and a pension. Bear in mind that in case of my death, the matter of finding out and getting what is possible should be energetically taken up by say Arthur Hugar, Henry Connor, or any friend of the family who can reach the ear of Congressmen or others in Washington.

In his Confederate veteran father's case, he noted specific Civil War incidents he believed should be included on his father's gravestone. In his brother Julian's case, he wanted the body to be brought home from Haiti (his brother had died there during an appendix surgery) to be buried next to his father. When Wells later died in action, he was laid to rest next to his brother and father in the family cemetery.[21]

Soldiers attended to more than just practical details because evangelical Christians did not leave their faith at home, instead carrying their beliefs into battle with them. Letters to parents, families, and friends assured them that the soldiers had lived sinless lives that allowed a family reunion, even if that death occurred far away. Georgian Lt. Harry Hanley wrote his mother from St. Mihiel, France, on October 23, 1918 (he died a month later from wounds received in the Argonne Sector), reminding her that grief had no place in her life if his death was in battle:

> I feel very proud at this moment and full of confidence over the result. If God chooses to call me now, I have tried to be prepared. You must not grieve unduly but just think that when I was born, God meant that I should leave you at this time. Always when you are at church, I will be there and I know that God, in his mercy, will make your burden lighter.[22]

Former newspaperman Frederick Malloy assured his mother that he was not going to die (even though the flu eventually did kill him). "Mother o' Mine," he jauntily wrote, "[I]t's going to take a whole lot more then [*sic*] the German Army to kill me—pneumonia failed twice, a Texas bronco gave up in disgust, and I have crossed Broadway and Forty Second street [in New York City] hundreds of times without being run over, so I am ahead of the game." Of course, Malloy, in his cheery fashion (and in response to the poor food he ate in the military), asked his mother and her friends to "pray not for my soul, but my stomach."[23] The next year, Malloy wrote his mother to remind her of his (potentially) good death:

> Well precious Mud [*sic*] of mine no more this time, but always that it has been your love and influence in this life that has made me do every decent thing I ever did, and without the loving comradship [*sic*] you have always shown me I would never have lived the very happy life I have always enjoyed. If anything should happen to me, please be proud that it was my chance to be in it all . . . And I was glad to pay the price for the fun I had out of it all. This isn't [*sic*] a will by a long shot, but I just thought I had better let you know for one can never tell when he will get run over by some foolish Ford—there are so many over here you know.[24]

While letters were the cheery, keep-a-stiff-upper-lip sort, diaries allowed soldiers to document their very real fears of dying. Future Memphis mayor Samuel Watkins Overton noted his fear of dying to his diary:

> Mr. Diary . . . you will help me, diary, I hope in two ways. First I will have a much needed outlet for my feelings and a chance to express myself in a limited way. I can't tell you, old top, all that I think and feel for I have to write to talk to you and there is no place I can keep you where you may not be found . . . there is a very small chance that I may live and grow old and then I can use you in my second childhood and thinking of these days can't help but make my future condition, whatever it may be, more cheerful.[25]

Soldiers also wanted to square their deaths with their religious beliefs about mortality, sin, and heaven. Correspondence from the time is relatively silent, but knowing that evangelical Christian soldiers might struggle with killing others, the Southern Baptist Convention (SBC) confronted those concerns directly in pamphlets they distributed to soldiers. Lazarus was Jesus's powerful example of raising the dead who were sinless. Those who died on a French battlefield would also be found by Jesus who knew where to find the deceased and escort him to heaven. In some ways, the SBC implied that death on a battlefield—considered noble, and therefore, the act of someone who was without sin—was good because Jesus had prepared a way to Heaven even in the chaos of war. The SBC told soldiers they were thus walking examples of Christ's promise of immortality for themselves, their peers and their enemies. It also told soldiers, "Just as you enlisted for serving Uncle Sam, and are living and fighting for the things for which Uncle Sam and our country stand . . . be a good soldier of Christ Jesus and His teachings. Not to be saved by them but to show you are His soldier."[26] Too, the linkage between sinlessness and being in right relationship with Jesus was a veiled attempt to keep SBC soldiers away from the delights of a distant land. At the same time as they were Christian soldiers at war for God's noble cause, abstaining from alcohol and prostitutes was required to make the noble death still possible and the vaunted family reunion secure.

Disease, Death, and the Military

When soldiers went to war, typically more—far more—died from disease than on a battlefield, causing substantial manpower shortages, especially in the Civil War. World War I was going to be that war where modern Progressive medicine would make dying from illness a thing of the past; only noble battlefield deaths would occur. The military's health work was in service to the war, but, in fact, its effects carried on for years after.

The military attempted to stave off illness the second soldiers arrived at training camps. Southern soldiers, because of the lack of strong, consistent immunization programs, went through an extensive vaccination process almost immediately, and with long-term effects since the effectiveness of immunizations did not cease with the war's end. Carl Brindley arrived at a training camp near Waco, Texas, and immediately noted in his diary:

> February 20, 1918: Physical Exam
>
> April 3, 1918: Trade test in A.M. First typhoid "shot" and vaccination in afternoon.
>
> April 4, 1918: Venerial [*sic*] inspection at 8 AM. Second such inspection since March 14 . . . sore as result of "shot." Not as sore as most others, however.
>
> April 9, 1918: . . . Veneral [*sic*] lecture, by 1st Lt. of medical corps at 6:45 p.m.
>
> April 10, 1918 . . . Second typhoid "shot" and smallpox vaccination. 1st vaccination did not take. Arm sore and felt bad at night.
>
> April 11, 1918: Went to sick call. Took dose calomel [*sic*] and salts. Felt bad all day. Better at night. Had "TB" examination in the afternoon. Was not told result.
>
> April 20, 1918: . . . Venereal [*sic*] lecture with lantern slides by Lt. of Med. Corps. . . . Weight with blouse 131 #[lbs.][27]

Immunizations did not hold off all epidemics, however. A major measles epidemic hit training camps in 1917, and officials at Camp Wheeler in Macon, Georgia, found that it led to pneumonia, the eventual cause of an uptick of soldier deaths. Then, in November 1918 at Camp Beauregard near Alexandria, Louisiana, a mumps epidemic broke out, halting any trips home right as the war ended. Louisianan Zeke Ellis caught the mumps, and wrote to his family that, "All of our clothes are taken away from us and won't be given back until we are discharged. This relieves them of any necessity of watching us about breaking quarantine . . . There are about 60 mumps patients in our ward and more coming in all the time."[28] And then the Spanish Influenza epidemic hit.

Soldiers confronted more than new vaccinations and health policies at their training camps. Training camps also introduced soldiers to the new weaponry made possible by the Industrial Revolution, a revolution that had transformed much of America from an agricultural economy to an industrial one in the nineteenth century. Now, in the twentieth century, the new machine age was harnessed to the purposeful killing of soldiers, often in horrific ways. Airplanes, although relatively rare in World War I, were a new machinery that could inflict that catastrophic injury. Carl Brindley, stationed in the Panama Canal Zone, described how one man was hit by an airplane propeller and lived a few hours before succumbing to his injuries, for example. But he was especially horrified by the deaths of two soldiers—listed only as Lieutenant Evans and Corporal Semsey—from another awful plane accident. From August 9, 1918, when the accident occurred until August 28, 1918, when Corporal Semsey was finally buried, Brindley described the accident and burial rites, "August 9, 1918: About 9 o'clock Leut. Evans and corporal [*sic*] Semsey were flying small land machine and fell a thousand feet or more into the bay, killed both men. The machine was actually broken into splinters and both bodies were mashed with almost every bone broken." Brindley had been schooled to bury the whole body intact, for it was the whole body that would reunite with family, not just a hand or an ear. But propeller and plane deaths meant substantial portions of the body were simply gone. How then could a body journey to heaven if it was not complete?[29]

While Brindley never tried to answer that question, the military provided its own answer: replace the body with a ritual that had military sanction, and then use it to encourage soldiers to grieve. Brindley recorded the ritual, noting that his commanding officer, "Major Wynne read a statement saying that we should feel the loss of Leut. Evans and Corp. Semsey." Then the military followed a set of rituals that mixed both familial preference and military requirement. In Semsey's case, his family requested he be buried where he died because they would "rather remember him as he was." Brindley's fellow soldiers attended the funeral (he had guard duty), and later reported back that the service was "good." Lieutenant Evans, on the other hand, was immediately shipped home with an escort who made sure his body arrived safely. No lonely coffins allowed here. Brindley's description of the sendoff is quite moving:

> August 24, 1918: Preparations are being made for escort for body of Leut. Evans from train to Transport tomorrow about 9 o'clock. I will be among men under arms—others will work on the plane.

> August 25, 1918: The escort for body of Leut. Evans took place as scheduled. The Navy band furnished the music and there was also a Navy escort of about 50 men. Taps was played as the casket was put aboard the [USS Army Transport] Kilpatric [*sic*]. Five of our planes circled about and dropped flowers.[30]

Subtle shifts had thus begun. The military established training camps and ensured (or at least tried to) that local health practices conformed to federal standards. Draftees benefited from induction healthcare, designed to ensure that deaths from disease would not harm battlefield readiness, even as new kinds of military weaponry promised catastrophic effects on bodies. What no one expected, however, was the sledgehammer that the Spanish Influenza epidemic turned out to be as it affected precisely those whose early deaths had been the focus of Progressive life extension efforts. It was a clear sign that there was work still to be done.

The Spanish Influenza Epidemic

What southerner Katherine Anne Porter called, "This funny new disease. Simply knocks you into a cocked hat," medical historians now believe was a bird flu (A, H1N1).[31] In 1918, contemporaries believed the Germans had weaponized the flu and brought it to the United States, offloading the germs in a Boston port. Historians now think that it was the very mechanisms to fight the war that gave the flu both its lethalness and its pathway from the military to the general population. The flu came in three waves, beginning most likely in Manhattan, Kansas, at Camp Funston, an Army training camp at Fort Riley, in spring 1918. This first wave was neither as contagious nor as deadly as later waves were. Historians believe the relatively benign virus evolved when the germ traveled to France. There it mutated, turning it into the deadly, contagious illness; and then it remigrated back to the United States, appearing at Fort Devens, Massachusetts, in September, 1918. Twenty-five percent of all soldiers eventually caught the flu. In the general United States population, approximately 25 million became ill with influenza, and more than 600,000 people died from the disease. This second, most deadly wave peaked in mid-October, slowly dying out, only for a third wave to reemerge in spring 1919, just as the negotiations for the Treaty of Versailles began, infecting negotiators like President Woodrow Wilson.[32]

The epidemic followed a unique mortality curve. Previous flu epidemics showed a "U Curve," meaning that only infants and the elderly, the weakest in any population, died from the flu. This new flu had a "W Curve." It not only killed babies and the elderly, but young people, aged 18–34, the age of most soldiers about to venture onto European battlefields. Death ensued when the patient developed pneumonia, and autopsies later found that the flu had destroyed the patient's lungs, describing its effect on them as violent and burning. Medical scientists now believe it was the patient's youth that caused the immune system to attack itself; the more virile the patient was, the more likely this immune system attack occurred. How many eventually died is unknown, given that the incipient health structures charged with counting the dead could not account for the epidemic; the numbers of ill and deceased, the ARC suspected, were vastly underreported. ARC reports out of Augusta, Georgia, suggest a reason. The sanitary engineer stationed there stated his morbidity reports were, "Very incomplete, causing considerable embarrassment in handling Influenza."[33]

Nationally, Progressive Era doctors and other scientists, victorious over yellow fever, cholera, and other epidemic diseases, believed the flu was a simple matter to resolve. No scientist was more ready to attack the flu than Alabaman William Crawford Gorgas, who was credited (along with another southerner, Walter Reed) with solving the mystery of yellow fever. Gorgas was the perfect Progressive Era medical officer who rigorously applied modern scientific practices, medical expertise, and the germ theory to health and wellness across the globe. Gorgas was also on the board of the Life Extension Institute. In light of his successes, Gorgas was placed in charge of the military's medical corps, running immediately into stubborn military practices that, in his view, fostered the spread of disease. He was later "retired" in early October 1918, most likely due to the epidemic as well as the medical department's inability to effectively contain the problem.[34]

Soldiers reported the flu's initial appearance in their barracks without realizing the devastation that would soon emerge. "There have been a number of cases of influenza among the soldiers and sailors on the one [*sic*] as well as among the civilians. There has been none in our squadron but a number of men have colds," Carl Brindley reported on September 23, 1918. Protected, at least at first, in the Panama Canal Zone, Brindley did not note any more flu cases until November 2, 1918, when he wrote, "A large part of the talk is about the Spanish Influenza or 'flu' as it is often called for short. Several of our boys here have had the influenza. None of them have been in the hospital more than a few days." His entry for November 21, 1918, notes the flu's first death while describing the senior officers' reaction to the epidemic: "It seems to be a fact that our squadron has the highest sick rate of any organization on the Zone. The medical men seem to think that our crowded quarters are responsible for this."[35]

From these initial cases among soldiers, the flu spread with a rapidity that caught many by surprise. The relative newness of southern camps and the lack of solid, well-established local sanitation most likely contributed to the spread. Camp Beauregard in Pineville, Louisiana, where Albert Abraham died from the flu, had one of the highest rates of illness although its death rate (294 soldiers died) from the flu was lower than other camps. Camp Taylor in Kentucky, on the other hand, had 768 soldier deaths from the flu. The post-mortem assessments after the war suggested that rural southern men in general were more susceptible to flu-inspired pneumonia, particularly whites, because they had been isolated on small southern farms and lacked exposure to common respiratory diseases that might have built some immunity.[36]

Camps' subsequent reputation for ill health infected military hospitals as well, earning them a bad reputation for their inability to provide safe, sanitary spaces. Samuel Watkins Overton wrote in his World War I diary that he was "in a little room in a basement with men with all kinds of diseases—no sheet—many not even undressed. It made me sick and angry. Why should we get such treatment merely because we have sacrificed our independence to fight for our country. I saw Dr. this morning but he refused to believe I was sick."[37]

Letters home reported on soldiers' experiences with the flu. One soldier, writing his mother in Baton Rouge from Camp Meade, Baltimore, reported the easing of the epidemic by mid-October 1918. "The *flu* is about over but many of the cases are developing pneumonia. Our death list yesterday was only 32. The daily rate was about 80 for a while. Several doctors, nurses, preachers, etc. were included."[38] Zeke Ellis wrote his aunt Sarah that at Camp Beauregard, Louisiana, "There are only two men left well enough to work in the kitchen and I have the good luck to be one of them." Later, he wrote that of the 250 men in his company, between 175 and 200 were ill, but "The medical inspector has just finished his rounds and pronounced none of the cases serious."[39] But the worry of illness was constant as was the rush to assuage that worry. "I'm glad you all are not worrying about this disease and guess it is a fizzle after all," Zeke informed his aunt.[40]

Racial assumptions about Black illness and death were perpetuated by the military, most likely adding to the flu death toll among Black soldiers. If Black soldiers did with less in the South, they did with less in the military, too. The federal government mandated segregated facilities for Black and white soldiers, including segregated medical facilities. Post-mortems later found that Black men were admitted to the hospital for the flu less often than whites because racial stereotypes led white doctors to believe Black men were inherently lazy and therefore given to lying about illness to avoid work. Black soldiers thus died more often than whites. Moreover, if training camps for white soldiers were bad, the training camps for Black recruits were nearly uninhabitable. White military doctors tried to blame the higher death rates on the tired eugenics arguments offered earlier in the century, arguing that if Black soldiers died, they did so because of their inferior genes, not because of substandard living facilities nor a lack of medical care. There were relatively few (only three hundred fifty) Black military doctors, too, and thus, white doctors with stethoscopes and racial stereotypes cared for the majority of Black soldiers.[41]

Civilians Become Ill and Die from the Flu

The flu quickly spread beyond the training camps because the pathways from soldier to citizen were easy and contagious. Military transportation, sometimes on general passenger trains, mixed soldiers and civilians indiscriminately in confined spaces. Neither were young men confined to training camps, scattering into local towns during off times that created efficient avenues that spread the flu. Katherine Dupre Lumpkin recalled that, "Outside my home city, Columbia [South Carolina], was huge Camp Jackson [that] mushroomed to enormous size in but a few months. Our streets were filled with soldiers, and not just southerners. Northerners by the thousands, officers and men, overran the town. It was all one to us. Or so it seemed."[42] The disease's easy spread meant an errant cough or sneeze could spread the virus as soldiers mingled. But a blasé attitude toward the flu did not help as some residents dismissed their symptoms as unimportant. Charlestonian Charlotte Ball reported to her friend, Edward Wells, that she had gone to a supper, and the woman seated next to her confided "to me that she had been ill all day and that she was sure she had it. I nearly threw her out, for you know how contagious it is."[43]

Panic ensued as the flu gripped men's hearts, and as thousands of civilians died, "Almost no family escaped and many families would all be in bed at the same time," recalled a history of Canaan Baptist Church in Bessemer, Alabama.[44] Textile mill worker Rosie Hutchins Ashley described the effect on her family:

> I guess you 'member ther flu epidemic. Back in 1918 I b'lieve. We was one o' ther fust families here abouts ter have hit an' ever boddy was so afraid o' hit they would not come in ther house but would call outin ther yard an' put food on ther porch fer us . . . Hit's a wonder I didn't die an' I've been not strong ever since. John [husband] had hit worse'n ther rest o' us an' he wasn't able ter work any a-tall ther nex' summer.[45]

William Wood, a Waco, Texas, doctor who had owned a sanitarium, recalled, "Civilians and soldiers died alike . . . were dying like sheep."[46] The litany of the dead was extensive. The flu killed Hattiesburg, Mississippi, resident Jessie Johnson's mother, and Ruth Davis, one of nine children, lost an older brother to the flu four years before she was born. Katherine Anne Porter nearly died from the flu, only to have her fiancé, who ministered to her as she coughed and wheezed, catch and then succumb to the flu, a story made famous by her book, *Pale Horse, Pale Rider*. Magnolia Le Guin's 16-year-old son, Charles Ralph, died from the flu on November 8, 1918. Southerners died in isolated areas like Edisto Island, South Carolina, where the flu carried off many without regard for age or race as Maulsey Stoney found when her mother, Molly, died. It killed young, healthy women like Nina Lynn Wood Friley, who died in College Station, Texas, and writer Thomas Wolfe's brother, Ben. Nathanial White Sr. recalled that his mother died from the flu at age 29, leaving four boys under the age of 10. A fifth son died during the flu epidemic and was buried with his mother in the same grave.[47]

Segregation and the lack of medical care for Black southerners, and for many rural residents, added to an already miserable situation. Doctors could not get out to rural areas, and were less likely to try if the care was for a Black family. One Lawrence County, North Carolina, woman recalled,

> That flu come along in World War I and killed out practically all my family . . . There wasn't too many colored doctors in the South. There was an old one named Dr. James. When my brothers was bein' sickly, all through the flu, you had to go 'bout ten miles to the little town and get him. Then he'd be out on call and he'd come the next day, or the day after. By the time he got there, everybody would be dead and you'd be goin' to the funeral.[48]

Louisianan Melinda Parker recalled her husband's death,

> My husband, Harry Parker, died on October 19, 1918. He was workin' at the shipyards in Algiers an' he got the flu an' in four days, he was dead from pneumonia. I was always a good church worker an' one night I went out to a meetin' an' when I came back, I found him in bed with fever . . . I called the doctor but he never gave me hope . . . He was buried in the Catholic church.[49]

It was only when Black leaders made an appeal that Black nurses were hired by the ARC and others. In Spartanburg, South Carolina, the ARC hired ten "colored" nurses specifically to care for Black patients, at once acknowledging segregation while simultaneously serving a clientele that was least served in the South.[50]

Incipient Healthcare Structures and the Flu

Once the impact became clear, newspapers reported the flu's trail from training camp to the general populace. The *Anniston Star* (Alabama) initially only reported positive news from its new training facility, Camp McClellan. It was not until September 18, 1918, that a small article appeared on its front page, noting "Spanish Influenza Strikes Atlanta." In a simple, understated title, it then announced on September 24 that the flu had come to Anniston: "Eleven cases of influenza shown" at Camp McClellan.[51] It also published various flu treatments, most of them quack remedies that paid for advertising space. Pseudo medical tonics like Tanlac urged readers to "Fortify Yourself Agains [*sic*] it [the flu] By Taking Tanlac."[52] Vicks VapoRub told druggists that it had been oversold due to the flu, noting "Tremendous Demand Last Few Days Has Wiped Out

Excess Stocks that We had Estimated Would Last Until Next January."[53] The implication, of course, was the sold-out stock reflected consumer belief that these products worked, with little or no science to back up that assumption. The flu's deadly impact and newspapers' reporting of it finally motivated some local officials to act. In Anniston, on October 6, 1918, local officials began enacting meaningful quarantine measures, closing movie theaters and other places of amusement while laying off teachers until the epidemic passed. In a true measure of fear, the newspaper announced on October 13, 1918, that the rest of the football season was postponed until the flu had run its course. Jostling the casualty lists for space, newspapers finally, but frantically, begged their readers to wear masks, find chickens to make chicken soup for the sick, and nurse the stricken. They also begged their readers to avoid common death rituals, for example, "refreshing the grief," or opening the casket to view a deceased soldier when he arrived home for burial in the family graveyard. According to the *Hartford Herald* (Kentucky), seven members of a family who did this were stricken with the flu and died.[54]

Eventually, cities established quarantines, closing schools and churches and halting public events. But quarantines had an unseen, deadly cost. Closing churches meant severing the main link between the South's incipient life extension efforts and serving those who were ill. The churches that remained open operated as pseudo hospitals where the ill could be cared for, but the makeshift effort with few extra hands was a vivid reminder that epidemic diseases could easily overwhelm the region.[55] The SBC rued its inability to adequately care for the sick during the "terrible flu scourge," blaming itself for not being Christian enough to build hospitals or train more nurses. It noted in its 1919 Convention report that "The thought of the thousands who have gone to premature graves because, as Baptists, we have not been alive to the call of our Master to minister to the sick and suffering should bring to our cheek the blush of shame."[56]

The ARC struggled to help as many as it could, but the lack of medical infrastructure, skilled nurses, and local support hampered it. In Chattanooga, Tennessee, ARC volunteers were sent from the "best" families to work in the local military camp, only to die themselves. One young woman worked only eight days before succumbing to it. In Augusta, Georgia, the ARC malaria truck did double duty as an ambulance until it broke down. Then volunteers used their own cars. In New Orleans, Louisiana, Harry Hopkins, the future head of the New Deal's Works Progress Administration, was named Division Chairman of the ARC's Influenza Committee, giving him a bird's eye view of the South's terrible health infrastructure. Faced with an overwhelming need for medical care at a time when many doctors had volunteered for war service, Hopkins called medical interns and medical school undergraduates into emergency service. Sick himself, Hopkins secured emergency beds for soldiers; scrounged for funds because the city had already drained its own health coffers; and published full-page ads in newspapers, pleading for nurses.[57]

Struggling to meet the overwhelming need, the ARC appealed to local businesses for help setting up emergency medical spaces. The Virginia Shipbuilding Corporation, along with subscriptions from local citizens, set up that space in Norfolk. Other emergency hospitals opened up in local clubs, including Elks Halls. Those spaces only helped those who were able to get to the hospital. By December 1918, the ARC reported the number of new flu cases had dwindled significantly, but also reported that its life extension work—malarial control, clean water, and milk supplies, for example—had been delayed until the flu emergency passed. In the meantime, the ARC took over the role of the family, caring for the ill, digging graves and burying the dead when families simply could not.[58]

The overwhelming numbers of dead required southerners to set aside some of their burial rituals as wave after wave of coffins went to the cemetery. It was the memories of those constant funerals that stayed with Estelle Williams, who recalled the constant parade:

> Now, the flu epidemic, in the first world war, was a great, great thing in this country, because nobody in this country had ever had the flu and the people just died, just, just . . . maybe five or six a day in Baton Rouge . . . And you see, we were right near that cemetery, and I can remember, we watched through the windows, one funeral after another, every day the funerals going by, and I think . . . that there were more people that died in the United States of that flue [*sic*] epidemic than was killed in the war.[59]

Louisianan Leona Spaht Huff recalled seeing the soldier dead arrive at the train depot during the flu epidemic:

> I think it [the flu] was spread a lot by the men being in service. A lot of them died in the service. We lived in Albany [Missouri], right near the depot and nearly everyday the train would bring some veteran back who had died. I can remember vividly seeing them take the body off the train and loading it into a hearse. People died like flies from that flu epidemic.[60]

Noble Death and the Flu

The flu conflicted with the noble death narrative that soldiers and the public had attempted to construct about the war. Cannons and guns were supposed to kill soldiers, not microscopic organisms. Cities continued to hold military parades, saluting their soldiers' heroism and creating a twentieth-century version of a super-spreader event. The lack of health departments and strong centralized health advocacy played a significant role in accelerating the flu's spread.

Newspapers reinforced the perception that the flu was out there somewhere, and dangerous, but not here. The Atlanta *Journal Constitution* reported that the flu had struck other regions in the nation, ignoring what was becoming a local epidemic with substantial, deadly costs. Indeed, the *Journal Constitution* published casualty lists from the war, but did not account for the casualties from the flu in equal numbers. One kind of death was appropriate; the other was to be hidden in a modern world where good health was supposed to exist.[61]

Although significant in terms of suffering, the flu's third wave in Spring 1919 was less virulent, perhaps owing to one of William Gorgas's final acts for the military: the quarantine of soldiers just back from European battlefields. Eventually hidden from view by postwar memorial activities, the flu's effect remained a significant, albeit implicit, motivation in catalyzing future life extension activities. Indeed, an indication of health reformers' later successes was the flu's virtual erasure from public memory. Only the noble soldier, dead from a battlefield wound, would be remembered well, a process that captured the nation's immediate postwar attention.

5 Remembering the War, Forgetting the Flu, Burying the Military Dead

Military ritual disrupted some southern families' assumptions of how soldiers should be buried, and no one was angrier than Henry "Grady" Abbott's mother, Alice. A white man from Van Vleet, Mississippi, Grady was killed in action in France on October 25, 1918, and buried in a temporary cemetery overseas until war's end. Then, the Quartermaster Corps followed relatively new protocols by contacting his next-of-kin, his widow, to decide his final resting place. The widow was about to remarry and did not want the inconvenience of a former husband. At first, she asked for his body to be buried in an Egypt, Mississippi, cemetery, but then decided to leave his body buried in France. Alice Abbott balked at the federal government's unwillingness to recognize Abbott's parents as his legitimate next-of-kin. "As we are the parents of Pvt. Henry G. Abbott—no. 1591678 we think we have the legal right to have his body sent to Van Vleet Miss. as our family burying ground is there. Mrs. Henry G. Abbott [Grady's widow] has no burying places and as she is to be married soon we think we have the first claim for his body," Alice wrote the Quartermaster Corps. But the former wife had the final say. Grady eventually was buried in the Meuse-Argonne American Cemetery in Romagne, France, among a new family of fellow soldiers and away from the family's plot in a rural Van Vleet cemetery.[1]

Charged with the eventual burial of some 116,000 soldiers, the United States Military Quartermaster Corps' burial practices collided with regional death care practices, a collision that challenged both familial and racial etiquette in the South and made the lonely soldier lying alone in his coffin far away from family a real possibility. At times, the military was able to redefine the image of the lonely soldier in ways that also redefined democracy. Because you died as an American, you were buried according to individual choice, albeit with some limits. Moreover, given World War I's special circumstances—a war fought overseas with a significant loss from illness rather than battlefield deaths—the military provided consistent models of burial while at the same time challenging some southerners to rethink death care, whether they wanted to or not. The later focus on memorialization firmly shifted attention away from the devastating flu epidemic to the repatriated bodies that began arriving in 1919, creating new spaces where southern ritual collided with military reality.

The Emergence of Military Death Care

Americans wrestled with daunting questions that overseas battles created. Should American bodies killed in Europe be left there? Did fighting and dying for democracy require individual choice or military practicality when it came to burials? Who would ultimately make these decisions? Who covered the cost, which would be extensive? Certainly, immediate war needs required bodies be buried in temporary cemeteries until war's end, but after that, what would happen? The Spanish American War played a part in answering these questions, to be sure, but more likely, the Quartermaster Corps did not want a repeat of the Civil War, where the burial of the dead was disorganized and chaotic. There had to be an order and process that would be a guarantee against chaos. In February 1918, the military issued General Order #30 that created a Graves Registration Service (GRS), to be part of the Quartermaster Corps. The GRS was tasked with keeping all death records, including burial case files (each deceased soldier's individual documentation); purchasing land for cemeteries; properly interring all American dead; and maintaining American cemeteries at home and abroad.[2]

New laws and personnel did not eliminate problems with burial completely, given the large number of dead. Identifying the body was the first problem. World War I military policy declared that soldiers were to wear two aluminum tags bearing their name, rank, company, and regiment, so that if they were killed, one tag could be buried with the body and one could be secured to the military-issued pegs that marked burial spaces. Soldiers still wrote notes and attached them to their bodies, however, as their counterparts did during the Civil War. William Abele, a Memphis, Tennessee, resident who was hit by an explosive shell in Samongneux, France, in October 1918, wrote a note that served a different purpose: "Never mind OD [*sic*] blankets, they've got me. If you get a chance, kill a couple of the b——. Notify my wife and brother that they've got me. Notify Col. Ashburn."[3]

The military standardized the notification process by informing the family first by telegram, then by letter, providing whatever details it might have. In the chaos of war where thousands died daily, however, many soldiers remained missing. Auther [*sic*] Acree's family, wanting to bring his body home to Andalusia, Alabama, inquired where his body was in 1920; the military finally found him in an isolated grave in Snippes, France, in 1924. How he was identified is unclear since the body tag was entirely corroded. He was subsequently reburied in Aisne-Marne American Cemetery in Belleau, France.[4]

The American Red Cross (ARC) assisted the military in finding soldiers killed or missing in battle, inundated as it was with many "sad search, sad letters" from families seeking information of their soldiers' welfare, beginning in 1917. A "woman searcher" had the responsibility of locating the missing, first interviewing men from the missing's company. Using that information in one case, the ARC then sent a detail out "to bury any of the men still unburied, and his body was found beside one of the guns, and he was buried there . . . without much ceremony, as it was just after a fight and we were then preparing to make an attack anew." In another instance, a searcher wrote that, "I hoped very much that I would not have to write as I must now, and tell you of his death." But she assured them that their son was buried decently and meaningfully: "His funeral was held the next day by Chaplain Billings, our Episcopalian Chaplain, who was very fond of your son . . . It was, of course, a military funeral, the coffin was draped with an American flag, taps were blown over the grave, and a salute was fired in his honor."[5] Not all soldiers were found. Even with the military's best efforts, 4,100 American soldiers remain missing.

One of those missing soldiers was Edward Wells, from the elite Charleston, South Carolina, family whose wealth and access to powerful people opened up other search opportunities. His family first contacted the ARC after he disappeared during the Battle of St. Mihiel; their last contact had been a letter from him dated September 19, 1918. The ARC later informed them, "The War Department sent us a report that a Lt. Wells died October 10, from wounds. We have not yet rec'd the full particulars; just as soon as we do we will communicate with you again. The Red Cross sympathizes with you in your sorrow and is glad to be of service." While the ARC did the best it could to find missing soldiers, Wells's mother sought information in other ways, writing to the editor of the *New York Herald*, beseeching the newspaper to run an ad for her missing son.[6]

The overwhelming number of deaths occurring nearly simultaneously meant mistakes did happen with regularity. Many times, it was simply a paperwork mistake when soldiers shared common names and initials. This is what happened to Wells, who was originally reported as a prisoner of war on a *New York Times* casualty list; that soldier turned out to be a native of Wichita, Kansas. Wells's body was finally found in January 1919, even though he had died October 10, 1918. The Wells family finally received a telegram on January 22, 1919, notifying them of Edward's death. Its message was similar to the many others sent during the war, in that the military "deeply regrets to inform that it is officially reported that Edward Wells, machine gun battalion, died."[7] The ARC followed up with its own notification once it had confirmed Wells's death. Its aid impressed Mrs.

Wells enough that she later donated her deceased son's clothing to the ARC for discharged soldiers.

The letters from searchers, describing the initial burials of soldiers, give the impression of a consistent set of interim burial practices, but, like the problems with confirming a soldier's death, that was impossible because of battlefield chaos. With German guns blasting in the distance, blowing taps and other burial rituals could make you a target. Thus, hidden in coroners' reports are the hasty attempts to bury the dead without getting killed. During the flu epidemic, the military tried to bury soldiers in uniform, per GRS orders, but soldiers were buried many times in whatever clothing they died in. Knoxville, Tennessee, native Christian Acklin died from pneumonia in England in October 1918, and was buried in a hospital shroud, for example. Mass numbers of deaths also required the hasty organization of temporary burial grounds, named for the battles the dead had participated in. Nurses serving in military hospitals reported the constant sound of trumpets as the dead were buried. Mary Dobson, an Army nurse, recalled, "The cemetery was just up the hill and every morning you could hear the bugle blowing as they buried the bodies. It was gruesome. It really was."[8]

With chaos ensuing and orderly ritual a goal rather than the reality, the Quartermaster Corps attempted to find consistency through paperwork, believing that, if there was a form for the dead, then mistakes would be minimized. These "burial case files" became the military's version of a Progressive Era funeral ledger. Each deceased soldier had one that included autopsies, descriptions of some burials, communications with the family and paperwork designating the body's final disposition. The GRS undertaker carefully noted how he ensured the body was identified correctly on those documents, and, when it was unrecognizable due to decomposition or damage to the body, he instead described the process he used to identify it, for example, noting "an envelope with grave tags as well as the tag on peg over body, and GRS plaque on body."[9]

The military tried to avoid at all costs sending the wrong body to the wrong family. This almost happened to the family of Bannockburn, South Carolina, native Sam Abraham. Abraham was scheduled to be shipped home from Finisterre, France, but the body found in his grave turned out to be Abraham Shore, not Sam Abraham. Sam Abraham's body was eventually buried in Arlington National Cemetery in its "colored" section, halting the potential of sending the wrong body back to a family. Mistakes did happen, of course. Raymond Acklin's mother filled out various forms for her son, who was gassed in Summer 1918 and died two days after returning to the states. The burial case file is a litany of errors. Clerks first misspelled his last name as "Acklem, Raymond." When his mother contacted the military because she wanted to accompany her son's body home from New York City to Huntsville, Alabama, the Quartermaster Corps misspelled her last name, referring to her as Mrs. Fannie Acklen.[10] These are small errors, to be sure, but they signal the potential for bigger errors in the midst of battle chaos and the immense amount of paperwork to be filled out when a soldier died.

How Did My Soldier Die?

Southerners—really, Americans in general—wanted to know how a soldier died, even as they relinquished death care to the military. One practice, probably resurrected from the Civil War, reemerged when the deceased's fellow soldiers wrote letters to the family, describing the final moments. Dry paperwork could not describe heroic efforts; the soldiers themselves had to create that narrative. Captain E. A. Kindervater wrote to Mrs. Wells in March 1919, assuring her that her son's death was a heroic one. Another soldier, Frank Parker, wrote that, "In the First Division no finer record of gallantry and efficiency in combat than that of Edward L. Wells can be found. He was the embodiment of those virtues which meet the reference [word unclear] test of an officer of combat troops."[11] Still another soldier wrote Wells's sister that "he was killed instantly. . . . I felt conscious from the first that he possessed all the qualities of an efficient officer and high-minded gentleman . . . If he had lived a hundred years he could not have accomplished more than he has, even though his life was short in years, and he gave it up gladly to make the supreme sacrifice."[12] Letters from the front assured North Carolina's Eugenia Ranson that her husband, John Oliver, had died a good death when he rushed a German machine gun nest. "Let me say that during our months since we left you there has not been a single day he did not live up to the standard of the true American that you know him to be. He was always helpful to his men and the officers with whom he was associated—his presence in any group was always appreciated," Lieutenant James W. Thompson informed her.[13]

Journalists like Frederick Malloy, the North Carolina newspaperman, wrote letters to his friends' families, capturing the battlefield drama and their sons' heroism. But more than informing of a death and constructing a narrative of honor, Malloy tried to define how southern families should grieve. If the death was on a battlefield, it was to be glorified, just as deaths in the South were ones to exalt for those who had been born again. It was not all right to grieve a noble death—understandable, of course, but not right. Upon learning of a friend named Harry's death, Malloy wrote his mother:

> There must be mingled with that deepest grief, a feeling of pride, glorious soul pride for having given to the world a man who valued his country's honor more than his life. Harry did not drift into the service of his country on the heyday of war's

> patriotism, he gave valuable service during peace times and worked upward until he reached the acme of perfection in his line of endeavor; then when war came, he as ever was ready to serve. Harry's death brought the horrors of this Hell-bred war before our very eyes, as he was my friend, and I will say for him, as I know he would have said for me—thank God he was not a slacker.[14]

The British military served as an example of honoring the sacrifice soldiers made on the field. Malloy described one incident to his mother, "I heard a 2nd Lt. of the British Army received news of his brothers [*sic*] death—his answer was a toast—Gentlemen, to my brother, he has had the honor of dying for King and Country."[15] In the midst of battle action, too, when deaths and injuries were common, grief was a luxury those who wished to survive did not have. "I have lost many friends lately, men that have gone thru the furnace with me, but it soon becomes a game and we dont [*sic*] have time to mourn, which in itself is a godsend," Malloy assured his mother.[16]

When the Spanish flu threatened to make soldier deaths incidental rather than honorable, letters home reassured families that the death, even though from disease rather than a bullet, was still an honorable death. Private Cecil Abner's lieutenant, Abraham K. Wrenshall, informed his family in Rockmart, Georgia, that his death from the flu in the spring 1919 in no way cast a negative light on Abner's service, sacrifice or manly honor. Wrenshall wrote,

> In admiration of your son's renowned service and with a heart that goes forth to you in your affliction, we extend out condolence for your loss is ours. Noble and great is the Sacrifice which America's brave have made in this grand Case that freedom might not perish. Private Abner distinguished himself in this great Attainment by this splendid courage and fully demonstrated the ideals of a loyal American soldier by having fought in his Country's great need and risked all for a righteous Victory.[17]

Frederick Malloy's captain, Walter Gaudinsky, cast his death as honorable, even though it was caused by the flu, not a gun. He wrote:

> On October 15, the day before his birthday, he had been promoted 1st Lieutenant in compensation for the most valuable services he has rendered to his country upon who altar he has laid his young life. The promotion came to him as a ray of sunshine for although the insidious disease had begun its deadly work, he got up from his cot for a while and walked around camp. The following day however he began feeling worse ... The boys of the troop fitted him out with everything for his comfort.

To comfort Mrs. Malloy, Gaudinsky linked the death to his service. Her son refused to acknowledge his illness and it was that refusal that finally killed him.[18] Other soldiers vested Malloy's mother with the honor due her for sacrificing a son. A compatriot, Captain Carl Hanton, wrote Mrs. Malloy in December 1918 that:

> I think it was that night [of a battle in which he had to go outside to deliver a communication] he caught the cold which developed into the illness that caused his death. So you see, Mrs. Malloy, that your boy gave his life to contribute to the success of a vital operation that hastened the end of the war and saved the boys of other mothers from the horrors of this awful thing we have just been through. Had he not had a brave heart that night, a brave heart and the endurance which your care of him in his boyhood had endowed him, he might not have delivered that order on time, we might not have broken the Boche line the next day and the war might still be going on.[19]

Planning for Repatriation

Armed with the knowledge that their soldiers died nobly, no matter the cause, many Americans demanded their dead be returned to them, forming groups like the "Bring Home the Soldier Dead League." The Secretary of War, Newton Baker, had many options for the repatriation of deceased soldiers, but in the end, gave the decision to the families, linking their choice of where to bury the dead to the democratic ideals the war had been fought for. In other words, one democratic right became the ability to choose *where* to bury your dead. Circumstance, however, determined *when* a body was buried. If a soldier died before leaving the United States, for example, he was sent home immediately, embalmed and casketed by a local funeral director contracted by the military. If a soldier died overseas, however, there was a long wait for the body's return.[20]

The grim task of repatriating thousands of American soldiers from European cemeteries began in 1919. At the end of the war, the multiple temporary European cemeteries used to inter soldiers overseas—military historian Lisa Budreau puts the number at more than 2,400 sites, a number that does not include an additional 15,000 individual burials—had to be consolidated into larger cemeteries where American soldiers were temporarily laid to rest, awaiting shipment home. The War Department then sent questionnaires to families, giving them four choices: burial in Arlington National cemetery; burial in another national cemetery; burial in a local or family cemetery; or leave the body overseas. All bodies buried in Germany, Luxemburg, and North Russia were disinterred and brought home, no matter the family's wishes. In the end, 45,000 families decided to have their sons disinterred and reburied at home while the rest left their sons abroad. By the end of the disinterment period (around 1924), the 2,400 temporary graveyards and 15,000 individual graves had been centralized into eight American cemeteries, mostly in France and Belgium; the remaining bodies were shipped home at a cost of $30 million.[21]

The Quartermaster Corps tried to find all families and discover their wishes, first making multiple announcements in newspapers. J. T. Adair reached out regarding the return of his son's body from the French battlefield where he had been killed in battle in September 1918. "I see in the papers where the boddies [*sic*] of soldiers that died in France would in the near future be sent back to the U.S.A.," Adair wrote, "I here with make [*sic*] application for my sons boddie [*sic*] . . . when it is brought back to the U.S.A."[22] Using the Next-of-Kin's information, the Quartermaster Corps also contacted families directly. Once contacted, the military required a dismaying set of documents that confounded many. The ARC helped some navigate the documents, but it put some Black southerners in awkward positions when they reached out to local white southerners for help. Ellen Adair, whose husband Luther died in France in January 1918, turned to Winona, Mississippi, lawyer Vernon Rowe who was the local ARC representative. Adair, who seems to have been able to read, but not write well (an extant letter from her shows a difficulty with spelling) turned to Rowe who wrote for her,

> Ellen Adair, to whom you addressed a letter on Oct. 5, and Nov. 15, 1928, with reference to removal of the body of the above named soldier . . . is in my office and directs that I answer your letters for her. She is an ignorant colored woman,

Figure 5.1. This is the view from the Suresnes American Cemetery, looking toward Paris, with the cemetery's memorial building to the author's rear.

Figure 5.2. The United States Military mixed its foreign burials without regard to religion or race. A Jewish star marks a grave amidst Christian crosses here at the Suresnes American Cemetery.

Figure 5.3. Luther Adair's widow, Ellen, approached local white officials in Mississippi in order to fill out the military's paperwork for World War I burials. In the end, she left her husband's body in the Suresnes Cemetery.

> and I represent the American Red Cross here and that is the reason she sought me out. This woman says that she prefers yhat [*sic*] her husband's body be removed to one of the permanent cemeteries, where his grave will be assured of perpetual care by the United States.[23]

In other words, the paperwork reinforced some Black dependence on whites even though the deceased's service was potentially revolutionary. Mrs. Adair got her wish, however. Luther Adair is honorably buried in the Suresnes American cemetery, just west of Paris, France, where his grave is carefully maintained a hundred years after his death.

Bringing the Soldiers Home

Paperwork once again guided the military after it turned its ships over to reinterment in 1919, coming through harbors such as Port Hoboken, New Jersey. All bodies were off-loaded there, and then escorted home on a train by a military representative like Corporal Henry S. Hoy. Hoy accompanied forty-five bodies from the port to North Carolina, South Carolina, Georgia and Florida, using paperwork to streamline the task of taking all of them at once, stopping in each soldier's town to deliver the body. He stopped in Darlington, South Carolina, to return Barney L. Abbott's body to his family; his father, Moses L. Abbott, then signed another official document, stating he had received his son.[24] Telegrams guided the process from start to finish as they ensured an appropriate military honor guard was present and that local undertakers and the family knew ahead of time. The lonely casket on a train platform was not the noble image the military wanted to portray, since escorting bodies home could—and did—lead to Americans confronting the real costs of war, namely the deaths of young men.[25]

Southern undertakers, newly vested as the South's death officers, were eager to affirm their status as they served as intermediaries between families awaiting a dead soldier at the train station and the military escort. E. H. Harleston Sr., the Charleston, South Carolina, funeral professional, for example, reburied Frank Thompson, a 24-year-old soldier who served with Co. A, 353 Eng., 144th Inf., and who arrived home in April 1919. The military paid for all services until Thompson arrived in Charleston; at that point, Thompson's Virginia Insurance policy paid for transferring the body, for the hearse and four cars to the cemetery, and for the cemetery plot and service fees, totaling $55. H. F. Hoover, in rural Shelbyville, Tennessee, reburied L. S. Haynes, who died in France and was brought home in April 1920, and charged his family for a robe, plank, and hearse ($32.50).[26]

Inevitably, a clash of cultures emerged when those who received the body assumed that southern practicalities (for example, taking bodies to distant family cemeteries on rural roads) would be paid for by the military. Funeral ledgers are silent on this clash, but burial case files are not. When Marion Abernathy died from pneumonia in March 1917 and was shipped from El Paso, Texas, to Cedar Bluff, Arkansas, the undertaker transported the body to the family home, some thirty-five miles away. "I hired a team to use on my own hearse," the undertaker, M. W. Phariss wrote, "This will be a loss to me unless paid by the Government. Please do what you can to have this paid to me." Phariss eventually lost the $25 he believed he was owed because the government made no provision for transportation from the train station to the burial ground.[27]

In another potential clash with the military, only certain family members were legally obligated to receive the body because of the military's strict accounting for next-of-kin. Spouses were the legal next-of-kin, then fathers, mothers, and finally, siblings. The military was so strict that George Acty's mother had to declare in a telegram that her husband was dead and Acty had no wife, after he died from the flu in October 1918 in France. Letters like those Alice Abbott wrote are particularly poignant as she saw her former daughter-in-law remarry and yet retain the right to bury Abbott's son. The GRS, while gentle in its response, was adamant. Captain R. E. Shannon wrote Mr. Abbott that, "it is regretted to have to inform you that your request must be denied in view of the fact that a contrary request has been filed by the widow of the late soldier. It is possible that you may be able to secure the consent of Mrs. S. M. Abbott [the daughter-in-law], to the delivery of the body of the late soldier to you."[28] The grief this caused Abbott's parents was profound. Schooled to believe a family reunion occurred if the family was buried together, their son's French burial suggested they might not see their son in heaven. Alice Abbott eventually found a superficial way to include her son in the family graveyard in that her obituary in 1941 mentions that she was a Gold Star mother.[29] Frederick Malloy's mother went a step further. She had a cement cross with his name on it planted next to her husband's gravestone (he died in 1915), even though her son's body remained in a French cemetery.[30]

For soldiers with no families, the military filled all of the roles that the family typically would, for example, by acting as the official mourning party or providing burial space. Charley Achee, Bellrose, Louisiana, died from pneumonia in Suresnes, France, in December 1918, and the military cared for him until it eventually located his sister. Because the military served as a new family for their soldierly kin, burial in national cemeteries was sometimes a reasonable option; the cemeteries were also ubiquitous in the region, making visiting a soldier an easy task. National cemeteries also provided the poorest soldiers, whose families were sharecroppers, a permanent place for their sons' bodies. Burial on sharecropping land had always been tenuous; sharecroppers, Black and white, could be evicted from the land without notice and there was no way to carry their dead with them. National cemeteries provided that permanent resting place. Virginian Roderick Acors was killed in action in Meuse-Argonne

Figure 5.4. Alice Abbott's grave site at the Asbury Cemetery in rural Chickasaw County (near Van Vleet), MS.

and his father requested he be buried in Arlington National Cemetery. John Franklin Acuff's family buried him in the National Cemetery in Chattanooga, Tennessee, while another fifteen World War I soldiers were buried at the National Cemetery in Knoxville, Tennessee.[31]

For all soldiers who served in World War I, no matter when or where they died, the federal government promised to pay for a headstone, a new commodity for southerners who marked graves with trees, rocks, and memories. When John Abraham died in 1928, his widow wrote the Quartermaster Corps, requesting that gravestone for her husband in Charentan, Louisiana. It permanently marked both his resting place and his service in the war. Moreover, the engraving of names on stones made the bodies buried beneath known to anyone who walked through the graveyard.[32]

Finally, the military processed the military insurance, ensuring all moneys owed were forwarded to the survivors. Private Isaiah Abernathy died from pneumonia in October, 1918, and his mother, Lizzie Abernathy, was named the beneficiary of his $10,000 government insurance. At his death, another set of paperwork was filled out and the money was paid out in weekly installments over many years, providing her a stable income.[33]

Figure 5.5. This is a typical World War I stone, provided by the federal government to all soldiers, no matter when they died.

Families Remember the Dead

For many, death remained a physical process, meaning the laying on of hands at death or viewing the body before burial mattered to them. Delayed repatriation—or in the case of Henry Grady, no repatriation at all—forced some southerners to reimagine death care, putting more energy into memorializing the dead than in burial. How could families ensure their soldiers would be remembered after their own deaths? Physical objects became stand-ins, replicating the bodies' physical presence in some cases and ensuring the soldier would be remembered in others. Frederick Malloy's mother had already placed a stone in her family plot to make sure she would see him in Heaven. She then took each of her son's wartime letters and retyped every single one, including the most poignant communication of all, the military telegram telling her he had died from the flu. The documents were then sent to the North Carolina Historical Commission for archiving in 1938 and 1944.

Families in urban areas also claimed their losses publicly so that neighbors and the random passerby would know they had lost a soldier. In rural areas, locals knew who grieved, but the migrations out of the region to war industry jobs as well as the overall expansion in city populations meant those who had lost a soldier had become invisible. Their loss had to be made visible so it could be acknowledged by a grateful nation. An Ohio officer, Colonel Robert L. Queisser made and patented an "in service" flag (the ubiquitous red and white flag with a blue star in the middle) to be hung in windows, announcing that this home had sent someone to war. Once that soldier died, a gold star replaced the blue star, announcing the death. Loss, then, became a public announcement. Eventually, the Gold Star Mothers, a national group organized by a mother whose aviator son had died in the war, emerged to guide the remembrance of the war's dead, finding a real home among southern mothers who fervently claimed the right to remember.[34]

Southern States Reclaim Their Soldiers

States reclaimed their right to memorialize the dead, rather than ceding that authority to the federal government. Both Alabama and Georgia produced massive memorial projects, documenting their state's dead. Alabama State Archivist Marie Bankhead Owen took charge of the project in Montgomery, using published newspaper casualty lists to contact families and then sending a "bio-form" to each family. Survivors filled in information about their soldier's service, ancestry, schooling, work life, and other information, sometimes sending photos and other documents. The paperwork eventually became the Alabama Department of Archives and History's Gold Star database (created well after the fact; it can be found here: https://digital.archives.alabama.gov/digital/collection/goldstar). In the letter she sent each family, Owen said she was going to publish a book, honoring the heroic Alabamans who died in the war, although there is no evidence the book was ever published. Writing to Belle McKenzie, whose son Arthur was killed in action in October 1918, for example, Owen noted that she was compiling photos and biographical information for those who "died for their country, either while serving in camp or on the field during World War I." Critically, Owen made no distinction between those who died in camp, a vague reference to those who died from the Spanish flu, and those who died in battle.[35] Moreover, Black Alabamans (there are fifty-two on Owen's list of the dead) were included on her list, and many Black families responded with photos, completed biographical forms, and notes, documenting their dead's service to the nation.

Georgia reclaimed its dead differently: the Military Department of the State of Georgia produced a memorial book, dedicated to the "Gold Star Mothers of Georgia in Memory of Their Heroic Sons Who Made the Supreme Sacrifice in the Cause of Humanity," but for whites only. Claiming to be an "authentic record," the book was a kind of coffee-table book, replete with photographs of white Georgians who had died as well as photos of the American cemeteries in France and Belgium where some Georgians still rested. The causes of death were listed, ranging from typhoid and flu to gunshot wounds received in training camp, being gassed, or being on a ship that sunk.[36] Invisible on those pages were the Black Georgians who also died, and memorial books allowed white southerners to manage the honor conferred on Black southerners by making them, literally, invisible in Georgia's pantheon of World War I heroes. Memory thus became segregated.

The book was to take the place of the visit to the family graveyard while simultaneously assuring the bereaved that a new family cared well for their dead. Modern photography portrayed beautiful images of American cemeteries, carefully evincing northern burial practices where cemeteries could be mistaken for parks and places of solace rather than a collection of bodies. The American cemetery at Le Mans, France, "shows how Uncle Sam cherishes the memory of the gallant heroes who answered their country's call to defend her liberty." At the American Expeditionary Force Cemetery in Romagne, France, authors noted, "Close to the battlefield on which they made the supreme sacrifice, sleep 26,000 immortal American heroes, whose deeds are deeply carved in gratitude in the hearts of America's grateful people." The French, the book noted, were grateful for the sacrifice, and photos displayed decorations placed by French citizens in gratitude.[37]

The book had to deal with another kind of lonely soldier, the unknown dead. Not since the Civil War had the nation had to reckon with unknown soldiers. Those soldiers were still buried decently, the book assured its audience, no matter who the (white) soldier was. At the American Expeditionary Force Cemetery at Le Mans, France, "Each grave is properly marked with a white cross on which is printed the name of the deceased, company and division, to which he last belonged. This plan has been followed out in all of the American cemeteries in Europe."[38] Authors noted, under the picture of a cross marked as "Unknown," "Although they were not able to identify the body laid at rest in this grave, the scouting party who found it made sure the unknown soldier was properly buried and the grave marked with a cross to distinguish it." In other words, all white soldiers, no matter who they were, were claimed and buried decently.[39]

The pictures could jolt the generally Protestant southern audience, however, because soldiers were buried without regard to religious denomination, southern burial practice, or racial practice. Southern burial grounds segregated themselves racially or denominationally, and intermingling Catholic or Jewish bodies alongside Protestants was never done. The military buried Christian soldiers with a cross in contrast to many southern burials; trees and rocks were not effective markers. But mixed in with crosses were Stars of David, which marked Jewish graves, suggesting indiscriminate burials that relied on military necessity rather than denominational loyalty. Photos hid another fact of overseas burials. Black and white soldiers were buried together, without regard for race. Luther Adair, whose wife sought help from a local white man and who is buried at the Suresnes Cemetery west of Paris, is mingled with other soldiers with no indication of his race.[40]

Other documents describe a darker story behind the noble photographs. Samuel Watkins Overton, the future mayor of Memphis, described his own cemetery work while stationed in France in his diary. Placed on an outside detail to "pretend" to fix up graves, Overton realized his labor was merely to make work for him and his fellow soldiers. "We worked on graves laughing, cursing and loafing. Our sensibilities have been deadened. Many French 'Mort Pour La France' [died for France] buried there—Amer. graves unkempt and many poorly marked," he wrote in his diary.[41] Staged photographs thus hid what was a rather chaotic process.

Photography and Other Postwar Memorials

Those whose kin did not appear in grand memorial books searched for ways to know about their burials. Photographs of a specific grave site became one new memorial. Photographing the dead was relatively rare in the South. Indeed, rural southerners did not go to photographers; rather, photographers tended to go to customers with their cameras, searching for locals who wanted their pictures "made." Photography thus became a relatively new tool in celebrating the dead as the GRS and ARC had photographs of military graves taken by professional photographers. Then, censors checked the photos because the dead could not look too dead. The approved photograph was ceremonially turned out in a good quality gray paper folder, folded into a gray paper mailing envelope, and sent to the family.

Photography was one kind of postwar memorial. Conferring medals like the Croix de Guerre and the unveiling of local memorials were others. Charlestonian Edward Wells received the Distinguished Service Cross twice; won the Croix de Guerre posthumously; his alma mater, the Virginia Military Institute, memorialized his death with a tablet in his honor; and his mother pursued awarding him the Congressional Medal of Honor (the answer was a gentle, but firm, no). Later, the family tried to have Water Street (where the family resided) renamed Wells Street in honor of his service, for the name would, according to one friend, "represent a tradition of active and positive influence upon the future." The city declined.[42]

Families also honored the dead by shifting their focus to the living. With the breakdown of class barriers on chaotic battlefields came the sponsorship of working-class folks by elite families. Ben Kuniawsky, a Russian immigrant, received Mrs. Wells's largesse once she discovered he had stayed with Edward as he died. It is not clear how she discovered Kuniawsky, but his death care replaced the family's on that distant battlefield, and sponsoring Kuniawsky became a way to memorialize her own son. She decided she would give Ben, who suffered from tuberculosis (TB), a thousand dollars from Edward's insurance money. Friends warned her that he might take advantage of her, writing, "This seems too large a sum to give Kuniawsky all at once. The boy is young and very imaginative and has been earning a living among people in different circumstance from those you have been thrown with enough to understand." Indeed, one friend said, "if Ben can procure light work and has to make a living, unless his health entirely fails, it will be better for him. This is a very large sum for a boy like that."[43] Mrs. Wells seems to have ignored them.

The military also shifted its veneration of the dead to those whose loss was perceived to be the most profound, Gold Star mothers. The military first made medals for mothers who had lost a child; Mary Acree, from Bayles, Alabama, whose son, Auther Acree, died in France in July 1918, asked the military to send her "the medal that the mothers are supposed to wear for their sons that died on the battlefield." For Acree, the medal served several purposes. Certainly, it was a constant, visual reminder to others of her loss. But in the case of Acree, whose body was lost for a while, the medal gave her something physical to cling to when her son's body could not be found. Later, after he was buried in the Aisne-Marne American Cemetery in Belleau, France, the medal came to be a representation of his final resting place.[44]

Death tourism became another way to honor mothers when their personal funds or the federal government allowed some Gold Star Mothers to visit their son's or husband's grave, becoming a kind of "death tourism" in the early 1920s. Frederick Malloy's mother visited his grave in 1922 in Romange, France, confirming for herself that her son's grave was well cared for. Friends also visited the graves of the dead and sent back descriptive letters to families. But the vast majority of mothers and friends could not afford the trip. Recognizing this, the national Gold Star Mothers Association successfully lobbied the federal government to take thousands of Gold Star Mothers or Wives to European cemeteries in the late 1920s and early 1930s. The military invited both white and Black mothers and spouses to attend, albeit on segregated trips, acknowledging the nobility of all mothers and wives who had lost a soldier. Eventually, the government spent $5 million sending mothers to overseas American cemeteries.[45]

The arrangements for the trips were extensive, for it would not do for a Gold Star Mother or Wife, each wearing the appropriate medal, to be harmed on her trip. The government arranged for transportation to France; for escorts both in Paris and in the cemeteries; for food; and then, for transportation home. One Texas mother later wrote, "I am glad I have come. Now I feel that my son rests at peace among his comrades, that he is a soldier."[46] But only some were able to go. Grady Abbott's mother, Alice, was invited in 1932. By then 69 years old, she was too ill to travel ("home, though a poor one, suits me better," she wrote), but she was "truly grateful for the interest manifested" on her behalf.[47]

Black mothers and wives were sent to France on a segregated trip. One of those women was Greenville, South Carolina, native Polly Adair, whose son, Rayford, was killed in action September 28, 1918, and reburied in the Meuse-Argonne American Cemetery in September 1921. The burial case file tracked Mrs. Adair's visit to France, carefully calling her and her traveling companions by the honorific "Mrs."[48] Once Black Gold Star Mothers arrived in France, the actual visits remained segregated, meaning if Black American mothers were in France, then Black French citizens were assigned to entertain them. A report of the visit noted, "This being the first contingent of colored pilgrims its arrival aroused considerable interest in Paris," and a group of "colored" musicians serenaded the travelers as they disembarked from the train.[49] But if the military believed that only Black French citizens could entertain Black Gold Star Mothers, it also believed that American Expeditionary Force leadership should acknowledge their loss. "Colored musicians" may have serenaded them at the train station, but General John Pershing, the American commander during World War I, and the French Military Governor of Paris were present at the various ceremonies honoring the mothers. The trip went so well that Adair wrote a thank you note to the Quartermaster Corps General, thanking him for "every courtesy shown me since leaving my home in Greenville, S.C."[50]

Not all southerners received the military's largesse. The military denied Auther Acree's mother's request that her daughter go in her place. Luther Adair's widow received an invitation to visit her husband's grave in France, but her subsequent marriage voided her right to travel to France. Other Black mothers such as Mrs. Loralee Cannon, an Athens, Alabama native, refused to visit her son, calling the segregation of mothers an "insult to the living."[51] Contradiction thus ruled the military's response to Black mothers when it acknowledged their grief, but then segregated the mothers themselves.

Reburying the dead and mourning the loss took a long time, given the unique circumstances of World War I, as the nation as a whole struggled to create a ritual capable of marking all soldier deaths as honorable. The final instances of memorialization did not occur until the early 1930s when the final Gold Star Mothers visited their dead overseas. Yet dying in World War I had some significant, but still subtle, effect on southern death rituals and on incipient life extension practices. Some southerners changed their death care to adhere to the military's strict ritual, even as it conflicted with local practice. Soldier repatriation also came with some challenges to the region's caste system, albeit not nearly enough. The changes in death care as well as the expanded manufacturing capacity the war fostered meant that in the Roaring Twenties southerners could invest in new death consumer goods. The exposure to deadly southern landscapes also meant military health officials maintained and expanded federal investment in life extension, hoping to create a healthier post–World War I South.

PART THREE

Death Care in the 1920s South

Although the fight abroad was short, the sale of American military goods to European countries expanded the already burgeoning industrialization of the South in ways that had implications for making death more of a consumer experience, for attacking its deadly environment when new epidemics appeared, and for extending life. The Southern Baptist Convention (SBC) warned its followers, "The South is predestined to be thoroughly industrialized—to become more and more the mill and shop center of the United States—and in so doing to be forced to take more active and strenuous measures against the encroachment of the great white plague [tuberculosis]."[1] Migrating to urban centers for munitions work during the war, many stayed as those factories shifted to producing new death (and other) goods. Death goods marked one as modern, important, and significant. But urban areas also hid a dark secret. They could be as deadly—or more so—than rural areas, and new funeral professionals had plenty of customers to bury.

The exchange of goods was the foundation for an exchange of ideas when Sigmund Freud's theories about mourning and melancholia became more known, when Emily Post claimed that respectable people used a certain kind of death etiquette, and when religious organizations updated their theology to account for a modern world. Grief and mourning became more accepted, albeit within strict limits. The shift in death care required a new focus on the comfort given to mourners, using newly available printing presses that produced personalized stationery and scrapbooks, cheaply and efficiently, that both acknowledged and privatized grief.

As the new consumerism transformed death care, the military and the American Red Cross (ARC) expanded their incipient investments in life extension, attacking stubbornly high mortality rates and coming to count the economic costs of dying young. More than a problem of insurance not being paid up, the death of so many young southerners was itself an economic problem.

For some, how you died did not matter, however. With the insurance paid up and your burial society ready to mourn you, what mattered was the purple throne that awaited you when you died.

6 Purple Coffins and Cadillac Hearses

Purchasing a Good Death

Purple became the color of death in the post–World War I South, mimicking Protestant theology where purple was the color of royalty and associated with Jesus Christ at Advent and Lent. After World War I, purple coffins were that manifestation of royalty for some Black southerners, especially women. Memphis housewives Bridie Davis (age 34, died November 1924) and Pearlina Stanley (age 39, died April 1925) were both laid out in plush, purple coffins, wearing silk dresses, and were resplendent as Christian royalty. There were, obviously, no consequences for claiming to be royal in a racial system that decreed otherwise. But, because many southerners believed they did not go to Heaven until the coffin was buried deep, these housewives-in-life/queens-in-death believed they would be at their funeral, at least in spirit, and would view their bodies laid out on their purple thrones.[1]

The shift from tangible burial practices—namely family-based death care to a death commercial system that did the actual death work—caused many southerners to vest death goods with the deceased's memory and personhood. Death goods also became emotional and political statements as well as religious and eschatological ones as domestic goods production linked a burgeoning network of funeral directors to factories which were only a telegram and a train ride away. Those who imagined their funerals endowed those goods with a political import that ignored racial hierarchies. Others believed that certain kinds of goods affirmed their place in that same racial system, dictating those wishes in wills and giving them legal import. Death goods thus became an alternative political system for Black and white, for middle class and working class people, to claim, affirm, or deny their status in an increasingly urban South.

Building a Modern South

Historians have long noted the expansion of the industrial South beginning around 1900, but point to the 1920s as an era in which industry, urbanization, and population explosions became ordinary rather than rare or evolving. Catalyzed by the wartime industrial infrastructure, factories now manufactured a variety of death products, including cheap coffins, metal vaults, clothing, and other goods. Moreover, the transportation networks necessary to the war effort became a way to quickly transport a coffin or other products to undertakers. Rather than having an "antagonistic" reaction to new consumer goods and technology, southerners readily purchased the new wonders that a modern industrial infrastructure brought.[2]

Urban population explosions accompanied industrial expansion as large cities added new residents to their population. Between 1900 and 1920, historian Blaine Brownell found that "the populations of Atlanta, Memphis, and New Orleans grew by 123, 59 and 35 percent, respectively."[3] Birmingham, Alabama, a small steel town in 1900 with 38,415 people, reached 178,806 residents by 1920. Churches in the area reported their own population explosions as they built or added on to existing church buildings. Ruhama Baptist Church in Birmingham announced that it had a thousand parishioners, and that it had built a new building "modern in every respect," with an auditorium for 1,000 and an education space for 2,000.[4] By 1930, twenty southern cities had reached metropolitan size (population of 100,000 or more) when very few had reached that mark by 1900.

Regional cities were not the only places southerners migrated to; migrating to the north or west was also an option. Out migration, however, meant coming home to the South when one died. The Harleston Funeral Home received multiple migrants from across the country, including New York, Connecticut, and Los Angeles, and then turned around and shipped them to rural South Carolina graveyards. Migration and urban areas came to be seen as deadly when migrant children came home in coffins. Edisto Island (South Carolina) residents Edward and Pauline Simmons sent three sons to New York City, having caught what one Federal Writers' Project (FWP) interviewer called, "Harlem fever," the promise that Harlem provided a rich experience for Black southerners. But two of those sons came home for burial in the family graveyard. The first time, Pauline's screams could be "heard across the creek. She wrenched herself free from supporting arms and jumped into the half-filled grave. It was a long time before her relatives could quiet her." Another son soon followed. This time, however, Pauline was stoic as she realized that Harlem fever killed as easily as yellow fever used to.[5]

Funeral Home Expansion in Cities

The migration from rural to urban areas as well as the professionalization of death officers catalyzed the growth of the death industry itself. In 1900, there were 16,200 funeral homes nationally; by 1920, there were 24,464. New funeral homes appeared across the South, for example, the Dauterive and Fremaux Funeral Home, in Crowley, Louisiana. Crowley, west of New Orleans, grew by 25 percent in the 1920s and the former furniture-store-turned-funeral parlor opened in 1923. Nationally, the number of dead bodies to bury increased 2.3 percent, but not enough, according to one expert, to counter the "number of undertakers [which] increased twenty-five times as fast as the total volume of business."[6] The number of funerals per undertaker per year thus dropped, at least nationally, from 83.5 in 1900 to 56.6 in 1920. Moreover, the larger client base did not protect against customers who did not pay their bills. Dauterive and Fremaux sent a large number of letters requesting payment and hired attorneys to track down customers; however, the debt caused this funeral home to close after only three years in business.[7]

Funeral directors who had already built up a good name capitalized on the growth, opening up branch offices in other towns or states. Charleston's Harleston Funeral Home opened up the Fleming-Harleston Funeral Home in St. Augustine, Florida, in the 1920s. The family was reasonably optimistic about their success, given that their "only present competition is way behind," meaning they lacked modern funeral practices.[8] Being modern meant licensed professionals. Edwin Harleston Jr. quizzed his student, Katie Fleming, every night after they completed their embalming duties so she could take her embalming exam in November 1929. She could then apply for a Florida undertaker's license and run the Fleming-Harleston Funeral Home by herself without needing another licensed embalmer on site.[9]

Black funeral professionals' businesses became anchors in burgeoning Black business districts, financially stable and protected from market whims by burial insurance and burial societies. Black business districts like Hayti in Durham, North Carolina; Greenville, Mississippi; and later, Nashville, Tennessee's famed music strip, Jefferson Street, were areas where funeral homes provided that economic stability, even during financial downturns. Funeral businesses were not the only businesses that rooted Booker T. Washington's self-help ideal into urban districts, of course. Black customers patronized Black-owned beauty shops, banks, restaurants, shoemakers, umbrella repair shops, pharmacies, and musical spaces, but funeral homes' relative isolation from financial pressure made them anchors on this new urban landscape.[10]

Funeral homes also doubled as financial institutions, turning many undertakers into pseudo-bankers who advanced money against future insurance payments. Many insurance policies seem to have been paid directly to the funeral director rather than to the deceased's family. Funeral directors advanced money to those families who waited until the insurance paid for the funeral to receive their remaining money. J. H. Hanley advanced Frank Summer's wife $25 in January 1922 to tide her over until Summer's Industrial Policy ($100), Pilgrim Policy ($99), Banker Policy ($50), American National Policy (no amount listed), and Estes State Policy ($64.35) paid for his $195 funeral. This system, however, could leave undertakers with outstanding debt on their books. One Hanley customer, Sarah Jones, ordered a $260 funeral for Will Hunter (it is not clear how they were related), and Hanley advanced her $150 to tide her over until her Metropolitan and other insurance policies paid out. Hanley remarked, "You know that Metropolitan Insurance Co. do not [*sic*] pay the Undertaker under any condition." Still owed money, he finally took Jones to court for the remaining balance.[11] But with the problems came a realization of opportunity. In its first year of business in 1921, Hanley's Bell Street Funeral Home in Atlanta closed out its funeral ledger, stating, "Year of 1921 closed with one hundred 24 cases [*sic*] handled throu [*sic*] our office for the first year in business. We consider it a fair deal regardless of what the future may bring further. Signed this 31 Day of December 1921, Saturday, J. H. Hanley."[12]

Deadly Cities

Ironically, it was these urban areas' deadly underpinnings that created new customers willing to purchase a lavender casket. Migrants moved to southern cities, but some believed—correctly, it turns out—that expanding southern cities were deadly because rapid growth and negligent regulatory control created contexts ripe for high death rates. Cities' neglect, in fact, fostered new spaces where disease and death flourished. Statisticians with the United States Public Health Service (USPHS), now a more visible presence after their wartime duties ceased, concluded that Black southerners were healthier in the rural South than in the urban South, particularly cities in Louisiana, South Carolina, and Mississippi. Tuberculosis was the usual suspect, in that cities incubated TB epidemics among Black rural migrants, who became "disobedient" city dwellers. Jacksonville, Florida, insurance collector Homer Jordan, a white man, believed that rural Black folks were "better n——-s—know their place. Ain none of them lazy smart-alecks . . . [C]ountry n——-s is ginneraly more healthy." Venereal disease was evidence to a white southerner like Jordan that Black sexuality manifested in disease and death. Indeed, tuberculosis (TB) and syphilis became co-joined in white southern minds as deadly, dangerous, and evidence of urban Black southerners' poor health.[13]

Disease killed many new urbanites, but industries provided new ways to die that caused catastrophic damage to the body. Trains had already plowed through the South, dismembering bodies as they reached further and further inland. Elise Forrest Harleston wrote to her husband, Teddy Harleston, about a particularly gruesome train accident in 1925. "Julian Weston was struck by the Carolina Special one night last week and died Friday. He was sitting on the edge of the cross tie—drunk—and the step of the engine cut him at the back of the neck which paralyzed his body and cause internal hemorages [*sic*] from which he died. He is to be buried Wednesday," Harleston wrote her husband.[14] Other industries inflicted both catastrophic and mundane damage to the body with lumber workers in Mississippi fracturing their skulls felling trees and Bridgestone Tire Company workers in Memphis, Tennessee, having heart attacks on the line. But capitalism and its emphasis on pushing labor to its physical limit caused workers to identify textile mills as especially deadly, particularly during a "stretch out," in which workers were required to manage more looms than was safe, leading to injury and death. A poem by North Carolina mill worker Mary Brit, called "Textile Life," was famous for its poignant honesty: "We have the stretch-out system/And it spreads throughout the mill/Two-thirds of the people it has sent to hospitals/And the other one-third it has killed." Another stanza states that millworkers owed money to the "Butcher, the Doctor, the Merchant," and sometimes the undertaker, too.[15]

Perhaps nothing symbolized this deadly era of urbanization better than the car. And perhaps no other single consumer item left southerners more dismayed, defining the 1920s as a deadly decade. Edisto Island resident Julia La Roche believed that "We Southerners are a fool race of people—working to support automobile factories . . . I wish we had our horses and buggies back." When asked if she liked the new roads, La Roche replied, "Don't like them at all . . . Pretty soon there will be nothing to the island but roads—I never saw such a thing. The world has gone insane on the subject of road building . . . I can't see what is to be gained by paving the roads. More automobiles, more smashes, more people killed just for speed's sake."[16] Another South Carolinian, Mamie Collins, believed that highways were "the worse [*sic*] curse the Lord ever sent on us good people," after her sister fell on a highway, broke or fractured every rib in her body, and died sixteen days later (cancer was the underlying cause).[17] Roads in other parts of the South were no better. Ray Campbell, writing from Mississippi to his friend, George Purvis, in 1919, noted the effect of rains and hail on the ability to drive his car, "You ought to be here to see the water. It is all over the fields[,] we have been having the bigest [*sic*] rains. And had two big hails. [*sic*] We have a car. But can't ride. [*sic*] The roads are so bad."[18]

Letters written during the 1920s and 1930s contain horrific descriptions of car accidents and the fruitless efforts to save those injured in this era before ambulances and EMTs. Lillian Parker Larsen described a gruesome car accident that left her husband, Driskell Larsen, cut and bruised, and another man dead, in Alto, Georgia. Larsen wrote that Driskell's stepmother "Margaret was behind them and managed to get Dris[kell] and Arthur Adams out but couldn't get the one that died. Rushed them to Jefferson for first aid and on to Dublin," Lillian wrote.[19] Speed, careless driving, and drunk driving were common causes of deadly accidents. Dr. L. M. Mitchell's wife, a Batesburg, South Carolina, native, drove to a church convention, but never made it home because a drunk driver killed her. Undertakers, among the first with a consistent access to cars, were also killed in accidents. Clarie Collins Harvey's father crashed when out on a "call" (picking up a body); his injuries eventually killed him. Traveling musicians, exposed to poor road conditions as they drove from one appearance to another, also died on southern roads. Bessie Smith, the famed blues singer, was in the front seat of a car driven by her husband, who misjudged the distance between his car and a truck he was attempting to pass. Smith bore the brunt of the ensuing impact, losing her right arm, and then her life, in September 1937. Cars' dangers caused one North Carolinian to write, "We almost take our lives in our hand every time we go on the road."[20] Car accidents became so prevalent that they became themes in local country music songwriting, for example, Dorsey Dixon's "Wreck on the Highway (I Didn't Hear Nobody Pray)."[21]

You did not need to own a car to die by one. Children playing in streets and men walking home all suffered the consequences of a car speeding down the road. Sidewalks were relatively nonexistent, leading to accidents like the one that befell Charles Jonas, who was hit while walking down a street. His son later wrote an acquaintance, "I am sorry to inform you that my father was struck by an automobile Saturday afternoon while walking home from the office. His injuries, while not fatal, are nevertheless serious and he is in the hospital where he will have to remain for at least a week or ten days."[22] Thanks to cars, some rural southerners thought they were taking their lives into their hands when they moved to town. The Epps family moved from rural Georgia to Athens so their children could attend school, Mr. Epps grudgingly so. "All right," he told his wife, "but as sure as we do [move to town], one of the children will be killed, sure." He was right. Their son was killed while playing in the front yard by a speeding car. Ironically, another modern invention—the airplane—killed Mr. Epps, an early aviator who died in a plane crash, leaving just enough insurance to "put him away decent."[23]

Children killed by cars made the driver's guilt—or at least the owner of the car, since many white elites hired Black men to chauffeur them—a new modern emotion. Emma Hale, a Memphis native, wrote to her friend, Annie Crutcher, after a boy ran out in front of her chauffeur-driven car in June 1920. She described the car accident:

> The week after I came home from Knoxville, I had a most horrible accident with my car. You know I don't drive at all. I have a negro chauffeur—the same one I've had for 8 years—the 24th of Nov. [*sic*] as I was on my way into the city, a little 4 yr old boy darted across the street in front of my car—he not running as hard as he could and looked neither to the right or left. My car (the left fender) struck him and the little fellow was instantly killed. I jumped out and ran to him, but oh! It was all so horrible. For days, I couldn't eat or sleep—that little child was with me every where [*sic*] I turned all the next day I was with the mother and at the funeral. It was a most harrowing experience. Then came the appearances before the Grand Jury, etc. It was just one of those unfortunate things that couldn't have been helped. There was no way on earth to have missed the child.[24]

What is intriguing in this litany is her assumption of guilt and responsibility. Most likely, the child was white, given the lack of racial descriptor. In another time and place, the Black chauffeur might have been physically harmed for the accident, but because Hale employed him, she assumed the responsibility for the child's death. Indeed, the chauffeur seems notably absent from the accident, absolved from guilt or responsibility.

New Palaces of Consumption—for the Dead

However the dead came to be at the funeral home, what awaited them there was a new array of funeral goods that promised to anoint the dead and their survivors as modern, tasteful, and respectable. The transition from rural burial practice to a consumer-based ritual was not seamless nor was it uncontested. To ease the potential disruptions, a new domesticity came to be associated with the funeral home, complete with a mother and father to care for the dead. It is no mistake that those who sold coffins and other goods sold them from funeral *homes*, vernacular that allowed undertakers and directors to claim themselves as one of the family. When Edwin Harleston Jr. established his satellite funeral home in St. Augustine, his partners believed that theirs was a model, respectable home. One partner wrote, "We fortunately secured Doctor Brown's old homestead and a better place could not be built. It will truly be a funeral home[,] a spacious nine room house of two stories."[25]

Appearances mattered in these new homes, and the funeral home and its employees had to look good before they could sell a coffin or drive a hearse. Harleston's reports of business included requests from a "middle aged lady whom they want buried *nicely*," most likely a charge to purchase the best goods from his respectable establishment.[26] He made sure his employees kept the funeral home neat and clean in appearance, with the stairs swept and the windows clean, while attending to their own personal appearance. He raised concerns about his hearse driver, who refused to look right when driving the dead. "Caleb," he reported to his wife, "is still uncouth, will *not* wear clean clothes. Drove the hearse at Malloy's funeral in a rusty brown coat and those filthy pants."[27] Later, Harleston reported he purchased chauffeur suits that fit the funeral director's desire for a clean, modern look, suits he insisted Caleb keep at the funeral home where they could stay clean. Other funeral directors required all who embalmed or cared for the body to assume a Christian demeanor of reverence. Stuttgart, Arkansas, funeral director Don Essex always demanded modesty for the body (for example, always covering a nude body with a cloth) and a dignified demeanor from the embalmer. His son, Frank, recalled that the cleansing of the body was "done with care. Always have the body covered. Always have an appropriate demeanor. And you always do things in a careful kind of way. You may know someone from growing up in the community . . . if it wasn't for Christian beliefs and practices there would be no modern funerals."[28]

Involving women in the business reassured customers that this was not crass business, but a solemn practice where a new family served the dead. Ruth Quisenberry, a white woman, had worked as a hospital technician before moving easily into being a Lady Attendant after she married Phillip Quisenberry, an Athens, Tennessee, undertaker, in 1937. In some rare cases, typically in a large city like Memphis, women opened their own funeral homes, as Mrs. Emma Wilburn did, promising "A Special Care for Women and Children," as well as being a "Most Complete Dresser." She included her photo in her City Directory ad so customers would know she was Black.[29] Lady Attendants promised more than reverence and good care; they also ensured that good taste reigned when funeral items were purchased, given that women were defined as a family's main consumers. Later at the services themselves, if held at the funeral home, the female organist played sweetly and sadly in the background, as if all were gathered around a hearth to sing. The fatherly funeral director made sure embalming and other practices were professional and scientific while the motherly Lady Attendant made sure the work was done in a homelike atmosphere, with taste and discretion.[30]

Embalming has been claimed by death scholars as the consumer item that wedged between family-based death care and a funeral professional, but it was just as likely, if not more likely, motorized hearses. In fact, it became a mark of a modern town to have an undertaker with a motorized hearse, as Katy Brumby believed of her town, Mt. Meigs, Alabama, because the undertaker was "not the horse-pulling kind."[31] Both the most expensive funerals as well as the cheapest ones included a hearse ride. Mrs. Mary Elizabeth Rice Thompson was chauffeured to her final resting place by a car and driver provided by Iredell County (North Carolina) Undertakers. Her funeral cost more than most, with the total for embalming, a casket, car and driver, steel vault, and other death goods coming to $349. But even the smallest of bodies, babies and toddlers buried without ceremony or fuss, still went to the cemetery in a motorized hearse; for example, the McPeters Funeral Home (Corinth, Mississippi) ferried children's bodies to the cemetery for $5. Some southerners set aside money in their wills to pay for cars, as Elvie McFadden did when she asked "that cars be provided as far as possible for all friends who desire to attend the burial."[32] The status conferred on deceased bodies came not only from being driven in a hearse, but by the kind of hearse one rode in. J. C. Oates in Memphis owned three cars to drive both the grieving and the deceased to the cemetery: a Cadillac, a Studebaker, and a Paige. When their rolling stock could not ferry a large funeral party, undertakers secured taxis to carry the rest.[33]

While motorized hearses quickly replaced horse-and-buggy hearses, horses were still better able to navigate the South's bad roads. Some funeral directors like an Athens, Georgia, funeral director recalled bringing both the motorized hearse and the "dead wagon" for particularly difficult rural areas, leaving the hearse at the main highway and using the wagon to venture into the hinterlands for a body. The first motorized hearses to appear in a neighborhood were a memory to be recalled later, but with the poor southern roads, the memory invariably involved getting stuck in the mud. Marian Miller Edmonds, Norfolk, Virginia, recalled,

> I remember the first time I saw a hearse. The lady on the next block died, and this big black thing came up with all this ornate design on the side of it to take Mrs. Randall away. We didn't have paved streets at that time, and the day my mother was buried, the hearse got stuck in front of our house in the mud.[34]

For Black customers, the motorized hearse ride was a political statement in an era when streetcars, buses and other motor vehicles were segregated, shameful urban spaces. Sit in the back, Black southerners were told; that is where you belonged. Segregation made you common, unimportant. Lying in the back of a hearse, on the other hand, and being chauffeured to a cemetery was an entirely different statement. The hearse became a royal coach and the body an important, modern person, ferried to a graveyard in style and class. The family who followed in another chauffeured car became by extension important modern people whose sorrow—and their status as consumers able to bury their dead decently—had to be acknowledged as they made their sad trip to bury their dead. Furthermore, Cadillac touring cars were wide-open cars (covers went on when it was raining), so people on the street could see the family as the car drove by. The purchase of three cars and a hearse for Mrs. Emma Johnson for her burial in Summerville, South Carolina (the entire funeral cost $135, all covered by burial society and insurance policies), was most likely a small expense in exchange for the feeling of importance that Black families gained from the expense.[35] It is not clear where the twenty-first-century tradition of pulling over for funeral hearses comes from, but, potentially, the amazing sight of a luxurious car may have prompted it.

But some old-timers refused to let their families use a hearse. When they went to the cemetery, they wanted to go via a horse carriage, the proper way in their eyes. One unidentified Black woman recalled, "Grandaddy told them before he died[,] don't take his body on no hearse, take him to church on horse power." But his family did not because, as she said, "It looked bad."[36] Claims to good taste may have trumped old-timers' desires in some cases, but in others, funeral directors did try to accede to the dying's wishes. Funeral director Teddy Harleston's Aunt Venie, a Flat Rock, North Carolina, native, told her family before she died: "Please tell Brother Edwin [Harleston's father] that she would love so much to have him put her away and wish it were possible to have a horse drawn hearse as she hates to think of being carried to her last resting place in an automobile."[37]

While hearses publicly restored dignity to Black customers, the hot and humid South and its quick effect on decaying dead bodies made embalming a welcomed, though carefully used, commodity. Embalming had become a common northern custom after the Civil War, but well into the twentieth century, older folks, whether Black or white, refused embalming at death and parents typically did not pay for infants to be embalmed.[38] For the skeptical southerner whose Christian beliefs required a body to molder to ashes and dust, fluid shot through the veins to preserve the body for, if not eternity, then for a long time, might have been a hard sell. In the North, Abraham Lincoln's embalmed body, on display to the thousands who watched his sad, weeklong train ride from Washington, DC, home to Illinois for burial in 1865, was a moving advertisement for the efficacies of embalming. In the South, the causation was different. World War I, in part, facilitated the acceptance of embalming as federal death practices influenced regional ones. The spread of life extension practices across the South also sold many on embalming because they believed that it quashed all potentially deadly germs still extant in a dead body. Dead from tuberculosis? Embalming ensured your body did not reinfect anyone who viewed your body, or so funeral directors said.[39]

Undertakers merged scientific advances in embalming with scripture in their advertisements that sold embalming as an integral part of an evangelical Christian's religious life. Winchester, Tennessee, funeral director, Jeff Moore, advertised his embalming services in the local newspaper, calling on the Genesis story of Joseph to sell the fluid. Claiming the "Antiquity of Embalming," embalming had allowed the Israelites to carry Joseph's intact and embalmed body to Canaan for burial, a journey that took forty years (KJV Gen. 50:26).[40] If Joseph's family could embalm, the ads suggested, then no one else should have a problem with it. Customers did not expect biblical methods of embalming, however; they expected the most scientifically up-to-date fluids to embalm their loved ones. Undertakers had a variety of fluids now to choose from, too, including Arlington, Favorite, Sterilol, Dermaform, Hemosol, Osmotone, and Satin Cream embalming fluids.[41]

Some suggested that draining the body of blood and replacing it with chemicals freed the body from a potential contagion, but a secondary outcome was the sense of permanence that embalming created. The dead, once seen as separating into a soul that went to heaven and a body that moldered to ashes and dust in the ground, now stayed whole, permanent in the ground. What did that mean for southerners? Along with name plates and coffin handles, the body was no longer a transitory item, but had a permanent place in this world rather than venturing off to the next one. Did that mean the dead remained longer, stalling the heavenly reunion? It is not clear, but there was an attendant rise in sales of boxes to surround and protect the expensive coffin in the grave, including cement caskets called Imperisho, that implied the coffins would be protected from the earth and not disintegrate into the ground.[42]

Embalming had more practical uses, too, when it came to lengthening Black funerals. While white funerals continued to follow rural prescriptions of burial within a day or two after death, Black funerals expanded the time between death and burial, so all who wished to attend could. In part, this was a custom handed down from slavery days when the enslaved had to wait until the master gave them time off to attend a funeral (typically Sunday). But embalming meant the body stayed in (relatively) good condition, even though dead, and could be laid out so the entire family could see the body before burial. There are dozens of examples where the date of death and the date of burial were at least five days apart; for example, Glover Brack, who died on March 1, 1924, a Saturday, was finally buried on March 6, 1924, a Thursday. Embalming made telegrams in his funeral director's ledger sent to distant places like Woodville, Georgia, and Pittsburg, Pennsylvania, the norm with funeral charges now coming to include Western Union charges, including for one woman who sent two succinct telegrams, "Mitchell is dead. If coming, answer. Azalena."[43]

Perhaps the most lavish changes to what really were utilitarian items came to coffins and caskets. They ceased to be simple handmade wooden objects fit to be covered in dirt, becoming a different kind of ornate death bed. Coffin and casket factories popped up throughout the South, including in small towns such as Cleveland, Tennessee. Coffins companies advertised their goods via catalogs that displayed new choices. The National Casket Company in Baltimore, Maryland, promised that it catered to the most discriminating tastes of the "funeral director and his customers," and claimed that its caskets were manufactured in modern factories, utilizing the most up-to-date machinery and "skilled designers" who produced coffins that were "architectural perfection." At the same time, all caskets were now built to uniform standards, meaning all adult coffins were five feet, nine inches in length, rather than custom made to fit a body as rural coffin makers did.[44]

Casket makers transformed the coffin into luxury items that catered to individual taste, providing a variety of colors including white plush, steel gray, silver doeskin, and copper, as well as a variety of baby caskets. For white southerners, they could now purchase caskets in Confederate gray, so they could be Confederate in death as well as life. In other cases, Christians could be buried in a Noah casket, an ark of one's own that the modern industrial complex made possible. Many interiors were also elaborately designed, with sunrises, for example, stitched into the pillows that adorned the coffin lid.[45]

The color of the coffin mattered, as death goods now had the sublime potential of undermining social hierarchies. Ornateness could symbolize luxuriousness, and by extension, status, but color, especially purple, could denote royalty. Coffin manufacturers also assumed southerners now wanted to bury babies and children well, albeit relatively cheaply given the high death rates, and promoted child funerals by claiming children's deaths were significant rather than common and not worthy of much attention. Funeral directors linked the belief that children were the lambs of God and Jesus Christ's favorite by creating white lambskin caskets for them. These were not expensive caskets: $5, according to Hanley's ledger and $25 according to the Robertson Funeral Home's (Tennessee) ledger.[46]

Only the best-dressed adult corpses were buried, with new silk dresses or burial robes, gloves, slippers, and hose outfitting them for their initial audience with Jesus. But more importantly for Black southern women required to wear gray, black, or white uniforms at work in white homes, vibrant colors proclaimed a different status in death. The Mickey Funeral Home provided ladies robes in white silk, purple, gray, and black. Men wore black or steel gray suits. Shoes were white, white calf, or gray slippers. J. C. Oates regularly outfitted corpses in all new clothes, for example, a 33-year-old woman who did housework and had a $347 funeral ordered for her; it included a burial robe, gloves, slippers, and hose.[47]

Death goods not only proclaimed a decent burial, but conferred a personhood when the deceased was anonymous, even if the body was horrifically mutilated. The body of an unknown child, most likely Black, was found near Charleston in 1919, and the Harleston Funeral Home embalmed the body and provided a hearse for the anonymous child. The child became somebody not only because he was buried decent, but because undertakers used death goods that established the child's identity when no name or family existed. They also listed the child on their ledgers, using another commercial space to make sure the child was known, in case someone searched for him. Harleston did the same with a man killed by a train near Charleston, South Carolina, in 1921. Because the African American man had no name, Harleston's funeral ledger became a place to remember the body in case relatives came looking for him. It simultaneously documented the railroad's purchase of funeral goods, with the ledger entry reading, "Atlantic Coast Line Railroad, burial of unknown man killed by train at Four Mile. [Description of deceased]: dark brown man, about 25 years old, ab 5 ft, 7 in., 150 lbs., Removal and interment at Elmwood Cemetery 25 [dollars]. January 13, 1921."[48]

Consumerism in the Cemetery

The new consumerism reshaped southern death landscapes visually, particularly as gravestones replaced trees and shrubs. The permanence of gravestones for many, not just the elite, made the body's presence seem permanent as well as visible for all to see and remember. Understanding that cemetery stones would exist for a long time, white southerners used their wills to ensure the best gravestones were purchased and proclaim them and their kin as elite in perpetuity. Maggie Muirhead left detailed directions for her family plot in Evergreen Cemetery, Murfreesboro, when she died in June 1920. Requiring a $500 monument be selected for her grandparents' plot (she was to be buried next to them), she named three female friends in her will who were to "assist my executor in the selection of said monument." She also required that the inscription say, "In memory of my grandmother, Mary S. Smith, my grandfather, William H. Smith, my brother, John B. Muirhead. This monument erected by Maggie Muirhead, who died (date to be filled in)." The date was never filled in, although Muirhead died June 27, 1920.[49] Sisters Miss Lou Nelson and Miss Charlie Nelson (most likely two white unmarried women as denoted by the title Miss), from rural Lavergne, Tennessee, desired their final resting places be marked with substantial death goods at their death. Their will said:

> Except $100.00 which we direct to be used by our executer in placing a concrete top upon the walls inclosing [*sic*] the graves of the family, and placing a monument over our graves, that is we direct that $500.00 shall be used in placing a top on the walls, the remainder to be used in purchasing said monument.[50]

The distinctiveness and ubiquity of certain markers visually transformed southern death landscapes. The Woodmen of the World Insurance Company's unique gravestone transformed a death landscape marked with trees and peony bushes to one populated with the Woodmen's cement gravestones, fashioned to look like a tree trunk. The Omaha (Nebraska) insurance company's distinctive markers taught other southerners that grave markers were a meaningful consumer item within the anonymity of a city or town cemetery. Their stone

Figure 6.1. Maggie Muirhead's will left detailed directions for her family plot in Evergreen Cemetery, Murfreesboro. She required a $500 monument be selected for her grandparents' plot (she was to be buried next to them), and that the inscription say, "In memory of my grandmother, Mary S. Smith, my grandfather, William H. Smith, my brother, John B. Muirhead. This monument erected by Maggie Muirhead, who died [date to be filled in]."

suggested another kind of permanence. A tree could be chopped down or a bush pulled out, but that stone stayed for a long time.

Some southerners used their deaths in the 1920s to modernize older family's burials, using their estates to align modern practices with past deaths. A white woman, Elizabeth Richardson Brenagh, required her executors demolish the vault on the family enclosure in Evergreen Cemetery (Murfreesboro), and erect a "rough gray granite monument, placing thereon the tablet to my grandfather, Henry Watkins Collier, now on said vault. They shall also erect suitable markers to my grandmother, Mary Anne Battle Collier, and my uncle, James Wyatt Collier."[51] Theresa Jacob, who died in January 1929, wanted her estate to buy "some larger and nicer foot-stones [to] be placed on the graves of my parents in Mt. Calvary Cemetery, Nashville, Tennessee, and the old ones be removed. I, also, desire that some nice larger corner stones be placed on the cemetery lot in Mt. Calvary Cemetery instead of the old ones which are there now."[52] Black women did the same. Lizzie Robinson Davenport directed that her body be buried in a

Figure 6.2. An example of the distinctive Woodmen of the World tombstone, found in Asbury Cemetery in Chickasaw County, MS.

Jackson, Tennessee, graveyard next to her husband, and that her dates of birth and death be inscribed on her tombstone. More importantly, she wished that her "mother at her death . . . be laid to rest at the feet" of her and her husband, again with the appropriate monument.[53]

Parents who bought into this ethic, literally, used consumer items to create an imaginary world where physical items stood in the place of the deceased. Lannett, Alabama, native Nadine Earles died from diphtheria just before Christmas in 1933, but her parents still celebrated, complete with songs, presents, and games. The guests could not play in the playhouse her father had built for her for Christmas, however, because it had been dismantled and removed to her cemetery plot. Every year thereafter, Christmas presents adorned the rather macabre house, tucked under a small Christmas tree where Santa placed them. Both parents were later buried in the house's front yard.[54]

Churches saw the creep of cemetery goods as a modern idol that distracted parishioners and their dollars away from the church's work. What was the most appropriate memorial: a stone at the head of a grave or a donation to the surviving church? The Southern Baptist Convention's fundraising drives suggested that money spent on gravestones was frivolous and unnecessary, particularly when purchases ate into church tithes: "WHICH IS THE BETTER MONUMENT—A

Figure 6.3. Nadine Earles died at age four from diphtheria in 1933. Her devastated parents took apart her playhouse and rebuilt it over her grave at the Oakwood Cemetery in Lanett, AL. Both parents were later buried in the playhouse's front yard and people drop by, leaving Barbie dolls and other toys for the child.

DEAD STONE BEARING THE WORDS 'AT REST,' OR A LIVING CHURCH VOICING THROUGHOUT THE YEARS 'AT WORK,'" it shouted from the pages of its 1920 Convention record. A tombstone would soon crumble, it decreed, using an image of crumbling stone surrounded by the sixty churches. The $500 marker (very expensive for the time) would support churches "until He comes! Which is the better monument?"[55]

Expanding the Funeral Ritual

The consumer goods were to be in good taste, but death goods meant little without a ritual incorporating them into funerals, especially for Black southerners. Ritual countered racial custom that dictated rank in the South's racial hierarchy, and restored a dignity denied by the broader culture. Burial society rules, for example, at the Bathsheba Grand Chapter of the Order of the Eastern Star (Meridian and Jackson, Mississippi) required all men to be referred to as Sir and all women to be referred to as Lady. Burial rituals also required society members to wear armbands to honor the dead, typically provided by the funeral home. Members had to attend memorial services, according to the bylaws of the Mississippi Benevolent/Standard Fraternal Aid Society (Lexington and Pickens, Mississippi), and in fact, were subject to a fine if she or he did not attend a funeral. One insurance man recalled burial society provisions not just for cars or caskets, but for "moaners and rental of black coats for pall bearers."[56]

The actual funeral services were also critical. Greenville, South Carolina, funeral director Edgar Biggs directed a memorial service for the Railway Employees Burial Association and the printed program—a rare find in funeral records before World War II—listed twelve musical performances, five different papers or responses, and a Bible reading. Ornate, organized, and tightly structured, the service used order and pomp to confer dignity upon the deceased. The grief displayed at funerals was now a public expression of worth, too. Although dismissed by whites as another example of an overly emotional Black community, grief claimed the deceased as worthy because mourners publicly stated that the deceased mattered enough to mourn in public and out loud.[57]

Because of the tight link between ritual and racial hierarchy, white funerals and obituaries became mini dramas that affirmed racial structures, casting a fictional antebellum past as a romantic, halcyon time where kindly white patriarchs managed their families, Black and white, with a firm but gentle hand. White southern writers like Tennessee State Librarian John Trotwood Moore published books that hailed the benevolent plantation South. At Moore's death, his funeral became a public performance of this myth as six current and former Tennessee governors served as honorary pallbearers, looking on benevolently while the Black porters from the State House did the actual heavy lifting, moving the casket from the State Capital to the graveyard. The services were described afterward in *The Tennessean*: "The simplicity of rites of the Old South marked the brief services honoring the man whose words and stories have made immortal the glories of the old ante-bellum South. The tender hands of beloved negro capital employes [*sic*] the faithfulness and love of whose race Mr. Moore has immemorably chronicled, bore the body to its last resting place on the beautiful hillside of the Southland of Mr. Moore's life-long devotion."[58]

Published obituaries in white newspapers were another arena for social dramas where white writers recalled the Black servant who served white families faithfully. Rose Lewis, who worked for the Wingo family in Virginia for forty years, was lauded by white writers for her willingness to serve in a rare obituary for a Black woman published in a white newspaper in 1917. "She was a typical old Virginia 'mammy,' born in slavery and spending most of her life in freedom, she retained an undying love for the family which owned her . . . She was noted for her loyalty to those for whom she worked," the Richmond, Virginia, obituary acknowledged.[59]

William Faulkner's *As I Lay Dying*

By 1930, rural ways of burial embarrassed some, were considered passé by others, and longed for by still others. William Faulkner recognized this new complex world of dying in his novel *As I Lay Dying*, published in 1930. Mississippian Addie Bundren lay dying in her room while her son, Cash, built her coffin just outside her window, holding up boards through the window for her to approve. After death, her unembalmed body was dressed in her wedding dress, and then carried across the state to her family burial ground in a wagon hitched to mules. The smell of her decaying body attracted buzzards and caused another son, Darl, to end the journey by sending the mules to their death, an act that landed him in a Mississippi insane asylum. What is important here is not the story Faulkner wrote, but the horror he imagined among his readers as they reacted to her body's lack of decent care. By its publication, enough southerners had bought into—literally—the new death consumerism that he knew this older, more rural way of putting the dead away decent would repel his audience.[60]

With the new goods came new ways to honor the dead, causing yet another shift in death care. Where the laying on of hands was once the focus, now southern communities shifted their focus to mourning the loss and comforting the grief stricken. In an urban South, there was now time to grieve—just not too much. Intellectuals provided standards for this new culture of grief and comfort that came from the same industrial processes that built coffins and hearses. What to use and how to use it thus became the work of psychologists, etiquette gurus, and theologians, accounting for this changed world and its bewildering array of products.

7 Indifference, Shame, Selfishness, and Wrong Living

New Ways to Grieve and Comfort

South Carolinian Amelia ("Melie") Mellichamp died from breast cancer one Friday in April 1926, and her sister Nell, devastated and melancholic, spent the next twenty years grieving her loss, captured with intense emotion in two large notebooks. Nell's deep grief permeates every page in a classic example of Sigmund Freud's definition of melancholia, a deep hysterical grief that kept her, it seemed to friends, family, and even her bishop, from functioning effectively in society. Her first entry sets the tone for the rest of the journal:

> Two weeks ago today at 10:15 a.m. the one human being whom I love with my whole heart and soul passed the portals of life. It is as if thirty five years had been spent in a dream and only since previous to Melie's illness, all the mists have cleared away; doubt disappeared and, laid before me in terrible clearness, are the years of indifference, shame, selfishness, and wrong living—too late to change and live for her—except for six short months—(less even) and now that the agony of separation is upon me even the atonement and love which I tried to put in those few months seems so small compared to the years of opportunity which I heedlessly let slip by.[1]

It is in Nell's journal that a number of 1920s trends coalesce, particularly for elite white southerners. Visible cross-racially in other documents, her grief journal exemplified new literature on grief and melancholy; a shift in liturgical assumptions about Christian burials for some elites; the evolving etiquette of comfort; and the creation of physical documents curated to replace a loved one now gone. In this way, southerners privatized death rather than denying it as grief, certainly never absent at a death, but never really focused on, came to have new weight in southern culture.

As grief was normalized, it was hidden in public spaces as southerners channeled their grief into good work, say, a nice scrapbook of condolence letters, so that others would not think poorly of them. And so the new messages were mixed: grieve, but be careful that you were not seen as grieving too much. "I am glad you are able to say to me that I did not betray the worry and apprehension surrounding me at the time," T. Brady Jr. wrote his friend Lucius Burch in 1938, given Brady's worry about his own father's illness and his grief at Burch's father's death.[2] Nell Mellichamp's journals, an extreme, but ultimately private example of what Brady hoped others could not see, opens up both this new material culture and the transformation of mourning, grief, and comfort in the 1920s South, indeed, in the United States as a whole.

Freud and 1920s Assessments of Grief

Emily Post's biographer argues that Austrian neurologist Sigmund Freud; Havelock Ellis, the British physician who studied sexuality; and etiquette maven Post were the three main intellectual gurus of the 1920s. While Freud's theories probably did not impinge on the daily consciousness of the average southerner, Post implicitly acknowledged his ideas in her more accessible, and infinitely more popular, etiquette manuals. Freud's psychoanalytic theories became popular in the 1910s and 1920s when he proposed that interactions between a psychoanalyst and a patient could effect some kind of curative of various neuroses; that, by uncovering the unconscious, one could explore and then heal from the pain. One of the obvious neuroses was grief. Freud's observations of patients caused him to identify a continuum of grief that moved from mourning to profound mourning and then to melancholia. In his 1925 work "Mourning and Melancholia," Freud argued that mourners "objectified" loss, meaning the deceased became an object that needed to be disassociated from the living's psyche. In a consumer world where literal objects—purple coffins, silk dresses—had become the markers of death, the deceased bodies themselves became objects that opened some fragile southerners up to profound mourning, a deep, persistent sense of loss that could dominate and overwhelm the ego.[3]

Freud did define loss more broadly than the death of a loved one; the loss of any meaningful relationship, for example, could evoke the same grief. But in objectifying the loss and using consumer goods to replace the dead, Freud worried about "obsessional states of depression" that distinguished melancholia from the other way stations on the continuum of grief. Melancholia's absorbing, obsessive quality could make the mourner incapable of anything but wallowing. The melancholics were thus those whose desires were not able to be transferred to another object. Nell's journals suggest both the absorption and an obsessive quality where the object of her grief—Melie—came to be objectified over and over again, as she wrote in her journals, sometimes multiple times a day. Certainly, Nell's friends were aware of her tendency toward melancholia as they watched her grieve over her sister's death, but one could argue that her journal came to represent her sister and simultaneously, gave her grief a physical space to express that extreme sadness.[4]

Freud assumed that those who were relatively healthy psychologically at some point finished their grieving and moved on. This was ironic to white southern families, whose dead remained active participants, at least imaginatively, in family conversation or in family tradition for decades. Indeed, Freud could have reasonably argued that much of white southern society was in a state of perpetual psychosis, mired as it was in a fiction of white racial superiority.[5]

Perhaps Freud's most unacknowledged contribution to southern death care was the implicit permission to grieve. At the same time, Freud's focus on melancholia put real limits on how much, where, or how long one should grieve. Family letters became one space where discussions of grief, rather than the simple passing on of news about those who had died, became normalized and mulled over. John Wilson McRaven, a Yazoo City, Mississippi, oilman who lost his wife suddenly in December 1921, wondered aloud to his children why she died. Clearly grief-stricken, McRaven wrote his son in January 1922, that "I miss her more and more and it is hard to realize that she will never return." While he realized that "Some day we may realize why she was taken in the prime of life," perhaps, too, they would also figure out "why she should be taken in such a vague way."[6]

White southerners used Freud's ideas of melancholia to cast those who grieved out loud as neurotic, harnessing psychoanalytic theory to justify racial and class structures. "Excessive" mourning came to be associated with Black southerners, particularly working-class ones whose vocal grief was an example of their less "civilized" selves. Invisible to white eyes was the dignity conferred on the dead by ritualized mourning as well as a healthy grieving process itself. Greenville, Mississippi, native William Alexander Percy made this distinction in his book, *Lanterns on the Levee* (1941), when reminiscing about his interactions as a white child with local Black children. With Percy as the corpse and leader as was appropriate to his racial status, he recalled, "As a corpse I was a fiasco, but as mourners my colored entourage displayed genius. Racially they are the best diers [*sic*] in the world anyway: they put more force and enthusiasm into the scene, being seriously aware it is the climax of the show, their curtain."[7]

The Etiquette of Mourning and Comfort

How, then, could people experience grief, but avoid melancholia? Etiquette and good manners could be that mechanism that channeled grief into socially acceptable practices and responses. In the dizzying changes of the 1920s, some bemoaned a broader "postwar deterioration of public morals," and turned to new etiquette experts because they thought good manners provided stability in a time of "social unruliness," according to historian Arthur Schlesinger.[8] Emily Post's 1922 book on etiquette provided a script for those seeking a stable way to comfort those who grieved and to ensure their mourning did not venture down the wayward path toward melancholia. If Freud tried to determine *why* people grieved, then Post, a Maryland native, attempted to describe *how* one should grieve and how others might proffer comfort. At the same time, Post also used etiquette to dismiss or sneer at some of the new death consumerism that had the power to challenge racial hierarchies. Good manners still were good politics in the South, since those manners marked one's place in the region's power hierarchies.[9]

Post's book, *Etiquette: The Blue Book of Social Usage,* catered to an audience, her biographer noted, of war wives, immigrants, the newly rich, and rural-to-urban migrants who desired to don the mantle of respectability. Post's prominent voice on the radio and in syndicated national columns made her work accessible to a variety of Americans, establishing a national etiquette rather than one exclusively for southerners. The assumption that she came from the South (Maryland) where better manners were reputed to exist did not hurt her popularity. For white southerners who fiercely guarded their privileged racial place, the exhibition of good manners reinforced their claims to racial power. For Black southerners, adherence to this evolving etiquette countered white claims of racial superiority.[10]

Post competed with others—funeral directors, for example—when she attempted to dictate what good taste in death care was. She proposed a uniform response to death, for example, that focused on relatively rigid, precise, and narrow standards of behavior because:

> Good taste or bad is revealed in everything we are, do, have. Our speech, manners, dress, and household goods—and even our friends—are evidences of the propriety of our taste, and all these have been the subject of this book. Rules of etiquette are nothing more than sign-posts by which we are guided to the goal of good taste.[11]

But it was "in the moment of deepest sorrow that etiquette performs its most vital and real service," she wrote. Rather than a superficial set of practices, etiquette countered the chaos of death, providing a soothing and expected order that dropped an anchor during the deepest sorrow. Mourning need not become melancholia because etiquette provided a path that could steer the grieving away from that deeper psychosis, she implied. "Unbalanced physically," she wrote, the "overstrained nerves" of the grief-stricken guided all reactions. The good friend or kind nurse helped best by "banish[ing] all consciousness of self," meaning they set aside their egos to care for the grief-stricken, to prevent them from traipsing down the garden path of deep melancholia.[12]

Post excised older rural traditions that no longer had meaning for urban migrants. There was no need for long vigils by the coffin, for example. Practically speaking, window screens were more common in cities, eliminating the concern for cats harming the unembalmed. She assumed a closed coffin during the funeral, and refreshing the grief was probably too vulgar because it could lead to an exuberant display. Post did not dismiss an expensive funeral as in poor taste, but she did concern herself with estates that could be depleted by the "vulgarly lavish and entirely inappropriate funeral expenses." She also challenged her readers to speak vaguely and euphemistically about death to "avoid unnecessary evidence of the change that had taken place."[13] In other words, do not talk about the deceased and avoid bringing notice to the loss, as if not talking would somehow make the death go away. Silence thus became an act of care that relied on a denial of mourning out loud.

Religious Responses to Grief and Mourning

Theologians wrestled with the philosophical implications of consumerism, mourning, and manners. Two denominations in particular grappled with death care's evolution in their liturgical tracts, updating their rituals in response to death care and life extension: the Southern Baptist Convention (SBC) and the Episcopal Church (dominant among Black and white southern elites). Both published new tracts on grief or provided revisions to funeral services, formulating a modern theology that recognized the family reunion, life extension, and mourning. While responding to new trends, the new documents still retained key practices and assumptions from the past about death, grief, and their place in modern psychology and theology.

Freud might have approved of a modicum of grief, but the SBC warned, not so fast. The SBC's publishing arm and libraries answered a critical theological question in a Freudian world: how should the grief-stricken evangelical Christian, who was not to question God's will, respond to a death or comfort survivors? Was it all right to grieve if a family reunion awaited one's own death and patience was all that was required? Rather than being how-to books, newly published SBC books sought to transform what their readers believed about God during the grieving process, fit for a modern world, but rooted in older prescriptions.

Dr. R. A. Torrey, an associate of evangelist Dwight Moody, wrote *Death Defeated and Defied: A Message of Comfort, Consolation and Cheer* (1923), an approved choice for the grief-stricken on the SBC's library shelves. Written as one daughter was dying and simultaneously acknowledging another daughter's death some twenty years before, Torrey exhorted his audience to be joyful and sound triumphant at these poignant moments. Jesus Christ's crucifixion and resurrection had made death a moment to exclaim, not mourn. "Oh death, where is thy sting? Oh grave, where is thy victory?" Torrey quoted from the Bible (1 Corinthians 15:55, KJV). Death had transformed the corruptible body into an incorruptible one; sin had been conquered once one had professed a belief in Jesus Christ. Grief was thus, he implied, a sinful act. But he was not without compassion for those who mourned, providing proscriptives that might help realize God's hand in death and avoiding melancholy. What could one expect from the trials of mourning if she or he truly believed in Jesus Christ? Death could bring three new or reinforced beliefs. First, death brought "radiant joy for the believer in Jesus Christ." Second, it brought the mourner into "personal communion with Christ." And finally, death brought "the believer in Jesus Christ a real likeness to Himself."[14]

In the midst of the SBC's theological depictions of grief and mourning, the Episcopal Church published a new *Book of Common Prayer* (BCP, its foundational document) in 1929, after an extensive, nearly sixteen-year process to revise its 1892 edition, a mild revision of the 1789 BCP. A liturgical tradition like the Catholic Church from which it descended, but affiliated with the Anglican Church in England, the Episcopal Church served the southern elite, including many United States presidents. Services focused on a common set of practices, or liturgies and offices, laid out in the BCP that provided a church-sanctioned order for prayers as well as appropriate biblical verses for Sunday services and life events including baptism, marriage, and death. The liturgy was driven primarily by the church calendar, beginning with Advent and ending four Sundays before Christmas. Its biracial congregations were rigorously segregated, as some of the architects of white southern racial politics in the pre– and post–Civil War eras were leading members. Leonidas Polk, for example, the Confederate general who helped found the University of the South and its Episcopal seminary, was an Episcopal Bishop before resigning to serve the Confederacy in the Civil War.[15]

The national Episcopal church voted to rewrite the BCP in 1913, at the height of Progressive fervor in the United States, naming northerners from Pittsburgh and Boston as committee leaders. The BCP's historiographer, E. Clowes Chorley, opined that an earlier revision published in 1892 was too "timid" and "conservative" in its revision and that the 1929 version finally eliminated antiquated medieval language that could not account for a rigorous devotional life in the twentieth century. Indeed, Clowes, given to writing with a flourish when describing relatively dry liturgical changes, wrote of the 1892's limited revision, "It hesitated to embark on a liturgical adventure."[16]

Revisionists first eliminated older language to reflect new translations of the Bible, especially the New Revised Edition, which used new translations of the King James Bible. The BCP also gave more "liturgical liberty" to priests in choosing scripture for various services, providing individual churches more freedom. Most importantly, the new BCP embraced the Progressive redefinition of sinfulness; it taught that context made basically moral human beings act immorally, rather than that humans are intrinsically sinful because of original sin (i.e., from Adam and Eve in the Garden of Eden). What this meant was the individual was no longer considered innately immoral and without redemption, which required a more hopeful, compassionate view of humankind to anchor the document.

Reflecting new perceptions of health, wellness, and grief, the book created devotional space for grief in multiple sections, including a new office, the Visitation of the Sick; the newly revised Burial Office; and another entirely new liturgy to be used "At the Burial of a Child." This final section suggested children's health had improved enough that their deaths were now a tragedy that needed its own liturgy, rather than being too common to recognize as spiritually significant. Moreover, unlike medieval writers of the BCP's previous editions who assumed that sickness and death were co-joined, the committee firmly eliminated that link. The insertion of the Visitation of the Sick reflected this, according to E. Clowes Chorley:

> As it appeared in the old Prayer Book it [the Visitation of the Sick] was so gloomy, so medieval in its theology and so utterly lacking in any understanding of the psychological approach to sick persons, that it had almost ceased to be used in the church. Its basic assumption was that not only is all sickness sent by God, but it is sent as a just punishment for some wrong done. The minister was directed to say to the sick person, Wherefore, whatsoever your sickness be, know you certainly that it is God's visitation . . . it be sent unto you to correct and amend in you whatsoever doth offend the eyes of your heavenly Father. This Exhortation, as unhappy as it is untrue, is omitted in the new Book.[17]

Chorley flayed older assumptions where illness was portrayed as not caused by germs, but as a punishment visited upon humans who were "miserable sinners." Prayers for recovery, another new addition, now made perfect sense to Chorley and his fellow Episcopalians in a world where illness was not linked to sinfulness, but to germs, diseases and a potential cure.[18]

Updates were already in use before the BCP's official publication and one can imagine that, for Melie's service, the Order of Service for the Dead was done. It assumed that her body was blessed by a priest at death, even if she was excommunicated or never baptized (neither seemed to be true in her case). Moreover, Paul's letter to the Corinthians (1 Cor 15:29 KJV) was eliminated in favor of new language that supplanted harsh words. Priests once intoned:

> Else what shall they do which are baptized for the dead, if the dead rise not at all? Why are they then baptized for the dead? And why stand we in jeopardy every hour? I protest by your rejoicing which I have in Christ Jesus our Lord, I die daily. If after the manner of men I have fought with beasts at Ephesus, what advantageth

> it me, if the dead rise not? Let us eat and drink; for tomorrow we die. Be not deceived: evil communications corrupt good manners. Awake to righteousness, and sin not; for some have not the knowledge of God; I speak this to your shame.

Priests omitted these words in favor of a more compassionate God, now praying, "All that the Father giveth me shall come to me; and him that cometh to me I will in no wise cast out" (John 6:37, KJV). Finally, Chorley claimed the most significant addition to the new office was the offering of this prayer:

> Remember thy servant, O Lord, according to the favour which thou bearest unto thy people, and grant that, increasing in knowledge and love of thee, *he* may go from strength to strength, in the life of perfect service, in thy heavenly kingdom; through Jesus Christ our Lord, who liveth and reigneth with thee and the Holy Ghost ever, one God, world without end. [The congregation responds *Amen.*][19]

A more just and forgiving God now anchored the Episcopal liturgy, providing comfort rather than judgment as well as the potential for recovery from illness, a more appropriate symbol for a modern world of death care and life extension.

Older Rites Transformed

Older acts of death care were transformed to reflect this new thinking about grief, etiquette and comforting theology. Diaries, kept by southerners, were older items of material culture that documented daily living, but in the 1920s, they were turned into physical expressions of death when the family provided the final entry, finishing both the diary's and the diarist's life. Extant diaries, written before the 1920s, do not seem to do this. George Monro [*sic*] Yoder was a farmer, merchant, teacher, coroner, surveyor, county commissioner of Catawba County, North Carolina, census taker, justice of the peace, postmaster, and an elder in his Lutheran church. Given all that he had to track, it is not surprising that Yoder kept a diary in a ledger book from 1916 until his death Saturday, March 13, 1920, at age 94. His son, Enloe, finished the diary for his father, noting the details of his death and burial on the last page of the diary:

> Saturday 13 Father died. Complained when dressing, said had a severe pain in stomach. Went to table drank some hot water, ate one sausage, left the table and lay on the bed. Died in fifteen minutes of heart failure. Said when he lay down down, he was going going [*sic*] to die . . . Sunday 14: Father buried at Grace Church at 3 p.m. One of the largest assembly of people ever gathered at a burying at Grace Church.[20]

South Carolinian Sallie Dorcas Brown Whitesides's diary has a similar poignant ending: "This is June 1 1929, Sister Sallie died May the 15 at 10 minits after 8 on Wens night 1929[.] I hope she is at rest with her heavenly Father. [signed] Fannie Land."[21]

Another common ritual, flowers and plants, had long accompanied funerals, as rosemary and other strong-smelling plants had practical uses. Held to the nose, rosemary's strong smell covered the smell of a decomposing body in days when embalming was not common. Flowers as a decorative element or a symbol of an absent friend's sentiment had rarely been considered, but with embalming's elimination of the smell, flowers became a new act of care, of love, and, eventually, of good taste. To fulfill the responsibility of caring for the dead, cutting flowers from a garden (if local) or sending them from a florist (if living far away) became a ritual in which the act of sending flowers itself was an important message to the family. Easter lilies, symbolic of Jesus Christ at Easter, lined up near Melie Mellichamp's casket and told onlookers that she had died and now rested with Jesus.[22]

In this era of mass migration, flowers came to stand in as the physical representation of a family member or friend who could not attend a funeral, a tangible item that came to be an acceptable substitute for distant friends. In a consumer culture of death where goods represented the deceased, it was a simple step for consumer goods to represent absent friends and family. Unable to attend her cousin's husband's funeral due to a broken hip, Sadie Gaither Anderson wrote, "We hope the flowers we ordered carried our loving sympathy for you all and our high esteem for Col. Harris."[23] Mattie Smith, a Winnsboro Mills, North Carolina, resident, told a Federal Writers Project (FWP) interviewer, "We send flowers to funerals when there's a death. Of course, maybe we oughtn't do that, but we work hard and enjoy giving in those ways. I think about when we are old or in trouble it would be nice to know our neighbor friends thought that much of us."[24] Newspapers reported the outcome of Virginia Reverend Charles Maddox's funeral where "many rich floral tributes attested the esteem in which Mr. Maddox was held."[25] Emily Post cast female friends in the role of arranging flowers, charging them to bring pencils to collect and inscribe the cards with descriptions (say, "Spray of Easter lilies and palm branches tied with white ribbon"). It would not reflect well on the family if the loving gesture was not acknowledged with a note afterward.[26]

Personal cameras, called "Brownie cameras," photographed the lavish displays of flowers, new mementos for a grieving family. Mattie and Tally Smith took photos with their Kodak camera of their cousin's husband's flowers after he was killed by a train. "I have never seen so many pretty designs of flowers, and the artificial ones are just as pretty as they were the day they were put there. They stand the rain and bad weather and will be pretty for weeks yet," Mattie said.[27] Will Henry McRaven could not attend his grandmother's funeral in 1923, but no matter. His sister, Margaret, photographed the flowers at the cemetery for him. Flower tributes became excessive enough that funeral directors began charging for extra hearses—$4 for Isaac Bernstein's funeral in 1919—to carry the many flowers that were sent. Emily Post cautioned against these lavish displays, saying, "It is very vulgar to fill open landaus with displayed floral offerings and parade through the streets."[28]

Flowers and diaries were transformed to meet the needs of the ordinary 1920s southerner. Still other technologies, relatively new but becoming accepted as part of daily life complicated private grief and had to be used carefully. The telephone specifically frightened southerners, given their expectation that the phone was to be used only in an emergent situation. One young woman, Ellie, a student at Sophie Newcomb College in New Orleans, wrote to her mother after a frightening phone call in 1926, "I'm so sorry if I worried you by ringing you Saturday evening but I really couldn't help it. I just had to talk to you and just hearing your voice made me feel better."[29] Faceless conversations over the phone where the callers did not see each other meant that some broke implied rules of intimacy where no mention of grief was allowed. Elsie Slopes sent Mary Daniel Moore a note, writing to "apologize for telling you over the phone that I'd been in constant sympathy with you lately. It was not a subject for a telephone conversation but my impulse to let you know how deeply I felt for you got the best of my judgment . . . but I do want you to know that I'm sorry I touched on the subject over the phone."[30]

Printed Material

Older rituals and technologies shifted meaning rather than being a completely new event. With the expansion of printing presses in the post–World War I era, new kinds of material culture could be purchased for a funeral, to provide words of comfort or to carefully preserve memories of the dead. Emily Post hovered symbolically over this new material culture of mourning that included scrapbooks, condolence notes and photographs taken of flower-strewn graves. What became most widely used was the sympathy note. There are very few collections of sympathy notes from World War I. The earliest sympathy notes that I found in a southern archive are in Robert Church's collection; he was credited as the South's first Black millionaire at his death in 1912. Other sympathy notes may have been sent before the 1910s, but not saved. Tennessee Governor Austin Peay, writing to a friend in 1921, mentioned receiving a condolence note from the friend's now deceased father twenty-three years earlier. What may have changed then is that sympathy notes became keepsakes, imbued with the memory of the dead and the love of a friend; hence the main change here was in the archiving of notes rather than necessarily in the writing of them. Moreover, in this new world of modern printing presses that could easily and inexpensively create personalized stationery, this expression of good taste became crucial as sympathy notes focused exclusively on the deceased rather than in combination with other news.

In the 1920s and thereafter, families could receive hundreds of sympathy notes, especially if the deceased was well known, like Congressman William Bankhead of Alabama or the John Trotwood Moore family in Tennessee. Indeed, letters of sympathy, written specifically in response to a death, recreated in writing the dead's daily, lived experience since those quotidian experiences required acquaintances, business partners, and friends to acknowledge a loss. Emily Post promised to be the good guide here. Following her etiquette manual, southerners made sure their stationary had an appropriate appearance, including matching paper and envelope, the correct salutation ("My dear Mrs. Smith" was the common suggestion), and the correct signature (Yours very truly was preferred over Respectfully). Most, but not all, were handwritten; typed letters were typically (but not exclusively) from business associates who saw the condolence note as acknowledging a business relationship. Post formulated content rules, too, admonishing her readers to avoid quoting "endlessly from Scripture or from poetry" (most southerners ignored that rule). But in their ability to write in the moment and be fully open to it, writers of condolence notes provide real access to the interior lives of those who sought to comfort the grief stricken, and in some cases, into the grief process itself.[31]

The initial decision whether or not to write was itself an act of good taste, particularly in the South where daily interactions included cross-racial ones; notes were potentially just as fraught as an encounter on a downtown sidewalk. Condolence literature thus merged southern racial etiquette with Post's death etiquette, as those who were white claimed the privilege of writing. Congressman William Bankhead received dozens of sympathy notes when his mother died in May 1922, many starting with phrases such as "My dear Mr. Bankhead," and ending with signatures such as Sallie Windham's which read (Mrs.) Sallie S. Windham. The ubiquitous (Mrs.) on these letters, as in funeral ledgers, was an etiquette that telegraphed whiteness.[32] The letter sent from a white southerner to a Black mourner was another act of racial privilege that allowed whites to cross that line with impunity while real care had to be exercised by Black southerners. It was a privilege rooted simultaneously in good manners and genuine concern. At funeral director E. W. Biggs's passing, R. L. Allen of the Palmetto Casket Company, a white man, recognized that a good customer had died and that business etiquette required it be acknowledged. "Gentlemen," he wrote, "We have just learned of the death of E. W. Biggs, and we want to take this means of expressing to his family and friends our most heartfelt sympathy during these sad hours of bereavement. We always thought lots of E. W. and we feel that his passing has caused a place to be made vacant that will be hard to fill. May God bless each of you is our prayer."[33]

Only rarely, it seems, did a Black southerner write a letter of condolence to a white southerner, and when those racial lines were crossed, it was an elite Black southerner who did so. A. F. Shaw, Fisk University dean, wrote Merrill Moore at his father, John Trotwood Moore's death, rather than Mrs. Moore. Perhaps the two knew each other, but Shaw, who was Black, did not write to Moore's mother, who was white. Moreover, he typed his note on stationary, citing his position at Fisk University, rather than a personal handwritten note of sympathy, an act of intimacy that seemed to be unthinkable between Black and white southerners.[34]

Who could or should write was an important question; when you wrote was another landmine of good taste. Writing soon after the death on good stationary with legible handwriting was appropriate. Post's popularity meant that when one went against the evolving etiquette of sympathy notes, an apology was necessary. Walter Hill was out of town when his friend, Floyd Jenkins, lost his wife. His hurried note includes a p.s. "Pardon [the] stationary but I am in Richmond and wanted you to know of my thoughts."[35] Post also may not have approved of family and friends who telegraphed their sorrow. But the speed of telegrams made them viable options. Typical was John Powell's telegram from Mountain Lake, Virginia, to his friend, Arthur Kirkman, after Kirkman's father's death. He said, "Would be with you today but impossible to make [train] connection. Will write at once. Dearest love to your mother."[36]

Several themes dominated the letters. Many began with how the writer heard of the death, which seemed to be as important as comforting the grief-stricken. The startled reaction at the news, framed as a "shock," came next. "I was so shocked and grieved to hear of your father's death. My heart goes out to you and family [*sic*] in this trying hour," wrote Mrs. Griffin to Nashvillian Sally Warner Frazier in 1927 (Frazier's father had died).[37] "I learned of the death of your mother through the columns of the Birmingham News last night," L. M. Dodds wrote to his friend, Alabaman William Bankhead.[38] Death was referred to euphemistically as "your trouble," "your great loss," or "sad information" by authors who understood letters to be intimate acts that carried a heavier sting. Euphemisms hinted, then, rather than stated that a death had occurred.[39] Finally, letter writers assured their recipients that the deceased had been a good person bound for heaven. Mary Childress wrote Nashvillian Mannie Howell when her aunt, Mrs. H. P. Burrus, died in 1913, stating she was a "beautiful character, a perfect lady, and a noble Christian woman."[40]

Even though Post admonished Americans to avoid scripture in their sympathy notes, southerners ignored this particular piece of advice. The most common of Christian expressions was the continued stoic acceptance of death, but mixed in were newer ideas about God and grief. Comments about God's will appeared in this modern format. "God Knows Best" was a common phrase in many letters.[41] Others wrote to tell of their love while mourners were "walking in this shadowy place on the road," a reference to Psalm 23 (KJV), a relatively new reference that acknowledged the grief ("this shadowy place") that was to come.[42] They also linked the death to southern evangelical assumptions about life after death ("What a glad reunion there was on 'the other shore' yesterday!") and then promised that God would provide some recompense for the mourning ("May God Bless and comfort you in this dark hour").[43]

But new assumptions about death appeared, too. Families "broken up" by death received letters from afar, bearing the writers' promises to help carry the burden of sorrow—to be "sincere friends," as Walt Crissman promised his friend, Arthur Kirkman—albeit at a distance.[44] Friends and Jesus Christ would be succor in a troubling time. Sadie Gaither Anderson wrote her cousin Cora Harris that she had "the healing presences of that Comforter whom the tender loving Savior and Heavenly Father send to those who mourn."[45] But mourners were charged with putting up a stoic front, to "be brave and cheerful for your mother's sake," as one sympathy note expressed to North Carolinians Jean and Janie Blue when their brother died in a polo accident in 1934.[46] It was all right to grieve, just not too much, and make sure it was in private.

Sympathy notes became so much a part of a southerner's day that writers noted the letters of sympathy written in their diaries—noting, too, their good taste in sending them. John Trotwood Moore wrote three letters of sympathy one day, recording in his diary, "Wrote 3 letters of condolence in one day—to Judge Wycle, Mrs. R. M. Dudley, and Mr. Caldwell (his grandson killed in an auto accident) but such is life—a game stacked on chance—and yet is it all chance? God reigns and all is in the plan of His purpose."[47] Teddy Harleston, the Charleston funeral director, reported his good letter-writing etiquette to his wife, Elise: "Sorry to hear of Charlie Brown's passing but am not at all surprised. He had been going down for sometime. Am writing Gertie today."[48]

For those who lived close to the family, what used to be the visit to the bedside before death evolved to be a visit to the front door after death, presenting an embossed card with the visitor's name on it. Many were inscribed with messages like, "Thinking of you with a great deal of love and sympathy."[49] For the elite white family, for example, railroad executive Wade Harris's family, one can imagine a doorbell rung, a Black servant opening the door and the card extended as a memento of the visit, sometimes accompanied by cut flowers. Judging by the thirty-five cards kept when Harris died, this scenario repeated itself many times over.

The well-mannered southerner acknowledged the letter or visit, thanking those who lent sympathy in a difficult time. Arthur Kirkman wrote Arthur Allen, thanking him for his thoughtful letter that expressed "sympathy for my mother and me in the saddest event of our lives."[50] Funeral directors also sold pre-printed cards to customers that could ease the task of responding, with vague statements like "Gratefully acknowledging and thanking you for the flowers and your kind expression of sympathy" printed on the front.[51] Emily Post offered examples of tasteful pre-printed cards that might easily fulfill the family's obligation to thank those who comforted them.[52]

Curating Grief and Death Care

In the private moments sanctioned by complicated views of when and how one should grieve, scrapbooks became the physical embodiment of new printing presses, good manners, and Freudian admonitions. In private, one could create an altar to a loved one without facing accusations of melancholia as one curated expressions of sympathy and gave them some order. Large collections of sympathy notes were saved and made permanent by pasting them into scrapbooks, and archives across the South have them. Scrapbooks required the creator to put an order to a death, typically of a close intimate like a spouse or sibling, giving it a "meaningful sequence" by creating a catalog of death ephemera.[53] These private albums do not seem to be intended for public display, as photograph albums of family photos, displayed in a living room or parlor were. They were private, intimate documents that were sites of personal grieving.[54]

Some scrapbooks were started for other purposes. New Orleans native Jeanne Sully Smyth began her scrapbook during her debutante season in the early 1910s, posting invitations and newspaper articles about her social activities. She later cataloged other life events, pasting invitations, guest lists, and wedding announcements from her wedding to her first husband, Dr. John Smyth. But at the death of her mother, Mary Rocchi Sully, in 1928, the scrapbook became a place to store condolence notes. She cut down the telegrams so that only the core message was showing, for example, a telegram from Marie L. Harolson, from Natchez, Mississippi, to Thomas Sully (Jeanne's father) on August 27, 1928: "Deepest Sympathy to you and Mrs. Smyth [Jeanne] in Your Sorrow." This enabled her to paste twenty telegrams on just two pages. The final seven pages were cards and flowers she received. In this case, the scrapbook documented a portion of her life she believed significant rather than documenting her entire life (e.g., her second marriage after Dr. Smyth's death, unmarked in this album).[55]

Later scrapbooks were created specifically for one death rather than evolving like the Smyth scrapbook. Scrapbooking was not a gender-specific craft, but one that helped both men and women grieve. Floyd Jenkins, County Superintendent of Schools in Southampton County, Virginia, buried his 45-year-old wife, Varina Bailey Jenkins, in August 1937 (breast cancer killed her), and his scrapbooks (the number of cards and letters received warranted two books to account for the many messages he received) are a poignant example of a man's grief at his wife's death. He began his scrapbook with her picture and birth and death dates, and then pasted in personal items of hers such as handkerchiefs. Then, a poem called "Not Changed but Glorified" claimed the book for his grief: "Oh beauteous language/For those who weep/Mourning the loss of some dear face, departed/Fall asleep."[56]

Scrapbooks served a practical purpose, too. When one received dozens of sympathy notes or flowers with cards, was it good etiquette to throw them away? Jenkins did not think so, and glued in the many cards and accompanying flower sprays, including those sent from the Southampton County Negro Teachers Association, a Sunday School class, the Ladies Aid Society, Courtland High School faculty, and many others (seventy-eight different people and organizations sent flowers). Then, he pasted a sympathy note on each page, including the letter's or card's envelope. Typical of condolence literature, the notes recreate Jenkins's daily interactions since the groups he worked with day to day all sent him notes, including a textbook publisher, his Congressman, the Virginia State Board of Education, local teachers, and his Sunday School class. Jenkins also pasted two photos of his wife's grave covered with the flowers he received.[57]

Jenkins's and Smyth's albums relied on privacy so they could fully expose their grief. Other albums, particularly photograph albums, instead used silence to grieve. Photograph albums kept images of beloved family members and were displayed for visitors; they became implicit grief scrapbooks after a death when the absence of photos, perhaps even the inability to open up the scrapbook itself, became a way to grieve. In the case of Tennessean Ken Sloan's family, photos of his older twin brothers litter family scrapbooks until one of the twins died in 1924. There were no further photos pasted into the book until Sloan was born five years later in 1929. New silences mark Sloan's mother's grief, in that she could not take pictures and document her remaining son's growth and development until there was a new baby to celebrate. Once Ken was born, she began keeping photos again, showcasing her growing family.[58]

Nell Mellichamp

These trends coalesce in Nell Mellichamp's journals, obsessive, forlorn, and most likely a superficial guard against her deep grief. Mellichamp (1890–1981), a native of Columbia, South Carolina, was a piano teacher, a founder of the local SPCA, and an unmarried woman who lived with her wealthy white family (Melie, too, was a spinster). The family was Episcopalian, with close ties to the local bishop, and were stalwarts in Columbia's white, elite community. They were also prone to nervous breakdowns. Nell was also an inveterate scrapbooker, keeping books on various social activities like her Mozart Music Club. Turning to a scrapbook to record her grief was thus an obvious choice.[59]

Nell began scrapbooking two weeks after Melie's death. The first volume is dated 1926–1927 (it ended up being 152 pages long) while the second volume, incorporated into one that had already been started, was labeled 1921–1947. The second volume especially came to serve multiple mourning purposes, as, by the mid-1930s, Mellichamp used the journal to note when her dogs died (for example), making the document a pliable one that could be applied to her general grief. Because the second journal was started earlier for other purposes, Nell rued the use of it, saying in February 1927:

> I've missed my little book since the last page was filled. This one doesn't seem right, but as no other can be found I must use it. The relief of putting into words—no matter how inadequately expressed—the pain and perplexities of daily livings, helps me so much. Tonight I need the constant assurance of the continuity of life. I must know that Melie's precious life is going on—touching mine. I must know that we are working together, loving, understanding each other and consciously carrying on.[60]

"The pain and perplexities of daily living" prompted Nell to write two times a day in volume I, at least during 1926, curating notes and poems alongside her journaling. She noted weekly anniversaries—Melie's death on a Friday made every Friday thereafter a day to mourn—and the holidays, like Easter, that Melie would never celebrate again. The new death ephemera like cards were glued side by side with her notations of grief. Nell pasted poems she had typed as well as letters that friends sent her, as if this was a collective document where the many who grieved were documented, rather than the intense melancholy of one woman. Also pasted into the document was Melie's obituary from *Southern Churchman*, noting her work as a former English professor and later running an Episcopal mountain school, and the long letters friends wrote Nell. Finally, photos of Melie on her sickbed reminded Nell of who died.[61]

The journals also document the ways that Melie's death and Nell's grief became a part of the household. In the evenings, Nell made a daily visit to the family garden, where lilies represented her sister. Melie's room became a monument, posed in such a way to suggest that she would be back soon (e.g., by leaving writing materials out). Nell thus constructed multiple altars in the house, not just in the scrapbook.[62]

Nell's journals are a barrage of self-incrimination, a clear indication that she had turned Melie's loss inward, in classic melancholia style. Heavenly reunions did not comfort here, with Freudian ideas perhaps adding a burden that might not have existed before. Written next to a pasted-in letter from the Right Reverend K. G. Finlay who begged, "Do try to get some rest," Nell bemoaned, "This is the last day of my 35th year—wasted years! Selfish."[63] In another entry she wrote, "How often the thought comes to me, that if I had gained and held my dear Melie's confidence by trying to control my bad temper and irritability that she would have trusted me and told me about her physical condition."[64] The loss highlighted her own limitations and neuroses. "If I had had more faith—if I had prayed hard—believing perhaps He would have spared my Darling to me longer; to love and cherish and do for. Did my faith waver or grow cold?" she wondered in June 1926.[65] In October 1926, Nell wrote, "Dear, the real loneliness is borne in upon me more and more each day for the world sympathizes only for a while and then sinks back into indifference and love of pleasure and gain . . . You know the heartache and tears which no one else knows or cares about."[66] Intriguingly, she never really used the terms grief or mourning. Always, she felt sadness and loneliness, as if her family, which had already suffered a number of losses (father, mother, a sister, and a brother predeceased Melie), had never had to account for grief. Melie's death in 1926, when grieving had found a place, meant all other sadness could also come out.

Like the writers of condolence notes, Nell used religious metaphors as she struggled with Melie's death. Nell was "high church," or more vested in the conservative order and ritual of Episcopal practices. Jesus Christ became her personal comforter and a Great Therapist, who could "alone comfort and sustain."[67] Yet her deep melancholy challenged what was supposed to be a joyful event—the family reunion—when Melie went to Heaven. While others wondered, "O death where is thy sting?" Nell bitterly wrote, "The sting of death is indeed regret [for the living]." As an Episcopalian, the Eucharist and absolution that Melie received on her deathbed also dominated Nell's early writing. Melie was a saint in this book and the reckoning back to those Episcopal rites was a moment when her sainthood was acknowledged. Flowers in Nell's writing also validated this: violets and lilies represented Melie as emblems of her "purity and truth."[68]

In Nell Mellichamp's grief journals, a number of 1920s trends coalesce as death care evolved to consider grief. As death consumerism made funeral directors key actors in preparing the body for the grave, friends and neighbors used new consumer goods, made possible by the same factory systems that produced elaborate coffins and silk dresses, to comfort the grieving. Gurus of good taste and manners like Emily Post dictated how middle-class and elite southerners cared for those who mourned, but gurus of good mourning like Sigmund Freud characterized grief as potentially morbid and melancholic. New or updated religious tracts like the BCP provided prayers for the grieving, more common in this modern world. Grief thus came to be acknowledged, but only in the privacy of one's home and scrapbook. The privatization of grief echoed practical health changes where some southerners idealistically supposed that good health and a long life were purchasable commodities, a generational change that became apparent as the federal government did not leave the region, but in fact stayed to help make the region healthier.

8 "Health Is Just Everything"

Expanding Healthcare in the South in the 1920s

Old vulnerabilities appeared in letters between families in the 1920s, a generational and transitional moment where the promises of good health seemed unfulfilled. Clydie Scarborough's mother, Irene Waller Fullwood, worried constantly about her family's health. In letters to her daughter who was married to Hayti (Durham, North Carolina) funeral director John C. Scarborough, Fullwood reported on another daughter's vaccination; a smallpox scare near her in Tuskegee, Alabama; the death of a local infant; and her own health. Mrs. Scarborough, with her husband's substantial funereal practice supporting her, was busy establishing nursery schools for poor Black children where they were taught proper healthcare practices that could ward off early deaths. It was ironic, of course, that her husband's funeral business supported her life extension work. Yet, in a generational shift, Mrs. Fullwood assumed, when she had not heard from a family member, that that person was ill, perhaps deathly so, whereas Mrs. Scarborough assumed she could stave off illness and in the long term, make healthcare more equitable for Black southerners.[1] Perhaps, too, life extension practices had begun to give the impression that death no longer lay around the corner, but was a long way off in some nebulous future.

Other letters had a different take on healthcare in the 1920s and 1930s, exposing the practical reality behind Mrs. Scarborough's optimism. At a mere ninety-two pounds when she entered a tuberculosis (TB) sanitarium in 1933, Lillian Parker Larsen's poignant letters show her struggling to fight off the invidious disease. But it was no use. "Health is just every thing. I realize more every day I should have stopped a year ago and gone to bed," she wrote to her mother just before her death at age thirty-one. She might have agreed with a South Carolina writer who said, "'Health is wealth,' is an old maxim, but health is also happiness and power; for whatever improves the health of the individual increases the sum of the life and enhances the happiness and wealth of the people collectively and a vast addition is made to the prosperity, the energy, and the power of the commonwealth."[2]

This post–World War I generational shift caused some younger southerners to ignore their parents' fears of an early death and invest in life extension. Pre-war efforts had been relatively superficial—really, the perception that life extension had biblical sanction was the most significant step—but had had some success, too, in coalition-building with private charities and local churches. But catalyzed by the war and armed with numbers, money, and educational pamphlets, the consumerization of death led to a belief that, if one could buy a good death, one might also buy good health. The diverse coalition that eventually emerged included federal officials; stubborn state and local officials who rued spending money on anything, let alone public health; industry leaders; national charities; death commercial actors; and local Progressives. They worked through the region's decentered system of health, rooted in churches, schools, and civic institutions as high mortality rates came to be seen as economic and political failures rather than simply theological ones. Attention thus shifted to diseases with economic bases, namely pellagra, malaria, and TB, all diseases that potentially indicated a declining health environment.[3]

The USPHS and the American Red Cross Discover a Deadly South

Generational shifts and practical realities relied on the continuing presence of the United States military and other federal officials in the region after the war ended. Even as it dismantled some training camps, health personnel did not turn away from the deeply disturbing health problems they had uncovered. In fact, they expanded their work after venturing into the cantonment zones and confronting the horrific living situations made not just by incipient urbanization, but also by the long-term neglect by municipalities. Lewis E. Foulks, the Chief Sanitary Inspector for the United States Public Health Service (USPHS), prepared a twenty-page report documenting the unsanitary conditions in Alexandria, Virginia, as well as his sense of horror that southerners had been allowed to live in these conditions in the shadows of the nation's capital. He argued for building a basic sanitary foundation in the region, hoping the exposure of filthy conditions would shame local authorities into cleaning up the area.[4]

It is hard to fully capture Foulks's horror at what he encountered. He and his assistants created block maps that marked the "open privies, manure piles, filthy sinks and holes filled with wash water from houses, mixed with decaying animal and vegetable matter, numerous mosquito-breeding areas and all other insanitary conditions."[5] Foulks and his inspectors wore military-issued gas masks to protect themselves from the smell as they ventured into Alexandria's alley system, finding open privies; garbage littering the streets, built up for many years; piles of manure that were prime breeding places for flies that caused typhoid; and stagnant and standing water that produced anopheles mosquitoes, the carriers of malaria. If these general conditions were appalling, the areas closest to the Virginia Shipbuilding Plant where Black workers lived exposed "conditions that are difficult to describe in the English language," investigators said. They found streets and alleys filled with "ashes, garbage, and all forms of waste material," and houses built so low to the ground that they were standing in the buildup of waste material, requiring some residents to build small trestles to walk over the waste to the street. The filth included the dead and rotting carcasses of cats, dogs, fish heads, rats, and chickens, and its dispersal throughout the area required children to wade through the mess in order to play. No garbage system existed in the city, save for the pigs that wandered freely, eating what waste they could.[6]

The USPHS made the obvious leap from filth and squalor to disease and death as investigators stood in piles of manure. Alexandria, according to its statistics, had the highest rate of typhoid deaths among all Virginia cities, for example. Foulks noted:

> Little children playing about these sink holes of death, their little feet and hands covered with poisonous filth, shouting and laughing in their childish innocence, little dreaming that grim death, with its clammy hands, was reaching out from the horrid filth to clutch them. Such sights as these should blanch the cheek and chill the blood of any father or mother beholding them—helpless innocence playing with merciless death! How long will the game last? Not long, it is too onesided; the odds are too great, and in the end fresh graves will indicate the score.[7]

He also said "without hesitation that each and all of them [sections of town] constitute a present and serious menace to the public health, and the danger will become greater as the summer season draws near."[8]

The death and disease these conditions caused were costly, literally, to the region. One man lost his wife and two children to typhoid, at a cost of $460 for doctor and hospital bills, the USPHS reported. These deaths could have been avoided for a mere $18.25, the cost of a sanitary privy that would contain epidemics. Indeed, inspectors noted, the "people of Alexandria have in recent years been paying a terrible penalty in human life for permitting such conditions to exist as we have above described." Assessing costs here allowed investigators to claim that "public health is a purchasable thing."[9]

Heavy-handed tactics and a willingness to invest in racial hierarchies in the name of good health were not beneath federal officials, however, even as they advocated for good health for all. Personnel used local law enforcement and the region's racial caste system, with one white clinic supervisor in Montgomery,

Alabama, sending the local Chief of Police with arrest warrants for Black patients. If patients did not show up for subsequent treatment, then the police arrested the person and put him or her in jail, a frightening prospect for Black southerners who knew a visit to jail could be deadly. But the ARC and other public health organizations also subverted racial structures. The ARC had already hired Black nurses as more than tokens during the flu epidemics, assuming that white nurses should care for white patients and Black nurses should be hired to care for Black ones.

More importantly, the organization found ways to pay for nurses after the war ended, using local industries' funds. As historian Douglas Flamming argued in his study of the Crown Cotton Mills in Dalton, Georgia, "World War I elevated southern consciousness about epidemics, and because wartime emergency production demanded a healthy work force, southerners everywhere became more receptive to measures aimed at alleviating mill village health problems."[10] With that in mind, Assistant Surgeon General Taliaferro Clark wrote G. A. Wheeler, a USPHS doctor staffing a venereal disease clinic in Spartanburg, South Carolina, that "It is very desirable, therefore, that you continue to bring pressure upon the local authorities with a view to securing their acceptance of the Red Cross laboratory and clinic equipment free of cost at the termination of this period provided the said authorities agree to continue [the work.]"[11]

Thus, the federal government's presence never fully disappeared, leaving some real changes in place. In fact, when it came to veterans specifically, the military expanded its care when it built the Veterans Administration (VA) hospital system nationwide. The federal government initiated a Veterans Bureau in 1918 and then a Veterans Administration in 1921 to provide healthcare for returning soldiers. Veterans Administration hospitals tended to be specialized facilities that grouped soldiers with similar problems together. The VA Hospital in Murfreesboro, Tennessee, for example, was built as a psychiatric unit when it opened in 1939 while the VA Hospital in Outwood, Kentucky, only treated tubercular soldiers when it opened in 1922.[12]

The ARC Saves Lives

The postwar generational shift, based on an expanded, though still decentered, healthcare apparatus, required a new vocabulary, especially from ARC personnel. Now that causes of death were more firmly known thanks to death certificates, personnel found that 100,000 deaths occurred nationally from swimming accidents. Given the number of floods in the region, being unable to swim was a significant issue. Armed with this knowledge, there was an attendant change in ARC language from life extension to "life saving," as it expanded its swimming lesson curriculum specifically. *The Red Cross Courier*, the organization's newsletter, showcased articles by certified swim instructors like Lieutenant Herbert Sparrow in Fort Bragg, North Carolina, who baldly called out those who could not swim. After describing the statistics on drowning—"forty, fifty, so many thousands of deaths each year"—the lieutenant then blamed ignorance for those deaths. "Think back a moment to little Johnny Hall, the druggist's son. Johnny dove from an inviting limb jutting out high above the river. Did he know of the sodden logs below its surface? A broken neck bears mute witness to his ignorance," he mused.[13]

The ARC chapters' individual focus depended on the county, of course, even as they embraced the swimming lesson curriculum. The language of lifesaving, however, was at the base. The ARC chapter in Richland County, South Carolina, taught 630 people of all ages to swim. Then they collected tin foil to donate to a Shriners Hospital and gathered fruit and canned goods for the local orphanage at Thanksgiving and Christmas. In its mission to "promote good health, to develop altruistic tendencies in children, to give practice in good citizenship, and to promote international friendliness among children of the world," it also taught first-aid skills to local businesses with the intention that those who learned the skills would then teach their fellow employees.[14]

The ARC also tackled the problem of car accidents, but only for small cities and large urban areas. Rural areas were left to their own devices. The main problem it addressed was the lack of medical care on the road. Emergency medical technicians and ambulances were relatively unheard of (the only ambulance services at the time were hearses from funeral homes). If there was a paid police force in a given area, the ARC set up first-aid training for police officers and firefighters. The belief was that if responders were trained in first aid, they could better care for the injured.[15]

Ignorance or Poor Hospital Care?

With this shift in language and approach—that death could be staved off with some reasonable precautions like learning to swim—came a new perceived cause of death: ignorance, at least among public health officials. As early as 1922, doctors believed that high mortality rates, particularly in rural areas, were a function of ignorance. It was easy to fix high mortality rates, the president of the Louisiana State Board of Health, Oscar Dowling, announced, but the "lack of knowledge" kept that easy fix from occurring because of a "lack of appreciation of the value of the right methods," in places like Louisiana.[16] What public health officials called ignorance, however, some southerners called a reasonable fear of poor medical care, especially in hospitals. White patients typically believed that new hospitals were a place to die, not be made well. One man wanted to take his wife to Duke Hospital for treatment for some unnamed illness, but she refused because she feared hospitals more than her illness. Judgment from doctors and nurses kept Black southerners from seeking medical care. Lois Lapiene, a New Orleans prostitute, attempted suicide by taking poison after she had been orphaned, caught gonorrhea that had taken away her ability to have children, and finally, was abandoned by her husband. As the doctors and nurses attempted to save her, Lapiene heard the nurse say, "'It's a pity she didn't know what to take.' They don't waste no pity on suicide cases."[17] Others recognized that white doctors used Black charity hospital cases to practice new medical procedures with impunity. Another New Orleanian, John Anderson Hill, told a Federal Writers' Project (FWP) interviewer that "Charity Hospital doctors jest experimenting wid me, thats [*sic*] all. I don't mind it . . . them white folks need all of that to hep [*sic*] make a better world."[18]

Maternity wards were perhaps the most dangerous places, with hospitals and doctors clearly to blame for high infant mortality rates, especially of Black infants. Health scholar Karen Kruse Thomas described the dangerous environment newborns and their mothers experienced:

> Well into the twentieth century, mortality rates for mothers and infants had been so high in many American hospitals that women often refused to deliver there . . . most maternity units were identical to units in the rest of the hospital, and small hospitals did not even segregate maternity cases in separate units . . . Infants were taken from their beds to be fed, bathed, and treated in the same nursery room, and the lack of separation between sterile and septic activities was "frequently a grave source of infection," particularly when babies were bathed in one common basin.

"Ignorance" was, in reality, a reasonable reaction to poor hospital conditions, and Black midwives remained a good alternative, if southern mothers wanted their children to survive.[19]

Healthcare in a Pamphlet, a Statistical Abstract, or a Seven Million Dollar Check

The USPHS was a catalyst for expanded health work; the American Red Cross and others provided a new vocabulary; public health officials and patients fought over whether ignorance was indeed a lack of knowledge or just good judgment. These changes occurred just as Congress appropriated seven million dollars (about $111 million in 2022 dollars) for the Sheppard-Towner Act in 1921 to support infant and maternal health in the United States, specifically through the Children's Bureau. Southerners, starved for real financial support, saw the money as a potential catalyst for lower infant mortality rates as well as more spending by local governments. From Louisiana, Oscar Dowling wrote the Bureau in December 1918 that, while he had "a limited force and limited funds," he was hopeful of "employing, [*sic*] a public health nurse for our Board who will supervise the nurses employed by the various towns, and [be] paid either by volunteer organizations or partly by the community and partly by the women's club or some other association."[20]

Following good Progressive practice, Sheppard-Towner moneys funded the published article, a public health report, or the statistical abstract counting illness and death. But the money gave the Children's Bureau a credibility it had not had before and the opportunity to finally (for example) complete the birth registration areas. Infant and maternal mortality information remained inconsistent, however. Some parents did not report stillbirths, deciding instead to quickly bury bodies on farmland without documenting the birth. At the state level, one might report overall causes of death while another state might report infant and maternal mortality by county. Moreover, in states like Louisiana where birth and death certificates were haphazardly filled out, public health officials could claim that infant and maternal mortality rates had dropped but could not give precise numbers because they simply did not exist. What is clear is that some southerners craved this information, sending missives to the Children's Bureau requesting information in far greater numbers than before the war, and beseeching the organization for whatever help it could proffer.[21]

Children's Bureau officials relied on these haphazard statistics to count the costs, literally, of high infant and maternal mortality rates. In a step that signaled the linking of high death statistics to poor economic conditions, the Department of Commerce then incorporated the Bureau's numbers into overall death rates in published pamphlets; having Commerce publish them implied high mortality rates were a problem because of the negative effect on business. One could only lose so many potential customers or workers after all. The Department of Commerce's *Statistical Abstract of the United States*, published every ten years, provided the fuller picture of death once the final states were added to the counts. In 1904 only 7.2 percent of Americans were in Death Registration Areas; in 1919, 52 percent; in 1929, 91.3 percent.[22] Still, by 1928, federal statisticians like Mary Gover could say more definitively, if not perfectly, who died and how. Black southerners, especially in cities, died earlier and in far greater numbers, with their mortality experience in rural areas somewhat better. The higher number of deaths in cities, linked firmly by statisticians to poor urban conditions, seemed to prove that segregation was, indeed, deadly.[23]

Rather than painting a bleak picture, however, solid numbers allowed Black insurance companies to reassess their actuarial tables, accounting for the cost differential in insuring a Black life. They invested in Black actuaries who created these new mortality tables, for example. North Carolina Mutual's actuary, Asa Spaulding, worked for the company before graduating from New York University in accounting in 1930, and from the University of Michigan with a master's degree in Mathematics in 1932. Appointed to the position of actuary in January 1933, he rewrote policy provisions and reassessed risks, actions that led to the company's significant financial improvement over the 1930s and 1940s.[24]

No matter the benefits of knowing numbers, the statistics were frankly appalling. Black women and men suffered significantly higher rates of TB, with 348.5 and 391.2 cases per 100,000 respectively. White women and men's rates were significantly lower, at 131.5 and 193.7 respectively. Louis Dublin, the Metropolitan Life Insurance Company actuary, and Jessamine Whitney, of the National Tuberculosis Association, blamed "hard headed municipal authorities" for the continued loss of life from TB. Perhaps by showing the economic loss, both believed that the "preventable" disease, if addressed appropriately, could decline and "life conservation" might happen. In particular, both claimed the loss of life among young people, which TB attacked more vigorously than those over forty, was especially costly since lost wages and lifelong productivity were greater in a 20-year-old than a 40-year-old. In fact, the losses numbered $26.5 billion annually, they claimed.[25]

Economic Diseases

But TB was not the only economic problem. A diverse coalition of Progressives, catalyzed by USPHS doctors, began focusing on pellagra, firming up the link between southern economies and high death rates. The implication came to be that if the economy was fixed, then pellagra, a disease later found to be caused by a lack of niacin in diets, might disappear. Contemporarily, however, it had a 40 percent mortality rate in South Carolina alone. Intrepid medical investigators like epidemiologist Joseph Goldberger and statistician Edgar Sydenstricker suggested that a disease that kept someone from working made that person a financial burden. Thus, alleviating that burden was an economic and health goal rather than specifically lowering mortality rates.[26]

Pellagra was different from TB in that TB sufferers, when they were not coughing, could hide the disease and therefore its shameful implications. Pellagra, because its symptomology included a nasty red rash that caused the skin to blister and peel, was more visible. That visibility and its lack of a known cause—was it caused by insects? A contagion of some sort?—made it a shameful disease among working-class people because some defined pellagra as a disease of shiftlessness. Pauli Murray, who grew up in Durham, North Carolina, recalled that having "pellagra was only a little less disgraceful than having 'the bad disease,' as folks called gonorrhea and syphilis. People thought it came from dirt and filth and that only ignorant poverty-stricken country folks got it. They considered it highly contagious and avoided those who had it as they would lepers or smallpox cases." When Murray's grandmother was diagnosed with pellagra, it was considered a "comedown" for the elite family.[27]

But because it could not be hidden, doctors like Goldberger could literally see its impact on the region. Goldberger was an intrepid investigator who sometimes used himself as his own lab rat. His research begat other long-term research by Sydenstricker, medical doctor G. A. Wheeler, and "junior" statistician Dorothy Wiehl in South Carolina textile mills. By his early death in 1929 (age fifty-four, kidney cancer), Goldberger had almost definitively proved that pellagra was an economic disease. When economies crashed or wages and hours were cut, southerners relied on unhealthy diets (fat back, cornbread or grits and molasses; no vegetables, protein, or dairy) because they could not afford better food. The health investigators thus could pinpoint where poverty was increasing simply by counting the number of pellagra cases.[28]

Goldberger's linking of high mortality rates to economics came from studying orphans in 1914 in Jackson, Mississippi, and Black Mississippi state prisoners incarcerated at prisons like Parchman Farms, which allowed him to narrow his focus quickly to diets. Fruit and vegetables were scarce in the poorly funded orphans' home, while prisoners always ate the infamous southern poverty diet. His longer view allowed him to chart spikes in pellagra cases region-wide, for example, when the cotton market collapsed in 1914–1915 and in 1920; with wartime inflation in 1917; and when the Mississippi River flooded in 1927. Because he could prove that pellagra came from the dietary insufficiencies that came with lower wages and layoffs, he decisively linked the disease to cotton production and sharecropping as well as to mill villages.[29] His solution was simple. Set aside a small portion of land and plant green peas (he did not know yet why green peas worked). Then, switch from the corn-based diet to a more wheat-based one or take a daily dose of pure yeast to combat symptoms.

Goldberger published his results in a pamphlet that was eventually republished eighty thousand times. Mississippi newspapers published his report so those who could not afford the pamphlet still could benefit from it. County agents, Goldberger's biographer noted, kept the pamphlets handy and spread the information at the county level. The ARC also carried it across the South and incorporated it into its lifesaving classes.[30] But when Goldberger suggested that poverty and economic conditions caused the South's high mortality rates, powerful legislators and capitalists took it as a challenge to their authority as white southern men. Both the Children's Bureau and Goldberger, who was married to a southerner and was usually more adept at navigating southern masculine traditions, ran into problems with white men whose racial policies helped beget the long-term poverty and mortality experienced in the South. South Carolina Congressman James Byrnes bristled at Goldberger's assumption that poverty made pellagra possible, calling it an "utter absurdity." Others, like Oscar Dowling who suggested that high death rates were something to be "ashamed" of in 1922, were summarily removed from their positions.[31]

State Health Department Responses

Some white officials and capitalists would not admit that their constituents deserved a better standard of living. Indeed, their refusal to believe Goldberger and others suggested that some were quite comfortable with high death rates because it benefited them. Instead of challenging them, then, the federal government caved, allowing states to rein in Goldberger and others, by the Children's Bureau responding to requests with information rather than providing substantial financial support, and by hamstringing any ability to effect real systematic change.[32]

Still, state health departments were one beneficiary of this pressure. Where southern states had once organized public health committees reactively (meaning once an epidemic like yellow fever appeared, a public health committee was temporarily created), now public health committees remained in place when no epidemic existed. As early as January 1918, well before the flu epidemic, North Carolina health officials laid out their goals for better health, including "1. Sanitary survey, including soil pollution, 2. Quarantine and disinfection, 3. Medical inspection of schools, 4. Life Extension, 5. Infant Welfare."[33] The state also reorganized its State Board of Public Charities as the State Board of Charities and Public Welfare, increased the number of board members, and created a new state position, the Commissioner of Public Welfare in 1919. The state also paid for a trained health staff, typically, but not always, white. South Carolina established its state board of health in 1919 with an initial $10,000 budget (augmented by Rockefeller Foundation funds), but the top-heavy organization vested authority in the state structure rather than in day-to-day public health, providing white officials a nice middle-class job.

Money troubles thus forced healthcare workers to imaginatively fulfill their health missions. The newly organized Bureau of Public Health Nursing in Mississippi, for example, planned a three-year project in which its public health nurses visited each county (all eighty-two) and spent three months in each, teaching good health practices, examining children, and doing maternal and infant health work. Mobile health units were another imaginative tactic. Dowling had a health exhibit car that taught good health practices in rural Louisiana counties. Efforts to curtail tuberculosis inexpensively caused the Mississippi State Board of Health to fund another truck called a "Motor Clinic." But the truck could only travel on hard surface roads which typically did not exist in the state, causing the truck to be nearly abandoned because of poor roads.[34]

The business of good health also appeared in large cities like Charleston, South Carolina, where deeper coffers led to its own division of child hygiene in

1920. By 1927, the city had established a Health and Social Work Health Center that included the departments of Sanitation, Public Health Education, Records and Statistics, Food Inspection, Communicable Disease Control, Laboratory, Child Hygiene, and Public Health Nursing, among others. The facilities were segregated, with two clinics each week, one for white patients and one for Black patients.[35]

And yet some municipalities recognized that health and wellness were good business. Anniston, Alabama, civic boosters claimed in 1913 that its low death rate was a good reason to invest in the area, and by 1922 proclaimed there was "no more healthful spot on the American continent." Indeed, "There is no better climate in the United States than that enjoyed by Anniston . . . Cases of prostration from heat are unknown. Anniston is surrounded by mountains and is blessed with pure mountain air and restful nights." But it also advertised its public health officer and its county board of health as indicators of both civic duty and business acumen. By 1924, it described its large, naturally draining sewers that freed the residents from contamination in the city's Polk City Directories.[36]

Secular and Sacred Sites of Good Health

The weak medical infrastructure in the South continued to dog Progressive health reformers who turned to secular institutions like schools and colleges as the new locus of good health. With public school attendance now required throughout the South—Tennessee did not require its elementary school–aged children to attend school until 1913—schools and colleges taught good health, with public health officials assuming the lessons would follow children home. Segregated schools meant that Black children had less opportunities because there were fewer schools for them, although the Rosenwald School building program helped mitigate that problem by building more than five thousand schools for Black children. By the 1920s, citywide kindergartens became more common in cities like Columbia, South Carolina, where indigent children, attended school while their parents visited the healthcare clinic attached to the school.[37]

Schools did not supplant the church's healthcare role, but motivated churches to shift their health work out of their buildings. One woman argued, "The church is the best institution we have, and the most necessary, and people should be glad of an opportunity of being identified with some church. They do so much good with the money that is given them. Not that I think unfortunate people should expect the churches to take care of them except in extreme cases of sickness, but I mean that churches help keep up so many other necessary institutions."[38] Recognizing the need for a more systematic approach to healthcare,

Southern Baptists continued to build new hospitals throughout the South—in Selma, Alabama, and Lynchburg, Virginia, for example—using "God as the Good Physician" language to justify their work. Authorized at a meeting of the Virginia Baptist General Assembly in 1919, the Lynchburg facility opened up in 1924. Jesus gave his special blessing to it, according to hospital literature that said, "The Hospital was conceived and organized by the Baptists of Virginia to render a complete Christian ministry of preaching, teaching, and healing, and every Virginia Baptist has an individual obligation to help support such an institution." Indeed, Jesus the great healer going among the people of Galilee (and Virginia) to cure both illness and sin (according to Matthew 4:23, KJV) justified the hospital's work.[39] The Southern Baptist Convention's fundraising arm more generally continued to raise money for God's good health work, setting aside $2,125,000 of a $75 million campaign for hospital buildings. While foreign missions were still the main financial focus (budgeted at $20 million), two million dollars was a substantial investment in healthcare in the South that promised to "increase greatly our hospital service to the sick."[40]

Private Charities and Educational Institutions

But church tithes did not pay for the less sexy work of public health, and frustrations with city, county and state governments caused private charities at least to shift strategy. Schools' investment in student health became a wedge when combined with private charities' money. Recall that the Rockefeller Foundation had attacked specific diseases like hookworm with a laser focus; but by the 1920s, the newly endowed Commonwealth Fund, another New York–based fund, thought more systematically about healthcare, experimenting with funding a health department in Murfreesboro, Tennessee, in 1924, in a county (Rutherford) that had little investment in public health. The Fund initially built a building; hired a doctor, Harry Mustard; and funded a Black and white nursing staff that spread out from the city to the county. The fund then built a hospital in Murfreesboro three years later.[41]

In many ways, what came to be the Rutherford County Health Department shifted healthcare strategy significantly. First, the Fund decreed that, if separate but equal was the law of the South, then the public health department (but not the hospital it built) was going to be separate and architecturally equal, a perfect mirror image of itself, with one side of the building for whites and the other side, equal in size and stature, for Blacks. Second, Mustard and his health staff focused on secular institutions, not churches, as avenues to good health, especially local white schools and their PTAs. Finally, the Fund hired one black nurse, the Tuskegee-trained Mary Ellen Vaughn, who capitalized on the Fund's presence to provide better healthcare for Black residents.[42]

Figure 8.1. The Commonwealth Fund in New York City built the Rutherford County Health Department in 1924. The building is a perfect mirror of itself because, if separate but equal was southern law, the Fund made sure the two branches of the building were equal. Among those hired to work was nurse Mary Ellen Vaughn, who looked after Black locals.

Given the shift to schools as health-education spaces, PTAs became obvious partners with the Fund. The Tennessee State PTA, fifteen years old in 1926, constructed a platform that reads like a typical Progressive era "to-do" list, including advocating for mothers' pensions, anti-smoking, and anti-child labor platforms. But in keeping with the Children's Bureau attacks on high infant mortality rates, the organization resolved in 1926 to "urge a more rigid enforcement of the laws requiring birth registration, and, if possible, make obligatory on both parent and physician to see that registration is done within a reasonable time after the birth of the child, thus placing Tennessee in the birth registration area."[43] Rutherford County PTAs sometimes mimicked the statewide organization's goals, founding Health Committees, using information from Mustard and his staff. They set up school-based health centers for nurses to examine the sick; created "loan closets" with appropriate healthcare materials (sheets, pillowcases, and nightgowns, for example) that were loaned and then returned; and used publicity to promote good health strategies. The Almaville PTA, affiliated with

Figure 8.2. Mary Ellen Vaughn's historical marker in Murfreesboro, TN.

the two-teacher school in the area, raised money to install two "sanitary privies," hung shades on the windows, and graveled the school's driveway to keep the school floors cleaner. But rural isolation continued to impede the Fund's work, with rural communities like Buchanan, for example, unable to address health issues meaningfully until a new school consolidated ten grades into one building around 1927. Then, the focus was more on paying off the school note than raising money for healthcare.[44]

Corporate Paternalism and Good Health

Mill owners and other corporate leadership invested in these generational changes as the costs of their employees' poor health became more apparent. Corporate paternalism, that set of employment practices capitalists increasingly invested in the 1920s to stave off union organizing, improved health in notorious mill villages where epidemics could break out. After all, a disease outbreak that shutdown a facility was as disruptive as a strike. Moreover, nothing exposed the economic consequences of mill village capitalism more than an epidemic. Still, local health officials had to give corporations a significant nudge. A tainted water supply caused a typhoid outbreak in a Bluffton, North Carolina, mill village, for example, and health authorities required the system be fixed in 1923. In this instance, no deaths seem to have occurred, but deaths were known to happen elsewhere because of poor sanitation.[45]

The corporate investment in health practices ranged from major investments in a hospital to funding doctors who visited the sick. The Winnsboro Mills in South Carolina had both a "little hospital" and public health nurse, according to residents Mattie and Talley Smith.[46] In Dalton, Georgia, the Crown Cotton Mills contributed $25,000 to a new thirty-bed hospital that catered, if not exclusively, then substantially, to the local workforce. That hospital, named for an owner, opened in 1920, and mill workers received a 50 percent discount on their bills. Because the mill only hired white workers, however, only white workers received healthcare at the hospital. Company-sponsored insurance was another mechanism for good health. The Crown Cotton Mills Burial Association was created in 1905 and put in the hands of a local employee. By the 1920s, the owners began offering company-sponsored life insurance, causing some to believe the owners would care for them. Mattie Smith recalled when a local man "got drowned in Wateree River[.] Well, there wasn't anything the mill didn't do to help out."[47]

Corporate welfare mimicked trends in public health, but that did not mean mill workers were healthier. Tuberculosis, caught while working on the mill lines in Concord, North Carolina, caused Belle Walter to go to a tuberculosis sanitarium for fourteen months. Her sister Lottie paid the $40 per month needed to keep her sister in the sanitarium, but she would not have been able to had the mill superintendent not helped her. Large influxes of workers to Crown Cotton Mills in Dalton, Georgia, in 1917 had health inspectors worried that a typhoid or malaria outbreak might occur because local sanitation practices could not keep up. Others believed mill owners themselves were the source of death in their families. Sarah Wall hoped she would "never to see a young'un I've got go in the mill for even one day's work . . . Because it's unhealthy work and it wears you out before yore time. Not getting' enough money to live decent don't help yore health neither."[48]

Others like union recruiter Ella Mae Wiggins, the author of the song, "A Mill Mother's Lament," who was shot and killed when she tried to organize in September 1929 in Gaston County, North Carolina, agreed. Sent to work at an early age after her father died, by age twenty-nine she had seven children and an absent husband. She worked at a mill in Gastonia, earning so little each week

($9) that her children suffered from various diseases stemming from malnutrition (rickets, for example). Two others died from respiratory diseases. Before her murder, she wrote "The Mill Mother's Lament" to capture the mill's poverty:

> We leave our homes in the morning,
> We kiss our children good bye,
> While we slave for the bosses,
> Our children scream and cry.
> But understand, all workers,
> Our union they do fear,
> Let's stand together, workers,
> And have a union here.[49]

Death Commerce Confronts Early Death

The South's death commerce industry invested in secular efforts at extending life, some superficially, others more concrete. In 1924, the North Carolina Mutual Company (NCM) opened up an office called Life Extension that was tasked with teaching good health practices to its customers. The largest investment NCM made was in its personnel, many of whom believed their insurance work was a service to their community, both in terms of selling burial and life insurance, and, simultaneously, promoting good health. Certainly, many NCM representatives believed the company provided them a stable middle-class living, but at the same time, they recognized, as NCM Norfolk, Virginia, representative Laurence "Zip" Johnson did, that their jobs provided "unlimited opportunities to serve my race with an essential need—security."[50]

Burial societies and insurance confronted a deep-seeded problem with white hospitals, opening another avenue for life extension. In the "colored wings" of white-owned hospitals, segregated healthcare was literally a name worn on the back, the sheets one slept on, and the door one used to enter the building. Milton Quigless, MD, recalled the Tarboro Clinic (North Carolina) had a wing for Black patients where the sheets, pillowcases, and gowns, threadbare and patched over, had the word "colored" stamped on them. Treatment like this kept Black patients from seeking help so that when a patient finally went to the hospital, Quigless recalled, "most of the time you were too late anyway. And it [the hospital] was synonymous with death, you might say."[51] Frustrated at a system that provided indecent healthcare to Black sharecroppers and town dwellers alike, Dr. Quigless opened his own hospital, albeit in 1947, that became well known throughout the state for its one door (no separate entrances for Black and white patients) and its good care of everyone.[52]

Black burial societies solved some of the problem by building private hospitals, treating their Black patients as someone who was ill and in need of good care. Burial society hospitals emerged across the South, for example, the Royal Circle Hospitals in Memphis and in Little Rock, Arkansas, where the hundred thousand members of the Supreme Royal Circle of Friends of the World ensured its financial stability. The Afro-American Sons and Daughters Burial Society, incorporated in 1924, built a modern hospital facility that opened in 1928 in Yazoo City, Mississippi. A fine brick building, the hospital featured thirty-six private rooms, two wards, and an operating room. Members who could find transportation to the hospital received free hospitalization as part of their dues. Non-members were required to pay for the services.[53]

Burial society hospitals were a good, but not perfect, response to poor healthcare for Black southerners for two reasons. First, because the hospitals were a matter of racial pride—"see what we were able to build," they proclaimed—they could be a mechanism to police moral behavior and to assert some control over rural Black southerners. The Ancient Moselites of the World, a Jackson, Mississippi, burial society, vowed to pay for illness and disability, unless the illness came from venereal disease or from injuries incurred when breaking the law. Secondly, the finances for all burial society hospitals remained precarious, with the fifty-bed Royal Circle hospital in Little Rock opening in an old house in 1921 and closing in 1934.[54]

Segregation and Tuberculosis

New hospital infrastructure continued to mimic racial structures in the South: this hospital for whites, that one for Blacks, and neither all that capable of treating one significant disease culprit in the 1920s. Tuberculosis continued to spread because of rapid migration, poor or no housing and ensuing close quarters. But motivated to segregate urban spaces by race, health officials segregated people by health, too, with the building of public and private TB sanitaria that gave some wealthy families hope of fewer contagions. It also allowed white families, shamed by their relatives infected by TB, to hide them from public scrutiny. After all, TB was a disease of the working-class Black men and women, not white, middle, or elite classes. Shame thus became part of disease management. Writing to his niece, Mary Ballard Creath, in 1928, one Virginian described how he told his wife she had the disease, the next steps he took to keep her from infecting the rest of the family, and the ways he managed the shame. "Uncle Louie" wrote:

> I know when the doctor told me your Aunt Mamie had TB, I was so distressed I could not say no word for several minutes. And I was alarmed for fear how it would affect her when she was told. So he [the doctor] came up to see her—and while sitting in our room he told her. She took it much more calmly than I did and asked very naturally what she would have to do. He told her that the only thing was to go

> to a Sanitarium—and she wanted me to take her on the next train but of course I could not. But after telegraphing to Blue Ridge and Catawba [both TB sanitaria] and could not get in we wired Mt. Regis and they could take her. So the next day I did take her. She was there four months—3 months in bed, the last month she was allowed to take some exercise and then came home and the doctors report [*sic*] is she is perfectly well . . . Now Mt. Regis will cost $37 ½ per week besides extras for x-rays . . . I suppose it cost about $700 for your Aunt Mamie for 4 months."

Uncle Louie knew how to treat TB, telling his niece, "besides you know T.B. is not hereditary. You can contract it—and I want to caution you to be careful with Virginia [a relative] and caution Virginia to be careful with herself." His wife, Mamie, underscored his good knowledge by writing a postscript to this letter, underlining her sentence, "TB is not hereditary," twice and reminding Mary Ballard that "Children and young people are susceptible to it *if exposed to it* so you, her husband and baby have been, I hope, *very* careful and she really ought to begin her rest cure at once."[55]

Once at a TB sanitarium, letters continued to share modern health information. Lillian Larsen described to her mother the care she received, including problems with roommates, significant weight increases, her love of the radio while she was confined to bed, and her final poignant letter, written by a nurse, that said goodbye to her children. Larsen also stayed quiet about her diagnosis, hoping to save her family, especially her father-in-law who was a congressman from Georgia, the shame of a relative with TB. They acted "queer," Larsen wrote her mother. "No one here knows I'm going and I don't suppose I'll tell them—people here are so queer—so I guess to them I'll be in Arkansas [her mother's residence]," she said.[56]

Perceptions of Life, Age, and Disease

Although early death remained a problem, some successes appeared, especially in infant and maternal mortality rates. If it was not yet a practical reality for everyone, Progressives still successfully sold southerners that the "life record," how long various family members lived, was expanding to meet the biblical sanction of three score and ten. John Trotwood Moore, the Tennessee State Librarian who romanticized antebellum slave life, looked back on earlier generations of his family, noting a "weak life record." Moore wrote in his diary about his mother's family's tendency to die young, "A weak life record on this side. Hard to make it with that." Moore used genealogies to chart his mother's family, claiming, "all died before my mother was 50 yrs. old." But he also noted his siblings had broken that curse. His sister, he wrote, died at age sixty-nine and his brother, born in 1855, was still living in 1924.[57] Some earned that longer life record, according to some eulogists at Moore's death in 1929. T. H. Alexander wrote, "To my mind there is usually nothing tragic or shocking in the death of a man who has attained his full three score and ten years, but there is tragedy in the death of Mr. Moore because his life had just entered his really productive era."[58]

Generational shifts allowed younger southerners to see some lowering of mortality rates. To be successful in extending life in the South, however, the New Deal had to eliminate the ad hoc, cash-starved, decentered nature of public health while simultaneously systematizing care. It needed to see beyond racial barriers as well. Its eventual success would be built on these sporadic attempts when Franklin Roosevelt came to power in 1933 and invested in the region during the New Deal and World War II.

PART FOUR

Death and the New Deal

The transformation of death care and the expansion of life extension in the 1920s motivated some to think that dying young could be staved off. But when the Great Depression hit, that initial optimism appeared to have masked an awful reality as death rates rose. It was Franklin Delano Roosevelt's optimistic tone that seemed to be the saving grace for Americans as he and other New Dealers redefined American citizenship at first to include some economic rights, for example, a federally mandated minimum wage. But in reimagining what rights Americans deserved, some health rights were also codified into law. New Dealers invested in a more general public good, willingly bringing all Americans under a big tent to secure a public good that seemed elusive at the time, albeit in flawed and incomplete ways.[1]

The federal government broadened its intervention into the region with the first of three New Deals, literally disentangling death from southern landscapes. As it built hydroelectric dams across the South, the Tennessee Valley Authority (TVA) dug up bodies and reburied them according to modern practice. Simultaneously, the Civilian Conservation Corps (CCC) began to control the region's mosquito problems while providing young men marketable skills. The Second New Deal became even more focused on codifying life extension practices with both practical infrastructures and a legal foundation. Simultaneously, its cultural work cast southern death rituals, particularly Black ones, as odd and different. The Third New Deal raised wages meaningfully with the passage of various labor acts, but also signaled that it would continue to focus on the South as the nation's most pressing economic problem.

It did not take much to see the deadliness of the Depression in 1930, however, surrounded as many were by young men who died suddenly from heart attacks.

9 Making Deadly Landscapes Healthier

The First New Deal

Virginian Mollie McLaughlin's fiancé, Pinckard "Heck" Heckman, died suddenly in June 1931, most likely from a heart attack, and condolence writers noted that his early death was not unexpected, even though Heckman was only forty-three. One writer said, "The past year or so has been a great strain on so many people, we have heard of so many young men being taken off suddenly that we have commenced to about dread opening the mail. At least five of our acquaintances have had sudden deaths, none over fifty years of age. One day they were playing golf and the next day gone."[1] The Great Depression, in other words, was not simply an economic event, but one that caused otherwise healthy people to die suddenly.

The New Deal proved that liberal democracy—focused on expanding rights rather than retracting them—still had vibrancy, potency, and durability as it made health and wellness a right of citizenship. With its impoverished cities and deep rural poverty, creating a healthier South became a special focus of the New Deal's agenda. Powerful forces in the South and in the Congress, where southerners dominated, supported these practices as long as racial hierarchies did not budge. New ideas of citizenship focused on lowering morality rates could thus exist side by side with racial segregation because Black southerners became patients rather than people with the right to vote, a "deluxe" kind of Jim Crow that made Black southerners healthier, albeit in separate hospitals and clinics.[2]

To lower death rates, the First New Deal tackled two core beliefs about southern land. The first was bodies buried on family land that secured political and racial systems and where locals rooted their community's identity. New Dealers, especially the Tennessee Valley Authority (TVA), just saw a lot of dead bodies. Across eight states, the TVA then removed more than ten thousand bodies as it built its system of hydroelectric dams, giving the image, at least, of ending the link between buried bodies and the land's deadliness.

The second belief was rehabilitating the land itself. The federal government could not stop hurricanes or tamp down the heat, but it could eliminate landscapes that made disease-carrying insects like mosquitoes common. The Civilian Conservation Corps (CCC) was especially prominent in making the land and its inhabitants healthier, caring for the young men who came into its ranks ill and poorly trained.[3]

Death, Grief, and the Great Depression

Many died from stress, economic deprivation, and poverty as the real ramifications of the Depression became obvious in fall, 1930. Of the most famous death stories associated with the Great Depression, deaths by suicide are ones with little factual information, most likely hidden by the shame associated with dying by one's own hand. Funeral ledgers, the place where the most honest assessment can occur, do not display any marked increase of suicides. But the collapse of the economy really did cause some to at least die from stress when they lost everything. Dr. Howard Fitts, born in Greenville, North Carolina, in 1921, recalled wealthy people dying as the Depression's ramifications became clearer:

> Some Blacks who had accumulated property and had built nice homes and they just lost them. And the experience was too much for many of them. They didn't live long after. There were some who were suicidal. At the time I didn't know who committed suicide and who died natural deaths but I remember a number of people were so affected by the losses and the severity of the Depression that they did not live long.[4]

The financially insolvent died, but so, too, did the most vulnerable of citizens, infants. The Children's Bureau had already claimed that infant mortality rates were a key indicator in assessing the nation's overall economic and political health. It was no surprise that, when it collated infant and maternal mortality rates for 1930–1932, the information provided a devastating picture for women and their children specifically and for the nation in general. Invariably, whether one measured Black maternal death rates versus white maternal death rates or rural rates (which had improved) versus urban rates (which were egregious), southern states invariably had the highest maternal mortality rates of 90–120 (or more) per 100,000; a "good" rate was under 59 deaths per 100,000. Only Nevada, New Mexico, and Wyoming ranked at the bottom with North and South Carolina, Tennessee, Mississippi, and Alabama. The Children's Bureau gave the rates a visual potency, with color-coded maps representing states with poor numbers by the colors purple and black and healthier states by red and yellow.

The North and Midwest were seas of red and yellow with some green (rates of 60–89 per 100,000) mixed in. Purple and black represented the South's deadly environment for pregnant women, giving administrators a sense of urgency.[5]

Sudden deaths added to Americans' financial woes as some turned to friends to help pay for an unexpected funeral, piling shame on top of economic woes. Textile worker Ellie Robertson recalled a woman whose husband was out of work, who had herself been cut down to one day's work a week, and whose mother died. She said, "Up to late Saturday they didn't know whether they was goin' to be able to bury her or not. Some of the neighbors went around and took up a collection to pay the grave diggers and buy the lot. Then this woman made arrangements with the undertaker and they got her mother buried Sunday morning . . . A collection come hard back then because so many people wasn't getting full time."[6]

The death commercial system should have been protected from financial whim, given that people still died and needed to be buried, but financial upheaval affected the most vulnerable death commerce, burial societies, which suffered deep declines in the 1930s. The M. W. Grand Lodge (Masons) members reported that it had been "a very strenuous year. Money has been scarce, banks have closed with our moneys in them, and many of our Lodges have not paid their dues, while others have paid only in part. The financial depression has hit us hard, yet we are glad to be able to face you and report that we have striven to do our best under this great strain." One of the luckier burial societies, it was still able to pay for its members' funerals at $50 and $25 each.[7] Other burial societies collapsed when dues-paying members simply stopped paying. This resulted in an attack against a burial society's ability to provide healthcare with hospitals like the Royal Circle Hospital in Little Rock, Arkansas, closing in 1934. The increasing availability of insurance probably had as much to do with the demise of burial societies as the Depression did, but insurance could not account for the meaningful ritual that acknowledged the deceased's worth. *National Baptist Voice* editors decried in 1938:

> Younger Negroes become less interested in funerals and "wakes" and monthly lodge meetings. Insurance companies developed offering security in sickness and death. Instead of the gayly-colored [*sic*] uniforms and the annual dress parade, the month meetings and the Grand Lodge session, the insurance agent quietly called around and collected the insurance premium at various homes. A shift began from the fraternal society to the insurance company, old members of the lodge died and they were not replaced by recruits from the new organization.[8]

Although many burial societies collapsed, funeral homes were relatively protected from the Depression with insurance and federal death benefits for World War I soldiers supporting their financial solvency. Moreover, new funeral homes

Figure 9.1. During the Great Depression, white funeral homes like the National Funeral Home, Memphis, TN, advertised their spacious, mansion-like homes to southerners who may have lost their homes during the crisis. Courtesy of Dr. Jim Moshinskie.

that looked like mansions provided a dedicated space that did not disappear (usually) with economic downturns. At a time when many had lost their homes, being put away decent from a mansion-like funeral home was recompense for those losses. When the Harrison Funeral Home opened in Lynchburg, Tennessee, in 1934, ads told new customers to "MAKE OUR STORE YOUR HOME."[9] The National Funeral Home, founded in Memphis, Tennessee, in 1935, promised white residents that its mansion-like facilities, pictured in local city directories and on postcards, that their funerals would show the truth of their status. J. C. Oates's Funeral Home, which predated the National Funeral Home by about twenty years, had done the same for Black Memphis residents for years.[10]

Having insurance and a desire to be buried from a nice home did not mean that families did not make cuts in death consumerism, however. Even those families who could still afford a modern funeral cut back. Whereas wealthier families were beginning to spend between $400 and $600 by the late 1920s, the $100 funeral became more common in the 1930s in J. C. Oates's ledgers. The expensive funeral was now one that cost $200, and it tended to be paid by insurance or in cash rather than by a burial society. Bad accounts also became common stuff on funeral ledgers as well as letters to attorneys charged with chasing down bad debt.

In the wake of financial catastrophe, insurance companies rushed to calm policy holders' fears that their insurance policies might now be worthless and their funerals no longer paid for. The North Carolina Mutual Life Insurance Company (NCM), for example, added the word "life" to the company's name, shifting from caring for the dead to promoting good health. It also published year-end reports, touting its financial and social strength in an era when decline seemed inevitable and persistent. Those assurances, of course, were also intended to sell insurance and ensure their customers kept up payments. North Carolina Mutual and other insurance companies also kept many employed, with "approximately one thousand Negro men and women gainfully employed, notwithstanding three years of depression." It paid out an average of $2,662.90 per day in 1932 in claims and made policy loans to its holders amounting to more than $210,000. "No home was complete without a North Carolina Mutual Policy," the annual statement said, because its financial stability reinforced a Black family's stability.[11]

A Grief Acknowledged

Within the limits placed on grieving in the 1920s, the Southern Baptist Convention (SBC) realized that the loss of money, jobs, and homes themselves was a kind of grief that needed a theological root. Douglass Scarborough McDaniel's *Stewardship of Sorrow* (1930) and other tracts were part of that new literature on grief, published by the SBC's Broadman Press. McDaniel argued that sorrow had to be borne silently, shared only with God rather than burdening others who had their own sorrows to bear. It was part of a Christian's lot in life. Expect sorrows of all kinds because the real paradise was in Heaven, not on earth. Keep your grief to yourself, she counseled, and be cheerful since outward displays of emotion dishonored the dead or, implicitly, the account lost when a bank closed.[12]

In a manner fitting for the time, McDaniel used banking language to prove her point. Sorrow could be a "liability," but really, it was an "asset." Grace was the result of "inheritance or endowment." Echoing earlier prescriptions against too much grief, she counseled her readers that worldly possessions were fleeting and that their losses could be borne because grief denied God's plans and she cast those who wallowed as "heathens."[13] Other SBC pamphleteers like

Mitchell Bronk used familiar phrases from the Bible, particularly Psalm 23:4's (KJV) well-known phrase, "the valley of the shadow of death," recognizing that familiar language could be an anchor in this new valley of financial losses. Assured that death was not to be mourned—indeed, calling grief a kind of sinful temptation—other writers like famed preacher A. C. Dixon wrote that death had a "bright side" in that it freed the soul to be with Jesus Christ, and was something to celebrate.[14]

But southerners countered attempts to make loss a quiet, prayerful relationship with God by relying more on secular ideas, especially sympathy notes. Wise words from the Bible no longer were sufficient; only "Time" would take care of losses. Capitalized or italicized similarly to evangelical Christians' capitalization of God, "Time," a vague passage of months or years (no one ever said specifically how much) would comfort those who mourned. "So little any one can say to comfort you. I have found that *time* is the only healer," Alice Selectman wrote Eva Smith when her husband died in 1934.[15] "Elsie," writing to North Carolinian Cora Harris after her father died in 1935 said, "My father and I had a very close understanding and somehow I never think of him as gone, but just away. Time is a great healer and work heals us from thinking."[16]

Volunteerism and the Great Depression

President Herbert Hoover remained unimpressed with American suffering because, as a firm believer in classical economic theory, he viewed economies as rocking boats. In the same way one could not right a rocking boat, one had to wait out a depressed economy, letting its waywardness subside on its own. As the problems spread, Hoover's suggestion that prosperity was just around the corner and that poor people were at fault for not saving for a rainy day (when banks closed down and those savings accounts were lost) struck many as callous.[17] Some of the callousness was rooted in his belief in individual goodwill, or "volunteerism," which stated Americans were people of good conscience, and when something tragic occurred, one only had to ask for help. The government should stand on the sidelines, only stepping in to manage the response. Meatless Mondays and Wheatless Wednesdays during World War I were Hoover's volunteerism applied to the need to feed Europeans embroiled in war, for example. By voluntarily giving up meat and wheat—rather than imposing a strict rationing system as would be done during World War II—Hoover managed to stockpile enough food to feed millions. He believed that this new crisis would be resolved by neighbor helping neighbor, with the federal government watching from the sidelines. The widespread suffering, however, meant neighbors could not help neighbors because they were suffering, too.[18]

As the Depression unfolded, however, the federal government faced a dearth of meaningful information about the real losses Americans faced. How many were unemployed? What were the general effects by 1933? Hoover asked a group of scholars, chaired by economist Wesley C. Mitchell with assistance from the University of North Carolina's Howard Odum, to research just these questions in fall 1929. Published as *Recent Social Trends in the United States,* one reviewer generously called it a "stout volume," with a compendium of statistics on population, family trends, crime, and education, as the twenty-nine chapters and thirteen auxiliary volumes formulated "a general sketch of complicated social trends which are remoulding American life." The group mentioned American death rates three times in the first forty pages, suggesting that the economic and social trends it described would be linked to poor health, illness, and mortality.[19]

In some ways, the report was a reactive one in that it was framed around changes in the 1910s and 1920s, using the decennial censuses to identify trends in families and industry. What, for example, was the effect of industrial processes on families as they evolved from primarily economic units to more social ones? Did the effect weaken the family's ability to function as a moral unit? The report's reactive goal made it somewhat out of date by 1933, at least in its ability to address the current steep decline in the American economy. But it did provide information that served New Dealers in their quest to address the underlying causes of the Great Depression. Moreover, *Recent Social Trends in the United States* made health a Depression-era issue while simultaneously linking it to contemporary economics.[20]

While the scope was national, the mortality portion had significant ties to southern life extension. United States Public Health Service (USPHS) statistician Edgar Sydenstryker, Joseph Goldberger's former research partner, wrote the chapter on death and the United States, titling it, "The Vitality of the American People." The shift in language here is telling. No longer was merely extending or conserving life the goal. Now, vitality, a more active word that implied a robust American nation, was. Sydenstryker struggled to define vitality, however, finally settling on what it was not. Vitality had to be more than living to one's three score and ten, a phrase he quoted. It was not the ability to reproduce nor was it any kind of biological process. It did mean not being depressed. Unable to come to any workable definition, Sydenstryker simply defined the term as not dying young. With this in mind, the editors and writers of *Recent Social Trends in the United States* forcefully proposed a more robust federal response, especially in the South, and it was in this context that New Dealers stepped in and systematically began extending life.[21]

The First New Deal

Sydenstricker's emphasis on the South foreshadowed another statistician, Margaret Jarman Hagood, who cast the South's main problem as one of rural land tenancy when she published her masterful study of white southern tenant women in 1939. "In an unhindered trend toward farm tenancy will be endangered the basic principles of Jeffersonian America, namely, land as the foundation of national wealth and the sturdy landowning citizen as the bulwark of national strength," she wrote in *Mothers of the New South.*[22] In other words, how could Americans in general define citizenship if the land that served as its buttress exploited and sickened more than it served? She did not necessarily suggest that life extension would be one of those new ways. However, to Progressives who had tried to lower the South's high mortality rates; to the commercial death industry that saved money when its clientele lived longer; and to those southerners who now experienced death care in different ways in 1930 than in 1900, living to one's three score and ten was itself a kind of citizenship, one that could reasonably replace land as American citizenship's firm basis.

These first New Dealers came to their work with a sense of urgency that was stoked by multiple violent tornadoes that cut a swath of destruction across Alabama, Kentucky, Louisiana, Mississippi, South Carolina, and Tennessee, beginning on March 14, 1933. In one Tennessee storm that spring, a tornado blew a path across the entire state, around four hundred and fifty miles. Tornados killed more than two hundred southerners, injured thousands more, and leveled homes without regard to state lines. Large hurricanes in North Carolina, Florida, and Texas that fall added insult to the already numerous injuries. The government's incipient, state-focused Emergency Relief Agencies aided the American Red Cross (ARC), which stepped in to help the injured and devastated, willingly taking over the care of the non-military dead and acting as the family when the deceased had no one else. It established burial committees, for example, after a Louisiana tornado in May 1933, where 36 were killed and 451 injured in Bienville and Webster Parishes. Churches were commandeered, "improvised," in the ARC's language, to become first-aid stations and hospitals until the injured could be moved to larger cities.[23] Dramatic language accompanied aid efforts, using grim scenes to conjure empathy and aid. "Seldom has grim tragedy been more evident. Children blow into tree tops, limbs torn from bodies, heads severed, whole families wiped out, scores of children orphaned, badly injured loaded on wagons and hauled weary miles in the rain," ARC documents reported, where they might find a paved road for an ambulance to take the injured away.[24]

The American Red Cross may have been the main responder, but as the New Deal built a presence across the South, the dividing line between ARC and New Deal personnel became more fluid, as personnel migrated to paid federal positions.[25] With the intertwining of ARC and New Deal personnel came social worker assumptions from typically white middle-class southerners about who received aid, how they received it, and whether they were worthy of it. Each family became a "case" that was investigated carefully before receiving funds. Certainly, this was to ensure that a loss had actually occurred, but in some cases, this was a moral assessment of whether the devastated were worthy of material assistance. Alice Dugger, sent to South Carolina in May 1933, was appalled at the conditions she viewed. "Really, it [South Carolina] is about ten years behind Va. from what I could see, but the people are human after all and with care they could be brought out of the winderness [*sic*: wilderness] along about the next century," she wrote an ARC colleague.[26] In any case, the ARC was slow in "closing," or investigating cases and then issuing checks. Of the 248 registered cases to be investigated after the May tornados, only 57 had been closed in the next few weeks after the storms blew through.[27]

The slowness came in part from aid workers' reporting mechanisms. Reports documented head of household (typically male), spouse, and children; described whether the family owned the house or farm or was a tenant farmer; documented the damage to the house and family; and then listed the goods the ARC gave to replace lost or damaged ones. The Broadus Thompson family, devastated by a tornado in Greenville, South Carolina, in May 1933, lost four family members including the mother and three children, while four other children were shuttled to a local hospital courtesy of the local mortician. The ARC noted, "Everything lost, except stock. Four in family killed, four injured and sent to hospital . . . sent two ambulances, two hearses to scene of storm."[28] Economics also hampered local branches. The Nashville ARC, responding to the loss of life and property in the March tornadic events, was able to raise enough money, but in areas like rural Sullivan County, Tennessee, there simply was no money to donate.

Divorcing Death from the Land

Tornadoes were the sort of lightning strike that forced New Dealers to focus on the region's mortality rates almost immediately. New Dealers began by first eliminating the dead's visual impact as it constructed a system of dams that provided hydroelectric power across the Tennessee River Valley. The TVA eventually moved more than ten thousand bodies in the 1930s from the southern cemeteries most likely to flood to new cemeteries above the flood line. The TVA, like most New Deal programs, served two purposes: to provide jobs for local men (for example, the four thousand hand-built caskets to rebury the dead were built by locals) while simultaneously building the South's hydroelectric infrastructure. By providing electricity, TVA administrators saw themselves as "creating a higher social and economic order in the valley" which the dams would provide.[29]

The TVA's elaborate system to disinter and rebury bodies from below the flood line began in earnest in summer 1933, with the Norris Dam Project on the Clinch River in Anderson and Campbell counties in northeast Tennessee. This project not only moved the most bodies—5,219 in all—but the project set the standard for future reburials, for example, the Wheeler, Pickwick Landing, Guntersville, and Chickamauga projects. The Norris Dam project took a full year to complete, from August 1934 to August 1935, and cost $149,407. The grave removal process required multiple steps before bodies were actually moved, with the ensuing paperwork designed to confirm a consistent process. The first step was a general survey to identify where the cemeteries were. The second, almost simultaneous step was a photographic survey that, in some ways, was an implicit argument for grave removal because many of the smaller cemeteries were ill kept. Families, in other words, had reneged on their promise to care for the dead and the New Deal implicitly suggested it could shoulder the responsibility. Next, the TVA contacted and interviewed the nearest kin, offering them three options: removal by the TVA to a location within twenty miles of the current resting place; removal by a local undertaker within the same twenty-mile limit, with a $20 budget; or leaving the bodies where they were. Bodies were to be moved as is, meaning the TVA constructed boxes to place remains in, no matter their state. Where bodies had become ashes and dust, grave diggers simply put dirt into the hand-built box before reburial.[30]

The TVA followed explicitly northern rituals, grouping as many burials together as possible into new park-like settings well away from the nearest city. For the Norris Dam project, four new cemeteries, Bakers Forge Memorial Cemetery (public), New Loyston Memorial Cemetery (private), New Indian Creek Memorial Cemetery (private), and Big Barren Memorial Cemetery (private), were created to rebury the dead from 226 cemeteries. About 95 percent of the disinterments, according to later reports, were moved to those four cemeteries. Only a few graves were left where they were. Administrators, many of them northerners, hoped that by making the new public cemetery, Bakers Forge, "very beautiful and attractive," the "memories of the region may be respected and preserved."[31]

The TVA constructed a ritual of respect to stave off any claims of being economic carpetbaggers, a term reminiscent of the post–Civil War era when migrant northerners were dismissed as mere exploiters of a ravaged postwar South. An undated report, most likely from 1933, stipulated that "Only those who possess an attitude of respect for the dead and the reasonable sentiments of their living friends and relatives be assigned to this work. Any one not manifesting this respect for the dead or behaving in such a way as to result in harmful comment by the relatives should be discharged for the cause."[32] The TVA hired local men so that friends seemed to act on behalf of locals rather than the federal government, and family members witnessed the reburials when possible, although the only official funeral service planned was a final one after all of the bodies had been reburied. Finally, the agency tried to keep family groups together, even though different relatives might have differing claims over individual bodies. Mrs. Addie Collins did not decide to move her daughter's body until her son agreed to move his other relatives. Her decision was motivated by his, to be sure, but also by her desire to keep her family together.[33]

In encountering burial practices dating back to the eighteenth century, the TVA encountered the hundreds of small family cemeteries as well as the haphazard marking of graves. The desire to bury the whole body also required the TVA to move the random leg or other body part in anticipation of the rest of the body's eventual death. Locals feared that unmarked graves were not adequately identified in the TVA's initial surveys and would be flooded by the new dam. There is reason to believe those fears were realized, in part because memories of some burials had faded or sites were inadequately marked. In 1943, for example, one family wondered where a small tract with five graves was, and the TVA could not help them because the graves had been marked only with rose bushes.[34]

But in its interactions with older burials, the TVA gave locals the rare opportunity to update older burials in accordance with evolving twentieth-century death care or to migrate bodies closer to where families had moved. The Watts Bar Project, for example, allowed Lavens M. Thomas to move his family members to the Chattanooga Memorial Park, a more modern park that was closer to him (he was a lawyer in Chattanooga), rather than the Leuty Cemetery (Morgan Springs, Tennessee) where his father and one-day-old son had been buried. The reburial in Chattanooga allowed him to join them when he died in 1946.[35]

Clashing Death Cultures

The clash of cultures between TVA administrators and locals was inevitable. Those hired locally did not use good grammar and spelling when writing reports, for example. The New Deal, like the Progressives before them, embraced precisely filled out paperwork to manage reburials, but found its laborers did not sign their paperwork, or made mistakes on the multiple forms that had to be filled out. Some of the concern was for the future. "Your reports," one administrator said in a meeting, "will be studied by professors, archeologists, etc., so do the best you possibly can. Keep your report sheet clean." Other behavior had to be managed, too. Drive carefully, administrators cautioned, to give the impression that care was taken even with the most mundane details.[36]

Care and respect toward the family was above all essential, with administrators wishing to avoid "kicks," or complaints. They tended to be successful, with many thanking the TVA for its good manners. "Relative to the burial grounds and the removal of the bodies," John D. Freeman, Executive Secretary and Treasurer of the Southern Baptist Convention wrote, "I wish to express my appreciation for the spirit manifested by you."[37] Another LaFollette businessman told a grave removal foreman, "You fellows are doing a lot better job than I thought you would. I was surprised at the way the bodies were being handled."[38] The high standards of respect carried over to other projects. Dye Seeley wrote to H. H. Turner, a TVA supervisor with the Watts Bar Project, to thank him for his "kindness in regard to the removal of my parents [*sic*] graves. Every thing was conducted in such a nice way and it made it so much easier to go through. I appreciated every thing so much and am so satisfied."[39]

The careful ritual did not stop some locals from causing trouble. Some fussed when the TVA pursued efficiency rather than catering to a family. It sent a car for I. R. Boruff on December 21, 1934, for example, so he could witness the reburials of his mother, father, wife, and daughter from the Big Barren Memorial Cemetery. Boruff refused to attend, citing his current wife's illness. The graves had already been excavated down to the coffins and had the TVA left them open, water would have run into them during the Christmas holiday. The TVA continued the reburial, but contacted Boruff's nephew, who stood in as witness. Boruff still complained.[40]

Southern assumptions about death care also caused tension when they believed that the removal of a cemetery would destroy the identity of their communities. The visit to the graves on Decoration Day; the desire to be buried next to a long-dead spouse or brother; the disturbing of bodies that needed to be intact for Resurrection Day, all challenged the TVA to move carefully when disinterring bodies. The new Bakers Forge Cemetery was thus problematic because it represented the end of an individual community's identity, as bodies from multiple communities were intermingled. Not only that, but other Protestant denominations, often in "jealous competition" with each other, overlapped in the cemetery. "We want our people buried together," as one TVA official characterized the feeling. Moreover, many locals did not have cars to drive to new cemeteries. But since a lack of a car or old age or infirmity made it impossible to visit the original graves, the ability to imagine that visit was crucial to the elderly. What ended up selling some of the more intransigent locals was the promise of perpetual care provided by the federal government. The forgotten family cemetery, something locals saw daily, seems to have frightened them and the federal government's promise of perpetual care was persuasive.[41]

The TVA also worked hard to include local undertakers, who feared both the TVA's competition and its higher standard of care. When approaching families for the Norris Dam Project, the TVA stressed that its agents had to offer each option (TVA reburial, undertaker reburial, or leave in place) without prejudice,

Figure 9.2. One of the stone memorials at the Bakers Forge Public Cemetery.

even though it was much easier for it to move the bodies. Public relations officials stressed that making local death commercial actors look good was critical to a successful project. But some undertakers did a terrible job reburying the dead, in one case, leaving a set of graves looking uncared for.[42] The problems were significant enough that, after the Norris Dam project was finished, the agency never included funeral directors again. It was simpler to have the TVA move the bodies. In fact, the process was "in general, more satisfactory to the relatives and to the Authority. It was also more economical for the Authority than having them removed by contract," TVA supervisors wrote after they finished the Pickwick Landing Project on the Mississippi/Alabama/Tennessee border.[43]

Patriotic Bodies and the New Deal

To counter any bad press, administrators saw the potential of moving older, patriotic bodies, foreshadowing the Second New Deal's emphasis on reviving "pioneering" values. The TVA argued that "hardy" pioneers, through hard work and a deep commitment to building the nation, had traveled across the Alleghenies in the westward push to settle America. "These qualities, it has seemed to me, bear emphasis at this time because of their value if they might be revived in our nation today. The fortitude, the courage and the endurance of the pioneers of the T[ennessee] V[alley] region seems to me to be an object lesson that will always be epic," one TVA official wrote his colleagues.[44] Locals defined pioneering differently, however. Whereas the TVA focused on eighteenth-century and nineteenth-century pioneers, especially Daniel Boone, Davy Crockett, and John Sevier, locals wanted Confederate soldier graves moved with equal reverence. J. B. Gaines, for example, asked if his uncle, a Confederate soldier killed at Sharp's Landing in September 1864, could be moved to a graveyard in his "native county," Union County, Kentucky.[45] In some cases, locals who linked those patriotic bodies to their family's status wanted it maintained. Sallie Cleveland, seventy-three years old, supported by the Morristown (Tennessee) Daughters of the American Revolution, wrote repeatedly to TVA agents regarding her great grandparents, Revolutionary War soldier Royal Jennings Sr., his wife, Katherine Jennings, and other family members whose bodies lay on their original land grant from the federal government. "*I must have the remains of Royal Jennings, Sr. & his wife Katherine,*" she wrote, while noting, "the march of Time brings advancement and I bow to the improvements without complaining."[46]

Paperwork Confirms Ritual

The TVA quickly established a raft of forms to be filled out before and after a body's removal. Paperwork would, to its thinking, confirm that everyone had been treated the same. Take the case of Helen Walker, who died in 1926 from "acute indigestion," just short of her first birthday, one of many infants the TVA reburied. On November 25, 1934, the TVA contacted her father, J. C. Walker, who signed a "TVA Grave Removal Contract." The body was moved from the TVA–designated Cemetery #10, known to locals as "Cedar Hill Cemetery" to Bakers Forge where space was set aside for her parents when they died (her mother died in 1956; her father in 1959). The paperwork assured the family that the TVA had the right "to go ahead at its own expense and disinter and remove the remains of the said deceased person and all markers of the grave from the said area, and reinter the said remains and properly replace the said markers in some other suitable cemetery, preferably"; and in the case of Walker, Bakers Forge Memorial Cemetery was typed in. The next bit of paperwork, the Grave Removal Record designated a local funeral home, Agee and Carden Undertakers, to proceed with the disinterment, with TVA inspectors (all local men) as witness.[47] Causes of death were also noted to discern whether grave diggers might be exposed to infectious diseases. It made for some gruesome moments, however, when one woman was described as having been "shot in edge of mouth by husband [*sic*] during 'drunken brawl.'" Her brother had also been killed in the same rampage and TVA reports thoroughly described the bodies before they were reburied together in a single grave.[48]

Figure 9.3. This is Helen Walker's gravestone, weathered by time and topped by a small lamb to denote infants as the Lamb of Christ.

Figure 9.4. As promised by the TVA, the Walkers were buried next to their infant daughter, Helen, even though her father died in 1959 and her mother in 1956.

Witness was critical to the disinterments. The field engineer who contacted Helen Walker's family described the TVA's work as "very satisfactory to the relatives who come to witness the removal."[49] Yet this, too, could be gruesome. After the body was dug up, the contents of both the grave and coffin, if it still existent, were photographed thoroughly, probably to avoid charges of grave robbing. Walker's body, dug up December 5, 1934, at 1:50 p.m., included the condition of the container ("Good"); the condition of the body ("Skeleton"); and an inventory and disposition of articles in the grave ("1 Set Handles Put in box"). By 2:15 p.m. that day, the body was ready to be transported three miles to the Bakers Forge Memorial Cemetery and was reburied at 2:45 p.m.[50]

Race and Southern Landscapes of Death

The TVA guarded its prescribed ritual ruthlessly. Helen Walker was going to be treated exactly the same as every other body without regard to class, gender, or cause of death. Race was another matter, however. As it moved south along the Tennessee River, the TVA confronted areas in Chickamauga, Wheeler, Watts Bar, and Pickwick Dam where the Black population was far more numerous (slavery had been relatively unheard of in the Norris Dam area) and where its roots reached back before the Civil War. The number of cemeteries of the enslaved needing to be moved increased substantially. Tennessee Valley Authority administrators also knew that southern congressional representatives, all white men, had to be kept happy if funding was going to be maintained, and thus signaled their willingness to affirm, and in fact, modernize racial segregation.

The TVA first labeled both the Black deceased and their descendants as "colored," distinguishing them from other families who were assumed to be white. Reburials were done according to race, with public cemeteries called "colored" remaining "colored" on TVA survey maps. Private letters also indicate a patronizing attitude toward Black southerners that likely affirmed the segregationist practices. Letters exchanged between TVA administrators like Fred Wendt and his superiors expose a mocking tone toward Black southerners. Wendt wrote, "'Zen' is o.k. and having a lot of fun with the 'Colord [*sic*] Brethern' as well as the young 'Sisters.'"[51]

Northern assumptions about marking graveyards also caused problems. Crews cleared out trees and shrubs from the Campbell Church Cemetery (listed as "colored") near the new Wheeler Dam in northern Alabama. Then, they asked church members where the bodies were. No one could tell them because the bushes, trees, and shrubs that marked those graves had been cleared. It happened a second time with the Chickamauga Dam in Harrison, Tennessee, albeit with crews who were not affiliated with the TVA. They cleared what seemed to be weeds and brush but were actually grave markers. The agency, with the help of church members, eventually identified 208 graves (of more than 300 burials) of which 199 were removed.[52]

But pre–Civil War cemeteries of the enslaved proved to be a problem, especially if they had been abandoned. Who owned the cemetery, the enslaver or the community that claimed them as ancestors? Who had the legal right to move the bodies? The TVA tended to value the enslaver's family over the enslaveds' relatives. The Frazier Cemetery, near the Chickamauga Dam, had five slave graves in it, but the owners, identified by locals as the Chattin family, had moved away before the Civil War. In that case, the TVA acted as the family and left the bodies where they were. Other cemeteries, where the master was clearly buried among his "faithful servants," were interpreted to fit white locals' assumptions about the plantation South and the white family was given control over the bodies.[53]

The Civilian Conservation Corps and Creating Healthy Men

While the TVA literally removed the dead from the land, the Civilian Conservation Corps (CCC) made that same land healthier. Environmental goals achieved health aims, specifically for the young men who worked on the project, and in general, for the region. Structured according to military hierarchies, the agency cleaned up swamps and graded roads, combatted the region's vast problems with erosion, and eliminated areas where standing water cultivated large swarms of mosquitoes. At the same time, the young men aged 17 to 23 1/2 were paid $30 a month ($25 went to their parents), and were fed, clothed, and cared for in segregated units. At night, administrators rectified learning and reading deficiencies. Later, when it seemed like America might be going to war again amidst strong isolationist sentiment, CCC camps became a way to begin military training without drawing the ire of isolationists. By the time the program ended in 1942, some three million men had worked in a CCC camp.[54]

The CCC's daywork addressed both emergent and long-term environmental problems. In 1937, when the Ohio and Mississippi Rivers flooded, the CCC's 346th Company, out of Kingston, Tennessee, moved to Kentucky where the "troops" worked for two weeks, strengthening levees and dikes. Longer term projects addressed problems emanating from the haphazard road building in the 1920s. In Murfreesboro, Tennessee, one hundred and fifty young men, all white, constructed terrace outlets, diversion ditches, and fences around most of the roads in Rutherford County, and then planted new saplings in worn and eroded areas. Building state and federal parks across the nation—the Blue Ridge Parkway, for example, in Virginia—the CCC also created access points so that users could commune with nature in healthy, vital ways.[55]

Figure 9.5. The Civilian Conservation Corps built parks like the Montgomery Bell State Park in Burns, TN. Later, some parks posted memorials like this one that described the CCC's environmental and health work.

But the young men themselves needed care, as administrators discovered substantial health problems, in particular malnourishment. Seventy-five percent of the young men who joined were underweight, with other maladies also in evidence, for example, tuberculosis and hookworm. The camps, modeled on World War I training camps, became health units, with food served in abundant quantities, and in the rigorous inspections of camps for potential hazards, like poor sanitation. Camp reports documented food costs, for example, but administrators measured both weight gain and the nutritious food the troops ate to ensure that fruits and vegetables, purchased locally, were healthy and fresh. In 1940, at the Murfreesboro camp, inspectors reported that each enrollee averaged a 9.5-pound weight gain in the six months they worked for the CCC.[56]

In the evenings, other deficiencies were addressed. From six to nine p.m. each night, instructors schooled the young men—fully one third in the CCC could not read—or trained them so they could receive a first-aid certificate. In one report, inspectors noted that 51 out of 157 young men were taught to read and write while simultaneously receiving job training. Indeed, one official reported that the "emphasis in academic [*sic*] is placed on illiterate and grossly undereducated."[57]

Once again, the federal government proved willing to follow white southern racial rules by segregating Black men into their own CCC companies, for example, the 1464th Company out of Fort Oglethorpe, Georgia, a troop that had mostly young men from Memphis. The 1464th planted 135,000 trees, reduced fire hazards, and did required road maintenance at the Chickamauga National Military Park. Another unit out of Fort Oglethorpe consisted of sixty World War I veterans who were sent to Shiloh National Military Park to build firebreaks, landscape, and plant some 325,000 trees. Black men also built state parks in Tennessee, including the Montgomery Bell Park in Burns, Tennessee, parks they most likely were not allowed to use as fully as whites. Thus, the CCC inherited both the best and worst aspects of the TVA. It was willing to make life easier for southerners while making sure that separate but (not really) equal remained in place.[58]

The heart attacks young men suffered at the beginning of the Great Depression did not foreshadow the meaningful changes to the South's deadly landscape. Alerted to its deadly spaces by tornados and other environmental catastrophes, the TVA and the CCC were quick solutions to the high mortality rates. The federal government then fashioned a new citizenship, albeit an incipient one, based on good health with the Second and Third New Deals institutionalizing that citizenship.

10 Revitalizing a Sick South

The Second and Third New Deals

The typical New Dealer was an idealist who believed her work was a "sacred mission" that would reinvigorate the sick and suffering, who were too focused on dying. In many ways they echoed the sense of potential Clydie Scarborough carried with her to work each day in the 1920s. One Arkansan, Anna Weir Layne, who worked for the Resettlement Administration, visited a small house in an Arkansas cornfield, assessing its need for relief and becoming dismayed to see two crosses adorning the family's mantle. Historian Alison Collis Greene described the interaction this way:

> In the center [of the mantle] was a framed print of Joshua Reynolds's *The Age of Innocence*, an eighteenth-century painting of a small girl. On either side of the painting stood a two-foot-tall wooden cross, painted white. "Sorrow" was lettered in green across one, "Adversity" across the other. Layne took offense. "Mr. Barclay, will you please tell me why you have those words on the crosses?" she recalled asking. "Yes, life is like that, most all sorrow and adversity," answered Barclay. Layne promptly retorted, "It is not, except as your thinking makes it so." She lectured Barclay on God's good intentions toward all creation, and then extracted a promise from the farmer: He would turn the crosses around and print "Love" on one, "Joy" on the other.[1]

Sorrow and adversity could no longer be the watch words of a South, mired in illness, death, and adversity; joy and love would be the words for a healthy and vital region and nation.

Franklin Delano Roosevelt embodied these same idealistic notions when delivering his Second Inaugural Address on January 20, 1937. "We of the Republic sensed the truth," he told Americans, "that democratic government has innate capacity to protect its people against disasters once considered inevitable, to solve problems once considered unsolvable." But, first, he said, the nation had to help folks like the Barclays, one third of the nation that was still "ill-housed, ill-clad, ill-nourished." Referring to the Depression as an "economic epidemic," his language of illness and death signaled the need for good health to become a right of citizenship.[2]

The Second and Third New Deals vested the common man and woman like the Barclays with significant political power. America would become healthy again as a nation if pioneering values of old, inherited by everyday common people, provided a steadfast rudder. But the common man and woman were too focused on death; they had to be cured first if they were to be worthy of their symbolic attachment to a reinvigorated nation. The Works Progress Administration (WPA), the Society Security Act of 1935, minimum wage legislation, and other programs were designed specifically to foster new cultural work, build new hospitals, and raise the standard of living. They also centralized life extension practices in federal hands, making good health a federal policy rather than local or state policy, using funding as the federal government eventually assumed nearly 50 percent of state health costs.[3] There were firm boundaries on that work, however. One Nashville, Tennessee, newspaper ad stated:

> There must be none of the dangerous belief that the Federal Government will take care of our needs. On the repeated word of the President of the United States and the Governor of Tennessee, the Federal Government will not assume any part of the responsibility for local charity or social work. [But] the Federal Government will help see that nobody dies of starvation. Further than that it cannot and will not go. The Federal Government will help that life is made possible. Nashville must see that it is worthwhile. A great task is ours and ours alone here in Nashville.[4]

The New Deal, with its sharp focus on the South as the nation's one economic and health problem, could finally attack mortality rates in a holistic way, building on the First New Deal's rejuvenation of a deadly landscape. Now, the Social Security Act codified life extension while the WPA's cultural work fetishized older forms of death care, casting those practices as pathways to poor health and deadly landscapes. Then, with the Third New Deal in 1937 and 1938, officials linked a more expansive economic policy to a healthier South, confirming an expanded definition of American citizenship that included both economic rights and the right to a reasonably healthy and long life.

The Works Progress Administration

The Second New Deal dates from 1935 with the passage of the WPA and the Social Security Act. Roosevelt chose someone familiar to southerners to run the WPA, once Congress passed the $4.8 billion bill: Harry Hopkins, who had directed the American Red Cross's response to the Spanish flu epidemic in New Orleans, Louisiana. Hopkins and others imagined infrastructure broadly, building schools and expanding hospitals at the same time as the WPA paid artists, musicians, writers, and actors to preserve American culture. The WPA invested especially in skilled people like nurses and public health workers. In the South, this typically benefitted white women and actively replaced Black midwives as rural areas' main healthcare providers.[5]

The WPA drew healthcare out of churches and schools and centralized it in hospitals, built by the thousands across the nation. Historian Karen Kruse Thomas noted that it built 2,000 health facilities, modernized more than 2,000 other facilities and added 107,849 beds to existing healthcare facilities. Modern medical facilities allowed professionals to segregate their wards by specialty so that patients of like concerns were housed together. Both new hospital buildings and renovations of older ones targeted Black Americans specifically, although that aid did not attempt to drop any racial boundaries. Indeed, Thomas argued that "medical and racial segregation developed alongside and reinforced each other." Yet she also noted that by the time Roosevelt died in April 1945, healthcare had become the least segregated space in the United States.[6]

Hopkins and others understood good health began at home, however. In surveying the South, New Dealers found that 86 percent of southern households did not have adequate plumbing, and that even though long focused on providing sanitary privies, it appeared that Progressives had made only a small dent in the sewage problems that begat typhoid epidemics and other illnesses. The WPA was able to fix the sanitation problems in significant ways. According to Thomas, it "completed 11,200 miles of water mains, more than 20,000 miles of new or reconditioned sewer lines, and more than 1,100 new water and sewage treatment plants . . . [and] constructed nearly 3 million sanitary privies by 1942, nearly two-thirds of these privies in the South."[7] In South Carolina, early iterations of public sanitation programs had worked on eliminating standing water which fostered some of the worst malaria rates in the country. By 1936, health administrators claimed the mosquito population was under control; by 1940, malaria rates had mostly disappeared along with significant decreases in mortality rates for both Black (a 75 percent drop) and white (an 80 percent drop) South Carolinians.[8]

Public Health Nurses

The WPA's new health infrastructure required experts who could guide locals through the array of changes while it cast federal intervention as merely the work of a family member. Through white women's work especially, and to a lesser extent, Black women's, the New Deal relied on women's symbolic status as mothers, only now of a new family with deep pockets. Federally funded public health units and nurses were not economic carpetbaggers, but a wholesome attempt to provide care.[9]

White nurses and social workers, who tended to be middle-class women who had fallen on hard times, used New Deal funds and their symbolic power as mothers to replace Black midwives and their healthcare as federal sanction now replaced biblical sanction. The WPA paid for skilled nurses and social workers down to the county level. Mabel Lawson Clark, a Patrick County, Virginia, resident from a prominent white family, became the county's first director of the Department of Public Welfare in 1934 (the New Deal paid her $100 per month), remaining in that position until her retirement in 1957. Born in 1890 and orphaned at a young age, Clark was widowed young with two children, taught school until her children were in college and then went back to school where she trained to be a social worker. Then the county, just south of Roanoke hired her to be its first county-level social worker for its Department of Public Health.[10]

Clark relied on community networks to find patients, oftentimes venturing into difficult terrain to reach remote parts of the county. One case required her to drive toward the top of a mountain; then, when the road ran out, she walked up a path until it, too, gave out, requiring her to climb over wire fences and through shrubs and bushes. When she finally reached the mountain top, she remarked on the view to the client, who responded, "Yes'm, but it don't fill the belly." At times Clark removed the back seat of her car so she could ferry the ill to the hospital. At still others, she chopped wood, bathed the sick, cooked and cleaned for them, and secured help from neighbors when there was no family. When parents neglected their children, she stepped in to care for them, too. In other words, she acted not only as the federal government's representative, but like family when none existed or was neglectful.[11]

Public health nurses and social workers focused quickly on Black midwives as an easy way to lower high infant and maternal mortality, bringing with them a healthy dose of judgment. States had already begun to regulate midwives in the 1920s, with licensing standards varying state by state. In some states, licensing required letters of recommendation by two doctors. In others, midwives were required to carry a manual in their medical bag and bring their registration certificate there as proof of the state's purview. In still others, one only had to be able to read a manual for midwives, be able to write out a birth certificate (which made reading and writing skills essential in a racial system where Black education was substandard), and attend fourteen births under the supervision of a doctor.[12]

New Deal–funded public health officers affirmed their own status by claiming midwives were responsible for the region's high infant and maternal mortality rates. No one questioned that babies died, and in great numbers, but there was significant disagreement over why. Doctors argued midwives' "voodoo medicine" and unclean environments caused high death rates. These challenges against vernacular medicine affirmed a new distinction: there was good medicine and there was bad medicine. Those who had gone to college and learned scientific methodology practiced good medicine. The rest was simply voodoo.[13] Midwives, correctly, told another tale. Poverty, starvation, and other kinds of racial violence were more likely the culprits. But doctors, social workers, and public nurses had the weight of the state public health apparatus behind them and a healthy dose of New Deal money.

Biblical sanction and generational knowledge no longer affirmed a midwife's status; a state-issued license did, affirming doctors' and public nurses' power over birthing systems. There were two purposes here. Licensing would resolve high infant mortality rates in the short term by forcing midwives to adhere to public health standards; in the long term, it would end Black midwives' dominance of rural births. The easiest midwives to eliminate were the ones who did not want to change from what one midwife called the "old law" to the "new law." The "new law," or broader health practices required by the New Deal, covered clothing, conduct, even the bag a midwife carried to each birth. Supervision was also necessary. Carrie Dykes, a Texas midwife, had already delivered fifty or sixty children, but by 1944, a white nurse had to meet with her and other Black midwives monthly to explain the "new" rules of delivering babies. Dykes wryly noted the new rules were necessary because "dey tell me chillun ain't born the way they used to be."[14] A Georgia midwife, called "Aunt Jeanie," summed up the new regulations this way:

> There are things you got to *be*: You got to be of good moral character and in your right mind . . . Another thing is you got to be clean in a personal way and clean in the way you work.
>
> There are things you got to *have*: You got to have a new midwife license every year and be ready and willing to show it to any person that wants to see it [a new level of scrutiny by the state].
>
> Then there are certain things you got to *do*: You can't have no midwife license without you take a blood test every year to see if your blood is moral and you ain't got no bad disease. You got to get a scar from vaccination if you ain't had smallpox."[15]

Other WPA programs like the Federal Writers Project (FWP) followed white nurses as they imposed the new regulations on both midwives and pregnant women, finding that white southern assumptions about venereal disease colored the treatment of Black pregnant women. FWP writer Chlotilde Martin followed Mattie Ingram, a white public health nurse, through her daily rounds in Beaufort, South Carolina, in 1939, as Ingram checked on her "colored prenatals," local Black women who were pregnant. Ingram described her fight against high mortality rates, which included "three venereal and three pre-natal and well-baby clinics each month, instruct a weekly class of mid-wives, examine and vaccinate school children and, in between times, do home visiting." It was enough, Ingram noted, to keep her "pretty busy." But she brought with her medical bag a healthy skepticism toward those who did not practice her modern form of medicine. It was returned in kind. One patient, a Black woman named Sara Roberts, viewed Ingram's work as a public nurse and her use of scare tactics skeptically. "If Sara doesn't come back for her shots, her baby is likely to be stillborn," Ingram told the interviewer. But Ingram's rant went beyond claiming Sara's child would die. She said, "It's a vicious circle. When they don't take treatment for venereal disease, the babies die and that makes the mortality rate for South Carolina appallingly high. And when they do take the treatment, the birth-rate shoots up just as appallingly. Although that makes the vital statistics records look pretty, it clutters up this part of the earth with thousands of ragged, half-fed children."[16]

The WPA's Cultural Work

The WPA imagined infrastructure broadly, meaning it did not simply build new hospitals or pay for new public health nurses. It also invested in the nation's cultural infrastructure, funding post office murals, concerts, and theater productions. It also invested in out-of-work writers who conducted oral interviews with everyday Americans and with the elderly former enslaved. Cultural work more generally vested the common man and woman with a symbolic vitality that could lift the nation out of its doldrums and were poised as authentic Americans whose values and perseverance could revitalize the nation. This shifted the nation's focus from businessmen—now deemed responsible for the Depression's misery—to touting the common man's and woman's pioneering roots. Indeed, if the nation looked to contemporary ancestors, then it could right itself. The new cultural assumptions accompanied the parks and greenways the Civilian Conservation Corps (CCC) and WPA built, creating a new, healthier environment for playtime. In these spaces, New Dealers like Eleanor Roosevelt thought, if people played in healthy spaces or listened to good music, they would become moral, wholehearted communities again, not crass individuals out for their own gain.[17]

The WPA's cultural work fashioned the South as an impoverished region, but with contemporary ancestors who were simultaneously the keepers of early British folk music, an older, purer culture imbued with pioneering values like perseverance and stubbornness in the face of adversity. They now lived in poverty and had to be made healthy before their cultural work could have meaning. Writers like Erskine Caldwell (*Tobacco Road*, 1932); Grace Lumpkin (*To Make My Bread*, 1932); and Caroline Miller (*Lamb in His Bosom*, Pulitzer Prize, 1934) foreshadowed the WPA's work. Nonfiction research by sociologists like Liston Pope on mill hands or Margaret Jarman Hagood's work on sharecropping women gave fictional works the imprimatur of truthfulness rather than cultural construction.[18] Believing in ghosts; folk beliefs with supposedly no basis in science; and evangelical religion all marked the characters in these fictional narratives as contemporary ancestors. Death at an early age was central, making these stories seem like it was 1900 all over again. Walking to their neighbors in *To Make My Bread*, for example, Emma and her daughter, Bonnie, passed the church with a "burying ground." Lumpkin wrote:

> The church, a small log building, was up a short trail at the left. Across the road, on a slope, was the burying ground. Emma's husband and the three children who had come between Kirk and Bonnie were laid away there. There were no flowers in the burying ground. The graves lay flat and plain on the slope. The dead were dead and there was enough to do caring for the living. There was not a woman around the country who did not have one child or more in the ground. When a woman was ripe she gave birth, and if the child died, it did not help much, after the first days of sorrow, to weep. What was done was done.[19]

These early narratives influenced FWP interviewers, who used life histories and slave narratives to collect stories, rituals, and music that needed to be preserved. Collecting stories from everyone, rather than just the wealthiest, vested them with democratic import—their words and their stories mattered. But in taking these interviews, FWP life histories identified who was sick and how they suffered. Interviewee Floridian James Kerby Ward said in his interview, "I reckon we done right well. We coulda done better though if we hadn't had so much sickness. You know that takes a lot of money for doctors and medicine and for hospital. I had to have my wife operated on a year or two ago and we are just now a-gettin' out of that debt."[20]

Interviewers incorporated racial and class assumptions, sometimes inconsistently, into their interviews from their initial choices of whom to interview to how they rendered the final transcripts. A constructed vernacular, for example, identified who was working class or who was black. But interviewers ran into trouble when Black interviewees refused to follow its racial script, for example, accomplished Black men whose language reflected an elite class status. J. H. Robertson (noted as Negro by interviewer Miss Grace McCune; the honorific Miss, of course, claimed her whiteness) was an insurance broker for North Carolina Mutual Life Insurance Company. McCune interviewed him three times in 1939, with Robertson describing his daily duties as well as whimsical stories of being an insurance collector. The interview is unique in McCune's inconsistent adherence to local (Augusta, Georgia) racial practice. She could not write the interview in the faux dialect associated with Black working-class southerners. At the same time, other parts of racial etiquette did appear: the notation of (Negro) next to his name, her claim of the title "Miss" while not noting his title (Mr.). Perhaps choosing him to interview made him seem an anomaly in a world where white southerners assumed all Black southerners were "ignorant" and incapable of "correct" speech. Black FWP interviewers, on the other hand, simply ignored racial etiquette altogether.[21]

Federal Writers' Project interviewers cast Black death rituals as survivals of a pre-modern era that had to be collected. Yet as they did, FWP writers festishized them as something odd, different, and weird. Ruby Pickens Tartt, a white interviewer from Livingston, Alabama, for example, attended "Aunt" Amy Chapman's funeral. A 95-year-old woman born into slavery, Chapman died suddenly from a stroke, and Tartt described the funeral, including the sitting up with the body, the digging of the grave by local men to create a mound, and the use of automobiles in the service. Without recognizing its import, she noted Chapman's purple coffin and matching purple robe. Tartt also captured a unique ritual whereby each grave digger took his spade and rested it against the burial mound's side, "iron point in the soft earth and handles pointing toward the sky." When she asked later why, the response was only, "It is customary in our race." Racial hierarchies were also apparent when she was pressed to bring her flowers to the grave first before anyone else, signaling the requirement that white people, no matter the occasion, went first.[22]

Federal Writers' Project writers also collected Black folklore, interpreted by anthropologists like Elsie Clews Parsons as savage and exotic, gathering music and sayings in the faux Black dialect assigned to respondents. Estelle Williams, for example, sang for her interview,

> Nothin' to live for
> Jes' one time to die;
> N——- does de work
> White folks gits de pie
> Spare me, dear Lord,
> For some o' dat dessert
> Den I don't give a d—-[*sic*]
> Eff I do git hurt.[23]

Black gravesites were another site of premodern disorder, seeming chaotic to white folklorists' eyes. Parsons was active in collecting Sea Island folk beliefs about death and dying. Her publications stereotyped them as quaint, marginalized folk who exhibited "primitive" beliefs far out of step with mainstream funereal practice. "Point yer finger at the graveyard, an' it will rot off unless you put it in water or in de groun," she quoted one. To be sure, buried beneath her elitism are real descriptions of Black death practices, but a modern healthcare world needed to archive these older traditions as different and then, moved onto more scientifically informed care.[24]

Travel Guides and Other Southern Car Narratives

Federal Writers' Project writers also produced travel guides for each state, part of the American Guide Series that accomplished work similar to the Life Histories. The New Deal developed new industries like tourism, investing in infrastructure and access, for example, via the WPA's Farm-to-Market Road Building Program that improved or created roads across the nation. Better roads made tourism possible. To draw Americans out of their homes, the FWP wrote travel guides for each state, highlighting interesting landmarks to visit on these newly improved roads. Roads themselves became a quaint and easy way to access not just the physical landscape, but the cultural landscape, too. The belief that these roads were safer and deadly accidents less likely for drivers was an important sub-context to these guides.

The guides documented medical beliefs and death as an intrinsic part of the southern landscape, even as the Tennessee Valley Authority (TVA) was eliminating that link. Older ways of death care became interesting artifacts or quaint relics, rather than part of a modern, healthier present, that travelers could view and move on from as they drove. As one toured Mississippi, for example, one might pass multiple cemeteries, giving the writers an opportunity to explain local folk medicine beliefs and death rituals. Black Mississippians were cast as oddities in the healthier world New Dealers were building. Knowing that scientists had determined illness came from known agents, white writers winked at their audience that the more "primitive" Black southerners thought illness came from the "conjuring power of an enemy," and folk medicine was the best medicine rather than scientific concoctions. Death rituals themselves were scrutinized by white writers with the Mississippi guide's story of an important Black preacher's death and his lying in state for nine days before Mississippi law required him to be buried. Quaint, odd, and now firmly in the past, death care in the early twentieth century became a roadside attraction for travelers to the South.[25]

Even as the guides sent tourists traveling those roads, that perception of road danger was still prevalent, according to other writers who used their FWP jobs to document deadly car accidents and drunk driving. William R. McDaniel, writing in the Knoxville (Tennessee) *Journal* an article saved in the state's FWP files, likened local death statistics to a new kind of war where "death meets its victims on these shores"; any highway or street was a battlefield and the weapons were "negligence, carelessness, poor judgment and incompetence." And no one seemed to care, according to McDaniel, even though the deaths were useless ones that could be curbed with better lighting, new law enforcement procedures on drunk driving, and safer cars with better brakes.[26] Automobile accidents thus were another kind of roadside attraction that travelers had to take care with.

The Social Security Act of 1935

While the WPA attacked the nation's cultural and physical infrastructure, the Social Security Act became the federal codification of life extension work that had been pursued in the South. Passed August 14, 1935, the act created a system of taxation that funded a variety of life extension practices and was steered to completion by strong southern congressional representation. Its preamble stated that it was an "act to provide for the general welfare by establishing a system of Federal old-age benefits and by enabling the several States to make more adequate provision for aged persons, blind persons, dependent and crippled children, maternal and child welfare, public health, and the administration of their unemployment compensation laws."[27] It excluded many Americans from its initial incarnation, particularly rural and domestic workers (many of whom were Black) because they did not receive a paycheck each week (these exemptions were later rectified), but did mimic the commercial death business by providing a death benefit for survivors of those who died before age sixty-five. Moreover, by providing funds for unemployment insurance, the act also countered the possibility, laid bare by the Great Depression, that poverty from unemployment caused poor health and death, recognizing the United States Public Health Service's (USPHS) close linking of poor economies and high rates of disease and death. Finally, according to historian Edward Beardsley, even though many identified it as a pension system, it really was "the foundation for a sprawling edifice of federal health initiatives carried out by local officials."[28]

Frances Perkins, the United States Secretary of Labor, led the committee that codified what had been done piecemeal in the 1920s. Now, the Children's Bureau's and the USPHS's work became funded policy as the act cared for the nation's most medically fragile. Certainly, it had the dual intention of drawing Americans older than sixty-five years of age out of the labor market so that younger Americans could raise families on those wages. But infant and maternal medical care were also part of the act, with money set aside for "medical, nursing, and welfare groups and organizations," especially in rural areas. Finally, the act and other federal programs required state governments to match federal dollars, forcing many to fund public health programs at higher levels.[29] Historian Edward Beardsley found that before the funding was available, of the 4,000 American counties, no more than 600 of them had full-time public health departments. After the act passed, that number was 1,371. Georgia, which had had few public health departments before 1933, now had 55 county public health programs, in 169 counties. Infant and maternal health also received a substantial increase in funding. The Children's Bureau had about $1 million a year to spend before 1935; with the act's passage, it had $14.6 million per year to fund well-baby clinics and prenatal care.[30]

Pensioners needed proof of their birthdates, a problem for those born before birth certificates were issued. Minnie Stonestreet, for example, had to rely on her mother's word for her birthdate. Others turned to family Bibles for proof. "Well, I'm trained to talk to government people. Lots of white ladies have called and they asked me everything about my life and that of the family. I know it by heart now. I even sent home and got a record of the families birth dates. I have them in my Bible," Patience Flucher, a Lakeland, Florida, native told an FWP interviewer in February 1939. What had been a sacred date to be memorialized in Bibles now came to have political and economic implications.[31]

The Third New Deal

The Third New Deal, a sort of last gasp coming in 1937, responded specifically to labor strikes that had dogged the administration throughout the decade. In 1937, Roosevelt began cutting social programs, causing what historians now call the Roosevelt Recession, a steep increase in unemployment rates and a sign that the New Deal's economic reformation was not complete. As this occurred, the New Deal's focus shifted more firmly to the South, catalyzed by social scientists who published numerous books on the South's poverty. Social scientists were probably motivated by Fisk University sociologist Charles Johnson, who published multiple books on southern Black life, including *In the Shadow of the Plantation* (1934). The wave of research that followed Johnson included social demographer Hagood's *Mothers of the South* (1939); anthropologist Hortense Powdermaker's *After Freedom* (1939); and psychologist John Dollard's *Caste and Class in a Southern Town* (1937). The studies utilized social science techniques like gathering statistical data, participant observation and ethnography, and psychological analysis to assess the reality of southern poverty.[32] Powdermaker, provided an entrée by Johnson into Indianola, Mississippi's Black society, used her outsider status to examine the town's rigid racial hierarchy. She described society through the eyes of her Black respondents rather than from the white elite and discerned a new response to the federal government. "For some Negroes," she wrote, "the government has taken over the responsibility of being 'good white folks,' meaning that the government has become the paternalistic arm that white people used to fulfill and that [B]lacks saw as their right under a system that kept them exploited." That change was a generational one, however, as younger Black Indianolans desired more immediate change and saw the federal government as a mechanism to achieve those changes.[33]

The clearest links between health and economic problems ultimately came from reports generated by the federal government itself. Roosevelt turned to noted academics, governors, and others to proffer suggestions for southern improvement, a report that was entitled, *Report on Economic Conditions of the South*. Stating in the introduction that "the South presents . . . now the No. 1 economic problem, the nation's, not merely the South's," Roosevelt determined that regional uplift would uplift the nation as a whole, elevating southern wellness to a national concern rather than just a regional one. Certainly, the Social Security Act and other New Deal programs had done the same. But this new focus allowed the federal government to "explore southern realities while bypassing its racial conundrums," providing an investment in the region past any nominal end of the New Deal, albeit within its racial system.[34]

The report's authors were all white and, with one exception, male. All policy experts working with the New Deal, they gathered in Alabaman Virginia Foster Durr's living room in Montgomery and included her husband, Clifford; Memphis native and SEC counsel, Abe Fortas; Congressman Lister Hill, a neighbor who later sponsored the Hill-Burton Act (1946)[35]; and other white southern New Dealers. The only woman was a scion of Virginia society, Lucy Randolph Mason, described by Durr as "a pretty, dainty, white-haired Virginia lady who wore glasses."[36] "Miss Lucy" used a polite southern lady's demeanor to hide a decidedly radical agenda, including rectifying women's lot by working with the Congress of Industrial Organizations (the CIO) by becoming its representative in Atlanta.[37]

The report's authors identified a paradox that existed at the South's core: "blessed by Nature with immense wealth, its people as a whole are the poorest in the country." The authors reflected new thinking about climate. It was as healthy as anywhere else, particularly after nearly five years of the TVA, CCC, and the WPA; however, land could not support a healthy society, more focused on adversity and sorrow than on love and joy. In some sections like the one called "Health" (which notes death rates three times in the first two paragraphs), the authors proclaimed a "low income belt" existed that was also a "belt of sickness, misery and unnecessary death." Using data drawn from death certificates, they argued costs from deaths due to malaria alone cost the country nearly $40 million per year, according to the writers. With the economic basis obvious, the authors claimed that industrial hygiene commissions could address problems specific to some industries (for example, the high rates of pneumonia and tuberculosis suffered by miners) as well as solutions to problems created by capitalist actions (e.g., the deforestation of large forests, turning them into malarial swamps). Yet only seven southern states had industrial hygiene commissions, and then, only thanks to new Society Security Act funds. These industrial areas had to be addressed (the report suggested spending $100,000), but only a deep-seeded, systematic attack costing millions could really address the problem.[38]

Mortality Rates

While not clear exactly why, by the late 1930s, death rates overall began to drop. Certainly, the previous thirty years of work had had some effect, with newspapers announcing lower death rates as early as 1934. "Birth and Death Rates Show Drop," one clipping from North Carolina stated, even as it tempered the good news with the increase in deaths from car accidents and deaths from tuberculosis. Memphis, Tennessee, newspapers later proclaimed that the "Health of the City Better; Death Rate Declines."[39] Mortality rates in general, the *Negro Year Book* said, had dropped substantially by 1944, with Black women gaining 23.95 years and Black men gaining 22.75 years since 1900. Now, a Black man could expect to live to 55.30 years and a Black woman to 58.99 years. The *Negro Year Book* also announced that infant and maternal mortality rates had declined substantially since 1930, although Black mortality rates remained higher than white ones. The Southern Baptist Convention (SBC) noted the decline, too, claiming that "Death marches on; But at a Slower Pace."[40] These lower mortality rates were later affirmed in 2001 by economists whose demographic data showed a real decline in infant mortality, especially among Black children.[41]

Public announcements were meaningless without evidence from the main place deceased bodies appeared, funeral ledgers. Ledgers confirm that there was a substantial lowering of infant mortality rates, especially when it came to stillbirths and deaths of children under one month old. The National Funeral Home ledger, for example, shows that its share of business from burying white children dropped from a third of its business and more from 1935 to 1939 to 11 percent in 1940 and 6 percent in 1943, even as the funeral home increased the number of funerals it conducted (see Table 1).

Other studies affirmed declines of specific southern scourges. Pellagra rates, for example, plummeted as the Farm Security Agency (FSA) took up Joseph Goldberger's mantra. Goldberger's experiments on nutrition, economics, and good health became FSA policy as it combatted farm tenancy in the South. Malaria rates also declined substantially, making it virtually disappear in places like South Carolina.[42]

In many ways, long-standing trends, like the expansion of Death Registration Areas, came to fruition, aiding the government's ability to count the dead. By 1933, for example, all states were finally included in the registration area,

Table 1. Child Burials, 1935–1945, National Funeral Home, Memphis, Tennessee.

Years Date Range	1935 2/22/1935 to 2/22/1936	1937 2/23/1937 to 2/22/1938	1938 2/23/1938 to 2/22/1939	1939 2/23/1939 to 2/22/1940	1940 2/23/1940 to 2/22/1941	1943 2/23/1943 to 2/22/1944	1945 2/23/1945 to 2/22/1946
No. of Burials (total number)	199	161	177	170	183	284	288
No. of Child Burials, aged 5 years, 11 months and less	37	36	37	31	14	17	37
No. of Child Burials, Less than One Month Old	26	24	28	22	7	1	21
Percentage of all child burials to total burials	32%	37%	37%	31%	11%	6%	20%

allowing statisticians to thoroughly pinpoint specific rates and causes of death and to identify real rates of mortality decline. Nationally, the United States' mortality rates dropped from 13.0 per 1,000 in 1920 to 10.6 per 1,000 by 1938. Regionally, however, the results were mixed. Alabama, Tennessee, and North Carolina showed some declines in their mortality rates. Alabama's mortality rate fell from 11.6 per 1,000 in 1925 (it was not included in the registration area until then) to 10.2 per 1,000 in 1938; Tennessee's fell from 12.1 to 10.1; and North Carolina's dropped from 12.6 per 1,000 in 1920 to 9.6 per 1,000 by 1938. Other states manifested persistently high death rates, at least until 1938, for example, Georgia's, Louisiana's, Mississippi's, and Florida's rates remained nearly steady. Moreover, the New Deal avoided legislating against violent deaths, like lynching, in order to keep white legislators happy and the money flowing.[43]

Living Past Three Score and Ten

Amidst these changes, an elite few wondered if southerners were going against God's word when so many now lived past his or her three score and ten. One Richmond, Virginia, editorial write in 1936 noted three people in their nineties had died that week and, as the editorial writer noted,

> The co-incidence emphasizes the modern tendency of human life to exceed the Scriptural bound of three score and ten, or perhaps by reason of strength, four score. Modern sanitation and other methods of disease prevention, coupled with modern curatives, are prolonging human existence. There are, indeed, many

> nonagenerarians [*sic*] among us, and a man or woman who is seventy cannot properly be designated as aged. All indications are that the span will lengthen—that in another generation those who have lived beyond the century mark will not be rare as they are today. Today's child may entertain reasonable hope of attaining the five-score mark. This thought impels wonder as to whether those who live through the next century will behold as many wonders as have those who die at ninety today.

For the editorial writer, the worry of living past the biblically allotted life span was tempered by the writer's belief that those who died in their nineties were upstanding citizens who "deserved" to live longer, in this case, Benajah [*sic*] T. Davis, who died at age ninety-three and who had taken up arms in the Civil War for the South. If those considered worthy in a white southern society lived longer, so be it.[44]

But Black theologians disagreed, arguing that the increase in life expectancy provided a fuller discovery of God's natural world which was applicable to all. The *National Baptist Voice* quoted geographer William Morris Davis on its editorial pages: "Reverent science is much concerned with making our life on earth as good, as unselfish, and as helpful to others as possible." Reverent science—meaning a science that was not divorced from the Bible but an intimate part of its promise—was not antithetical to God, but a full exploration of the world that God had created. Editorials argued that Moses was the "Father of Preventive Medicine," that Christ was a "Good Family Physician," and that the ministry of medicine "is more than a great profession; it is a sacred calling."[45] Living longer lives then was biblically ordained.

On the eve of World War II, babies did not die as easily and many southerners began to enjoy a longer lifespan than had been thought possible even ten years before. Older traditions had given way to new ones as Joy and Love replaced Sorrow and Adversity. The Second New Deal built a centralized healthcare infrastructure while creating a cultural infrastructure that defined older death care as odd, different, and certainly premodern. The Third New Deal suggested that federal intervention in the South would not cease with the end of the New Deal. But the past still continued to haunt some who recognized good health as a valuable commodity. South Carolinian Mary Jordan's father wrote to her, "Take care of your-self no matter what happens, for your and Nathans [husband] health is worth more to you than any-thing else."[46] It was within this context that a new kind of mass death experience emerged, young men and women of military age now fighting a world war and, perhaps, dying in it.

PART FIVE

Dying in World War II

The irony of providing a healthier life for southerners specifically and for Americans in general was the drafting of military-age men to die on distant battlefields. Had the New Deal extended life, assuring a vital populace, only to expend that vitality far away? The promise of extending life now conflicted firmly with a war that promised the death of exactly those people Progressives and the New Deal said might live—and in fact, were living—longer. World War II's unique nature contributed to this irony. It was the first war to fully utilize the airplane, which expanded where a battle might be fought and who might be bombed as a combatant. Moreover, the war in the South Pacific caused sunken ships to become watery cemeteries in areas where no reasonable effort could raise the ship. The significantly larger forces (sixteen million in World War II versus four million in World War I) as well as its length (almost four full years rather than a year) promised a higher death toll, with about 400,000 Americans eventually dying with 79,000 Missing In Action.

Honoring the dead guided the United States military as it repatriated Black and white World War II dead between 1947 and 1955. Death care itself was now a mix of the past and present, with military escorts accompanying the repatriated dead and bearing witness to those changes. Two southerners, Captain William J. Faulkner Jr. and First Lieutenant Harold Leazer, one Black, one white, provide us an intimate view of these issues before, during, and after the war.

11 Flying and Dying as Americans

Virginian Harold Leazer's last letter to his mother was a poignant reminder that while he was tired of war ("Really I'll admit that I've had enough of this life and I'm ready to come home"), he assured her that, "And, too Mother, we still remember our prayers."[1] The next day, on June 26, 1944, he took off from Italy, piloting his B-24 Liberator to bomb a ball bearing plant in Moosbierbaum, Austria. On Leazer's bomber, ten men took their positions at the controls—two Virginians, two New Yorkers, a Minnesotan, a Floridian, an Alabaman, a Georgian, and two Michiganites—flying as Americans united in a single purpose. On their return, other pilots saw Leazer's plane fall out of formation and crash, although some parachutes, "marshmallows," in military terms, did emerge as the plane tumbled down and exploded. For the next few months, his family lived anxiously, hoping he might be found in a German Prisoner-of-War (POW) camp, but on September 30, 1944, the adjutant general, Major General J. A. Ulio, confirmed that Harold had indeed died in the crash. The information about his nine crew members remained unclear, at least to the military. But the Leazers already knew what had happened. The ten families had been in constant contact with each other since the plane went down, and the Leazers already knew who had survived and who had not.[2]

Perhaps one of the P-51 Mustangs that guided Leazer's B-24 into his last battle was Captain William J. Faulkner Jr.'s plane. Nearly six months later, the Nashville native flew his P-51 Mustang over another bombing target on November 7, 1944, crashing near Griffen, Austria. One of the famed "Red Tails," or Tuskegee Airmen, "Billy" flew his single pilot plane with stellar success and heartbreaking loss. The Faulkners first received a telegram, alerting them that Billy was Missing in Action (MIA) in November 1944, and soon after, a letter from General Ulio arrived, telling them that their son had died on his 56th mission, similar to the one received by the Leazers with the same grim purpose.[3]

In a Hollywood movie, Faulkner would have been Leazer's escort on his last mission, attempting to save his crew from an ugly end, but in the real world of pilots and planes crashing over Austria in 1944, there is no way to know. What is clear is the United States military segregated Black pilots and white pilots in cockpits, but standardized the death experience, no matter their race or manner of death. Rather than a story exclusively about the South in World War II, this story then becomes more of an American story told through the eyes of southerners because the vast effort to inform and bury the dead applied an assembly line–style thinking to death that required treating everyone the same, at least as much as possible. But the deaths of young men challenged the basic assumptions of life extension as World War II reinvigorated an older marker of citizenship earned by dying in military service. This military citizenship ended up working well with the new health citizenship because it extended the health work, begun by the New Deal, in order to field a healthy fighting force.

Preparing for War

Once the Japanese bombed Pearl Harbor and the Nazis had declared war on the United States, some southerners, in a classic case of understatement, declared the coming war was "upsetting everything." Writing to his daughter in Greer, South Carolina, in January 1942, Mary Jordan's father foretold doom, that "times are going to get harder and harder, every-thing being taxed and living expenses going higher and higher, and I fear that every able boded [*sic*] men under 65 will be called into the Army, and that will include [family members] Nathan and Dick being married will have nothing to do with it, even Women will be called to service . . . And we just must win or be made slaves, under Hitler." His dark vision caused him to add, "I tell you this War is serious . . . every business is changing and people and factories and whole-salesmen are being out to the core."[4] The fears of a large death toll prompted Mary's sister to write, "Don't kid yourself, we are loosing [*sic*] plenty of men in this war and all are going to see battle before its over."[5]

There was some truth to these fears when it came to the special nature of World War II and the need to field a healthy military. Airplanes, tanks, aircraft carriers, and battleships brought the battle to any urban street, over obscure islands in the middle of the ocean, or into dense forests where few humans had access. American soldiers thus had to be physically ready to fight in these diverse conditions as good health became a strategic goal. The military also could not afford the debacle of World War I where 50 percent of the deaths came from illness. But it quickly found that the New Deal's health work had not gone far enough. The 1947 *Negro Year Book* reported that the "prevalence of physical defects among men of military age (18–37 years) . . . indicates that all too frequently good medical care has been lacking."[6]

Of the 17 million American men examined before being drafted, the military had to do substantial rehabilitative work among a significant number of them. The new recruits, the army found, were deficient in terms of eyesight, tooth health (army dentists fitted 2.5 million dentures), and literacy. Immunizations had to be updated, if any existed, blood pressure measured, and childhood illnesses documented.[7] James Beck, a white staff sergeant from Memphis who was examined at Fort Benning, Georgia, exemplifies the problems. Beck had suffered malaria, chicken pox, and measles as a child (as well as Dengue fever as a soldier); was out of date for his typhoid, typhus, and yellow fever immunizations; was missing four teeth; and was three and a half pounds underweight. Because he did not meet the military's strict height/weight requirements—he was 64 inches and 116 pounds in 1943—the doctors had to recommend a waiver for him so he could serve. Three years and a wealth of military meals later, he was 65 inches and 135 pounds. Historian David Kennedy argued that the "army improved the standard of living of many recruits. Not only did they receive proper medical attention, some for the first time in their lives, but at the garrison food ration of 4,300 calories per day, many ate better than they ever had before."[8]

In camps, as the military created a healthy force, it also had to account for the catastrophic effect of war machinery on military bodies, particularly from airplanes. The National Funeral Home in Memphis noted the catastrophic effect of plane crashes as dead soldiers were sent home from training camps. "Crushing injury of skull with extrusion of brain," read one lieutenant's entry after he was shipped home from Alamogordo, New Mexico.[9] Funeral directors took special care with bodies killed in training camps before shipping them home as their practice of "restorative arts," or the reconstruction of mutilated bodies, became military strategy. Frank Essex, whose father had the Stuttgart (Arkansas) Army Base's funeral contract, recalled his father's approach to a soldier's mutilated remains. Essex's father buried sixteen men killed in plane crashes and three others who committed suicide. Working in a system where southern families buried a complete body, but facing a reality that little remained of it after a plane crash, his father used clothing to recreate disintegrated bodies, even though the military required the caskets to be sealed shut. Essex thus tucked socks into pants where legs or feet no longer existed, and knotted ties around throats where little else remained. The ritual mattered, even if the body no longer lent itself well to it.[10]

A Modern Military Goes to War

The strong Confederate identities that white World War I soldiers carried into battle were noticeably absent in this war. In part, it was a purposeful military strategy that helped integrate white soldiers without regard to region or state (but with regard to race) onto B-24 fighters or troop ships. Begun during World War I, but really coming to fruition in World War II, the military created "stand alone" units, or units that existed even when the United States was not at war. The Big Red One (the 1st Infantry Division) in Manhattan, Kansas, and the 101st Airborne Division in Clarksville, Tennessee, were two units created during World War I that remained after it ended. Into these units the army mingled together soldiers from across the United States rather than placing soldiers from the same place into the same unit. That way, one place or region did not suffer from multiple deaths, as occurred during the Civil War where units tended to be mustered from the same towns and then sent to war. Now, the misery was spread geographically, so one hometown did not bear the exclusive burden of suffering.[11]

Once units were sent overseas, southerners were killed in all major battles of World War II. They died when the Japanese bombed Pearl Harbor; when Americans stormed Omaha Beach; and drowned in submarines and battleships struck by kamikaze fighters. They died in Japanese and German POW camps; fighting along the Siegfried Line; and at the Battle of the Bulge. Soldiers died before June 1944, to be sure, but the numbers increased substantially after D-Day as the United States and its allies began their march east toward Germany. Deaths also increased as America's island-hopping strategy in the South Pacific brought the military closer and closer to the Japanese mainland, with long, especially devastating, battles at Iwo Jima and Okinawa in spring 1945.[12]

As deaths increased, the military relied on World War I's rituals to acknowledge the loss, albeit on a vastly expanded scale. The family's reasonable questions—what happened to *my* soldier, how did *he* die?—were propaganda problems for the home front. The military engaged in domestic propaganda in its one-to-one correspondence with surviving families so that all Americans, not just southerners, maintained their support.

Paperwork and information came to the military's rescue as geographic and other informative details took the place of a body. The military inundated the Leazers, the Faulkners, and others with mail, first, notifying them that their sons were missing; then that they had died; and then where they were buried, along with other final details (insurance settlements, for example). Intriguingly, the Army used geography to replace the son who had died. "[Leazer's] B-24 (Liberator) crashed at Stossing, Austria, approximately ten miles east southeast of St. Polten (48 Degrees, 12' N—15 degrees 37' E). These records further state that Lieutenant Leazer was interred on 27 June 1944 in the Cemetery of Stossing," Brigadier General Leon Johnson wrote his family.[13] Six months later, the Faulkners received similar notifications from Johnson. The general wrote that Captain Faulkner had crashed "near Griffen (46 Degrees, 43' N, 14 Degrees, 43' East), Austria. This village is approximately twenty-one miles east northeast of Klagenfurt. These records also state that on 7 November 1944, your son's body was interred in the cemetery of Griffen."[14] The Navy did the same, providing the map coordinates when sons were buried at sea. Writing to Edward La Flamme's family, naval observers pointed to the exact spot on the globe where his body rested, "Burial Services conducted at sea from U.S.S. Lyman, Latitude 15 degrees, 33', No. Longitude 143 degrees 35' East, with full military honors."[15]

In some cases, information could not confidently pinpoint where a deceased soldier's body was. The military erred, according to its own documents, "on the side of caution. More than 17,000 men who died for their country in World War II now lie in graves officially marked "Unknown."[16] The lack of knowledge was a great source of anxiety for some families, for example, Virginian Asher Colburn Taylor's mother. "This is all that I know about overseas . . . When my boy was killed I got a letter telling me that they had buried him and had a burial service, and that he was a good man and a good soldier . . . I do not know how he was killed. They did not tell me how long he lived [*sic*]," she wrote.[17] No body caused some families to believe their son was not dead. Virginian Sue Foster Blakemore reported:

> Even though the War Dept. has officially reported my son lost his life in the Southwest Pacific Area, I have never, and do not now, believe he is not living. There was never any tangible proof of death of the men on his plane. No trace whatsoever has been found of the plane or its passengers. I have met the brother of one of the men on this plane who said goodbye to them the morning they left New Guinea and he also believes they are alive.

Information in this case simply was not enough.[18]

While the military attempted to confirm a death and pinpoint precise details, battlefield chaos made their efforts less than perfect. South Carolinian Nathan Jordan Jr. and North Carolinian William McFadyen Jr. were both listed as MIA, with the military declaring both dead in 1946. McFadyen's plane crashed near New Guinea on November 27, 1942, as he was bombed by the Japanese and as he dodged large thunderheads. For his family, at least there was a date. The Jordans did not have a date for their son's death or last known action until after the war ended. Nathan Jordan Jr.'s last letter told his parents on August 11, 1944, that he had been assigned to a heavy weapons unit, had been promoted to staff sergeant, and was in charge of a machine gun squad in France.[19] General J. A. Ulio telegraphed the Jordans on August 30, 1944, that Nathan had gone missing as of August 14, 1944, but the military could not look for his body until war's end. In the meantime, his mother kept writing to him as if he was alive, "We haven't gotten any more mail from you since you wrote us on the 11th. Hope I have a letter from you when I return home."[20] Other friends believed that Nathan had "always been lucky and I believe he will come thru this. He has a wonderful mind."[21] But his brother, Richard, was more matter of fact:

> Have you all not heard anything yet about Jr.? Surely we should hear something before long. The way I see things now, I have very little doubt of Jr. being alive. He has been missen too long now. This missen in action doesn't mean a thing about him being alive (more than likely dead). I hate to write you this, but I have already seen too much.[22]

After the war was over, the military found him, deceased and buried temporarily in an American cemetery, and informed the family of his final disposition in January 1948. He had been seriously wounded just south of Cherbourg and had been left when the platoon leader was forced to advance with his unit. Once found, he was reburied in the Brittany American Cemetery in Montjoie-Saint-Martin, France.[23]

Confirmed Deaths and Notifications

Once a death was confirmed, the military contacted each soldier's family to resolve three final issues: the return of personal effects like letters and clothing; the payout of final salaries owed by the government; and the payment of insurance to the dead soldier's next of kin. All of the deceased soldiers in this study have the exact same documents regarding these three issues. The Office of Special Settlement Accounts contacted the Jordans to pay them the six months Death Gratuity Pay ($473.66) owed Nathan Jr., while the Veterans Administration wrote to detail the payment of his life insurance to his mother, Mary, who would receive payments over 199 months. To McFadyen's family, the Army Effects Bureau sent an inventory of his clothing including a pair of sweatpants and four pairs of khaki trousers, after his B-25 bomber disappeared. Once the family filled out official paperwork, the items were sent home from the bureau in Kansas City. The Leazers received Harold's wallet, his address book, his social security card, and other documents that he left behind when he took off in his B-24 bomber, items that became the core of his Virginia Museum of History and Culture collection.[24]

Then, families announced the deaths in local newspapers, becoming fodder for local politicians. Edward H. "Boss" Crump, who ran Tennessee's political machine from Memphis, had a secretary scour local newspapers for the sad announcements of soldiers missing or killed in action, and then used his own loss, namely the death of his son in an airplane crash in 1939, to write to surviving kin. Letters were almost exactly the same, except for different names, for example, "Dear Mrs. Mathis: My heart goes out to you in the tragic loss of your husband. The fact that he died a hero's death in the gigantic struggle for world freedom is a consoling thought, but I know it cannot assuage the poignant grief and terrible loss you feel. I want you to know how deeply I sympathize with you and yours. Only those who themselves have experienced the loss of loved ones can plumb the depths of sorrow that is yours." Dozens of letters mimicked this form letter, although in some cases a donation was made to a local charity.[25]

Flying and Dying Overseas: Harold Leazer

William Faulkner Jr. and Harold Leazer were part of a modernized military force that flew from Italy to bomb targets over Germany, Austria, and other parts of Central and Eastern Europe, beginning in 1943. The B-24 was the work horse of the war, able to fly longer range bombing runs than its predecessor, the B-17 bomber. But if, as David Kennedy argues, the military was "the mother and father of all melting pots," meaning the military intermingled soldiers without regard to hometown, the B-24 bomber was where that melting pot met, ten men at a time.[26] The relationships built on those planes became the defining experience for this generation of men. But in creating that melting pot, white southerners' belief in their racial superiority guided military hands when assigning personnel. Ten white men of various ethnic backgrounds flew them; Black southerners piloted the single-pilot P-51 Mustangs (no integration here) to keep white southerners back home committed to the war.

The experiences of the Faulkner and Leazer families, then, exemplify both the melting pot and the color line as the military managed them with real tension when heroic deaths occurred. The older of the two men, Harold Leazer was born in November 1916, in Kannapolis, North Carolina, and later moved to Remington, Virginia. He attended college for two years before becoming a well driller. He joined the Army Air Corps in February 1942, starting as an engineer and later transferring to pilot training in September 1942. He spent most of 1943 and early 1944 working as a flight trainer before shipping out to Italy in May 1944. Serving with the 15th Air Force, Harold completed seventeen missions, and in fact, had been shot down over the Adriatic Sea on June 11, 1944. The crew was rescued within an hour. A few weeks later, on June 26, 1944, his crew set off for a bombing run over Moosbierbaum, Austria, and was shot down.[27]

Like the Jordans and the McFadyens, the first evidence of a death typically came from the lack of mail rather than the military's own paperwork. Harold wrote to his parents in Virginia; his brother serving with the D-Day invasion forces in France; and his girlfriend, Claire Weir, in Texas at least every two to three days. He wrote his mother, for example, on Sunday, June 11, 1944, that "it's just another day as far as work is concerned. However, I still remember what the Sabbath stands for and I am thankful for that."[28] When the mail stopped, his family and girlfriend suspected something was wrong. His brother, Leon, serving in England, wrote, "I'll really appreciate it when he [Harold] starts writing again."[29]

Then, the military's processes kicked in, initially determining that Harold and his crew were MIA, and informing the Leazers via telegram. Of the many documents his family saved and donated to the archives, this telegram is noticeably absent. Letters from Ulio followed, describing in greater detail whatever declassified information he had, making it possible, some said, to live "from rumor to rumor," not knowing what was true and what was not.[30] New provisions, which seemed to have been passed in 1944, allowed the Quartermaster Corps to do the next best thing. It sent the names of the other missing crewmen and their next of kins' addresses so the families could be in contact with each other. They became fonts of information for each other that the military simply did not have the labor for. This exposed the Leazers to strangers who shared a common purpose (finding their sons), the families of the other nine soldiers becoming a sort of support group and information bastion, albeit via letters.[31]

Table 2 lists the soldiers who were on the plane with Harold with their hometowns and their next-of-kin. The * denotes which personnel died, either in the crash or once the soldier parachuted to the ground.

The first inkling this relationship would emerge came from John Morgan's mother, Helen, who wrote Mrs. Leazer from Traverse City, Michigan, in July 1944. "As we are all going through the same string of anxiety regarding our boys, I believe it would be a good idea for us all to keep in touch with each other," she wrote.[32] "Dear Mrs. Leazer," Freda Dyson wrote July 31, 1944, "Your son was the pilot on the ship my son was a bombardier on . . . We are hoping all the

Table 2. Soldiers on B-24 Plane Identification #42-50312

Name	Rank	Plane Duties	Next of Kin	Next-of-Kin's address
Oliver Volk*	2nd Lt.	Navigator	Mother	Houston, MS
Frederick Dyson*	2nd Lt.	Bombardier	Mother	Sanford, FL
John Morgan*	2nd Lt.	Co-Pilot	Mother	Traverse City, MI
Harold Leazer*	2nd Lt.	Pilot	Father	Remington, VA
Donald Johnson	T. Sgt.	Radio Operator	Father	Minneapolis, MN
Mario Damiani*	S. Sgt.	Engineer	Brother-in-law	New York, NY
Arthur Kremer	S. Sgt.	Waist Gunner	Brother	South Ozone Park, NY
Robert King*	S. Sgt.	Waist Gunner	Mother	Lawrenceville, GA
Charles Heinzel	S. Sgt.	Ball Turret	Mother	Rogers City, Michigan
Jennings Titus	Sgt.	Tail Gunner	Mother	Stratford, NJ and Richmond, VA

boys got out safely and are either prisoners of war or with the underground. If you hear anything about your son that can be told will you please let us know and we will do the same."[33] Jennings Titus's mother wrote several days later, telling Mrs. Leazer that "we received a telegram that Jennings is a prisoner of the German Government." She added, "I feel sure that you received the same message and I can well imagine how happy and relieved you are. We are going to try and check thru the Red Cross here and hope that before long we can be writing to the boys . . . If I do receive any more news soon I will write you."[34] Charles Heinzel's parents telegrammed from Michigan to let the Leazers know that Charles, too, was a German prisoner, and that they, too, hoped the Leazers had received the same news.[35]

This turned out to be an effective process even as it elicited bad news. In this case, four families of the ten reported to the other six that their sons had been captured and imprisoned in German POW camps, where they remained until the end of the war (the International Red Cross provided the information). By September 30, 1944, the Leazers received official confirmation that Harold had died because his body, with dog tags still attached, had been found; Oliver Volk's family received this same information. Four others, Frederick Dyson, John C. Morgan, Mario Damiani, and Robert L. King, continued to be MIA because their bodies could not be officially identified due to the catastrophic plane crash (the military waited one year and a day to declare an unidentified soldier dead).[36]

Once the death was confirmed, the relationship did not end. Bonded through a plane crash thousands of miles away, families celebrated when some were discovered to be alive and grieved when others were found dead. Each family also wrote to bolster sagging spirits when information was delayed. The Heinzils wrote Mrs. Leazer that they were sorry no news about Harold had been received. Brooklyn-based Italo Damiani, Mario's brother, wrote the Leazers that, "Mrs. Morgan in her last letter to me [*sic*], seemed as though she was becoming discouraged. I tried to cheer her up a little by writing an encourageing [*sic*] letter. We sure admire you for the way you took the news."[37] Don Johnson's mother also wrote to Mrs. Leazer in October 1944, after the official confirmation of Harold's death had been made, sharing good news from Jennings Titus's family as well.[38]

Gracious people, they rejoiced over good news and grieved over losses. "I am so happy to write you this letter," Damiani wrote the Leazers, even as his brother remained missing and later was confirmed dead, "just to let you know that the Kremer boy has also been found."[39] At other times, however, they purposely withheld information to avoid upsetting the others. Damiani wrote the Leazers to say his brother had been mistakenly listed as wounded on a casualty list, "I had only written to Mrs. Morgan about this, but after I had, I was sorry. I thought it would be best if I withheld this news from you people, until I had

Figure 11.1. Families shared news and photos of missing soldiers. This is the photo Jennings Titus's sister shared with the other families on board Harold Leazer's B-24. Leazer is fifth from the left. Courtesy of the Virginia Historical Society.

received word from Washington, confirming."[40] Families also shared keepsakes. The crew had had a photo taken in Cuba, for example, and Beryl Titus, Jennings's sister, made sure the families all had a copy.[41]

The families used their own personal networks to find out more information about the missing flight crew, sharing what they found. Damiani had connections with the American Red Cross (ARC) and promised to pursue them. Harold's girlfriend lived near the Texas airfield he had trained at and she sent letters to various soldiers she knew stationed in Italy, who did their own investigations. Claire's letter, quoting word for word an unnamed soldier (most likely because he shared sensitive military information), gave the family some real information about the plane's demise. Her letter said:

> This is what he wrote. "I received your letter a few days ago, was very sorry to hear that Harold went down . . . His field is right next to mine, his group and mine fly the same missions. Yesterday, I went over and talked to his Commanding Officer and from all reports it looks very bad. Here it is: The raid was to Blechhammer, Germany. The target was an oil refinery, which was the priority target in Germany at the time, but after the raid there was not a refinery there. Harold's plane was

hit by flak and set afire, there were only two chutes seen to leave the plane before it hit the ground and exploded. I was on the same raid but went over target 10 minutes before Harold's group."[42]

The relationships continued after the war ended. The Kremers announced their son's release from his prison camp, and Freda Dyson and Italo Damiani continued to update the Leazers on their sons' status. They also exchanged Christmas cards at Christmas time. Moreover, the surviving soldiers felt that intimate bond well after the war and embraced their deceased friends' families as their own. This was literal, it seems, because after the war, Don Johnson, who spent the war in a POW camp, sent Mother's Day cards to Harold Leazer's mother well into the 1950s. In claiming those new familial boundaries, they also applied their own regionally and ethnically specific death care rituals. The Damianis, for example, enrolled Harold in the Society of the Little Flower, a Carmelite mission, and in honor of that, a Catholic mass was said for him as well as a series of novenas. The director then sent an enrollment card and a photo of the "Little Flower" to the Leazers.[43]

The warm relations between the families did not account for the significant tensions on Leazer's B-24, however. Tail gunner Jennings Titus was interviewed in 1984, possibly by Harold's younger sister, and described a tense atmosphere on the plane. Class differences manifested themselves as soldiers made friends with those who seemed to be like them. Johnson and Titus became good friends because, according to Titus, they were more of the "same class." The easy racism of the time caused crew members to refer to Mario Damiani as a "guinea," a derogatory term for Italian Americans, another problem. "Back then, that's what you called them," Titus said. Leazer told the crew to stop, and then told Damiani he was going to be replaced. War weariness and fear was another problem among the crew. Georgian Robert King, described by Titus as speaking like a redneck, came to the plane with alcohol on his breath and wearing two flak jackets at times, one on his head and the other on his body. Leazer also told him he would be replaced. In both cases, however, there was no time to replace them before that last fatal flight.[44]

Flying and Dying Overseas: William J. Faulkner Jr.

The death experiences for Black families were different because they were the outcome of segregating Black pilots. The single-pilot P-51 Mustangs allowed the military to integrate its forces without actually integrating them, meaning the Tuskegee Airmen could fly those planes out in front of the B-24s without actually sitting in a cockpit with a white soldier. Because of this, the Faulkners lived without the support network that the B-24s automatically set up. A national community gathered instead, to support the family as they grieved Faulkner's death, one that willingly crossed racial lines when they recognized Faulkner's heroism.

William Faulkner Jr. came from a more elite background than Leazer's solid middle-class upbringing. Born on August 11, 1918, "Billy" was the son of Fisk University's Dean of Men and Dean of Religion. Reverend William J. Faulkner Sr. and his wife, Elizabeth, were both active in interracial reform circles nationally, meaning groups of Black and white ministers (as well as others) worked cooperatively across the color line against racial segregation. Captain Faulkner attended Morehouse College, and then moved to Los Angeles, where he worked for Lockheed Vega Aircraft in 1941. In August 1942, he enlisted with the Tuskegee Airmen, the famed "Red Tails" for their P-51 Mustangs with tails painted red, that was part of the 332nd Fighter Group. Just after graduation, he married Martha Owens.[45]

The Red Tails' job, once in Italy, was to guard the cumbersome B-24 airplanes as they bombed strategic sites. The P-51 Mustang, a faster, nimbler plane than its German counterpart, could protect bomber streams much more effectively, and in fact forced the German Luftwaffe to change its strategy in 1943 when the first P-51s were introduced. The Red Tails flew, knowing they had something to prove. Their commanding officer, Benjamin O. Davis Jr., told them, "Don't come back if you lose a bomber," giving the Red Tails a sense that their good work had more than strategic purpose; it also had racial purpose as they proved they could withstand the rigors of war in profoundly heroic ways. Certainly, Captain Faulkner did, with his fifty-six missions.[46]

In its quest for standardized death notifications, the military treated Billy's family similarly to Harold's family, albeit with some exceptions due to the different planes they flew and the different circumstances of their deaths. After his plane crashed on November 7, 1944, in Griffen, Austria, a telegram informing Billy's family that he was MIA came quickly to his wife, who then informed her in-laws. In the time between reporting him as missing and reporting his death (confirmed eventually by the International Red Cross), the military treated his family with the same news and form letters that Harold's family received.[47]

Military paperwork elicited a unique response from the Faulkners, however. Reverend Faulkner, it seems, ignored the form letters sent to him, and wrote personally to the generals to thank them. He wrote Major General J. A. Ulio, thanking him for the kind letter "in which you spoke so comfortingly of our son who was missing in action at that time."[48] Later, Ulio received a thank you note from the Faulkners for his soldiers' good care of the family when they presented Billy's medals to his parents. Ulio wrote back, hinting at the cost of sending out those thousands of utilitarian notifications. "May I again express my thanks for your letter," the general wrote, "which is an encouragement to me in the performance of my sad duties. It is gratifying to know that my efforts have brought some measure of comfort to you in your bereavement."[49]

Letters from the military were not the only ones the Faulkners received. The fluidity and flexibility of condolence literature meant a note of comfort could be written to the family whose soldier was MIA or a POW; to families whose soldiers were confirmed Killed In Action (KIA); and to the family who awaited their deceased soldier after the war was over. The dominant themes in the letters shifted as the soldier's status shifted, although the ironies of a young man dying in a life-extension world were not lost on letter writers. Southerners had worked hard for years to make some deaths unthinkable (of children and young people, for example) and now, a youthful death was one they had to live with once again. "The sacrifice of those we thought of as the future is one of its [the war's] tolls. Destruction of the peace of mind of uncounted thousands is another," a friend wrote Reverend Faulkner.[50]

Condolence literature's ability to bend and flex with the moment caused letters to bend and flex as more information arrived from the military. While Billy was MIA, for example, letters carried a sense of hope that he would be found. Willie Drake wrote she prayed "for strength and faith to believe, to know, that God can and will be merciful to our Boy even in foreign prisons."[51] "I hope that it was a false alarm, and that you have had reassuring reports since. If it is true then I would have you and Mrs. Faulkner know that my heart is bleeding with yours and that I'm bearing your sorrow with you," Fred Brownlee, a New Yorker, wrote Reverend Faulkner.[52] Others reminded the Faulkners that the news was not firm yet. "So many sons reported missing have returned," a friend told them.[53] Perhaps, Billy, too, would be found alive and well in a POW camp. Hoping against hope, one family member sent Billy a Christmas card (and later reported to the Faulkners that she had done so) because she truly believed he was alive.[54]

Others avoided some common rituals—sending a telegram in sympathy, for example—because what was once a message of comfort could now be bad news from the military. The desire to reach out immediately, albeit from a distance, was now quashed out of sympathy for the fear it might inspire. "I wanted to call or wire you, but was afraid knowing how you must feel and that it might upset you to get a wire. I do hope he is just missing in action. I do hope as much that he is not fatally injured. It certainly brings this terrible thing close to our hearts," Faulkner friend John Cork wrote.[55] Others continued to uphold other rituals like avoiding confronting personal, private grief by calling on the phone. "I won't disturb you by calling, but I wanted you to know that I'm thinking of you and hoping and praying with you that he will be all right," a Nashville friend wrote.[56]

The fear of a missing son was one many writers shared because they had family serving overseas, too. Willie Drake noted she had three nephews as well as friends serving overseas and she *understood* (emphasis hers) how terrifying the experience was. Others wrote in trepidation that their own sons might end up in the same situation. In fact, condolence literature during World War II is an obvious juxtaposition of "I'm sorry your son died/was missing," and "my sons, grandsons, family members are there, too, and I fear this will happen to them, too." Mrs. Margaret Barren wrote to Mrs. Faulkner that she had "a boy, too, who is ready to go, so you know how we feel. Be brave, my dear! Be strong! Remember God always knows best."[57] James Lightbourn noted his son's service in Africa and Italy and a son-in-law's service in an airborne division in Europe. "The same tragic news that has come to you may come to us," Lightbourn wrote.[58]

As the news shifted from MIA to KIA, the fear of losing a loved one became more than just that family member's death. An extended war like World War II meant what was visited upon one family could be, and was, visited upon many, many others. Making those young deaths noble thus made them understandable. "His record of service and his meritorious achievement will live on and inspire others," one friend wrote the Faulkners.[59] Another friend, Margaret McCulloh, sent a handwritten poem to them, noting the unique sadness of their son's death:

> We will not let him die. His life shall live
> To fight a thousand battles year by year
> For all the values that he holds most dear.
> We too have lives, and these [illegible] we give
> We will not let him die. He still shall fight.
> The entrenched evil, the insidious wrong.
> His courage sings through many a youth its song
> Of brave defiance in the face of might.[60]

McCulloh reminded Faulkner's parents that they would be "glad in the nobler world his gift has won, Blest in the world, he gave himself to give."[61] Not all parents were so sanguine, as poetry published in Black newspapers questioned the necessity of soldier deaths. "A mother to her son/Was it for this I brought you in the world/A few short years ago? That I should suffer all this pain and anguish/ That only mothers know," written by May Bennett Spottwood and published by Mrs. Lula Fennie in memory of her son, PFC Joe Childs, killed in action in April 1944.[62]

More than noble, however, young men's deaths were sacred ones that brought the war into one's front room or church pulpit. Ruth Harper learned of Billy's death when her husband read aloud the news from their local paper. "The war never came quite so close to home as it did to me today," Harper reported. But the news became sacred and even more personal once the announcements went to church. Harper reported that her husband "took the notice to church and Rev. Ledbetter read it from the pulpit weaving it very beautifully into the sermon."[63]

Yet a note of uncertainty and helplessness entered condolence letters. How could friends comfort a family experiencing such a contradictory loss, of a young man dead when he was supposed to live a long and fruitful life? Their deaths were "tragic," not an example of God's divine will to be accepted without question. "In times like these one hardly knows what to say that may help or comfort, and there seems to be little that can be done," Bertram and Pansy Doyle wrote the Faulkners.[64] The deep sense of ambivalence (why did such a fine young man die?), and of helplessness (I am unable to comfort you about something I simply do not understand) caused some letter writers to simply avoid writing. Thelma Allison wrote her good friend, Elizabeth Faulkner,

> I've put off writing this letter just as long as I can. I simply can't let you go on thinking that I haven't been with you from the very first minute of your grief. I've just prodded myself with trying to think of something comforting to say to the best friend I have in this world. There is just nothing to say my darling. I can only pray earnestly and continually for you.[65]

One family simply noted, "There is sadness everywhere and it seems that the year 1945 will be full of sorrow."[66]

Older references to scripture—such as "In my father's house are many mansions"—still showed up in letters, but new references did, too, ones that did not promise an easy road. Some rejoiced that Heaven was just "as near from Austria . . . as it is from Nashville. Since you have a heroic son up there, it will seem more like home when you arrive," the pastor of First Baptist Church, East Nashville, wrote the Faulkners.[67] But with the shifts in death care in the 1920s that focused more on grieving, the Faulkner's earthly grief had to be acknowledged and biblically sanctioned. John 1:5 (KJV: "and the light shineth in darkness") and the 23rd Psalm (KJV: "The Lord is My Shepherd") became common scripture quotes that would guide the grieving through the coming years. The Reverend Charles Dinkins wrote to the Faulkners, "The Light is still shining in the darkness, for the darkness can never put it out."[68] Others hinted at the 23rd Psalm, saying "in a sense each of us must walk through this valley of deep shadows alone."[69]

The main response condolence writers deemed necessary was courage. In an era when young men marshaled courage to fly planes or invade beaches, courage was the core value required of families. Grief, then, was patriotic, not melodramatic and not melancholy. Cards and notes urged the Faulkners and others to be courageous, and, by extension, patriotic. "Be of good courage," Miss Henri Young wrote, "God in His own time will give us understanding."[70] Grief, especially obvious grief, could be used for the enemy's purposes. One unnamed correspondent to Nashvillian Ben Clay Espey's family claimed, "Our grief is their victory."[71] Writing to Mrs. Leazer once Harold had been confirmed dead, his brother wrote, "I know too that he wouldn't want us to take his death hard and I am doing my best to make it that way. As you know this is the first time we have ever had to undertake anything like this but I am sure we can manage. We are not as bad off as we think we are."[72]

In letters of condolence, young men's deaths were sacrifices to the altar of democracy and necessary losses, but Black and white writers defined sacrifice differently. For white southern soldiers, their deaths were a sacrifice to more generalized democratic ideals. South Carolinian Olin Dorn's death was the "supreme sacrifice that we may continue to enjoy the blessings of democratic freedom," Myrtle and Garris Thompson wrote the Dorns.[73] But for Black southerners, those democratic values, denied them in their everyday lives, meant something vastly different. When Billy Faulkner died, his death became a "challenge to all, who, in giving vent to their racial prejudice, belittle the worth and capabilities of Negroes in the Armed Services. It is sure the young flyer went to his death believing implicitly that his country will fittingly honor Negro boys who fight and die on battlefields by being wholly fair and honorable in its dealings with the race, with whom these heroic dead are identified," one obituary noted.[74]

Other Black organizations noted Billy's death's meaning for racial politics in the United States. His fraternity said his death was important because he had "fought bravely and brilliantly for the rights of his people and for the world peace which would ultimately mean so much to all mankind. His life and achievements, despite handicaps of race which he may have encountered, stand out as a shining example of what the youth of the race can hope to attain through preparation and hard work. May God enable us to perpetuate his ideals in our own services to humanity."[75] Perhaps the most poignant reminders came from other Black families who had also lost sons. Suffering their own loss, Mr. and Mrs. R. A. Hundley wrote that they understood that the Faulkners, too, had "laid a costly sacrifice upon the altar of Freedom and while the grief is singularly your own, to do with as best you can, the loss is not yours along; it is all America's loss; it is mine, it is my next door neighbor's. May I, nor any free American, never prove unworthy of the great gift of life itself that your son had given. Perhaps, if we do not live in vain, he will not have died in vain."[76]

In what was not a breach of etiquette, particularly between southerners of similar class status by World War II, elite white southerners wrote elite Black southerners in recognition that they shared something unique: pride over soldierly accomplishment and, later, grief over their noble deaths. Nashville's mayor, Thomas L. Cummings, wrote to the Faulkners in early 1944, congratulating them for Billy's military accomplishments. He wrote, "I wish to extend the congratulations of its citizenship upon the recent promotion of your son [to lieutenant] . . .

Nashville is justly proud of the splendid record of its native sons and daughters now serving our Country." He wrote again in November to express his regret over their loss.[77]

Death in service caused some whites to set racial hierarchies aside when confronted with Billy's obvious heroism. Billy's death also raised significant problems for white Tennesseans. How could they affirm local racial practices when young men like Billy Faulkner died as heroes? White civil rights activists in fact saw Billy's death as their own atonement for their willingness to uphold racial hierarchies. Writing to a third party, Janet Wynn, a New Hampshire native, feared writing directly to the Faulkners, "knowing the added pain of the bitterness of such a possible sacrifice for a 'democracy' that is not lived."[78] Smyrna, Tennessee, resident Adeline King, a white woman, wrote to the Faulkners in December 1944, recognizing that her letter, if not a breach of racial etiquette, might be a breach of death etiquette. Who, after all, was she to write the Faulkners? Thus, her letter began with the bold statement, "My name will have no meaning for you; but, in explanation, I will identify myself as *secretary* to *Mr. Bruce Overton* during the days of NYA [National Youth Administration]." King wrote, "Reading your son's record, I felt there surely were instilled in him the *high ideals* and purposes I have known in his father."[79]

In other letters, white southerners spoke to the Faulkners as one parent to another, recognizing that their loss was one that mimicked their own. "As one father to another, I want to express my sympathy over the loss of your son and also share with you a little of the pride you have in the service he rendered his country and the splendid quality of his life," Walter Stone, a doctor, wrote Reverend Faulkner.[80] Other families sent photos of their deceased sons imprinted on stationary that claimed they shared the same familial grief. Ruth Fahn Hundley, a white woman whose son, Wyatt, was killed in action in New Guinea in January 1943 (his photo adorned her stationary), wrote to the Faulkners in March 1945 that she understood their grief. "I know what it means to lose a beloved son and I know, too, what it means, months afterward, to face each day anew, standing guard over the portals of my heart lest I betray to the world that the pain and the anguish have never lessened," she wrote. There is no evidence that Hundley knew the Faulkners, but because they shared heroic children, their loss was the same and she extended her hand in comfort.[81]

Perhaps the most significant change in condolence literature was the prevalence of printed cards that took the place of handwritten letters. The greeting card industry added cards with military themes to its already significant number of condolence cards in anticipation of the war's deadly costs. Alongside cards with James W. Riley quotes ("He is only away!") were cards stating, "A Tribute to One Who has Served." Inside the card, the greeting cards reminded the recipient that, "What greater tribute could we offer than to say HE GAVE HIS LIFE

FOR HIS COUNTRY."[82] The Faulkner collection has at least fifty pre-printed cards; the Espey collection has a like number. Rendered in muted colors of gray and purple and tied with matching ribbons, the pre-printed card supplanted the written note for many, perhaps because they were at a loss for words. Gray denoted a somber tone; the muted purple, less the political statement of Black women in the 1920s and more the color of suffering and repentance associated with Lent. Perhaps, too, these were useful cards, given the large number of them that had to be written. Some considered the cards superficial and easy, however, in light of the letters written in the past. "Dear friends," Theo Williams Anderson wrote to the Faulkners, "I could have bought a card of sympathy with some stereotyped phrases, but I felt I knew you too well for that."[83]

Conclusion

As the news rang out over the radio that the war had ended, first in early May 1945 for Europe, and then in August 1945 for Japan, southerners stopped and pondered the war, its meanings for them and the consequences of so many soldiers dead. "We have fought four long years," Agnes Scott College student Sara Jean Clark wrote in her diary. "Men have suffered; men have died; even worse, men have lost their faith and their hope. Men and women have been lonely, but tonight they are one," she claimed.[84] The next phases—remembering the dead, repatriating them, and accounting for them—took almost as long as the war itself, evincing the changes of the previous fifty years.

12 Muddy Roads and Sacred Duties

Bringing Home the World War II Dead

The military hired embalmers like Dalton, Georgia, native William Willis to prepare dead soldiers for repatriation. Willis was a former Marine who had served in the military for thirty-three months and then became a Supervisory Embalmer with the Graves Registration Services in 1949 in Honolulu, Hawaii. As a Black man, he understood the men he sent home to the South were his responsibility, as a former soldier, as a funeral professional, and as a representative of the federal government. He willingly complied with the staunch and rigid ritual intended to confer nobility on the war dead, no matter their race or class, upholding the military's desire to claim all of its heroes.[1]

Once prepared, military ritual required bodies to be escorted home by fellow soldiers. But escorts, typically from outside of the South, reported on an uncomfortable occurrence once they brought the bodies Willis and others prepared home. Families insisted on opening the caskets and viewing their dead. Escort James R. Bowles brought soldier Telmer Knight home to Mississippi in August 1948, and reacted in horror when the family opened the casket. "The family of the deceased insisted on opening casket in spite of advice against it. They were convinced that the remains were properly identified because of bullet wound in the temple which they had been told he was killed and his teeth. Only the skeleton was left. The brother and uncle of deceased with undertaker and escort viewed the remains, the NOK [father] being ill at his home," Bowles reported.[2] While Bowles interpreted the Knights' act as one of knowing that *their* soldier had come home, what it really was, as it was repeated time and again, was a family saying goodbye one last time before the body was buried to refresh their grief, to molder to ashes and dust with other family members in the cemetery. That last look had evolved, however, as it reincorporated the body, killed overseas and away from family eyes, back into the family just before it was lowered into the ground.

The decision of where to bury World War II dead was a fraught one. If death was no longer a constant, current circumstances aside, did it matter where the southern dead were buried? Was the same familial ritual required? The answer to these questions was inconsistent. For the Leazers, there was no choice because of the nature of his death. The bodies were too tangled together after the B-24 crashed for individual burials, and five of the crew members were buried en masse in Arlington National Cemetery in 1951. For the Faulkners, while there was a body to be buried, they desired to root their son's death in broader meanings. This meant his heroism required his burial among other soldiers, Black and white, in eastern France, without regard to race. For the rest, temporary cemeteries held the bodies until the massive push between 1947 and 1955 to repatriate American soldiers, a job carried out by military undertakers like William Willis.

No matter the choice of burial, the professionalism and ritual were a compendium of practices that had changed over the course of the twentieth century, through two world wars, epidemics, and life extension efforts that defined a young death as remarkable and uncommon rather than a common, though miserable, part of daily life. World War II's special nature required southerners to find ways to remember the dead in their daily lives when a death occurred thousands of miles away. Resurrecting older rituals (if they ever left) like refreshing the grief became a way for southerners to reincorporate the body back into the family. The response then was a continued morphing of southern death care to more closely resemble American death care that would meet the exigencies of a postwar suburban South, yet with a nod every once in a while toward the past.

Declaring the Missing Dead

The final disposition of the body began with the finalization of death notices for the missing. In many cases, those soldiers' bodies were later found—South Carolinian Nathan Jordan Jr., for example. Family members wrote to Mary Jordan that "it is certainly hard to accept such fatal news—however, I believe it is best to do so . . . To accept it is to conserve one's energy to avoid future trouble."[3] With that finalization, many bought the argument that grief over their soldiers' loss was a patriotic act. But not all southerners considered their sons' deaths patriotic, and in fact, anger could define their grief as much as sadness and patriotism. It was not noble for their sons to die young, according to Virginian Wilson Tyrrel's father's seething letters. His son:

> Was with the ill fated and exploited 106th Infantry Div. at the German Bulge . . . Yes we like thousands of others lost our boy and we won the war. I doubt if we deserve it. One thing is sure he will not have to face the prospect of selling apples on the St. Corner . . . (Tell the truth and shame the devil).[4]

Families negotiated the military's rigid funereal policies next, first managing next-of-kin decisions. Martha Owens Faulkner, Captain Faulkner's widow, believed that her father-in-law, Reverend Faulkner, should be the military's main contact. Revealing a close family relationship and a real concern for her in-laws' grief, Martha wrote "dad" (Reverend Faulkner) that, "I don't like to bring this subject up, but I feel that you should know that I have received Billy's gratuity pay."[5] The military required her to remain the next of kin. Other families asked for wives to sign over next-of-kin status to them, such as Olin Dorn's family. As hard as their daughter-in-law tried to care for her in-laws, Olin's mother was angry about documents she believed should be hers that were in her daughter-in-law Mary's possession, in particular, copies of awards, theater ribbons and other medals of valor. Mrs. Dorn Sr. wrote the Special Information Section in August 1947, asking for duplicates as was her right, "In fact, if there is any thing that you, in the form of records or history of my son, send me I shall be rewarded in a small measure for being robbed of my only heir."[6]

The Continued Search for How Soldiers Died

The end of the war transferred the military's attention from fighting to searching as it tried to find the 270,000 bodies buried in thousands of cemeteries, disinter them, and then centralize the bodies in the approximately fourteen American battle cemeteries. From there, they would be moved to their final resting places. "Searching units" of the American Graves Registration Service (AGRS) were deployed after the war to find remains buried haphazardly in the heat of battle. The AGRS used enemy records, reports from commanders, and fellow soldiers as well as reports from American Prisoners of War (POW) to find those temporary burial grounds.[7] Plane crashes were a special problem, with the military treating each downed plane as a mystery that could be solved. The AGRS interviewed surviving soldiers to find out as much information as possible, both for its own necessity and for the families. These interviews later became a core component of "Missing Air Crew Reports." Writing to former bombardier William Goldberg, who lived Bennettsville, South Carolina, in September 1948, QMC Lt. Colonel T. H. Metz officially requested any information regarding the crash of his B-24 in Istres-Le Tube, France, on January 27, 1944. Metz wanted to know the exact place of the crash, the names of crew members known to have parachuted out of the plane, and information about the remains of those killed. A stamped, self-addressed envelope was included to make sure Goldberg responded.[8] After an extensive investigation with eyewitnesses, surviving crew members (if any), and enemy documents, the investigators concluded typically that the missing bodies most likely disintegrated in the plane crash and declared them legally dead.

It is in these Missing Air Crew reports that some of the mysteries of Harold Leazer's and his crew's deaths are resolved. After the war, the military contacted Sergeants Charles Heinzel, Arthur Kremer, and Jennings Titus for their eyewitness accounts. The first mystery to solve was why the plane crashed, and the survivors' descriptions are harrowing about the plane's final moments. Space does not allow me to quote the documents fully since Heinzel's, Kremer's, and Titus's reports are thorough and extensive. But in summary, after dropping its bombs, the plane broke formation as chaos and fire reigned on board, and German fighters attacked the plane from both the front and back, causing the No. 4 engine to fail and the communication system to fade. Titus believed that the pilot and copilot were killed by the German fighters before the plane crashed because, as it went into a tailspin, the pilots never tried to correct out of the spin. The oxygen tanks then exploded, and five crew members parachuted out, first Heinzel, then Kremer, then Titus and Johnson, who almost simultaneously jumped last. How Oliver Volk, the navigator, got out is unclear, although his death, which seems to have occurred after he jumped, was later recorded. The other four were immediately captured by German troops and spent the rest of the war in a POW camp.[9]

Europeans who buried the dead after crashes provided information to the families or to the AGRS and the Quartermaster General. Helen Morgan, whose son, copilot John Morgan, died with Harold Leazer, wrote to the Leazers that she had met an Italian surgeon who helped identify where her son and the others were initially buried and who had alerted American officials to their graves in Austria. The surgeon introduced Mrs. Morgan, via mail, to an archbishop at the Vatican, who used networks of Catholic priests across Europe to identify what happened to Harold's crew (save Oliver Volk). The information provided by the surgeon and his wife, Yvonne Balboni, was difficult. Locals reported that after the plane crashed, the "bodies were so thrown about that it was impossible to identify them."[10] In 1946, American officers disinterred the bodies and took them back to Vienna, but no one knew what happened to them from there. Mrs. Morgan later copied all of the letters and sent them to the Leazers, and most likely to the other families as well.

Because of the extensive damage to the bodies, investigators eventually assumed the four others, John Morgan, Frederick Dyson, Mario Damiani, and Robert King, were dead because there was no way to determine definitively whose body parts were whose. Only Harold's body was positively identified, most likely through the readable dog tags that were found near body parts (the other dog tags were burnt and unidentifiable). No funeral director was going to be able to recreate these bodies. Interred together in Stossing, the soldiers were eventually reinterred together as a group at Arlington National Cemetery.[11]

The second mystery was how navigator Oliver Volk, a native of Houston, Mississippi, died. Volk made it out of the plane, but died once he landed. The military confirmed the death and notified his family, who then notified the other families. How he escaped the plane in the first place is unclear. Kremer reported in his affidavit:

> A member of another crew said he saw a navigator who fitted the description of Lt. Volk, in a German truck with what seemed to be a 20 mm hole in his stomach. At an airfield where I was taken they had Lt. Volk's bent up dog tag, but all they would say was that he was dead. A member of another crew said that a German officer who questioned him had a wallet which contained a newspaper clipping about some soldier who was awarded either the CMH or DFC.[12]

Jennings Titus reported seeing Volk's "Mae West," his inflatable life vest with his name stenciled on it, after they were on the ground. Because Volk died away from the plane, he was buried away from his crewmates in Michelbach, Germany, and eventually reinterred in the Ardennes American Cemetery in Neupre, Belgium.[13]

Information about the deaths was more than an act of needing to know. In a world where the material culture and consumerism of death vested objects with the deceased's personhood, information was a material object. George Burchett wrote to Olin Dorn's parents in September 1946, about his service. "In my spare time the past 3 weeks I've tried to remember some of the few things which happened during the time your dear son was commanding our great company," Burchett wrote, before including a nine-page, single-spaced typed history of Olin in World War II, the words intended as a poor replacement for their son.[14]

Honoring the Dead

Well before the deceased were repatriated, Americans integrated memorials to them in their daily lives, a tangible reminder that a soldier had lived here, but died there. Military officials sent personnel to award families posthumous medals personally, for example. The military awarded Captain Faulkner an Air Medal with four oak leaf clusters, given posthumously to his father in a special ceremony at Nashville's airport. The event appeared in the local newspaper and included the family's home address, which locals used to write letters of condolence. The Leazers had a similar ceremony, receiving Captain Franklyn

Hendrickson at their home on March 5, 1945, to be awarded Harold's posthumous Air Medal. Both men were also promoted postmortem to Captain and 1st Lieutenant, respectively.[15]

Assembly lines continued to produce planes and battleships that became flying and floating memorials to the deceased. In Faulkner's case, the Los Angeles Lockheed plant he worked for named a Lockheed P-38 Lightning in his honor, giving his widow a plaque. She wrote a detailed description to her father-in-law afterward, telling him the plane was "a slick looking P-38, had Billy's name on it in blue and gold letters. Pictures were taken of me placing the scroll on the plane . . . The scroll was placed beside his name. These pictures will go to make up an album for Lockheed. You will receive an album within the next three or four weeks."[16] Other ships and planes bore the names of deceased World War II soldiers, too. The Junior Women's Club of Kannapolis, North Carolina, the Leazers' hometown, sold enough war bonds to name three Thunderbolts (the P-47, a short to mid-range bomber). One was named for Harold Leazer, and the family was invited in February 1945 to attend the service of dedication. The club paid for two other planes that were named for other local soldiers also killed in the war.[17]

Colleges, universities, and high schools, hit especially hard by World War II's losses, fashioned their own memorials on campuses across the South. Clemson University, for example, inscribed alumnae Olin Dorn's name on its "Roll of Honor" and told his parents that "a permanent record of his service will be kept here at the college."[18] After the war, a football trophy, called the "Harold 'Lug' Leazer Memorial Trophy," in honor of Harold's prowess as a football player and in remembrance of his service to his country, was dedicated at his North Carolina high school that was (and still is) awarded to the football player who is Most Valuable Player.[19] County courthouses followed suit with memorials to their World War I and II soldiers, like the one in Chickasaw County for Oliver Volk. Unfortunately, his neighbor, Henry "Grady" Abbot, the World War I soldier who also lived in Chickasaw County, was left off the stone.

Families also decided that preserving the letters and other documents of their soldiers' service was an adequate memorial, only now in much greater numbers. The Jordan family copied out all of the letters received regarding Nathan Jordan Jr.'s service and death. They then donated them, along with other family papers, to the South Caroliniana Library at the University of South Carolina. The Dorns also gave Olin's papers to the same archive. The Leazers gave Harold's documents to the Virginia Museum of History and Culture.[20]

Archives and historians were motivated to document each southern state's dead after World War I, but the impetus seems to have been muted after World War II and only Virginia seems to have published a *Gold Star Honor Roll*. The intention was to reclaim Virginia's soldiers' heroism for the state of Virginia rather than for the country. The authors from the Virginia Conservation Commission's

Figure 12.1. The Soldier Memorial outside of the Chickasaw County Courthouse, MS. Oliver Volk's name is on it. World War I soldier Henry "Grady" Abbott's name is not, although his family lived in the county.

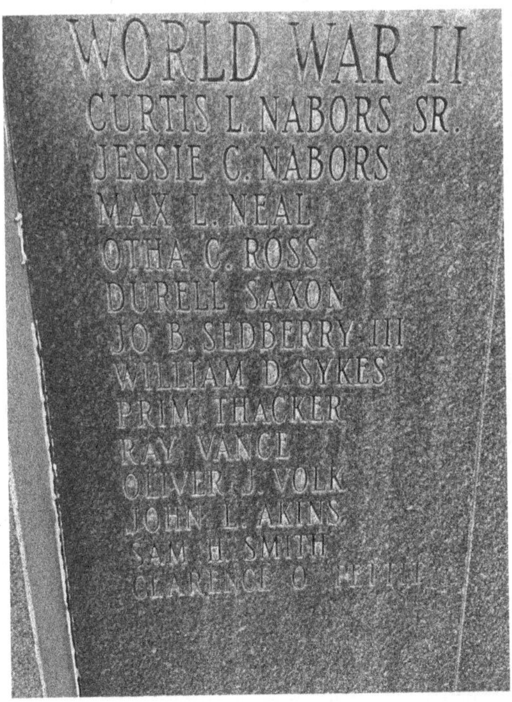

Figure 12.2. Close up shot of Oliver Volk's name on the Chickasaw County Courthouse memorial. He is buried in Belgium.

Division of History were an integrated group of historians that included the editor, University of Virginia professor W. Edwin Hemphill, and Luther Porter Jackson, the chair of Virginia State College's Department of History. In their view, those who had died for the "preservation of democratic civilization" should not be nameless. They also thought that the war had engendered a nobler sentiment that tended to dissipate once war was over, and the book was intended to be a reminder of those ideals.[21]

Relying first on casualty lists published by the military, the editors placed announcements in state newspapers to make sure they included every dead soldier. After creating a master list of the dead, they then sent forms to families, detailing their soldiers' experience in World War II. Harold Leazer's father filled out the paperwork for him, noting the crash in the Adriatic Sea a few weeks before he died. As they had after World War I when Marie Bankhead Owen had gathered similar information for the Alabama Archives, families responded once again with letters and photos of their dead soldiers, recognizing the opportunity to share their grief and memories.[22]

Virginians had gone to war to fight for their state, but they came home with a more nationalized identity. The editors tried to redefine that experience as a statewide one with limited effect. Joseph Sarnoski, a Congressional Medal of Honor winner, was actually born and raised in Pennsylvania. It was his training at Langley Field, Newport News, that made him a Virginian. Others pushed back at attempts to make their dead Virginians. Mrs. Ellen Phipps, from Ames, Iowa, thanked the commission for wanting to include her husband on their rolls, but "as it is he really wouldn't belong to the state of Virg."[23] In fact, one state claiming another's dead seemed to offend some survivors. Daniel Budd's father wrote the commission that "Don was born and lived all his life in New Jersey, and I feel that his war service should be recorded in that state, and of course, it should not be duplicated."[24] In both cases, the Honor Roll editors ignored the families.

Official casualty lists did not distinguish between Black and white soldier deaths; in the military's eyes, all soldiers' deaths were something to be mourned with relative equality. But the Gold Star Honor Roll gave Virginians the opportunity to resegregate Black from white. The presence of Luther Porter Jackson on the editorial board justified editors' desire to resegregate because they wanted scholars like Jackson to be able to write histories specifically of Black soldiers. They were therefore coded as Black using an asterisk next to their names.[25] But in a direct rebuke of white southern etiquette, Black women signed this paperwork using the title Mrs.: Mrs. Viola Ford's son, Lafayette; Mrs. Harrison Lassiter's son, Arthur; Mrs. Mattie Perry's brother, Lawton, all died. If their kin were "fearless in battle," then their survivors claimed the right to be fearless at home. The editors responded in kind by listing Black soldiers' female next of kin as Mrs., although not consistently.[26]

Bringing the Bodies Home

World War I's precedents and overseas cemeteries meant the military had already determined how it would interact with families in the post–World War II era, with paperwork attempting once again to make the process orderly. Pamphlets entitled "Disposition of World War II Armed Forces Dead" described the family's choices, and forms like "Request for Disposition of Remains" and "Relinquishment of Disposition Authority" legally vested the military with the responsibility for the body until it reached its final resting place.[27] The documents were relatively intense, and so the military named local experts who could help fill out the documents, including funeral directors, local American Red Cross Chapters, and veterans organizations like the Veterans of Foreign Wars (VFW).[28] The documents gave the next of kin three reburial options: remain in an American cemetery overseas, being cared for in perpetuity by the American government and the American Battle Monuments Commission (ABMC); disinter the body and bring it to a national cemetery (like Arlington) in the United States; or disinter the body and bring it to a family-designated graveyard. The ABMC eventually reported that 61 perecnt of the 270,000 overseas bodies came home. Of those that remained overseas, a significant number were unidentifiable.[29]

For those bodies left overseas, the military issued the family documents marking where their kin were buried. The Faulkners learned that their son was buried in Row 7, Grave 74 at the Lorraine American Cemetery in St. Avoid, France. The ABMC explained that 113.5-acre cemetery "contains the largest number of graves of our military Dead of World War II in Europe, a total of 10,489. Most of these lost their lives while fighting in this region. Their headstones are arranged in nine plots in a generally elliptical design extending over the beautiful rolling terrain of eastern Lorraine and culminating in a prominent overlook feature."[30] The bodies buried were cared for using rituals that were commonly associated with New England or the upper Midwest, but now familiar to southerners. The military created park-like settings, extolling the virtues of the "graceful trees and hedges" that lined the cemeteries and documenting the solemn structures (chapels, for example) that honored the noble dead. It also buried them without regard to race as the Faulkners received what they hoped for in Captain Faulkner's death: an acknowledgment of his worth as a human being as well as his heroism in the war.[31]

The Faulkners saw leaving their son among his new military family a reasonable choice. Other southern families left the bodies overseas because they did not want to re-open what was a "closed" grieving process, meaning they had grieved, it was over, and they did not want to revisit the death. For some, too much melancholy was associated with bringing the bodies home. Effie Vredenburg wrote the Virginia Gold Star Honor Roll editors about her son, Ivan, killed at Bastogne, Belgium, in January 1945, "I do not think that we (my husband, 3

Figure 12.3. A view of the Lorraine American Cemetery in St. Avold, France, with the mix of military burials without regard to race or religion.

Figure 12.4. From a distance, Tuskegee Airman Captain William J. Faulkner Jr.'s marker at the Lorraine American Cemetery.

Figure 12.5. The author next to Captain William J. Faulkner Jr.'s marker.

sons, and myself) will have him brought back to U.S.; as that would be reopening old wounds."[32]

The reburial of some deaths, especially those from plane crashes, had to be handled differently because of the nature of the deaths. The Leazers wanted to disinter Harold's body and ship it home, but his remains could not necessarily be distinguished from the other crewmen, and in this case, with other families involved, the military determined they would be buried together. In February 1947, the families were informed that the military was moving the bodies from their temporary burial in Stossing, Austria, en masse to an American cemetery. Moving the bodies was hampered by worsening relations with the Russians who controlled that area of Austria. Finally, Leazer, Mario Damiani, Frederick Dyson, John Morgan, and Robert King arrived home to be buried in Arlington National Cemetery, near other plane crews also buried together. Copilot John Morgan's mother, Helen, wrote to Harold Leazer's mother that "It has been a long time and very difficult for us all, but I know you feel as I do and will be thankful to have them in our own country." When they arrived at Arlington Cemetery, the Morgans and Leazers planned to meet. After a correspondence that lasted more than seven years, it was about time since these strangers, now friends via mail, were burying their sons together.[33]

Figure 12.6. Harold Leazer and his crew's tombstone from a distance. Arlington National Cemetery.

Figure 12.7. Harold Leazer and his crew's tombstone, Arlington National Cemetery.

The Arlington service reinforced the standardization of American military rituals, in that the same service was read over all of the soldiers, with each individual's name, rank, and branch of service typed into the first line. The service itself reflected changes in death care, where John 14:1 ("Let not your heart be troubled" [KJV]) was read, followed immediately by the Twenty-Third Psalm. The service most likely lasted ten minutes, if that. Afterward, Arlington's chaplain sent the Leazers, and most likely the other families too, a copy of it in memory of their sons.[34]

Escorting the Bodies Home

The third option—bringing bodies home to a family graveyard—was available to those whose kin had not died in a catastrophic plane crash or in a naval boat sunk to the depths of the South Pacific. "I know, however, that it is a great comfort to you to have his precious body buried in your own cemetery, where you can look after the grave and beautify it and its surroundings," Courtney Atkinson wrote to Olin Dorn's family.[35] Telegrams, that harbinger of immediate support in the 1920s and 1930s and of terrible news during the war, now became the way the military informed soldier families that their soldier was on the way home. The telegram's receipt began a difficult time of waiting, of seeing the truth of a soldier's death. "Cousin Mobley" wrote Olin Dorn Sr. in October 1947, acknowledging just this: "I am sure you are trusting in Jesus for grace through faith to carry you through this trying period."[36]

The military escorts assigned to each body ensured that the standard ritual was followed as consistently and precisely as possible. The first bodies were shipped home in October 1947, on the USAT Honda Knot. From that first shipment until the final one in 1952 (individual bodies were still found and shipped home until 1955), coffins bound for the South were first escorted to transfer points, Memphis, Tennessee; Atlanta, Georgia; or Fort Worth, Texas; and then shipped to smaller towns. Each body had its own escort, a soldier still in uniform, even if multiple bodies went to the same place, a possibility when the Quartermaster at Fort Worth sent 141 bodies home to Mississippi in March 1949 and another 115 bodies in April 1949.[37] In many ways, the escorts were part of a symbolic marking of the young dead. These young bodies needed the ceremony to brand their youthful deaths as honorable, noble, and now, relatively rare. The care, which was labor, time, and cost intensive, was an implicit nod at life extension's successes over the previous fifty years as the deaths of thousands of young men had to be marked as special cases with special rituals.

The military once again used paperwork, a lot of it, to ensure a consistent rendering of nobility on the dead. Another War Department pamphlet, "Conduct of a Military Funeral," dictated policy on the train and at the gravesite.[38] Other documents for the escorts, the next of kin, and the chaplain directing the service established the orderly system by which deceased soldiers were to be buried once they reached the gravesite. Where the chaplain should stand (at the head of the casket); how he should proceed from the church to the cemetery; and how he should read the service were all dictated by policy. The ritual required careful handling of the body itself: always carry the coffin feet first, not head first; ensure others did not treat the coffin with anything less than respect; and never leave the body alone. Railroad employees especially treated coffins with respect. "The Illinois Central RR baggage men were the very best I have ever seen for carefully handling remains," escort Thomas Veasey said.[39] In other cases, however, "The men at the Central Station who handle the casket [*sic*] are very lax about removing hats and gloves while handling shipping cases," escort John Fletcher reported.[40] Precision created little wiggle room when it came to brothers escorting brothers home or friends escorting friends. Donald Munn escorted his brother, Charlie, home to Kosciusko, Mississippi, in May 1948, most likely assigned at his own request. In this instance, Donald mingled with the family and allowed the firing squad commander to take charge, so he could be both escort and recipient of his brother's remains.[41]

Within these boundaries, chaplains tended to handle the services while funeral directors cared for the practical details, with the escort overseeing all of them. Pastor Richard Potter arranged for a bugler and an honor guard for Olin Dorn while serving as the minister. A local Veterans of Foreign Wars or American Legion group provided buglers and a firing squad for the three volleys that were fired after the service (never over the heads of the mourners, the directions said) as a bugler sounded "Taps." Then, the flag was removed from the coffin, folded, and presented to the next-of-kin.[42]

Preprinted scrapbooks, provided by the funeral home, documented the services, another intimate act usurped by the commercial death system. The Shelley-Brunson Funeral Home provided one for the Dorn family, for example, functioning as an elaborate thank-you for choosing the funeral home. But it was more than that; called a "memory book," the book documented the attention given to the parents and was to be a comfort in the coming years. Quoting Alfred Tennyson ("Crossing the Bar") and William Penn ("Life Everlasting") while featuring a colorized picture of a white Jesus walking on water, the book brought more national standards and language into remembering the dead. The standard, John 14:2 (KJV), appeared, but so, too, did Psalm 23 (also KJV). The quoting of Revelation 21:4 ("And God shall wipe away all tears from their eyes; and there shall be no more death, neither sorrow, nor crying, neither shall there be any more pain," KJV) was a new addition. The funeral home also listed the music sung ("Lead Kindly Light," "Abide with Me," both standard hymns from

Figure 12.8. Ben Clay Espey's gravesite, Woodlawn Memorial Park, Nashville, TN. This is an example of a government-issued headstone.

the Methodist Hymnal); the 83 visitors who signed the book; and the 146 who called on the family personally.[43]

Tucked into the Dorn scrapbook are yellowed notebook pages that list those who brought food, something not typically documented before the war. Gifts of food had long been an obligation of a community; what differed here was the acknowledgment of that gift. All of the donors were women, and in all but three cases, they were listed with the title Mrs., suggesting they were white women bringing food to the Dorns, who were also white. But three women, Henrietta (pie and cookies), Eunice (cake and flowers), and Jeanette (canned peas), could have been Black. Black women helping out with food probably was not new. What was most likely new was the public acknowledgment that they had helped.[44]

The military's final act of care for the dead was marking the grave with a military headstone, transforming the death landscape of the South further with a flat, bronze marker. Even when families chose another, more ornate headstone, they still asked for the military headstone that was typically placed at the feet with the ornate stone at its head. Olin Dorn's family purchased him an ornate

$600 stone, but the nondescript military marker, listing branch of service, rank and birth and death dates, also adorns the grave. Both families—military and natal—now claimed the body as their own with permanent markers.[45]

Mississippians Escorted Home

Escorts bringing Mississippi soldiers home unwittingly witnessed the dramatic shifts in death care over the twentieth century. The first change was the families who desired the body be buried without fuss and fanfare or decided against the "government headstone," rare enough that the escorts noted it. "No military service desired and memorial service conducted at time of death notification 2 yrs. ago," escort Donald Ahle wrote when he brought Claude Dean home in August 1949.[46] "About 10 people attended the funeral. The family did not want a government headstone," escort Harris C. Cotten [*sic*] reported when he brought Wyatt Wood home to McComb, Mississippi, in May 1948.[47]

The vast majority of the escort paperwork, however, documents the easy acceptance of military ritual. The soldiers first escorted their sad cargo to the nearest train station, and then, typically, were met by a funeral director who ushered the escort and coffin to the funeral home or cemetery, sometimes as far as forty-five miles away.[48] Many of the trips were difficult, but perhaps no more difficult than when Carl Reeves escorted Willie Hopson home on October 26, 1948. He described his trip:

> Enondale, Miss., the place of final burial, is 30 instead of 14 miles from Meridian and is on a dirt road. Due to the heavy rain storm Sunday, it was impassable and the grave caved in from the storm; and so the funeral was not held until Nov. 2. The NOK [*sic*: Next of Kin] sent a telegram to the Distribution Center requesting permission for me to remain for the funeral, and the telegraph operator informed me by telephone that a message granting the extension has been received.[49]

Reports contain a litany of complaints on the difficulty of navigating local bus systems, long delays, and difficult-to-find relatives. In bringing home Benjamin Collum to Choctaw County in January 1949, escort Richard C. Slankard wrote that the "roads were not passable and the relatives of the deceased said the funeral would be held when the roads dried out so the funeral director told me it was not necessary I stay and he was unable to give me any plans concerning the funeral."[50] Clarence Clark's mother was nowhere to be found when the escort brought him home to Belzoni, Mississippi, in June 1948, and the escort and funeral home director had to spend most of the day searching for her. It seems she had moved several times since receiving the paperwork and had not informed anyone.[51]

Other problems also emerged with the local VFW representatives or with the funeral director. Usually, the honor guards were commended with the highest praise, but at times, escorts complained about the abrogation of military etiquette. Clifford Corder reported that, "At Proper time while folding Flag, I stepped up to grave[;] instead of pallbearer giving Flag to me, he laid Flag in the Mother's lap and stepped off. Immediately the undertaker dismissed the family. All being done in a matter of seconds, the family being well tied together as one, I as Escort, did not change anything that would cause them added grief. The National Guard Unit needs instructions on proper steps to conduct a funeral."[52] In some cases, the local troops did not show any interest in honoring the dead; in others, the American Legion decided its rituals would be the focus, telling the escorts, "If the Army wants a military funeral, the Army can give it. We give a Legion funeral."[53]

The escort also became a sort of guardian against unethical funeral directors, using his power as the federal government's agent to stall cheats. Escorts typically reported the funeral director was "very cooperative and helpful to both the family and me. He is above the average in helpfulness and below the average in expense to the family."[54] But in other cases, the funeral director seems to have colluded with the family in securing more than their share. "It has been reported to me that a Mississippi Funeral home has been burying deceased service men under insurance contracts, and allowing the next of kin to claim burial expenses from the government also. Escort would like to give personal report on above," Walter Marshall reported in August 1948.[55] At other times, the funeral director could be "very unfriendly," as Clarence Crafton found when he brought Davis Beard home to Tupelo in July 1948.[56] Edward Jackson wrote to his superiors after he brought Isaiah McCarroll home in June 1948 that "The funeral director was not cooperative and treated me as if he wanted me to leave. I tried to talk to the Next of Kin whom I saw only at the funeral home, and the funeral director kept interfering. The NOK told me I could stay if I wanted to but seemed quite indifferent, and I felt that I really wasn't wanted. Their attitude was different from any I experienced before, and I felt it best to leave."[57]

The escorts, as military agents, also helped families navigate paperwork. Harry Watson escorted Ben Blackley home to Greenville, Mississippi, in July 1948, and stayed to help his widow fill out application forms for funeral expenses and the government-issued headstone. In other cases, escorts helped find military decorations (for example, medals) and personal effects that had yet to be delivered. The escorts were happy to help, and in fact, saw it as their job to mediate for families. In response, families welcomed the escort into their families, inviting him for dinner, asking him to be a pallbearer, or introducing him to the extended family. The Phagan family insisted Bruce Nunnally remain an extra day so he could meet some of their friends when he brought their soldier, Doyle, home in June 1948.[58] The family "thanked the government—[through] the escort for all that had been done in returning their son," escort Clarence Crafton reported after delivering Jewel W. Woodall home to McComb, Mississippi.[59]

Billie Jefcoat's family invited escort Otis Truitt to Thanksgiving dinner. Other families expressed "much satisfaction with the services rendered," escort Thomas Gray noted when he brought Delma Bishop home.[60]

The documents give us a glimpse, however, at the process by which deceased Black bodies were reincorporated back into Mississippi's racial system by the escort, the government, and the local community. Reincorporation began when families filled out paperwork for burial, particularly if a family, Black or white, desired a burial at the national cemetery in Vicksburg. Granted, only a small number requested that their soldiers be buried there. In February 1949, three of the 101 burials were completed at the military cemetery; in April 1949, 19 of the 134 burials were done there.[61] The military acceded to some racial hierarchies in these cemeteries, with the Vicksburg cemetery superintendent, James R. McConaghie, scheduling funerals for white soldiers and Black soldiers on separate days so that grieving families did not see each other. One set of paperwork for a Black soldier read: "One funeral, that of the late Pvt. J. D. Goss . . . is scheduled for the Vicksburg National Cemetery . . . The race of the deceased is Negro. The next of kin has requested a military funeral. Your usual cooperation will be appreciated." It seems that the "usual cooperation" was providing a Black firing squad, chaplain, and bugler at the gravesite. District Chaplain E. E. Price responded "The firing squad, bugler and chaplain will be present . . . for the funeral of Pvt. J. D. Goss . . . Negro. Thank you."[62]

But moving thousands of bodies back to the states came with the potential of making so-called mistakes, in particular, of sending a white cortege to welcome a Black soldier home, guided by a Black escort. To contain this, escort paperwork came with asterisks next to the names of those who were Black, with a footnote for non-southerners stating the asterisk denoted a "colored" soldier.[63] Jerry Exum, a white escort, wrote on his paperwork that in escorting L. C. Dinkins home, "a mistake was made in race identification, and I was sent instead of a colored escort. In accordance with instructions . . . The Supt. of the National Cemetery quickly arranged for [*sic*] negro undertaker and pall bearers after telling NOK that the funeral would be delayed. The NOK did not realize that an error had been made, and there was no embarrassment on either side."[64] For Dinkins's burial, the Tyner-Ford American Legion Post (Colored), in Vicksburg, Mississippi, was probably called to provide the firing squads, floral wreaths, and pallbearers. The post certainly received a letter of commendation for its efforts on behalf of Black soldiers from the Superintendent of Vicksburg's National Cemetery.[65]

In the midst of a military ritual that bespoke the tremendous changes in death care in the twentieth century, nothing more obviously remained an artifact than families' insistence on opening their soldiers' caskets. Sealed shut with screws, the military knew that dead bodies would cause Americans to question the war and ordered coffin lids sealed and bodies hidden from sight. Escorts, typically not local men, reacted with horror when Mississippi families opened the caskets. This was not a single incident, but happened over and over again. Escorts tended to interpret the act as one of confirming the deceased's identity, through a bone broken when younger or by a missing finger. "The casket was opened in spite of the facts told the father and two brothers. They were satisfied after they identified the body themselves," escort William Van Camp said when he escorted John H. Ray Jr. home.[66] "I was asked to help funeral director open casket for widow and her father to view remains. They were satisfied and made positive identification by dental work," Thomas Gray reported.[67] Not all families were satisfied with what they saw when they opened the casket, however. Jesse Bennett's family in Winona, Mississippi, thought his body had been embalmed because he had died in a hospital. His widow was distressed enough to deny that it was her soldier and refused to bury it "as belonging to them." She changed her mind the next day, however, and accepted the remains "as belonging to the deceased."[68]

Escorts assumed that families were identifying the body. But it was probably the continuance of that older southern practice in the new world of death care: refreshing the grief. For all of the changes that had occurred in southern death care over the previous half century, by the early 1950s, the most humane part of burying the dead remained that desire for one last look before burial. The ritual's persistence mitigated against some of the most significant changes in the first half of the twentieth century. From fights over family cemeteries to promises of a family reunion; from a desire to live to one's three score and ten to the lowering of mortality rates through life extension; to the rise of a death consumer system that provided purple thrones to grief being allowed in precise ways; from two world wars that killed and maimed from afar to the military's preparation of the body for burial, all made death care vastly different from the rural funeral conducted in 1900. Indeed, the federal government's witnesses—these escorts—to these changes reinforced this post–New Deal and World War II world where American citizenship would include the right to a relatively long life. Escorts were also an example of the government's willingness to continue to care for southerners as well as all other Americans. And yet this remnant of tradition—refreshing the grief—was persistent against unrelenting change, a leftover from the past, where saying goodbye one last time prepared the family for the newly imagined grieving process ahead.

Epilogue

Death in the Twenty-First-Century Suburban South

When I initially drafted the epilogue to this book, death care and life extension in the suburban South looked like this: death is now a quaint relic in a rapidly developing region rather than a common part of it. Within a mile of my house, for example, there are three graveyards or memorials to the dead. The graveyards—one from the nineteenth century, the other from the 1930s—have been carefully preserved among the suburban houses that now populate my neighborhood. The third is a memorial to a mother and baby who died in an F-4 tornado that destroyed our neighborhood in 2009. Recently, however, the crosses were taken down so the city could add a stop light at what has become a busy intersection, and developers used the opportunity to build a house there. Death care, then, is both traditional and adaptive in my neighborhood.

In this suburban area, the requirement that drivers pull over as a funeral cortege passes is a charming story in the midst of a landscape that was transformed before and after World War II. The war and its end only added to the momentum. Passing in 1946, the Hill-Burton Act provided federal funding for a mass expansion in hospital facilities; Lister Hill was the United States Senator from Alabama who had helped craft the 1937 manifesto that claimed the South was the "Nation's #1 Economic Problem." The bill provided low-cost loans for building or modernizing hospitals and nursing homes in exchange for low-cost care for people meeting certain income requirements. A massive wave of hospital building ensued throughout the nation, adding almost 500,000 beds to the nation's health infrastructure. The Centers for Disease Control, begun as a wartime malaria control program, opened up in Atlanta, Georgia, in 1946, giving it a special window into the continued improvement of southerners' health. New laws, affirming and extending the health citizenship of Americans, continued to be passed, including multiple amendments to the Social Security Act; the creation

Figure 13.1. Green Cemetery, an old cemetery, amidst suburban development, Murfreesboro, TN.

of Medicaid and Medicare in the 1960s; the passage of the Americans with Disabilities Act in 1990; and the Affordable Care Act in 2010. Each has expanded the health rights Americans have under law. Finally, in a region once associated with death, the urban South, especially Atlanta, Georgia; Nashville, Tennessee; and Memphis, Tennessee, now offers first-rate healthcare, with the surrounding suburbs benefitting from close proximity to cutting-edge medical practice. The shift that Progressives hoped for—from focusing on imminent death to living a vital and relatively long life—has been built into the suburban South.[1]

My more idealistic view was upended by the Covid-19 pandemic, however, as it exposed the limits of what I viewed as the significant transformations regionally and nationally. Old rituals, new laws, and expert healthcare centers hid the real health problems that continue to dog the South, including the very real dismantling of local medical care. Echoes of the past, of practices not fully embraced, of a racial landscape that has not yet adequately addressed the region's entrenched poverty, remain, especially in rural areas. In fact, state legislatures in many southern states have turned their backs on the decades of work, and the pandemic exposed both reemergent health problems and the unwillingness to address them.

The hints were there in the reinfections of old scourges; a still significantly high maternal mortality rate; and the closing of hospitals. Hookworm, for example, has reemerged in poorer sections of Alabama where health officials once thought it had been fully eradicated. Lowndes County, Alabama, a predominantly Black county, uncovered a widespread infestation in 2017. It is nowhere as serious as it was in the early 1900s when John Rockefeller spent a million dollars on hookworm control, but its reemergence is still daunting. The fix is equally daunting. An appropriate septic system that would eradicate the worm costs $15,000 per household. The county's average income is just over $18,000 per year.[2]

Infant and maternal mortality rates are also still high, although not as high as in the twentieth century, and healthcare advocates are once again linking infant mortality rates to the nation's general healthiness. In 2010, the national infant mortality rate was 6.1 per 1,000, but 8.8 per 1,000 in Tennessee. The implication, of course, is that a civilized nation cares for its weakest citizens and high death rates suggest that we are not able to do so. Health practitioners have devised programs to challenge those significantly higher infant mortality rates, especially among Black women, who continue to suffer from a much higher maternal mortality rate than white women. Forty Black women per 100,000 die from childbirth while only 13 white women do.[3]

Finally, rural hospitals across the South are closing rapidly, forcing those with medical complaints to drive significant distances to obtain healthcare. According to recent reports in the *New York Times*, the closing of hospitals in areas such as Ohio and West Virginia have had lethal consequences for locals who have died before they could reach a still-open hospital.[4] In Cookeville, Tennessee, the Cumberland River Hospital, built in 1965, closed in 2019. While there is another hospital in town, there simply were not enough beds when Covid-19 hit.[5] The Tennessee state governor's response has been tepid at best, claiming that "it's time for government to get out of the business of public health interventions."[6]

But Covid-19 did not expose the most significant shift in mortality over the last five years: the claiming of a new American region as one uniquely associated with death, usurping the South's early reputation. Demographers and others have identified a sharp decline in life expectancy, especially among working-class whites with only a high school education and who die in their middle age (defined as ages 46 to 59). Called "deaths of despair" and based on Princeton economists Anne Case and Angus Deaton's work, these early deaths are centered in post-industrial states like Ohio, Pennsylvania, and other Old Northwest areas. Deaths tend to come from suicide, alcoholism, and drug overdoses and are linked to a "red state–blue state" divide, meaning an early death can be linked to one's political beliefs, particularly if one votes Republican.[7]

As I finished a round of revisions of this book in 2020, I was in quarantine from the coronavirus and astounded at the echoes from the past, not just from the Spanish Influenza Epidemic, but from government's complete abrogation of responsibility, especially at the state level. As I recovered from a likely case of the virus, rallied my students whose families had fallen on hard economic times, and cared for a student whose roommate died suddenly, all the while dealing with my own breast cancer diagnosis, I have been dismayed, deeply so, at the casual dismissal of the epidemic's fallout. It went against a century's worth of work to retool death care and focus more insistently on life extension. I had hoped in a future draft that I would be able to say something more positive, but the deaths of first 74,000, then 129,000, then 550,000, and now one million in the United States alone is nothing to celebrate. Perhaps, the reminder of this earlier, deadlier time will motivate some to turn this around and provide some strategies on how to do so.

In Murfreesboro, drivers still pull over for a funeral cortege and the increased number of ambulances racing through our streets has slowed down those who used to try to outrun them. This leftover ritual remains after the Progressives' efforts to lower mortality rates and the New Deal's impact transformed the South's landscape of death. Those changes are the foundation of our modern healthcare system where patients now go, assuming they can be cured. I certainly did with my own cancer diagnosis. But while the high death rates in the South motivated these changes, they had significant implications for the nation as a whole as the federal government, two world wars, a massive pandemic, and a simply miserable health experience fostered new assumptions about how and when one should die. The Covid-19 pandemic has exposed the faults in this system, and I hope that new federal and state policies will address them, as being put away decently should be the last resort in a country that values its citizens' health.

Notes

Introduction

1. Melissa Locker, "Why You Should Always, Always Pull Over for A Funeral."

2. The South is defined here in a fairly traditional way, using the core states of the former Confederacy as my focus. At rare times, documents from southern Missouri, Kentucky, and Maryland are also included.

3. The literature on death includes Philippe Aries, *The Hour of Our Death*; James Farrell, *Inventing the American Way of Death, 1830–1920*; Gary Laderman, *The Sacred Remains: American Attitudes Toward Death, 1779–1883*; and Gary Laderman, *Rest in Peace: A Cultural History of Death and the Funeral Home in Twentieth-Century America.* For southern specific studies, see Christopher Crocker, "The Southern Way of Death"; and Charles R. Wilson, "The Southern Funeral Director: Managing Death in the New South."

4. Karen Kruse Thomas, *Deluxe Jim Crow: Civil Rights and American Health Policy, 1935–1954*.

5. Karla F. C. Holloway, *Passed On: African American Mourning Stories*; Suzanne E. Smith, *To Serve the Living: Funeral Directors and the African American Way of Death.*

6. Karen L. Cox, *Dixie's Daughters: The United Daughters of the Confederacy and the Preservation of Confederate Culture*, 1–6; Janet S. Hasson, *Widows, Weepers and Wakes: Mourning in Middle Tennessee*; Elizabeth Kubler-Ross, *On Death and Dying*. Thanks to Steven M. Stowe who helped with some of this language.

7. Jessica Mitford, *The American Way of Death.*

8. Aries, *The Hour of Our Death.*

9. Louise Aronson, *Elderhood: Redefining Aging, Transforming Medicine, Reimagining Life.*

10. King James Version, the common Biblical translation used by evangelicals.

11. Mrs. Omie Williams Epp to Sadie Hornsby, *An Air-Minded Family*, March 6, 1939, FWP, https://www.loc.gov/resource/wpalh1.12080715.

Part One. Death and the New South

1. Drew Gilpin Faust, *This Republic of Suffering: Death and the American Civil War.*

Chapter 1. Selling Our Dead

1. Durwood Dunn, *Cades Cove: The Life and Death of a Southern Appalachian Community, 1818–1937*, 288, fn. 35.

2. Philippe Aries, *The Hour of Our Death*, 46, 49.

3. Price V. Fishback et al., "The Impact of New Deal Programs on Black and White Infant Mortality in the South," 97; James C. Cobb, ed., *The Mississippi Delta and the World: The Memoirs of David Cohn*, 32.

4. Todd Savitt and James Harvey Young, eds., *Disease and Distinctiveness in the American South*, 4–5.

5. Edward Ball, *The Sweet Hell Inside: The Rise of an Elite Black Family in the Segregated South*, 47.

6. James C. Cobb, *The Most Southern Place on Earth: The Mississippi Delta and the Roots of Regional Identity*, 126–130; oral interview, Ellen Bryan Moore to Mary Hebert, October 8, 1995, LSU.

7. Julia LaRoche to Chalmers S. Murray, *Mistress of Magnolia Hall*, South Carolina, January 5, 1939, FWP, https://www.loc.gov/item/wpalh002107.

8. Cobb, *The Most Southern Place on Earth*, 9, 25; Tom E. Terrill and Jerrold Hirsch, *Such As Us: Southern Voices of the Thirties*, 83.

9. Terrill and Hirsch, *Such As Us*, 83–84.

10. Christine Stansell, *City of Women: Sex and Class in New York, 1789–1860*, 8–10.

11. James O. Breeden, "Disease and Southern Distinctiveness," in Savitt and Young, *Disease and Distinctiveness in the American South*, 10–11.

12. Mother Jones, *The Autobiography of Mother Jones*, Mary Field Parton, ed; Cobb, *The Mississippi Delta and the World*, 34.

13. Sylvia D. Hoffert, "'A Very Peculiar Sorrow': Attitudes Toward Infant Death in the Urban Northeast, 1800–1860," 602.

14. Lillian Smith, *Killers of the Dream*, 106.

15. Pauli Murray, *Proud Shoes: The Story of an American Family*, 27.

16. Cobb, *The Mississippi Delta and the World*, 32.

17. Molly Kensey to Geneva Tonsil, *I Got a Record*, Georgia, December 1, 1939, FWP, https://www.loc.gov/item/wpalh000561/.

18. Ted Ownby, *Subduing Satan: Religion, Recreation, and Manhood in the Rural South, 1865–1920*, 110–111; Elizabeth Harris Pointer [a.k.a. Ann S. Pointer] to Paul Ortiz, July 22, 1994, BTV.

19. Terrill and Hirsch, *Such As Us*, 29.

20. Maulsey Stoney to Chambers S. Murray, *Martha Joint, Occasional Servant*, South Carolina, March 3, 1939, FWP, https://www.loc.gov/item/wpalh002102; Smith, *Killers of the Dream*, 26; Randy J. Sparks, "The Southern Way of Death: The Meaning of Death in Antebellum White Evangelical Culture," 32–50.

21. Glenda Gilmore, *Gender and Jim Crow: Women and the Politics of White Supremacy in North Carolina, 1896–1920*, 128, 278, fn. 50.

22. Stoney to Murray, FWP.

23. Treeby Miller Andress, *When I Was a Little Girl: Memoirs of My Life and Family*, 39.

24. William H. Chafe, ed., *Remembering Jim Crow: African Americans Tell about Life in the Segregated South*, 49; James Weldon Johnson, *The Autobiography of an Ex-Coloured Man*, 79.

25. James K. Crissman, *Death and Dying in Central Appalachia: Changing Attitudes and Practices* 27; Chafe, ed., *Remembering Jim Crow*, 48.

26. Miss Dromgoole Ham, August 31, 1936, WPA Collection, SCL.

27. Andress, *When I Was a Little Girl.*

28. Federal Writers' Project, *These Are Our Lives: As Told by the People and Written by Members of the Federal Writers' Project of the Works Progress Administration in North Carolina, Tennessee, and Georgia*, 47–48.

29. LaRoche to Murray; Onnie Lee Logan, *Motherwit: An Alabama Midwife's Story*; Walter King Harris Funeral Ledger, 31–32, AGRC; 1920 Census Records, Ed Gregory and John Potts, Civil District 5[6], District 118, Smyrna, TN. The source for the Smyrna census record is Ancestry.com.

30. Terrill and Hirsch, *Such As Us*, 67.

31. Miss Minnie Stonestreet and Leila H., *In Lieu of Something Better*, Georgia, December 19, 1939, FWP, https://www.loc.gov/resource/wpalh1.13050127/.

32. Oral interview, Mary Johnson to Daisy Greene, May 8, 1977, MDAH; Georgeanne Runblad, "From 'Shrouding Woman' to Lady Assistant: An Analysis of Occupational Sex-Typing in the Funeral Home Industry, 1870–1920"; Logan, *Motherwit*, 48–49; Clifford M. Kuhn et al., eds., *Living Atlanta: An Oral History of the City, 1914–1948*, 240.

33. Sally Russell, ed., *Roots and Ever Green: The Selected Letters of Ina Dillard Russell*, 141.

34. Caroline Miller, *Lamb in His Bosom*, 161; Elizabeth Kytle, ed., *Willie Mae: A Poignant First-Person Account of a Black Woman's Life in the Segregated South*, 41.

35. John D. Combes, "Ethnography, Archaeology, and Burial Practices Among Coastal South Carolina Blacks," *Conference on Historic Site Archaeology Papers* 7:52–58, n.d., in "Burial Practices" Folder, Avery; the Avery burial files document the two pennies, one showing the birth year and the other the death year, on the child's eyes. Elaine Nichols, "Introduction," in Elaine Nichols, ed., *The Last Miles of the Way: African American Homegoing Traditions, 1890–Present*, 20–21; Mamie Garvin Fields with Karen Fields, *Lemon Swamp and Other Places*, 129; Chafe, *Remembering Jim Crow*, 84; Kytle, *Willie Mae*, 41; Eudora Welty, *One Writer's Beginnings*, 18–19.

36. Terrill and Hirsch, *Such As Us*, 84.

37. Dunn, *Cades Cove*, 191; Robert A. Clouse, "The Relocation and Restoration of Lucas Hill Cemetery, a Historic Cemetery near the Community of Waugh, Montgomery County, Alabama," 5; Laderman, *The Sacred Remains: American Attitudes Toward Death, 1779–1883*, 49.

38. Comments regarding cats and window screens were provided by participants at a lecture I gave at the Adams Place Retirement Community, Murfreesboro, TN, on October 15, 2010; Louis Armstrong, *Satchmo: My Life in New Orleans*, 91–92.

39. Crissman, *Death and Dying in Central Appalachia*, 69; David Roediger, "And Die in Dixie: Funerals, Death, and Heaven in the Slave Community, 1700–1865," 163–183; Elsie Clews Parsons, *Folk-lore of the Sea Islands*, 214; Kytle, *Willie Mae*, 94, 137.

40. Erma Calderon with Leonard Ray Tell, *Erma: A Black Woman Remembers, 1912–1980*, 38; Smith, *To Serve the Living: Funeral Directors and the African American Way of Death*, 27; Sparks, "The Southern Way of Death," 4; Parsons, *Folk-lore of the Sea Islands*, 213; Jean Ritchie, *Singing Family of the Cumberlands*, 214.

41. George Lafayette Tenpenny Jr., to Alexander W. Tenpenny, in Cannon County High School, *Old'uns' Stories Told to Young'uns*, unpaginated; Dunn, *Cades Cove*, 191.

42. Terrill and Hirsch, *Such As Us*, 250–251; Ritchie, *Singing Family of the Cumberlands*, 214; Dunn, *Cades Cove*, 191.

43. Laderman, *The Sacred Remains*, 49; Smith, *To Serve the Living*, 15–31; Terry G. Jordan, *Texas Graveyards: A Cultural Legacy*, 6.

44. Dunn, *Cades Cove*, 191.

45. Dunn, 288, fn. 35; Michael J. McDonald and John Muldowny, "Reburying the Dead: Disinterment and Reinterment at TVA's Norris Dam," 119.

46. Ted Ownby, *American Dreams in Mississippi: Consumers, Poverty and Culture, 1830–1998*, 36; Oral Interview, Jerry Gaither to Kristine M. McCusker, October 29, 2009, AGRC.

47. Cobb, *The Most Southern Place on Earth*, 91, 113; Clipping, "Old Cemeteries Can Hold Up Development," *The Post and Courier* (Charleston, SC), June 20, 2001, in "Burial Practices" folder, Avery; Oral Interview, Revonda Rucker to Kristine M. McCusker, October 13, 2009, AGRC.

48. Kenneth B. Young to Paul Ortiz, July 12, 1994, BTV.

49. Clipping, Bill Davis, "Down by the Riverside," *Charleston City Paper*, January 23, 2003, in "Burials" folder, Avery; Ross Hill Cemetery, https://www.findagrave.com/cemetery/62427/memorial-search; Stacey Graham, "The Plantation Community Cemetery: Reading Black and White Relationships in the Landscape," 68–91.

50. James Farrell, *Inventing the American Way of Death*; Roediger, "And Die in Dixie"; John Michael Vlatch, *The Afro-American Tradition in Decorative Arts*, 139–140.

51. Family property of Robert P. Roysden, shown to the author on a personal visit; Terrill and Hirsch, *Such As Us*, 258.

52. Jordan, *Texas Graveyards*, 30; D. Gregory Jeane, "Folk Art in Rural Southern Cemeteries," 163; Smith, *To Serve the Living*, 21.

53. Jordan, *Texas Graveyards*, 14–15; Dale L. Couch, "Confluence of Regional Cultures in the Savannah River Basin: Reflections of Settlement Patterns in the Decorative Arts," 64; Jeane, "Folk Art in Rural Southern Cemeteries," 163.

54. Bernard Fielding, Speech, in "Burial Practices" folder, Avery; Vlatch, *The Afro-American Tradition in Decorative Arts*, 139, 145; Jeane, "Folk Art in Rural Southern Cemeteries," 163; Jordan, *Texas Graveyards*, 20–22; Dorothy Jean Michael, "Grave Decoration," 129–136; Elizabeth Feen, "Honoring the Ancestors: Kongo-American Graves in the American South," in Elaine Nichols, ed., *The Last Miles of the Way*, 45, 47; Roediger, "And Die in Dixie," 163–183; Parsons, *Folk-lore of the Sea Islands*; Combes, "Ethnography, Archaeology and Burial Practices Among Coastal South Carolina Blacks."

55. William Alexander Percy, *Lanterns on the Levy: Recollections of a Planter's Son*, 345–346.

56. Margaret Jones Bolsterli, *Born in the Delta: Reflections on the Making of a Southern White Sensibility*, 5.

57. Jones, *Born in the Delta*, 49.

58. Murray, *Proud Shoes*, 56.

59. Laura C. Blalock to Mannie Howell, May 28, 1913, Joseph Toy Howell Sr., Papers, TSLA.

60. Eliza Kelly Brady to Rose Shepard, *Mrs. Eliza Kelly Brady*, November 23, 1919, FWP, https://www.loc.gov/item/wpalh000453/.

61. Meeting Minutes, May 1908, Midway Baptist Church, MFC 38, SUSC.

62. Russell, *Roots and Ever Green*, 142.

63. Charles A. Le Guin, ed., *A Home-Concealed Woman: The Diaries of Magnolia Wynn Le Guin, 1901–1913*, 190–191.

64. Grover Cleveland Goodwin to My dear Mother, July 2, 1916, Viola Wood Goodwin Papers, VHS.

65. Grace Lumpkin, *To Make My Bread*, 42.

66. Ball, *The Sweet Hell Inside*, 60; James Seay Brown, *Up Before Daylight: Life Histories from Alabama Writers' Project, 1938–1939*, 97; Oral Interview, Lorita Rocca to Pam Rabelais, August 19, 1995, LSU; Stoney to Murray, FWP; Lizzie Lineberger to Ethel Deal, *Lizzie Linberger*, July 23, 1939, FWP, https://www.loc.gov/item/wpalh001774/.

67. Audrey Colsen Faulkner, et al., *When I was Comin' Up: An Oral History of Aged Blacks*, 85.

68. Cook Family to Unidentified Federal Writers' Project Interviewer, January 3, 1939, FWP Project Papers #3709, Folder 1021, SHC.

69. Le Guin, *A Home-Concealed Woman*, 29, 199.

70. Sister to Carrie Purvis, December 11, 1901, Box 4, Folder 27, George C. Purvis Papers, LSU.

71. Mother to Carrie [Purvis], December 11, 1901, Purvis Papers, LSU.

Chapter 2. Heavenly Reunions and Progressive Reform

1. Alice Nashburn to A. S. Long, *Sarah Long*, July 10, 1939, FWP, http://www.loc.gov/item/wpalh001812/.

2. Samuel Kelton Roberts Jr., *Infectious Fear: Politics, Disease and the Health Effects of Segregation*, 70.

3. Dewey Grantham, *Southern Progressivism: The Reconciliation of Progress and Tradition*, 5, 15–16.

4. Susan L. Smith, *Sick and Tired of Being Sick and Tired: Black Women's Health Activism in America, 1890–1950*, 9; Bill J. Leonard, Baptists in America, 36–37, 54.

5. Donald G. Mathews, "The Southern Rite of Human Sacrifice"; Wayne Flynt, *Alabama Baptists: Southern Baptists in the Heart of Dixie*, 246, 254, 266, 268, 274.

6. Randy J. Sparks, "The Southern Way of Death: The Meaning of Death in Antebellum White Evangelical Culture"; James R. Goff, *Close Harmony: A History of Southern Gospel*, 16–18.

7. Ted Ownby, *Subduing Satan: Religion, Recreation, and Manhood in the Rural South, 1865–1920*, 9.

8. Charles A. Le Guin, ed., *A Home-Concealed Woman: The Diaries of Magnolia Wynn Le Guin, 1901–1913*, 116–117.

9. Tom E. Terrill and Jerrold Hirsch, eds., *Such As Us: Southern Voices of the Thirties*, 12.

10. Charles S. Johnson, *Growing Up in the Black Belt: Negro Youth in the Rural South*, 138.

11. William H. Chafe et al., eds., *Remembering Jim Crow: African Americans Tell About Life in the Segregated South*, 96–97, 98.

12. Ibid.

13. Neille Wesenger to Mrs. Ada Radford, *The Sunshine Lady*, December 29, 1939, FWP, http://www.loc.gov/item/wpalh000548/.

14. Federal Writers' Project of the Works Progress Administration, *These Are Our Lives: As Told by the People and Written by Members of the Federal Writers' Project of the Works Progress Administration in North Carolina, Tennessee, and Georgia*, 264.

15. Terrill and Hirsch, *Such As Us*, 130.

16. Terrill and Hirsch, 37.

17. William H. Brackney, *Baptist Life and Thought: A Source Book*, 277–278, 313–315.

18. National Baptist Conference, USA, Inc., "History of the National Baptist Convention, USA, Inc.," https://www.nationalbaptist.com/about-nbc/our-history, accessed October 3, 2022; Evelyn Brooks Higginbotham, *Righteous Discontent: The Black Women's Movement in the Black Baptist Church, 1880–1920*, 3, 6, 11.

19. David Hempton, *Methodism: Empire of the Spirit*, 1–10; H. Richard Niebuhr, *The Social Sources of Denominationalism*, 59–72; James J. Farrell, *Inventing the American Way of Death, 1830–1920*, 40–42.

20. "Short Talks on Music: Music and the Church," *National Baptist Union-Review* (January 11, 1919), 3.

21. E. P. Alldredge, "Scope and Need of a Tuberculosis Sanitarium," *Annual of the Southern Baptist Convention 1919* (Nashville: The Marshall and Bruce Company, 1919), 108–109, SBHLA; Charles E. Rosenberg, *The Cholera Years: The United States in 1832, 1849, and 1866*.

22. Elsie Wall to I.L.M., Elsie Wall, July 27, 1938, FWP, http://www.loc.gov/item/wpalh001860/.

23. William Link, *The Paradox of Southern Progressivism, 1880–1930*, xii, 25, 31; *Annual of the Southern Baptist Convention 1919* (Nashville: The Marshall and Bruce Company, 1919), 93, SBHLA.

24. Brackney, *Baptist Life and Thought*, 255–258, 266–268.

25. Robert Wiebe, *A Search for Order*; Judith Sealander, "Curing Evils at Their Source: The Arrival of Scientific Giving," 220–21. Thanks to Mark McGarvie for help with this citation.

26. Smith, *Sick and Tired of Being Sick and Tired*, 8–10.

27. Glenda Elizabeth Gilmore, *Gender and Jim Crow: Women and the Politics of White Supremacy in North Carolina, 1896–1920*, 108, 150, 152.

28. Higginbotham, *Righteous Discontent*, 168–169.

29. George Brown Tindall, *The Emergence of the New South, 1913–1935*, 4–32; Gilmore, *Gender and Jim Crow.*

30. Ida B. Wells, *Southern Horrors: Lynch Law in all its Phases*; Gilmore, *Gender and Jim Crow*, 147–150.

31. Higginbotham, *Righteous Discontent*, 174; Flynt, *Alabama Baptists*, 275, 278, 282–283, 312, 341.

32. Sheila Rothman, *Living in the Shadow of Death: Tuberculosis and the Social Experience of Illness in American History*, 3–6; Jimmie Rodgers and Raymond Hall, "TB Blues," The Essential Jimmie Rodgers, RCA 07863-67500-2.

33. Rothman, *Living in the Shadow of Death*, 3–6, 8, 179–183, 212–213; Exhibit narrative, Thomas Wolfe Memorial State Historic Site, Ashville, NC.

34. Oral Interview, Leroy Beavers Sr. to Kieran Walsh Taylor, August 7, 2002, Southern Oral History Project, R-0170, UNC.

35. York David Garrett to KM, BTV; A'Lelia Bundles, *On Her Own Ground: The Life and Times of Madame C. J. Walker*, 193–194.

36. Belle and Lottie Walter to MLW [*sic*], *Belle and Lottie Walter*, September 12, 1938, FWP, http://www.loc.gov/item/wpalh001921/.

37. John and Martha Belk to Robert V. Williams, *The Belks*, December 8, 1938, FWP, http://www.loc.gov/item/wpalh001905/.

38. Alldredge, "Scope and Need of a Tuberculosis Sanitarium," 115, 123, SBHLA. The numbers from 1915 were published in the 1918 proceedings.

39. Alldredge, 127.

40. Alldredge, 98, 121.

41. Alldredge, 124–125.

42. Alldredge, 110, 114, 112. Three hospitals were in Oklahoma, two in Texas, and one each in St. Louis, Missouri; Memphis, Tennessee; Atlanta, Georgia; Alexandria, Virginia; Columbia, South Carolina; and Jackson, Mississippi.

43. Polk City Directory, 1913–1914, MDAH; Polk City Directory, 1918, TSLA.

44. Historical Marker, Jane Terrell Baptist Hospital, https://www.hmdb.org/m.asp?m=86566;see also "Meharry News," *National Baptist Union-Review* (January 25, 1919), 4, SBHLA.

45. "Health Notes," *National Baptist Union-Review* (February 8, 1919), 4, SBHLA.

46. Ad, "Pellagra," *National Baptist Union-Review* (December 1, 1917), 12, SBHLA.

47. Smith, *Sick and Tired of Being Sick and Tired*, 38.

48. Smith, 33–34, 41, 43. Quote on page 41.

49. Smith, 44–45, 53.

50. Louis Armstrong, *Satchmo: My Life in New Orleans*, 91; Wells, *Southern Horrors.*

51. "Flaunting the Red Flag," *National Baptist Union-Review* (April 5, 1919), 9, SBHLA.

52. James O. Breeden, "Disease and Southern Distinctiveness," in Todd L. Savitt and James Harvey Young, eds., *Disease and Distinctiveness in the American South*, 14.

53. Link, *The Paradox of Southern Progressivism*, 142–144, 150–151.

Chapter 3. Life Extension and the Emergence of a Death Commerce System

1. Settlement time was the end-of-the-year division of money between landowner and sharecropper.

2. A. D. Pool to unknown interviewer, *He Never Wanted Land Till Now*, November 10, 1938, FWP, http://www.loc.gov/item/wpalh001885/.

3. David Roediger, "And Die in Dixie: Funerals, Death and Heaven in the Slave Community, 1700–1865," 163.

4. Suzanne Smith, *To Serve the Living: Funeral Directors and the African American Way of Death*, 8–9.

5. Mrs. Albert P. Boyer, Account Books, Mss. 1258, LSU; Edwin A. Harlston Papers, CHS; Oral Interview, Mary Scales to Kristine M. McCusker, November 9, 2005, AGRC.

6. Charles R. Wilson, "The Southern Funeral Director: Managing Death in the New South," 55–58; National Funeral Directors and Morticians Association, Inc., https://nfdma.com/; Calvernetta Beasley Williams, *Historical Archives: The Last Century of the Millennium: The South Carolina Morticians Association, Inc.*, 5.

7. Chapter 159, House Bill No. 125, in *Acts of the State of Tennessee Passed by the Fifty-sixth General Assembly*; Fletcher H. Fielder, License #498, May 7, 1917, Tennessee State Board of Embalmers Records, RG 104, TSLA.

8. Karla F. C. Holloway, *Passed On: African American Mourning Stories*, 16; Charles Johnson, *Shadow of the Plantation*, 197.

9. Smith, *To Serve the Living*, 49–53.

10. Oral Interview, Clarie Collins Harvey to John Dittmer and John Jones, April 21, 1981, MDAH.

11. Ted Ownby, *American Dreams in Mississippi: Consumers, Poverty, and Culture, 1830–1998*, 11; Tom Terrill and Jerrold Hirsch, *Such As Us: Southern Voices of the Thirties*, 75.

12. *The American Funeral Ledger's* "Ethics Page" lists this rule, J. C. Oates Papers, MPL.

13. Walter King Harris Funeral Ledger, AGRC.

14. Helen C. and Timothy R. Marsh, Hoover Funeral and Burial Records of Bedford County, TN, 37.

15. Marsh and Marsh, 144.

16. Robertson County Funeral Ledger, 4, 18, TSLA.

17. Benson Funeral Home Ledger, July 1, 1930, 1, ADAH.

18. Grave Removal Records for Bettie Hatmaker, October 15, 1934; Bart B. Heatherly, October 9, 1934, Box 16, Norris Dam, TVA Papers, NARA-SE.

19. J. C. Oates Funeral Ledger, Box 1, p. 54, MPL; Harris Funeral Ledger, AGRC.

20. Steven M. Stowe, *Doctoring the South: Southern Physicians and Everyday Medicine in the Mid-Nineteenth Century*, 104–106.

21. Ownby, *American Dreams in Mississippi*, 52; Jennifer Ritterhouse, "The Etiquette of Race Relations in the Jim Crow South," 20–21; Daniel Funeral Home Ledger, 78, 290, GSA.

22. J. H. Hanley Funeral Ledger, 1924, 111, and 1930, 351, Emory; Smith, *To Serve the Living*, 4–10.

23. Mr. and Mrs. Tally Smith to Lucile Clark Ford, *An Evening in the Smith Home*, February 14, 1939, FWP, https://www.loc.gov/item/wpalh002073/.

24. Pauli Murray, *Proud Shoes: The Story of an American Family*, 15–16.

25. Harris Funeral Ledger, 92, 102, 117, AGRC; Oates Funeral Ledger, Box 3, p. 71, MPL.

26. "Constitution and Rules of Humane Brotherhood," June 19, 1843, Avery.

27. Stone Square Prince Hall Masons Lodgebook, Burnt Corn, Alabama, 1920–1980, Volume 73, p. 45, 51, 95–96, SUSC; Boyer Account Books, 301, LSU.

28. The United Order of the Tents, "Heritage" section, http://www.unitedorderoftents.org/heritage/; Ruth Davis to Chris Stewart, n.d. [ca. 1990s], BTV.

29. Elaine Nichols, ed., *The Last Miles of the Way: African American Homegoing Traditions, 1890–Present*, 24; Burial Ritual: Association Confederate Soldiers [*sic*], Tennessee Division, TSLA; A. C. Seavers, Bodkin Funeral Home, Account #40, Microfilm Collection 1786, Roll #3, TSLA.

30. Elizabeth Henry to McKinney, Folder 1024, January 11, 1939, FWP Papers (#3709), UNC.

31. Benevolent Aid and Burying Society, Glendora, MS, 1935–1950, Mississippi Department of Insurance: Fraternal Benefit Society Annual Reports, Folder 5, MDAH.

32. Knights and Daughters of Tabor (Mound Bayou), Mississippi Department of Insurance: Fraternal Benefit Society Annual Reports, Folder 17, MDAH; Knights and Daughters of Tabor, Folder 7, MDAH.

33. Nichols, *The Last Miles of the Way*, 24.

34. Julia LaRoche to Chalmers S. Murray, *Mistress of Magnolia Hall*, January 5, 1939, FWP interview, https://www.loc.gov/item/wpalh002107/.

35. Walter B. Weare, *Black Business in the New South: A Social History of the North Carolina Mutual Life Insurance Company*, 23

36. Oral Interview, John L. Berry to John Fleming, October 12, 1979, Duke; Weare, *Black Business in the New South*, 16, 30–31.

37. New York Times, "National Society to Conserve Life; Life Extension Institute Formed to Teach Hygiene and Prevention of Disease," December 13, 1913, 2, https://timesmachine.nytimes.com/timesmachine/1913/12/30/100415073.html?pageNumber=2; Lee K. Frankel, "Conservation of Life by Life Insurance Companies," 77–79.

38. Irving Fisker and Eugene Lyman Fisk, How to Live: Rules for Healthy Living Based on Modern Science. Authorized and Prepared by the Hygiene Reference Board of the Life Extension Institute, Inc.

39. Weare, *Black Business in the New South*, 64.

40. Ibid.

41. T. K. Gibson to Edwin Harleston, February 25, 1911, on Atlanta Mutual Insurance Letterhead, Edwin Augustus Harleston Papers, CHS.

42. Weare, *Black Business in the New South*, viii, 14, 50, 86–7, 101.

43. Mickey Funeral Home Ledger, Page 13, Box 4, Folder 2, Avery.

44. Federal Writers' Project of the Works Progress Administration, *These Are Our Lives: As Told by the People and Written by Members of the Federal Writers' Project of the Works Progress Administration in North Carolina, Tennessee, and Georgia*, 206.

45. Mary McLeod Bethune, *Building a Better World: Essays and Selected Documents*, 3–9.

46. Richard Wright, *Black Boy: A Record of Childhood and Youth*, 161.

47. T. J. Marshall to Alberta Johnson, *T. J. Marshall*, February 16, 1939, FWP, https://www.loc.gov/resource/wpalh1.11050212/.

48. Homer Jordan to Stetson Kennedy, *Mister Homer*, February 3, 1939, FWP, http://www.loc.gov/item/wpalh000423/.

49. Louis I. Dublin, "Life, Death and the Negro," 77–85.

50. American Journal of Public Health, "Editorial: Louis I. Dublin: November 1, 1882-March 7, 1969," vol. 59, no. 7 (July 1969): 1083–1085; Dublin, "Life, Death and the Negro," 39, 42–43; Dublin, "The Health of the Negro."

51. Dublin, "The Health of the Negro."

52. Ibid.

53. Louis I. Dublin, "The Present Status of Birth Registration in American Cities and its Relation to the Infant Mortality Rate," 533–547; Berry to Fleming, Duke.

54. Louis I. Dublin and Jessamine Whitney, "On the Costs of Tuberculosis," 445; James O. Breeden, "Disease as a Factor in Southern Distinctiveness," in Todd L. Savitt and James Harvey Young, eds., *Disease and Distinctiveness in the American South*, 1–29 (see page 8 for quote).

55. Chapter 341, House Bill No. 140, in *Acts of the State of Tennessee Passed by the Fifty-sixth General Assembly* (Nashville: McQuiddy Printing Company, 1909–1910), 1256–1259. The bill is online at the Tennessee State Library & Archives Catalog, https://tnsla.ent.sirsi.net/client/en_US/tnslapublic, under the title, "Acts and ordinances of the governor and judges of the territory of the United States of America south of the River Ohio."

56. Louis I. Dublin and Edwin W. Kopf, "The Improvement of Statistics of Cause of Death Through Supplementary Inquiries to Physicians," 175–191.

57. Robyn Muncy, Creating a Female Dominion in American Reform, 1890–1935, xiii, 38, 39, 55.

58. Grace Meigs, MD, "Editorial," *Journal of the American Institute of Homeopathy* (March 1918), 1064–1065, Box 96, 1914–1920, Folder 8-6-7-2-2, CB.

59. Meigs, "Editorial," CB.

60. L. M. Bristol to Julia C. Lathrop, March 14, 1919, 1914–1920, Box 35, Folder 4-12-3, CB.

61. Mary L. Railey to Julia C. Lathrop, November 25, 1914, 1914–1920, Box 35, Folder 4-13-1, CB; Finding Aid, Frances Sage Bradley Papers, Emory; Frances Sage Bradley to Grace Meigs, February 3, 1918, Box 35, Folder 4-12-3, CB.

62. Memorandum, Margaretta Williamson to Miss [Julia] Lathrop, April 5, 1919, 1914–1920, Box 96, Folder 8-6-7-2-2, CB; Memorandum, April 7, 1919, 1914–1920, Box 96, Folder 8-6-7-2-2, CB.

63. That claim can be found in Lydia Allen DeVilbiss, MD, *Handbook of Child Hygiene* Bulletins No. 8&9 (Topeka: Kansas State Board of Health, August–September 1918), 120–122, 1914–1920, Box 126, Folder 11-108, CB.

64. Marsh and Marsh, *Hoover Funeral and Burial Records of Bedford County, Tennessee*, 37; *These Are Our Lives*, 206.

65. James E. Cosby Jr. and Jean Burns Cosby, *Record of Caskets: Bennett-May and Company, 1924–1994* (no publisher, no date), TSLA.

66. Hanley Funeral Ledger, Box 1, p. 54, AGRC.

Part Two. World War I and Challenging Southern Death Care

1. Pauline Boss, *Ambiguous Loss: Learning to Live with Unresolved Grief*, 20, 29; Drew Gilpin Faust, *This Republic of Suffering: Death and the Civil War.*

Chapter 4. Lonely Coffins

1. Margaret Mitchell, *Lost Laysen.*

2. Albert Abraham, Burial Case File.

3. Drew Gilpin Faust's *This Republic of Suffering: Death and the American Civil War* describes the haphazard and decentralized process both sides used to bury the dead.

4. Carol Byerly, Fever of War: The Influenza Epidemic in the U.S. Army during World War I, 10, 126–127, 186.

5. Adam Hochschild, *To End All Wars: A Story of Loyalty and Rebellion, 1914–1918*, 267, 311, 330; David Kennedy, *Over Here: The First World War and American Society*, 10, 169–177.

6. Rupert Blue, Surgeon General, to Director, Bureau of Sanitary Service, December 21, 1917, Box 588, Folder 591.3; H. C. Robles, Acting Medical Officer in Charge, to the Surgeon General, November 2, 1918, Box 589, 591.3; "Report of Helen B. Fenton, Chief Nurse, with Red Cross Sanitary Unit No. 25, from January 10 to February 1, 1918," Box 588, Folder 591.3; H. D. Ward, Director, Sanitary Unit #17, to Director, Bureau Sanitary Service, November 13 and December 7, 1918, Box 587, Folder 591.3; "Report of Camp Hancock Extra-Cantonment Zone at Augusta Georgia for the Month of November, 1918," H. H. Wagonhalls to Surgeon General, USPHS, December 3, 1918, Box 588, Folder 591.3, all documents in ARC.

7. Church Bulletin, Ensley Baptist Church, February 3, 1918, and December 22, 1918, MFC 1051, SUSC; John M. Barry, *The Great Influenza: The Story of the Deadliest Pandemic in History*, 128–129, 142; Church Bulletin, Ensley Baptist Church, January 20, 1918, January 27, 1918, SUSC.

8. Allen Tate, "The New Provincialism: With an Epilogue on the Southern Novel," *Virginia Quarterly Review* (Spring 1945), quoted in Clay Motley, "Minnie Pearl and William Faulkner: Southern Music as Part of the Literary Renaissance."

9. Walter Edgar, ed., *The South Carolina Encyclopedia*, 147.

10. "Report of Helen B. Fenton, Chief Nurse, with Red Cross Sanitary Unit No. 25, from January 10 to February 1, 1918"; Ward to Director, Bureau Sanitary Service; "Report of Camp Hancock Extra-Cantonment Zone at Augusta Georgia for the Month of November, 1918"; both documents ARC.

11. Richard Wright, *Black Boy: A Record of Childhood and Youth*, 66.

12. Emmett Emmanuel Cheri to Kate Ellis, June 23, 1994; Harvey Johnson Jr. to Blair Murphy, August 4, 1994; Mrs. Lil Hooten to Paul Ortiz, July 11, 1994; all sources BTV.

13. 1st Lieutenant E. B. Garey, To Whom it May Concern, May 24, 1917, Edwin Augustus Harleston Papers, SCHS.

14. Monroe N. Work, *Negro Year Book: An Annual Encyclopedia of the Negro, 1918–1919*, 416.

15. Katherine DuPre Lumpkin, *The Making of a Southerner*, 197.

16. This nickname was his mother's maiden name rather than a derogatory comment on Malloy's sexuality.

17. Scope and Content Note, Wells Papers, SCHS, https://schistory.org/wp-content/uploads/2015/06/Wells-Edward-L.-papers-1111.00-1.pdf; Edward Wells to Richard S. Whaley, House of Representatives, January 27, 1917, Folder 4; Wells to Bob [no last name], July 17, 1917, Folder 5; Wells to Mother, August 10, 1917, Folder 5, Wells Papers; all Wells papers are at SCHS; Obituary appended to Notary Public documents, May 5, 1927, Folder 5, Frederick "Fagg" Malloy Papers, UNC.

18. Jeanette Keith, "The Politics of Southern Draft Resistance, 1917–1918: Class, Race, and Conscription in the Rural South," 1335–1361 (quote is on page 1343).

19. H. L. Harper to F. Donald Atwell, *The Man Who Was*, February 1, 1939, FWP, http://www.loc.gov/item/wpalh002013/.

20. Carl Brindley Notebook, RG 1675, NCSL; Byerly, *Fever of War*, 44.

21. ELW to Dr. Edward Rutledge, January 27, 1918, Folder 6, describes his mother as "nervous"; Edward Wells to Lil [Wells], December 2, 1917, Folder 5; Lily Wells Rutledge to Fannie [Wells], March 13, 1920, Folder 10, Wells Papers; all sources CHS.

22. The United States World War I Centennial Commission, Georgia Memorial Database notation for Lt. Harry Hanley, https://www.worldwar1centennial.org/index.php/georgia-memorial-database.html (search for Hanley); *The Georgia State Memorial Book*, Adopted as the Official Record by the Military Dept., State of Georgia, 15, GSA.

23. "Fagg" to Mrs. Theodore F. Malloy, September 11, 1917, Malloy Papers, UNC.

24. Malloy to My Own Dearest Mother, July 26, 1918, Malloy Papers, UNC.

25. Diary quote is dated December 14, 1918, Samuel Watkins Overton Papers, Ms. 58, Box 16, UMSC.

26. W. H. Hubbard, arranger, "If a Man Die, Shall He Live Again? A Chaplain Answers Some Religious Questions Asked by Service Men About This and Related Subjects," 1920, SBHLA.

27. Byerly, *Fever of War*, 14–23, 32, 50–51; Brindley Notebook, NCSL.

28. Byerly, *Fever of War*, 54; Zeke to Aunt Sarah, November 29, 1918, Box 18, Folder 48, Buck-Ellis Papers, LSU.

29. Brindley Notebook, August 9, 1918, NCSL.

30. Ibid.

31. Katherine Anne Porter, *Pale Horse, Pale Rider*, 126, 129.

32. Barry, *The Great Influenza*, 4, 91–97, 101–103; K. David Patterson and Gerald F. Pyle, "The Geography and Mortality of the 1918 Influenza Pandemic," *Bulletin of the History of Medicine* 65 (Spring, 1991), 4–21; Byerly, *Fever of War*, 1–6, 80–81 87–88.

33. Byerly, *Fever of War*, 70–71, 78–79, 89, 94; Barry, *The Great Influenza*, 35, 247–250; "Monthly Report for October, 1918 to Surgeon General and Doctor Clark," H. H. Wagonhalls to Surgeon General, n.d. [ca. November 1918], Box 588, Folder 591.3, ARC.

34. Byerly, *Fever of War*, 7, 15–21, 65, quote is on page 67; Barry, *The Great Influenza*, 57, 137–139; J. N. Baker, State Health Officer of Alabama, *The Journal of the Medical Association of the State of Alabama*, December 1936, William Crawford Gorgas Papers, Box 1, Folder 3, LSU.

35. Brindley Notebook, NCSL.

36. Byerly, *Fever of War*, 76.

37. Entries for January 14 and 15, 1918, Overton Diary, Overton Papers, UMSC.

38. George to Mother, October 13, 1918, Lewis Papers, LSU.

39. Zeke (Ezekiel Parke Ellis) to Aunt Sarah [Sara [*sic*] Ellis], September 30, 1918, and Zeke to Aunt Sarah, no date [ca. October 1918], Box 18, Folder 46, Buck-Ellis Papers, LSU.

40. Zeke to Aunt Sarah, October 2, 1918, Box 18, Folder 47, Buck-Ellis Papers, LSU.

41. Byerly, *Fever of War*, 167–173.

42. Lumpkin, *The Making of a Southerner*, 198.

43. Charlotte I. Ball to Edward Wells, October 10, 1918, Wells Papers, CHS.

44. Simon J. Smith and Fanna K. Bee, *Canaan-Garden Spot by the Cuttacochee, 1818–1968*, 77.

45. Rosie Hutchins Ashley to Clalee Dunnagan, *Roxie Owens*, August 30, 1939, FWP, https://www.loc.gov/item/wpalh001799/.

46. Dr. William W. Wood to Effie Cowan, *Dr. William Wood*, n.d., FWP, http://www.loc.gov/item/wpalh002262/.

47. Byerly, *Fever of War*, 13; Porter, *Pale Horse, Pale Rider*, 113–165; Charles A. Le Guin, ed., *A Home-Concealed Woman: The Diaries of Magnolia Wynn Le Guin*, 351–352; Maulsey Stoney to Chalmers S. Murray, *Martha Joint, Occasional Servant* March 3, 1939, FWP, http://www.loc.gov/item/wpalh002102/; Dr. William W. Wood to Effie Cowan, *Dr. William W. Wood*, n.d., FWP, https://www.loc.gov/item/wpalh002262/; Nathanial White Sr. to Paul Ortiz, February 17, 1995, BTV.

48. Audrey Olsen Faulkner, *When I was Comin' Up: An Oral History of Aged Blacks*, 158.

49. Melinda Parker, *Melinda Parker*, Louisiana Folklore, FWP, http://www.loc.gov/item/wpalh000584.

50. H. D. Ward, Director, Sanitary Unit #17, to Director, Bureau Sanitary Service, December 7, 1918, Box 587, Folder 591.3, ARC.

51. "More than 22,000 Prisoners are Captured; French Launch New Attack Astride Ailette," *Anniston Star* (AL), September 14, 1918, 1; "U-Boats Charged with Spread of Influenza: Members of Crews Believed Landed to Spread Epidemic Germs in Crowds," *Anniston Star* (AL), September 19, 1918, 1; "Eleven Cases of Influenza Shown," *Anniston Star* (AL), September 24, 1918, 3; all sources SUSC.

52. "Sixty-Nine Cases of Influenza Reported: Birmingham," *Anniston Star* (AL), October 10, 1918, 7; "More Influenza Cases Reported in South: Birmingham, Atlanta and Huntsville Hard Hit," *Anniston Star* (AL), October 11, 1918, 1; Ad, *Anniston Star* (AL), October 11, 1918, 5.

53. Ad, *Anniston Star* (AL), October 27, 1918, 9; all sources SUSC.

54. "Picture Houses Close Saturday," *Anniston Star* (AL), October 6, 1918, 1; "Teachers Should Receive Full Pay," *Anniston Star* (AL), October 13, 1918, 2; "Football Season Postponed," *Anniston Star* (AL), October 13, 1918, 1; "Pastors Decide Not to Open Churches: Anniston and Oxford Schools Will Also Remain Closed Another," *Anniston Star* (AL), 1; all sources SUSC.

55. James F. Sulzby Jr., *Annals of the Southside Baptist Church, Birmingham, Alabama, 1886–1936*, 150.

56. *Annual of the Southern Baptist Convention, 1919* (Nashville: Marshall and Bruce Company, 1919) 92, SBHLA.

57. Arkwright, "Red Cross Care of Influenza Epidemic Throughout Southern Division"; "Report of Camp Hancock Extra-Cantonment Zone at Augusta, Georgia, for the Month of November, 1918"; "Monthly Report for October, 1918 to Surgeon General and Doctor Clark"; W. J. Leppert, Acting Chairman, Division Influenza Committee, to Willoughby Walling, October 31, 1918, Box 688, Folder 803.08; all sources ARC.

58. Monthly Report, H. D. Ward, Director, Sanitary Unit #17, to Director, Bureau Sanitary Service, December 7, 1918, Box 587, Folder 591.3; Robles to the Surgeon General; all sources ARC.

59. Oral Interview, Estelle Williams to Pamela Dean, August 3, 1994, LSU.

60. Oral Interview, Leona Spaht Huff to Katherine Huff O'Neil, January 14, 1995, LSU.

61. "Friday Morning's List," *Atlanta Journal Constitution* (October 18, 1918), 12, ProQuest Historical Newspapers.

Chapter 5. Remembering the War, Forgetting the Flu, Burying the Military Dead

1. Mr. and Mrs. L. L. Abbott to Captain Charles J. Wynn, August 26, 1920, Burial Case File; https://www.abmc.gov/decedent-search/abbott%3Dhenry, ABMC.

2. Michael Sledge, *Soldier Dead: How We Recover, Identify, Bury and Honor our Military Fallen*; Drew Gilpin Faust, *This Republic of Suffering: Death and the American Civil War*, 65–90; American Expeditionary Forces, General Orders #30, February 15, 1918, Box 605, Folder 619.1, ARC.

3. William H. Abele, Burial Case File.

4. Mary Acree to War Risk Insurance, Treasury Department, September 24, 1920; Report of Disinterment and Reburial, February 25, 1924; both documents in Auther Acree, Burial Case File; https://www.abmc.gov/decedent-search/acree%3Dauther, ABMC; Record for Auther Acree, https://digital.archives.alabama.gov/digital/collection/goldstar/id/644/rec/5, ADAH.

5. "Photographs of World War I Graves in France Made for Families by the Red Cross"; "Information Especially Prepared for *The American Funeral Director*," February 8, 1961, 2–3, Box 605, Folder 619.1, ARC.

6. W. R. Castle, Director, American Red Cross to Mrs. Ida [*sic*] Wells, March 15, 1919, Folder 8; Telegram, W. R. Castle Jr to Mrs. Ida Wells, November 21, 1918, both sources in the Wells Papers, SCHS.

7. No author, note to Mrs. Wells, March 14, 1919, Folder 8; The Adjutant General's Office to Edward Rutledge, MD, December 31, 1918, Folder 6; Retyped Telegram on Rutledge and Hude letterhead; Adjutant General to Mrs. Wells, January 22, 1919, Folder 7; The American Red Cross to Mrs. Wells, January 15, 1919, Folder 7; Telegram, Congressman Whaley to Dr. Edward Rutledge, January 22, 1919, Folder 7; Telegram, Adjutant General Harris, January 22, 1919, Folder 8; Ruth Symonds, Assistant Hospital Director, American Red Cross, to Mrs. Wells, December 10, 1919, Folder 9; all documents in Wells Papers, SCHS.

8. "Report of Disinterment, Preparation and Shipment of Body," Christian Acklin, Burial Case File; Carol Byerly, *Fever of War: The Influenza Epidemic in the U.S. Army During World War I*, 179.

9. "Report on Disinterment and Reburial," September 28, 1921, John H. Abney, Burial Case File.

10. "Compilation of Disposition of Remains Data," Sam Abraham, Burial Case File; Raymond Acklem, Burial Case File; Bioform, Christian Acklin, ADAH, https://digital.archives.alabama.gov/digital/collection/goldstar/id/199/rec/4; "Report of Disinterment, Preparation and Shipment of Body," Christian Acklin, Burial Case File.

11. E. A. Kindervater to Mrs. Wells, March 9, 1919, and Frank Parker to Mrs. Wells, March 13, 1919, Folder 8, Wells Papers, SCHS.

12. Redmond C. Stewart to Miss Sabina Elliott Wells, May 10, 1919, Folder 19, Wells Papers, SCHS.

13. James W. Thompson to Eugenia Ranson, October 1, 1918; Newspaper Clipping, "Lt. J. O. Ranson Dead in France: Young Officer from Huntersville Was Leading His Men into Face of German Attack When End Came," October 22, 1918, Ranson Family Collection; both of the foregoing sources are at UNC; R. I. Francisco to Mrs. Wells, March 12, 1919, Folder 8, Wells Papers, SCHS. Monty Kelly added a postscript to this letter.

14. Frederick "Fagg" Malloy to Mrs. Hood, January 1918, [no date listed], Malloy Papers, UNC.

15. Frederick "Fagg" Malloy to Mother precious [Mrs. Theodore F. Malloy], June 30, 1918, Malloy Papers, UNC.

16. Frederick "Fagg" Malloy to My Own Dearest Mother [Mrs. Theodore F. Malloy], July 26, 1918, Malloy Papers, UNC.

17. Major John A. Nelson to Abner Family (written by Abraham K. Wrenshall, 1st Lt.), May 26, 1919, Cecil Abner, Burial Case File.

18. Captain Walter Gaudinsky to Mrs. Malloy, January 1, 1919, Malloy Papers, UNC.

19. Captain Carl Hanton to Mrs. Malloy, December 30, 1918, Malloy Papers, UNC.

20. Lisa M. Budreau, "The Politics of Remembrance: The Gold Star Mothers' Pilgrimage and America's Fading Memory of the Great War," 372, 377–378; Jeanette Keith, "The Politics of Southern Draft Resistance, 1917–1918: Class, Race, and Conscription in the Rural South," 1343.

21. Byerly, *Fever of War*, 130; Budreau, "The Politics of Remembrance," 372, 377–378, 379.

22. Chester P. Adair, Burial Case File.

23. Vernon D. Rowe to War Department, December 8, 1928, Ellen Adair to War Department, June 22, 1929, Luther Adair, Burial Case File.

24. Barney L. Abbott, Burial Case File.

25. Isaiah Abernathy, Burial Case File.

26. E. H. Harleston Funeral Ledger, Volume 1917–1919, page 309, Avery; Helen C. and Timothy R. Marsh, *Hoover Funeral and Burial Records of Bedford County, Tennessee*, 103.

27. M. W. Phariss to Chief, QM Corps, April 5, 1917, Marion Abernathy, Burial Case File.

28. Telegram from Mrs. Alice Acty, Rodwin, VA, George W. Acty, Burial Case File; R. E. Shannon to Mr. L. L. Abbott, June 2, 1921, Henry Abbott, Burial Case File.

29. Obituary and photo, Find a Grave, "Alice Manard Bishop Abbott," https://www.findagrave.com/memorial/24682696/alice-manard-abbott, accessed August 10, 2022.

30. Fred F. Malloy, Meuse-Argonne American Cemetery, https://www.abmc.gov/decedent-search/malloy%3Dfred, ABMC; and Find a Grave, "Frederick Fagg Malloy," https://www.findagrave.com/memorial/36541379/frederick-fagg-malloy, accessed August 10, 2022.

31. Byerly, *Fever of War*, 133; Charley Achee, Roderick Acors, John Franklin Acuff and Christian Acklin, Burial Case Files.

32. Major J. McClintock to Mrs. Mary P. Abraham, November 5, 1928, Box 7, John P. Abraham, Burial Case File.

33. Isaiah Abernathy, Burial Case File.

34. Lisa Long, "I Found it in the Archives: Blue Star Banner," History Blog, December 2, 2010, Ohio History Connection, https://www.ohiohistory.org/i-found-it-in-the-archives-blue-star-banner/.

35. Marie Bankhead Owen to Mrs. Belle T. McKenzie, November 4, 1921, and Bioform, https://digital.archives.alabama.gov/digital/collection/goldstar/id/2828/rec/1150/.

36. *The Georgia State Memorial Book*, Adopted as the Official Record by the Military Dept., State of Georgia, 10, 11, 19, GSA.

37. *The Georgia State Memorial Book*, 18, 42.

38. *The Georgia State Memorial Book*, 70.

39. *The Georgia State Memorial Book*, 30.

40. Ibid.

41. *The Georgia State Memorial Book*, 58; Overton Diary, November 15, 1918, Samuel Watkins Overton Papers, Ms. 58, Box 16, UMSC.

42. Memorial, Capt. Edward Lawrence Wells, Find a Grave, https://www.findagrave.com/memorial/33421367/edward-lawrence-wells, accessed August 20, 2022; Description of Edward Wells' Croix de Guerre nomination, March 25, 1919, Folder 8; Virginia Military Institute to Mrs. Edward Rutledge, November 1, 1927, Folder 9; Adjutant General to Mrs. Edward Rutledge, October 30, 1925, Folder 15; C.S. Coulter to General [Frank] Parker, April 6, 1923; Parker to Theodore [no last name, ca. 1923–1924], Folder 13; Frank Parker, Brig. General, to [no addressee], July 7, 1924, Folder 13, Wells Papers; all documents, except Capt. Edward Lawrence Wells Memorial, SCHS.

43. Ben [Kuniawsky] to Miss Wells, February 10, 1922, Folder 12; Fannie Wells to Lily, March 14, 1920, Folder 10; Fannie Wells to Lily, March 22, 1920, Folder 10; Ben to Miss Wells, August 23, 1921, Folder 12, Wells Papers; all sources in the Wells Papers, SCHS.

44. Mrs. Mary Acree to War Department, January 30, 1920, Auther [*sic*] Acree, Burial Case File; Bioform, Author [*sic*] Acree, https://digital.archives.alabama.gov/digital/collection/goldstar/id/644/rec/5; Author Acree, https://www.abmc.gov/decedent-search/acree%3Dauther, ABMC.

45. Letter, April 21, 1922, Folder 5, Malloy Papers, UNC; Lisa Budreau, "The Politics of Remembrance," 373, 390–393.

46. Budreau, 398–399, 404, 407.

47. Mrs. Alice Abbott, n.d. [ca. September 29, 1931], to Gold Star folks at Government, Henry Abbott, Burial Case File.

48. Budreau, "The Politics of Remembrance," 403; "Report of Disinterment and Reburial," Rayford Adair, Burial Case File.

49. "Itinerary of Meuse Argonne Group, Part L," Adair Burial Case File.

50. Ollie Adair to Quarter Master Gen [*sic*], War Dept. July 19, 1930, Adair Burial Case File.

51. A. D. Hughes to Mrs. C. H. Davis, September 27, 1929, Acree Burial Case File; Correspondence dated June 22, 1929, Adair Burial Case File; quote is from Budreau, "The Politics of Remembrance," 401.

Part Three. Death Care in the 1920s South

1. *Annual of the Southern Baptist Convention, 1918* (Nashville, TN: Marshall and Bruce Company, 1919), 127, SBHLA.

Chapter 6. Purple Coffins and Cadillac Hearses

1. J. C. Oates Funeral Ledger, Box 7, p. 23, 181, MPL.

2. Chad E. Seales, "An Old Love for New Things: Southern Baptists and the Modern Technology of Indoor Baptisteries."

3. Blaine A. Brownell, "The Commercial-Civic Elite and City Planning in Atlanta, Memphis, and New Orleans in the 1920s," 342.

4. Blaine A. Brownell, "Birmingham, Alabama: New South City in the 1920s," 21–22; Church Bulletin, February 17, 1924; Church Bulletin, January 21, 1923; "Annual Conference," January 13, 1924, Ruhama Baptist Church Collection; all sources SUSC.

5. Harleston Funeral Ledger, Reel 2, pp. 203 (express body), 201 (Connecticut), 244 (Los Angeles, CA), 295 and 308 (New York), 254 (Summerville, SC), Avery; Edward Simmons to Chalmers S. Murray, *Go to Go Crik*, February 8, 1939, FWP, http://www.loc.gov/item/wpalh002104/.

6. John C. Gebhart, *Funeral Costs: Miscellaneous Contributions on the Costs of Medical Care #3* (Washington, DC, November 1930), 6; John C. Gebhart, *Funeral Costs: What They Average; Are They Too High? Can They Be Reduced?*

7. George Fremaux to Mr. L. J. Dauterive, June 18, 1925, and Dauterive to Fremaux, October 20, 1926, Dauterive and Fremaux Funeral Record Book, LSU.

8. Teddy Harleston to Elise Harleston, August 23, 1929, Box 2, Folder 4, Harleston Papers, SCHS.

9. Teddy Harleston to Elise Harleston, September 19, 1929, Box 2, Folder 4, Harleston Papers, SCHS; Oral Interview, Clarie Collins Harvey to John Dittmer and John Jones, April 21, 1981, MDAH; Calvernetta Beasley Williams, *Historical Archives: The Last Century of the Millennium: The South Carolina Morticians Association, Inc., Formerly Known as The Colored Funeral Directors and Embalmers Association*, 9.

10. Oral Interview, John C. Scarborough III to Kristine M. McCusker and Lauren Pate, August 4, 2010, AGRC; Oral Interview, Evelyn Caldwell to Daisy M. Greene, June 12, 1978, Washington County Oral History Project, MDAH; Oral Interview, Florence

Bailey to Daisy Greene, December 4, 1976, MDAH; Suzanne E. Smith, *To Serve the Living: Funeral Directors and the African American Ways of Death*, 9.

11. Letter, J. H. Hanley to Messrs. Hendrix and Buchanan (law firm), December 18, 1928, Box 25, Book 1, J. H. Hanley's Bell Street Funeral Ledger, Emory.

12. Harvey to Dittmer and Jones, MDAH; Kelsey Pharr to Bertha R. Comstock, *Kelsey L. Pharr, Negro Undertaker*, January 11, 1939, FWP, https://www.loc.gov/resource/wpalh1.10120109/; Hanley Funeral Ledger, Box 24, p. 88, Emory.

13. Mary Gover, *Mortality Among Negroes in the United States*, 4–5, 16–18; Oscar Dowling, "Some Phases of Rural Health," 424; Homer Jordan to Stetson Kennedy, *Mister Homer*, February 3, 1939, FWP, http://www.loc.gov/item/wpalh000423/; Samuel Kelton Roberts Jr., *Infectious Fear: Politics, Disease and the Health Effects of Segregation*, 17, 216.

14. Elise Forrest Harleston to E. G. "Teddy" Harleston Jr., August 28, 1925, Folder 13, Harleston Papers SCHS.

15. Funeral record for Robert? ("Negro"), n.d. and Archie Buie, June 26, 1921, *Hulett Funeral Home: Records of Funerals, Volume 1, 01 January Through 31 December 1924*, 1, 22; Mary Britt to I. L. M., *Description of a Mill Village*, September 20, 1938, FWP, https://www.loc.gov/item/wpalh001871/.

16. Brownell, "Birmingham, Alabama," 33; Corey Todd Lesseig, "Automobility and Social Change: Mississippi, 1909–1939," 97; Julia La Roche to Chalmers S. Murray, *Mistress of Magnolia Hall*, 1939, FWP, https://www.loc.gov/item/wpalh002107/.

17. Mamie Collins to Annie Ruth Davis, *There's No Place Like Home*, 1938, FWP, http://www.loc.gov/item/wpalh002032/.

18. Ray Campbell to George Purvis, March 10, 1919, Box 4, Folder 50, George C. Purvis and Family Papers, Mss. #2971, LSU.

19. Lillian Parker Larsen to Mother, n.d. [ca. September 1933], Folder 6, Mss. 158, 1933–34, UMSC.

20. L. M. Mitchell, MD to F. Donald Atwell, *Small Town Doctor*, February 18, 1939, FWP, http://lcweb2.loc.gov/mss/wpalh3/30/3004/30040611/30040611.pdf; Harvey to Dittmer and Jones, MDAH; Michelle R. Scott, *Blues Empress in Chattanooga: Bessie Smith and the Emerging Urban South*, 135; Charles P. Cober [*sic*], to O. Arthur Kirkman Sr., July 30, 1930, Box 6, Folder 79, Kirkman Papers, UNC.

21. Patrick Huber, *Linthead Stomp: The Creation of Country Music in the Piedmont South*, 216–275.

22. C. R. Jonas to Mr. Voit Gilmore, March 20, 1939, Charles Andrew Jonas Papers, Collection 4536, UNC.

23. Omie Williams Epps to Sadie Hornsby, *An Air-Minded Family*, March 6, 1939, FWP, http://www.loc.gov/item/wpalh000513/.

24. (Mrs. E. W.) Emma R. Hale, Whitehaven, Tennessee, to Annie Crutcher, June 8, 1920, Box 4, Folder 5, Annie Crutcher Papers, TSLA.

25. Susan Porter Benson, "Palace of Consumption" in *Counter Cultures: Saleswomen, Managers, and Customers in American Department Stores, 1890–1940*; Robbie to Teddy [Harleston], February 8, 1927, Harleston Papers, SCHS.

26. Teddy Harleston to Elise Harleston, August 26, 1929, Box 2, Folder 4, Harleston Papers, SCHS.

27. Teddy Harleston to Elise Harleston, August 31, 1929, Harleston Papers, SCHS.

28. Teddy Harleston to Elise Harleston, September 8, 1929, Box 2, Folder 4, Harleston Papers, SCHS; Oral interview, Frank Essex to Kristine M. McCusker and Jim Williams, September 10, 2008, AGRC.

29. *Quisenberry Funeral Home, 1931–1954*, viii; Ad, *Consumer Directory for Jackson, Tennessee*, 2:47 (Jackson, TN: Baldwin Consumer Survey Company and the *Jackson Sun*, 1937), 54, TSLA; Ad, Memphis City Directory, 1923, p. 1770, TSLA.

30. Kristine M. McCusker, "Funeral Music and the Transformation of Southern Musical and Religious Cultures, 1935–1945," 426–452.

31. Katy Brumby to Mary Chappell, *The Story of Katy Brumby*, n.d., FWP, http://www.loc.gov/item/wpalh000016.

32. Will, Elvie McFadden, Probated May 16, 1926, RCA.

33. Gary Laderman, *The Sacred Remains: American Attitudes Toward Death, 1799–1883*, 158–161; Iredell County Funeral Registers, pp. 1, 29, 55, NCSL; Hanley Funeral Ledger, Box 25, Book 1, last page for Mrs. Sallie Sheats, Emory; Oates Funeral Ledger, Box 7, p. 25, MPL.

34. Marian Miller Edmonds to Kisha Turner, August 11, 1995, BTV.

35. Oates Funeral Ledger, 25, MPL; Elise Harleston to Teddy Harleston, August 31, 1929, Box 2, Folder 4, Harleston Papers, SCHS.

36. Audrey Faulkner et al., eds., *When I was Comin' Up: An Oral History of Aged Blacks*, 78; James J. Farrell, *Inventing the American Way of Death*, 1830–1920.

37. Elise Harleston to Teddy Harleston, July 2, 1926, Box 2, Folder 1, Harleston Papers, SCHS.

38. Hanley charged $12 to embalm an adult; J. C. Oates charged $20, according to the Hanley Funeral Ledger, Box 24, Book 3 (Emory) and Oates Funeral Ledger, Box 8 (MPL). See also Daniel Funeral Home Ledger, records 1586 and 1589 for a white southerner who refused to be embalmed, GSA; and Oates Funeral Ledger (MPL), Box 6, p. 14, for a Black southerner who refused to be embalmed.

39. Laderman, *The Sacred Remains*, 158–161; Robert G. Mayer, *Embalming: History, Theory, and Practice*, 59–60.

40. Ads, "Antiquity of Embalming," October 13, 1921, in Joe Casey et al., *J. C. Moore and Sons Funeral Home Records, 1931–1966*, Winchester, Tennessee.

41. Mickey Funeral Home Ledger, inventories, Folder 6, Box 3, Avery.

42. Oates Funeral Ledger, Box 7, page 22, MPL; Ad, Memphis City Directory, page 24, 1923, TSLA; Gebhart, *Funeral Costs*, 7–8.

43. David R. Roediger, "And Die in Dixie: Funerals, Death and Heaven in the Slave Community 1700–1865," 166; Hanley Funeral Ledger, Box 24, Book 2, p. 67, 69, Emory; Oates Funeral Ledger, Box 8, p. 66, for an embalmed body shipped home from Cleveland, Ohio, MPL; Hanley Funeral Ledger, Box 24, Book 2, 40, Emory; Telegram, n.d., Hanley Funeral Ledger, Emory.

44. Mickey Funeral Home Ledger, Invoice from Rockwell Furniture Company, February 3, 1926, Folder 1, Box 5, AI, Avery; National Casket Company, 1922, p. 3, VHS.

45. Mickey Funeral Home Ledger inventory, Folder 6, Box 3, Avery; Vicki B. Roach, *McPeters Funeral Records, 1916–1919, 1921–1923* (Corinth: Alcorn County Genealogical Society, n.d.), 9, MDAH; Noah Casket, Daniel Funeral Ledger, GSA.

46. Hanley Funeral Ledger, Box 24, Book 1, 152, Emory; Record for "Infant of Zeb Jackson," date of burial, April 11, 1919, Robertson County Funeral Ledger, MF 268, TSLA.

47. Mickey Funeral Home Ledger, Folder 6, Box 3, Avery; Oates funeral ledger, Box 7, p. 124, MPL.

48. Harleston Funeral Ledger, Reel 2, p. 211, 306, Emory.

49. Will, Maggie Muirhead, Probated July 1920, RCA.

50. Will, Miss Lou Nelson, Miss Charlie Nelson, Probated November 20, 1934, RCA.

51. Will, Elizabeth Richardson Brenagh, Probated January 1924, DCW.

52. Will, Theresa Jacob, Probated January 26, 1928, DCW.

53. Will, Lizzie Robinson Davenport, Probated October 14, 1929, *Abstracts of Last Wills and Testaments, Madison County, Tennessee, 1927–1937*, abstracted by Jonathan K.T. Smith (2000), TSLA.

54. For a picture of the playhouse, see "Memorial," Roselind Nadine Earles, Find a Grave, https://www.findagrave.com/memorial/11332/roselind-nadine-earles, accessed August 10, 2022; for her mother's burial, see Alma L Moody Earles, Find a Grave, https://www.findagrave.com/memorial/17261278/alma-l-earles.

55. *Annual of the Southern Baptist Convention 1920* (Nashville, Tennessee: Marshall and Bruce Co, 1920), 434, 428, SBHLA.

56. Bathsheba Grand Chapter, Order of the Eastern Star (Meridian and Jackson), Folder 2, Fraternal Benefit Society, Dead Files, Mississippi Department of Insurance, MDAH; Mississippi Benevolent/Standard Fraternal Aid Society (Lexington and Pickens), Folder 7, Fraternal Benefit Society, Dead Files, Mississippi Department of Insurance, MDAH; T. J. Marshall to Alberta Johnson, *T. J. Marshall*, February 16, 1939, FWP, http://www.loc.gov/item/wpalh000421/.

57. Contract, Grand United Order of Odd Fellows of Key of the West no. 1692; Program, June 26, 1932, E. W. Biggs Papers, Folder 7, Box 1, SCL; William Alexander Percy, *Lanterns on the Levee: Recollections of a Planter's Son*, 53.

58. "Last Rites for Trotwood Moore Held at Home: Negro Capitol Employes [*sic*] Bear Casket to the Grave," *The Tennessean*, May 14, 1929, 1, 5; Fred Arthur Bailey, "John Trotwood Moore and the Partician [*sic*] Cult of the New South," 28.

59. Death notice, "Rose Lewis, Died Nov. 1, 1917, at the home of her grandson," Scrapbook, Wingo Family Papers, Section 20, VHS.

60. William Faulkner, *As I Lay Dying*.

Chapter 7. Indifference, Shame, Selfishness, and Wrong Living

1. Nell V. Mellichamp Journal, 1926–1927, Volume 1, 1, SCL; Death Certificate, Miss Amelia E. Mellichamp, April 29, 1926, SCL.

2. T. Brady Jr. to Lucius Burch Jr., August 30, 1938, Burch Papers, UMSC.

3. Laura Claridge, *Emily Post: Daughter of the Gilded Age, Mistress of American Manners*, 248; Sigmund Freud, "Mourning and Melancholia," 239–258. My thanks to Stacey Owen for her help with Freud.

4. Freud, "Mourning and Melancholia."

5. Margaret Jones Bolsterli, *Born in the Delta: Reflections on the Making of a Southern White Sensibility*, 49; Pauline Boss, *Ambiguous Loss: Learning to Live With Unresolved Grief*, 9.

6. John Wilson McRaven to Will Henry, Easy and Lucile [McRaven], January 29, 1922, McRaven Papers, TSLA.

7. William Alexander Percy, *Lanterns on the Levee: Recollections of a Planter's Son*, 53.

8. Arthur M. Schlesinger, *Learning How to Behave: A Historical Study of American Etiquette Books*, 50–52.

9. Ibid.

10. Emily Post, "Funerals," in *Etiquette in Society, in Business, in Politics and at Home*, www.bartleby.com/95/24.html; "Emily Post," Emily Post Etiquette, http://emilypost.com/about/emily-post/, accessed August 10, 2022; Claridge, *Emily Post*, unpaginated photo of Post on CBS radio.

11. Post, "The Growth of Good Taste in America," *Etiquette*, ch. 38.

12. Post, ch. 24.

13. Ibid.

14. R. A. Torrey, *Death Defeated and Defied: A Message of Comfort, Consolation and Cheer*, 43–46, SBHLA.

15. E. Clowes Chorley, "The Antecedents of the American Prayer Book," *The New American Prayer Book: Its History and Contents*, ch.1, http://anglicanhistory.org/bcp/chorley1929/01.html, accessed August 10, 2022.

16. Chorley, *The New American Prayer Book*, ch. 7.

17. Ibid.

18. Ibid.

19. Chorley, *The New American Prayer Book*, ch. 7.

20. Email communication, Steven M. Stowe to Kristine M. McCusker, October 6, 2015; Diary, George Monro Yoder, UNC.

21. Diary, Mrs. Sallie Dorcas Brown Whitesides, SCL.

22. Mellichamp Journal, v. 1, 76, SCL.

23. Sadie Gaither Anderson to Cousin Cora [Harris], September 17, 1935, Folder 9, Harris Papers, UNC.

24. Mr. and Mrs. Tally Smith to Lucile Clarke Ford, *An Evening in the Smith Home*, February 14, 1939, FWP, http://www.loc.gov/item/wpalh002073/.

25. Clipping, "Funeral of Reverend Maddox, n.d. [ca. July 1927], Maddox Papers, VHS.

26. Post, *Etiquette*, ch. 24.

27. Smiths to Ford.

28. Funeral record for Isaac Bernstein, November 7, 1919, *Fisher Funeral Home*, 4, MDAH; John Wilson McRaven to Will Henry McRaven, November 18, 1923, McRaven Papers; Post, *Etiquette*, ch. 24.

29. Ellie (no last name), Newcomb College, to Mother dearest, October 4, 1926, Box 19, Folder 15, Buck-Ellis Papers, LSU.

30. Elsie M. Slopes to Mrs. Moore, May 30, 1929, Box 17, Folder 7, Moore Papers, TSLA.

31. Post, *Etiquette*, ch. 27; Kristine M. McCusker, "From 'Behind the Dark Clouds, the Sun Is Shining' to 'He's Only Away': Condolence Literature and the Emergence of a Modern South, 1913–1945," 207–228.

32. (Mrs.) Sallie S. Windham to My Dear Mr. Bankhead, May 13, 1922, Bankhead Papers, ADAH.

33. R. L. Allen, Palmetto Casket Company, September 14, 1932, Folder 8, Box 2, Biggs Papers, SCL.

34. A. F. Shaw, Fisk University, to Dr. Moore, May 13, 1929, Box 17, Folder 7, Moore Papers, TSLA.

35. Floyd Jenkins scrapbook, VHS, unpaginated.

36. Telegram, John Powell, Mountain Lake, Virginia, to Arthur [Kirkman, Jr.] August 2, 1930, Series 1, Box 6, Folder 79, Kirkman Papers, UNC.

37. Mrs. Griffin to Sally Warner Frazier, July 11, 1927, MF#1190, Reel 3, Sally Warner Frazier Papers, TSLA.

38. LM Dodds to My Dear Friend [W. B. Bankhead], n.d. [ca. May 1922], Bankhead Papers, ADAH.

39. Annie Hughes to Jean and Janie Blue, November 20, 1934, Blue Family Papers, Collection #04955, UNC; Mary W. Harris to Mrs. Wade H. Harris, Folder 8, Harris Papers, UNC; John Lord to Mannie Howell, April 22, 1913, Folder 8, Box 1, Howell Family Papers, TSLA.

40. Mary L. Childress to Miss Carter, April 22, 1913, Howell Family Papers, TSLA.

41. Harry M. Davis to William Bankhead, May 14, 1922, Bankhead Papers, ADAH.

42. Mary Tarbell Gordon? [signature illegible] to Mannie Howell, n.d. [ca. May 1929], Howell Family Papers, TSLA.

43. Windham to Bankhead, Bankhead Papers, ADAH.

44. Hughes to Jean and Janie, for the language "broken up"; Walt Crissman to Arthur Kirkman, August 1, 1930, Kirkman Papers, UNC.

45. Anderson to Cousin Cora, Harris Papers, UNC.

46. Hughes to Jean and Janie, Kirkman Papers, UNC.

47. Moore diary, December 23, 1924, TSLA.

48. Teddy Harleston to Elise Harleston, August 26, 1929, Harleston Papers, SCHS.

49. Envelope with 35 embossed cards, Folder 8, Harris papers, UNC.

50. Arthur Kirkman to Arthur Allen, September 30, 1930, Series 1, Box 6, Folder 79, Kirkman Papers, UNC.

51. Klumpp's, Inc., to Gentlemen, n.d. [ca. 1923], Oates Funeral Ledger, Box 4, MPL.

52. Post, *Etiquette*, ch. 24.

53. Alan Trachtenberg, "Albums of War: On Reading Civil War Photograph," 6.

54. Post, *Etiquette*, ch. 24.

55. Jeanne Sully Smyth diary and scrapbooks, LSU.

56. Jenkins scrapbook, VHS.

57. Record for Isaac Bernstein, *Fisher Funeral Home*, 4, MDAH; Photos, Moore Papers; Jenkins scrapbook, VHS.

58. Private family papers of Ken Sloan; Jeffrey Ruggles, *Photography in Virginia*, 146–190.

59. Obituary, Amelia Mellichamp, pasted in the interior of Mellichamp Journal, SCL.

60. Mellichamp Journal, Volume 2, 1921–1947, SCL.

61. No author, "Miss Amelia Mellichamp," *Southern Churchman*, January 15, 1927; James Higgins to my very dear friend, no date; all documents pasted into Mellichamp Journal, v. 1, SCL.

62. Mellichamp Journal, v. 1, SCL.

63. Mellichamp Journal, 32.
64. Mellichamp Journal, 64.
65. Mellichamp Journal, 30.
66. Mellichamp Journal, 109.
67. Mellichamp Journal, 2–3.
68. Mellichamp Journal, 4–5, 21.

Chapter 8. "Health Is Just Everything"

1. Oral Interview, John C. Scarborough III to Kristine M. McCusker and Lauren Pate, August 4, 2010, AGRC; Mother to Clydie, March 1, 1925, November 24, 1925, December 6, 1923, November 26, 1923, Folder 2; Clipping, *The Carolina Times*, May 1, 1982; both sources in the Clydie F. Scarborough Papers, Duke.

2. Lillian to Mother, [ca. February 1934], p. 8, Folder 11, Lillian Parker Larsen Papers, UMSC; Sheila Rothman, *Living in the Shadow of Death: Tuberculosis and the Social Experience of Illness in American History*, 227, 239; Myrtle C. Berry, "Diphtheria," February 12, 1940, Gertrude Chandler Peterkin Papers, SCL.

3. Karen Kruse Thomas, *Deluxe Jim Crow: Civil Rights and American Health Policy, 1935–1954*, 13.

4. Louis E. Foulks, MD, Chief Sanitary Inspector, to Assistant Surgeon R. P. Sandidge, Medical Officer in Charge, U.S. Public Health Service, Alexandria, VA, "General Sanitary Survey," March 15, 1919, 1, Box 589, Folder 591.3, ARC.

5. Ibid.

6. Foulks to Sandidge, ARC, 3.

7. Foulks to Sandidge, ARC, 11.

8. Foulks to Sandidge, ARC, 9.

9. Foulks to Sandidge, ARC, 11.

10. Douglas Flamming, *Creating the Modern South: Millhands and Managers in Dalton, Georgia, 1884–1984*, 137; Robert Olesen, Passed Assistant Surgeon, to the Surgeon General, August 4, 1918, Folder 591.3, Box 589; Monthly Report, Spartanburg, 2, ARC.

11. Taliaferro Clark to G. A. Wheeler, March 12, 1919, Box 587, Folder 591.3, ARC.

12. Oteen Veterans Administration Hospital Historic District, https://files.nc.gov/ncdcr/nr/BN0041.pdf; Charles M. Meacham, "The U.S. Veterans Hospital, no. 79, Out Wood, Kentucky," *Meacham's History of Christian County, Kentucky*, http://www.westernkyhistory.org/christian/meacham/chap47.html, accessed August 10, 2022.

13. Annual Report of the Richland County Chapter, American Red Cross, July 1, 1931-July 1, 1932, Box 656, Folder 758, ARC; Lieutenant Herbert G. Sparrow, "Clutching Hands," *The Red Cross Courier* (November 1934), 1, Box 819, Folder DR 560, ARC.

14. Herbert G. Sparrow, "Clutching Hands."

15. Clipping, "Murfreesboro Firemen Graduate in First Aid," n.d. [ca. 1930s], ARC Papers, Metro.

16. Oscar Dowling, "Some Phases of Rural Health," 427.

17. The Renns to ILM, *The Renns*, July 19, 1938, FWP, https://www.loc.gov/item/wpalh001861/; Lois Lapiene to unknown, May 1 & 2, 1939, FWP, Folder 1022, UNC.

18. John Anderson Hill to McKinney [no first name], n.d., FWP, Folder 1025, UNC.

19. Thomas, *Deluxe Jim Crow*, 81–82.

20. Oscar Dowling, president, Louisiana State Board of Health, to Miss Julia C. Lathrop, Chief, CB, December 4, 1918, Box 39, Folder 4-15-2-1-20, CB; Frances Sage Bradley to Grace Meigs, January 30, 1918, Box 35, Folder 412-3, CB; Price V. Fishback, Michael R. Haines, and Shawn Kantor, "The Impact of the New Deal on Black and White Infant Mortality in the South," *Explorations in Economic History* 38 (2001), 97–98.

21. Fishback et al., "The Impact of the New Deal on Black and White Infant Mortality in the South," 97; Mary L. Railey, Executive Secretary, Child Welfare Association, to Grace Abbott, Chief, Childrens [*sic*] Bureau, February 24, 1928, CB; Questionnaire, "Improvement in Infant and Maternal Welfare from July 1, 1922, to June 30, 1927," Box 267, Folder 4-2-2-0, CB.

22. United States Department of Commerce, *Statistical Abstract of the United States: 1919, 42nd Number* (Washington, DC: United States Government Printing Office, 1920), 74–81; United States Department of Commerce, *Statistical Abstract of the United States: 1929, 51st Number* (Washington, DC: United States Government Printing Office, 1929), 77–82.

23. Mary Gover, *Mortality Among Negroes in the United States.*

24. "Biographies of Presidents and Secretaries of the National Negro Insurance Association, 1921–1949," 29, Box 8 and Folder 50, Duke; Asa T. Spaulding to C. C. Spaulding, January 9, 1936, Box 53, Folder 1, Asa T. Spaulding Papers, Duke.

25. Louis I. Dublin, and Jessamine Whitney, "On the Costs of Tuberculosis," quote is on page 441.

26. Alan M. Kraut, *Goldberger's War: The Life and Work of a Public Health Crusader*, 156; Joseph A. Goldberger et al., "A Study of the Relation of Family Income and Economic Factors to Pellagra Incidence in Seven Cotton Mill Villages of South Carolina in 1916"; Edgar Sydenstricker and Dorothy Wiehl, "A Study of the Incidence of Disabling Sickness in a South Carolina Cotton Mill Village in 1918."

27. Pauli Murray, *Proud Shoes: The Story of an American Family*, 252.

28. Kraut, *Goldberger's War*, 56–59, 99, 104, 189–190; Jacquelyn Dowd Hall et. al., *Like A Family: The Making of a Southern Cotton Mill World*, 150–151.

29. Kraut, *Goldberger's War*, 105, 113, 123, 168, 174.

30. Kraut, 11, 227.

31. Obituary for Oscar Dowling, *Jena Times*, January 8, 1931, https://libguides.tulane.edu/ld.php?content_id=44434262; Memorandum, Margarita Williamson to Miss Lathrop, April 5, 1919, RG102, Box 96, Folder 8-6-7-2-2, 1914–1920, CB; Kraut, *Goldberger's War*, 126, 177, 192–193, 196.

32. Kraut, *Goldberger's War*, 126, 177, 192–193, 196.

33. Roy N. Brown, *Public Poor Relief in North Carolina*, 100–118; Monroe N. Work, *Negro Year Book: An Annual Encyclopedia of the Negro, 1921–1922*, 360; Frances Sage Bradley to Grace Meigs, January 30, 1918, Box 35, Folder 412-3, CB (quote).

34. Nannie Lackland to Anna Rude, August 13, 1920, CB.

35. Dowling, "Some Phases of Rural Health," 425; Ruth Dodd, RN, Supervisor, to Anna E. Rude, Chief, Division of Hygiene, November 22, 1920, Box 40, Folder 4-15-2-3-44, CB; J. O. C. Tiedeman, "Health and Social Work Health Center for City and County of Charleston, S.C.," [n.d.], Peterkin Papers, SCL.

36. Polk City Directory for Anniston, Alabama, 1913, 1922, 1924, ADAH.

37. Mary Hoffschwelle, *The Rosenwald Schools of the American South*; W. E. Moore, "The Columbia Children's Clinic," February 26, 1936, Peterkin Papers, SCL.

38. Miss Emma Hood and Mrs. Melissa Hood to Luline L. Mabry, November 18, 1938, FWP, Folder 1028, UNC.

39. Pamphlet, "Interesting Facts About Your Hospital," The Virginia Baptist Hospital, Smith Family Papers, LVA.

40. Hight C. Moore to J. H. Anderson and Campaign Announcement, "Millions for the Master," July 14, 1919, E. P. Alldredge Papers, SBHLA.

41. "Foundation History," The Commonwealth Fund, https://www.commonwealthfund.org/about-us/foundation-history, accessed August 11, 2022; no author, *Cross-sections of Rural Health Progress*, 1927, RCA; Harry S. Mustard, *Cross-sections of Rural Health Progress; Report of the Commonwealth Fund Child Health Demonstration in Rutherford County, Tennessee, 1924–1928*.

42. Harry S. Mustard, *Cross-sections of Rural Health Progress*; "Mary Ellen Vaughn Marking," Rutherford County Tennessee Historical Society, http://rutherfordtnhistory.org/mary-ellen-vaughn-marking/, accessed August 11, 2022.

43. Tennessee Congress of Parents and Teachers, Inc., "Resolutions," *Tennessee Bulletin* 4:1 (November-December 1926), 9, Anne Crutcher Papers, TSLA.

44. Mustard, *Cross-sections of Rural Health Progress*.

45. Enoch Ball to Anne Winn Stevens, *Shave Them*, August 1, 1939, FWP, http://lcweb2.loc.gov/mss/wpalh2/28/2809/28091634/28091634.pdf; Miles T. Mathis (et.al.) to Robert V. Williams, *Mathis Family*, November 1, 1938, FWP Interview, http://www.loc.gov/item/wpalh001907/; Hall et al., *Like A Family: The Making of a Southern Cotton Mill World*, 173–174.

46. Flamming, *Creating the Modern South*, 132–133.

47. Flamming, *Creating the Modern South*, 138–139; Lizzie Linberger to Ethel Deal, *Lizzie Linberger*, July 23, 1939, FWP, https://www.loc.gov/item/wpalh001774/; Mrs. Mattie Smith to Lucille Clarke Ford, February 14, 1939, *An Evening in the Smith Home*, FWP, https://www.loc.gov/item/wpalh002073/.

48. Linberger to Deal, FWP; Belle and Lottie Walter to Murial Wolf, September 12, 1938, FWP, http://www.loc.gov/item/wpalh001921/; Flamming, *Creating the Modern South*, 89–91, 137; Elsie Wall to ILM, July 27, 1938, *Belle and Lottie Walter*, FWP, https://www.loc.gov/item/wpalh001860/.

49. Mary E. Frederickson, "Wiggins, Ella May," NCpedia, January 1, 1996, http://www.ncpedia.org/biography/wiggins-ella.

50. Questionnaire, Laurence "Zip" Johnson, Box 1, Folder 10, C. C. Spaulding Papers, Duke.

51. Milton Quigless to Paul Ortiz, October 12, 1993, BTV.

52. Quigless to Ortiz, BTV; "The Quigless Clinic-Hospital," https://pubmed.ncbi.nlm.nih.gov/19378638/.

53. "Examination: Knights and Daughters of Tabor, Mound Bayou, Mississippi, as of December 31, 1935," Mississippi Department of Insurance/Fraternal Benefit Society Annual Reports, MDAH; "Report of Examination of the Afro-American Sons and Daugh-

ters, Yazoo City, Miss., As of December 31, 1935," Mississippi Department of Insurance/Fraternal Benefit Society Annual Reports, 1928–1938, MDAH.

54. Class B Policy, Ancient Moselites of the World, 1930, Mississippi Department of Insurance/Fraternal Benefit Society Annual Reports, MDAH; J. C. Oates Funeral Home Ledger, Box 7, p. 31, MPL; "Supreme Royal Circle of Friends of the World," Encyclopedia of Arkansas, http://www.encyclopediaofarkansas.net/encyclopedia/entry-detail.aspx?entryID=5861, accessed August 11, 2022.

55. Uncle Louie to Mary Ballard (Fontane) Creath, August 16, 1928, Hankins Family Papers, Mss 1 H 1946b 1391–1433, Section 34, VHS.

56. Lillian Parker Larsen to Mother, n.d. [ca. June 1933], Folder 3, Mss. 158, 1933–34, Larsen Papers, UMSC.

57. John Trotwood Moore diary entries, February 3–6, 11, for quote, see March 1–2, 1924, TSLA.

58. T. H. Alexander, "I Reckon So," n.d., John Trotwood Moore Papers, TSLA.

Part Four. Death and the New Deal

1. My thanks to one reviewer for this language.

Chapter 9. Making Deadly Landscapes Healthier

1. Robert, Cleveland, Ohio, to Mollie McLaughlin, June 16, 1931, Mollie McLaughlin Papers, VHS.

2. Ira Katznelson, *Fear Itself: The New Deal and the Origins of Our Time*, 32, 36, 149, 156–193; Karen Kruse Thomas, *Deluxe Jim Crow: Civil Rights and American Health Policy, 1935–1954*.

3. Jarod Roll, *Spirit of Rebellion: Labor and Religion in the New Cotton South*, 161.

4. Dr. Howard Fitts to Paul Ortiz, June 8, 1994, BTV.

5. Elizabeth C. Tandy to Mrs. Hopkins, July 2, 1934, Record Group 102, Box 492, Folder 4-2-2-2, CB.

6. Ellie Robertson to ILM, *Ellie Robertson,* September 28, 1938, FWP, https://www.loc.gov/item/wpalh001865/.

7. Annual Report of the Executive Committee of Masonic and O. E. S. Home for the Year 1930–1931, Submitted by A. M. Townsend, August 25, 1931, Prince Hall Grand Lodge Papers, MS 267, Box 1, Folder 2, UMSC.

8. "Supreme Royal Circle of Friends of the World," Encyclopedia of Arkansas, https://encyclopediaofarkansas.net/entries/supreme-royal-circle-of-friends-of-the-world-5861/, accessed August 22, 2022; "Our Fraternal Societies," *National Baptist Voice* (June 4, 1938), 2, SBHLA.

9. Joe and Jewel Casey and O. B. and Joyce Wilkinson, J. C. Moore and Sons Funeral Home Records, 1931–1966, Winchester, Tennessee, TSLA.

10. Ads for National Funeral Home (p. 31) and Thompson Brothers Mortuary, (p. 23), City Directories for Memphis, Tennessee, 1935, TSLA; James Mack to Grace McCune, March 9, 1939, FWP #3709, UNC.

11. Thirty-Fourth Annual Statement, North Carolina Mutual Life Insurance Company, December 31, 1932, Folder 8, NCM-5, Asa Spaulding Papers, Duke.

12. Douglass Scarborough McDaniel, *Stewardship of Sorrow*, 13–14, 19, 22–23. See also John Marcus Kester, *The Life Beyond Death.*

13. McDaniel, *Stewardship of Sorrow.*

14. McDaniel, *Stewardship of Sorrow*, 13; Mitchell Bronk, *Light in the Valley: Messages of Christian Hope and Consolation*, Foreword; Dr. A. C. Dixon, *The Bright Side of Death.*

15. Alice J. Selectman to Eva Smith, March 25, 1934, Smith Family Papers, LVA.

16. Elsie to Cora, September 18, 1935, Folder 9, Wade H. Harris Papers, UNC.

17. Alison Collis Greene, *No Depression in Heaven: The Great Depression, the New Deal, and the Transformation of Religion in the Delta*, 25; David Kennedy, *Freedom from Fear: The American People in Depression and War, 1929–1945*, 43–91.

18. Greene, *No Depression in Heaven*, 68.

19. President's Research Committee on Social Trends, *Recent Social Trends in the United States*, xlii-lii, lxxi, xciii; Arthur N. Holcombe, "Report on Recent Social Trends in the United States."

20. *Recent Social Trends in the United States.*

21. *Recent Social Trends in the United States*, xxix, liv, lix, lxvii, 602–603.

22. Margaret Jarmon Hagood, *Mothers of the New South: Portraiture of the White Tenant Farm Woman*, 3.

23. Official Report of Relief Operations of the American National Red Cross, "Tornadoes of March and May 1933, In Kentucky and Tennessee," November 1933, Box 814, Folder DR 484.08, ARC.

24. Louisville Chapter, American Red Cross, "Fellow Kentuckians Are in Dire Need," ca. May 1933, Box 814, Folder DR 484, ARC.

25. Official Report of Relief Operations of the American National Red Cross, November 1933; Colin Herrle, Assistant Manager, Eastern Area, to Mr. W. I. Jones, Red Cross Representative, May 25, 1933; W. I. Jones to Mr. Colin Herrle, May 18, 1933; Box 814, Folder DR 484.08; ARC Disaster Relief Report for Madison Parish (Louisiana) Tornado [tornado dated May 2, 1933; report dated August 6, 1933]; Clipping, "Storms Again Hit North Louisiana," May 5, 1933, Box 814, Folder DR 473; Official Report of the American Red Cross, "Hurricane Disasters of August and September, 1933," Box 816, Folder DR 516.08; Official Report of Relief Operations of the American National Red Cross, "The Tornado of May 1, 1933, in Webster and Bienville Parishes, Louisiana," Box 814, Folder DR 477.08; Report, Mr. W.I. Jones to Mr. Harris, May 10, 1933, Box 815, Folder 484.11; all sources ARC.

26. Alice B. Dugger to Miss Petersen, May 31, 1933, Box 814, DR. 480–08, ARC.

27. Official Report of Relief Operations of the American National Red Cross, "Tornadoes of March and May 1933, In Kentucky and Tennessee"; Herrle to Jones; Jones to Herrle; all sources ARC.

28. "Report on Windstorm Which Occurred in Dunklin Township, Greenville County [South Carolina], Friday May 6th, 1933 at 3:30 P.M.," Box 814, Folder DR 480.11, ARC.

29. Katznelson, *Fear Itself*, 254; Kennedy, *Freedom from Fear*, 148–150; the Tennessee Valley Authority Act of 1933, National Archives, https://www.archives.gov/milestone-documents/tennessee-valley-authority-act#:~:text=This%20act%20of%20May%2018,in%20the%20Tennessee%20Valley%20basin.

30. Maurice Henle, "5,219 Graves Removed for Norris Dam," *Association of American Cemetery Superintendents* 5(April, 1936), 1; Mrs. John F. Barksdale, "Immortal Pioneers," *Chattanooga Sunday Times (*September 13, 1936), 1; Harry Wiersma, Report, "Removal of Graves in Norris Reservoir, June 15, 1934"; W. E. Woolrich to H. A. Morgan, August 31, 1933; Gomer D. Hoskins to John F. Barksdale, May 4, 1934; Copies of Captioned Photographs; all documents in Box 1, Norris Dam, TVA Papers, NARA-SE.

31. Henle, "5,219 Graves Removed for Norris Dam"; Office Memorandum, C. A. Bock to Mr. Sayford and Mr. Woolrich, September 5, 1933, Box 1, Norris Dam; both sources in the TVA Papers.

32. David E. Lilienthal, *The Journals of David E. Lilienthal: The TVA Years, 1939–1945*, 144; No author, "Cemeteries in the Norris Dam Area," n.d. [ca. 1933] Box 2, Norris Dam, TVA Papers.

33. Mrs. Addie Collins to Mr. H. H. Turner, April 14, 1941, Box 154, Watts Dam, TVA Papers.

34. "Relocation of Cemeteries," Box 3, Norris Dam; Ned H. Sayford to J. Ed Campbell, November 20, 1943, "Norris Reservoir Area—Unregistered Graves—Tract No. NR-2144"; Burial Record for Leg of Rufe Polston, Box 18, Folder 5, Norris Dam; Memo, Fred Allen to Harry Wiersema, July 16, 1935; all papers in TVA Papers.

35. Lavens M. Thomas to Mr. H. H. Turner, March 31, 1941, Watts Bar Project Resource Group, Box 155, Folder 7, TVA Papers; "Lavens Mathewson Thomas II," Find a Grave, https://www.findagrave.com/memorial/117486045/lavens-mathewson-thomas, accessed August 22, 2022.

36. "Meeting of the Foremen and Clerks of Grave Removals," January 31, 1935, Box 1, Norris Dam, TVA Papers.

37. John D. Freeman, Executive Secretary and Treasurer, Tennessee Baptist Convention, to Professor W. R. Woolrich, November 28, 1933, Box 1, Norris Dam, TVA Papers.

38. "Meeting of the Foreman and Clerks of Grave Removals," TVA Papers.

39. Dye Seeley to H. H. Turner, June 10, 1941, Watts Bar Project Resource Group, Box 155, Folder 4, TVA Papers.

40. "Mr. Barksdale's telephone conversation with Frank Martin, Undertaker, of Coal Creek, Tenn.," November 19, 1934, transcribed by L. H. Greer, Secretary to J. F. Barksdale; Horace M. Irwin to John F. Barksdale, November 8, 1934; Zen K. Snodderly to John F. Barksdale, December 27, 1934, re: Interview with Mrs. Frank Norton, 1820 Woodbine Ave., Knoxville; Thaddeus A. Adams, Attorney, to I. R. Boruff, January 29, 1935; all documents in Box 1, Norris Dam, TVA Papers.

41. Luther C. Harris to Harry Wiersema via John F. Barksdale, June 18, 1934, Box 1, Norris Dam, TVA Papers; Gaines to Granville, TVA Papers.

42. W. R. Woolrich to L. L. Campbell, August 10, 1934, re: H. T. Lucus; Memo, Marshall Wilson, Aide, Public Relations, to John F. Barksdale, November 19, 1934; Meeting Minutes, January 31, 1935; all documents in Box 1, Norris Dam, TVA Papers.

43. Summary, "Relocation of Cemeteries—Pickwick Landing Reservoir," n.d., Box 45, Pickwick Dam, TVA Papers.

44. Arnold Kruckman to Dr. W. R. Woolrich, September 8, 1933, Box 1, Norris Dam, TVA Papers.

45. TVA Press Release, August 22, 1933; J. B. Gaines to Granville Hunt, February 14, 1934; W. R. Woolrich to Arnold Kruckman, November 15, 1933, Box 1, Norris Dam, TVA Papers; all sources TVA Papers.

46. Sallie Cleveland to Fred Allen, March 30, 1936, Sallie Cleveland to Mr. H. Wiersema, April 27, 1936, Sallie Cleveland to John Snyder, May 1936, Sallie Cleveland to Fred W. Allen, September 1936; all documents in Box 1, Norris Dam, TVA Papers.

47. Grave Removal Contract for Helen Walker, November 22, 1934; Tennessee Valley Authority Relative's Grave Removal Contract, November 22, 1934; Grave Removal Record for Helen Walker, November 30, 1934; documents in Box 1, Norris Dam, TVA Papers; all sources in the TVA Papers.

48. Cemetery Record for Silas Arthur, Grace No. 602, Baker Forge, Box 13, Norris Dam, TVA Papers; Photographs included in Field Book No. NR-10036, Cemetery Survey, Box 4, Norris Dam, TVA Papers; Reinterment Record for Margaret McHone and George Stanfill, Liberty Cemetery, November 13, 1934, Box 18, Norris Dam, TVA Papers.

49. John F Barksdale, Field Engineer, to J. C. Walker, LaFolette, Tennessee, November 25, 1934, TVA Papers.

50. Grave Removal Record for Helen Walker, TVA Papers.

51. See, for example, paperwork for Emaline Bell (Col) and her relative, J. Waddie Westfield (Col), Box 55, Chickamauga Dam; Summary, "Relocation of Cemeteries—Pickwick Landing Reservoir," n.d., Box 45, Pickwick Dam, both documents in the TVA Papers.

52. "Grave Removals in the Wheeler Reservoir," July 9, 1935, Box 42, Wheeler Dam; "Summary of Work performed in Each Cemetery," January 1941, page 3, Box 54, Chickamauga; Summary, "Relocation of Cemeteries—Pickwick Landing Reservoir," n.d., Box 45, Pickwick Dam, all documents in the TVA Papers.

53. "Summary of Work performed in Each Cemetery," January 1941, page 8, TVA Papers.

54. Kennedy, *Freedom from Fear*, 144–145; Neil Maher, "A New Deal Body Politic: Landscape, Labor, and the Civilian Conservation Corps," 435–461; *Official Annual: Civilian Conservation Corps, "C" District, CCC Fourth Corps Area*, 113.

55. Official Annual: Civilian Conservation Corps, "C" District, CCC Fourth Corps Area, 71.

56. J. C. Reddoch, Special Investigator, Camp Inspection Report and Work Project Report Supplement to Form 11 for Murfreesboro CCC Camp, April 7, 1941; J. C. Reddoch, Special Investigator, Supplementary Report for Murfreesboro CCC Camp, February 3, 1942; T. J. McVey, Special Investigator, April 30, 1940; Ira B. Daniel, Camp Educational Adviser, CCC Camp Educational Report, n.d. [ca. 1941], all documents in Records of the Civilian Conservation Corps, RG 35, Box 17, NARA; Maher, "A New Deal Body Politic," 438–441.

57. Thomas E. Sibert, Camp Educational Adviser, CCC Camp Educational Report, April 30, 1940, all documents in the Records of the Civilian Conservation Corps, RG 35, Box 17, NARA.

58. Official Annual: Civilian Conservation Corps, "C" District, CCC Fourth Corps Area, 152–153, 170–171, 200–201; Maher, "A New Deal Body Politic," 4.

Chapter 10. Revitalizing a Sick South

1. Alison Collis Greene, "The Faith of the 'Flotsam and Jetsam.'"

2. Franklin Delano Roosevelt, "Second Inaugural Address," January 20, 1937, Franklin Delano Roosevelt Library, https://www.fdrlibrary.org/documents/356632/390886/1937inauguraladdress.pdf/7d61a3fd-9d56-4bb6-989d-0fd269cdb073.

3. Edward Beardsley, *A History of Neglect: Health Care for Blacks and Mill Workers in the Twentieth-Century South*, 156.

4. Karen Kruse Thomas, *Deluxe Jim Crow: Civil Rights and American Health Policy, 1935–1954*; Ad, ARC Scrapbook, METRO.

5. Richard Pells, *Radical Visions and American Dreams: Culture and Social Thought in the Depression Years*; Benjamin Filene, *Romancing the Folk: Public Memory and American Roots Music*, 47–75.

6. Thomas, *Deluxe Jim Crow*, 69–73, 75.

7. Thomas, 48.

8. Beardsley, *A History of Neglect*, 158.

9. Eugenia Martin to Geneva Tonsill, *I Managed to Carry On*, November 1939, FWP, https://www.loc.gov/resource/wpalh1.13070112/.

10. Oral Interview, Ruth Clark Blevins to Kristine M. McCusker, June 30 and July 2, 2009, AGRC; *An Economic Survey of Patrick County*, 93; "Social Services," *A History of Patrick County, Virginia*, 42; *Patrick County Heritage Book*, Volume 1, 139; "Mrs. Mabel Clark Drowns in Philpott Reservoir," *The Enterprise*, October 4, 1962; all Patrick County documents courtesy of Patrick County HS.

11. Blevins to McCusker, June 30 and July 2, 2009, AGRC.

12. Debra Susie, *In the Way of our Grandmothers: A Cultural View of Twentieth-Century Midwifery in Florida*, 43; Marie Campbell, *Folks Do Get Born*, 18–19.

13. William Link, *The Paradox of Southern Progressivism: 1880–1930, 89–90*; Susan Smith, *Sick and Tired of Being Sick and Tired: Black Women's Health Activism in America, 1890–1950*, 124.

14. Susie, *In the Way of our Grandmothers*, 34–35; Ruby Pickens Tartt, "Carrie Dykes, Midwife," in Mody C. Boatright and Donald Day, eds., *From Hell to Breakfast*, 21–28. Quote is on page 22.

15. Campbell, *Folks Do Get Born*, 18–19.

16. Mattie Ingram to Chlotilde Martin, *The County Health Nurse*, January 31, 1939, FWP, https://www.loc.gov/item/wpalh002096/.

17. Filene, *Romancing the Folk*, 47–75; Kristine M. McCusker, *Lonesome Cowgirls and Honky-Tonk Angels: The Women of Barn Dance Radio*, 82–102.

18. McCusker, *Lonesome Cowgirls and Honky-Tonk Angels*, 14; Grace Lumpkin, *To Make My Bread*, xiv, xxxiii.

19. Lumpkin, *To Make My Bread*, 42. See also Martha Emmons, "Walk Around My Bedside," 130–136; Gertrude Chandler Peterkin, WPA documents, SCL.

20. James Kerby Ward to Lillian Stedman, *James Kerby Ward*, February 17, 1939, FWP, https://www.loc.gov/resource/wpalh1.12010113/.

21. J. H. Robertson (Negro) to Miss Effie Cowan, *John H. Robertson*, October 12, 1939, FWP, https://www.loc.gov/item/wpalh002257/; Mr. Thomas J. Henry to Geneva

Tonsill, *Mr. Thomas J. Henry*, October 1939, FWP, https://www.loc.gov/resource/wpalh1.13070511/; Andrew Johnson to Mrs. [Leola] T. Bradley, *A Good Investment*, October 12, 1939, FWP, https://www.loc.gov/item/wpalh000499/; Lisa Johnson to Mrs. [Leela] Bradley.

22. Ruby Pickens Tartt, Amy Chapman's Funeral, September 28, 1938, FWP, https://www.loc.gov/resource/wpalho.07012908/.

23. Elsie Clews Parsons, *Folk-lore of the Sea Islands*, 211–217.

24. Ibid.

25. Federal Writers' Project of the Works Progress Administration, *Mississippi: A Guide to the Magnolia State*, 28–29.

26. William R. McDaniel, "Murders of the Machine Age," *Knoxville Journal* (TN), April 25, 1937, Federal Writers' Project, Tennessee, Records, 1941, Microfilm Accession Number 1067, TSLA.

27. *Social Security Act (1935)* (Act of August 14, 1935), National Archives, https://www.archives.gov/milestone-documents/social-security-act, accessed August 11, 2022; Ira Katznelson, *Fear Itself: The New Deal and the Origins of Our Time*, 258–259; Beardsley, *A History of Neglect*, 163.

28. Ibid.

29. Social Security Act (1935); Beardsley, *A History of Neglect*, 163.

30. This paragraph relies heavily on Beardsley, *A History of Neglect*, 163–164.

31. Price V. Fishback et al., "The Impact of the New Deal on Black and White Mortality in the South"; Patience Flucher and Family to Paul Diggs, February 24, 1939, FWP, https://www.loc.gov/resource/wpalh1.11011313/?sp=1; Miss Minnie Stonestreet and Leila H., *In Lieu of Something Better*, Georgia, December 19, 1939, FWP, https://www.loc.gov/resource/wpalh1.13050127/.

32. Charles S. Johnson, *Growing Up in the Black Belt: Negro Youth in the Rural South*; Charles S. Johnson, *Shadow of the Plantation*; Margaret Jarman Hagood, *Mothers of the South: Portraiture of the White Tenant Farm Woman*; Hortense Powdermaker, *After Freedom: A Cultural Study in the Deep South*; John Dollard, *Caste and Class in a Southern Town*.

33. Powdermaker, *After Freedom*, 138, 325–331.

34. Rebecca Woodham, "Southern Conference for Human Welfare," Encyclopedia of Alabama, http://www.encyclopediaofalabama.org/article/h-1593 accessed August 11, 2022; Virginia Foster Durr, *Outside the Magic Circle*, 34, 117, 121–123; *Report on Economic Conditions of the South*, prepared for the President by the National Emergency Council, July 25, 1938, Internet Archive, https://archive.org/details/reportoneconomicoonati/page/4, accessed August 11, 2022; Katznelson, *Fear Itself*, 169.

35. The Hill-Burton Act, also known as the Hospital Survey and Construction Act, invested billions of dollars into building more than 10,000 hospitals nation-wide. Karen Kruse Thomas, "The Hill-Burton Act and Civil Rights: Expanding Hospital Care for Black Southerners."

36. Durr, *Outside the Magic Circle*, 116–123, quote is on 118.

37. *Report on Economic Conditions of the South*, 119.

38. *Report on Economic Conditions of the South*, 8, 29–32.

39. Clipping, "Birth and Death Rates Show Drop," C. C. Spaulding Papers, Box 2, Folder 2, Duke; Clipping, "Health of City Better; Death Rate Declines," March 13, 1940, Vital Statistics Folder, MPL.

40. Jessie Parkhurst Guzman, *Negro Year Book: A Review of Events Affecting Negro Life, 1941–1946*, 320, TU; *Annual of the Southern Baptist Convention of 1939* (Nashville: The Marshall and Bruce Company, 1939), 131, SBHLA.

41. Fishback et al., "The Impact of the New Deal on Black and White Infant Mortality in the South," 93.

42. Alan M. Kraut, *Goldberger's War: The Life and Work of a Public Health Crusader*, 251.

43. LeVern Beales, Chief Statistician, Compiler, *Statistical Abstract of the United States 1939*, 82, 84, 86–87.

44. Scrapbook, Editorial clipping, April 13, 1935, Wingo Family Papers, VHS. See also A. W. Patterson to Dr. Douglas Freeman, February 11, 1935, Freeman Papers, VHS.

45. Quote, *National Baptist Voice* (February 3, 1934), 2, SBHLA; Editorial, "The Voice Pulpit," *National Baptist Voice* (April 30, 1938), 4, SBHLA.

46. Father to May [Mary Jordan], January 27, 1942, Folder 14, Jordan Family Papers, SCL.

Chapter 11. Flying and Dying as Americans

1. Harold to Mother, June 25, 1944, Leazer Papers, VHS.

2. Major General J. F. Twining to Mr. H. L. Leazer, July 28, 1944; E. A. Bradunas to Mr. Hugh L. Leazer, August 9, 1944; J.A. Ulio to Mr. Hugh Leazer, September 30, 1944; Mrs. Charles Johnson to Mrs. Leazer, October 16, 1944; all sources in the Leazer Papers, VHS; Jennings Titus to unknown interviewer, July 31, 1986, August 24, 1986, VHS.

3. Clipping, "Famed Negro AAF Officer Dies in Action," *Knoxville Daily*, n.d. [ca. 1944]; Reginald Jones to Kenneth Crist, Lockheed Martin, Los Angeles, January 12, 1945, both documents in the William J. Faulkner Sr. Papers, MSRC; J. Todd Moye, *Freedom Flyers: The Tuskegee Airmen of World War II.*

4. Father to May [Mary Jordan], January 27, 1942, Folder 14, Jordan Family Papers, SCL.

5. Kate to May [Mary Jordan], May 3, 1942, Folder 18, Jordan Family Papers, SCL.

6. Jessie Parkhurst Guzman, *Negro Year Book: A Review of Events Affecting Negro Life, 1941–1946*, 328, 331; Lizzie Collingham, *The Taste of War: World War II and the Battle For Food.*

7. David Kennedy, *Freedom from Fear: The American People in Depression and War, 1929–1945*, 710–714.

8. Kennedy, *Freedom from Fear*, 713; Report of Physical Examination for James M. Beck, October 14, 1943; Immunization Register for James Beck, last dated August 1947; Report of Physical Examination for James M. Beck, August 26, 1946; all Beck documents in the James Beck Papers, UMSC.

9. Robert G. Mayer, *Embalming: History, Theory, and Practice*, 50; Frank Essex to Kristine M. McCusker and James Williams, September 10, 2008, AGRC; National Funeral Home, Record #3224, 3231, TSLA.

10. Essex to McCusker and Williams, TSLA.

11. Kennedy, *Freedom from Fear*, 712.

12. Pearl Harbor: Virginia Gold Star Honor Roll paperwork for Melvin Jefferson Smoot; D-Day: Virginia Gold Star Honor Roll paperwork for Clarence William Bloxom Jr.; Japanese and German POW camps: Virginia Gold Star Honor Roll paperwork for Cornealius Zane Byrd, Albert Kenneth Newsome, and William Lawrence Sligh; Siegfried Line: Virginia Gold Star Honor Roll paperwork for Jesse James Padgett; Battle of the Bulge: Archivist's note, Olin Dorn Papers; all documents SCL.

13. Leon W. Johnson to Mr. Hugh Leazer, May 13, 1946, Leazer Papers, VHS.

14. Leon W. Johnson to Reverend William J. Faulkner, Sr., June 7, 1946, Faulkner Papers, MSRC.

15. Virginia Gold Star Honor Roll paperwork for Edward Paul La Flamme, LVA.

16. Atlanta General Distribution Depot, U.S. Army, September 7, 1947, Folder 20 "Public Information," Box 9944, Record Group 58, MDAH.

17. Virginia Gold Star Honor Roll paperwork for Asher Colburn Taylor, LVA.

18. Virginia Gold Star Honor Roll paperwork for Neville Dean Blakemore, LVA.

19. Lt. H. S. Shearer to Mr. and Mrs. McFadyen, February 1943, Folder 3, McFadyen Papers, UNC; Nathan Jordan Jr., to Mother and Dad [Mary and Nathan Jordan, Sr.], August 11, 1944; Letters returned marked "Deceased" or "Missing" include Audrey Jordan to Nathan Jordan, August 24, 1944, and Mary Jordan to Nathan Jordan, August 9, 1944, August 29, 1944, all Jordan letters in Folder 33, Jordan Family Papers, SCL.

20. Nathan and Mary Jordan to Nathan Jr., August 30, 1944, Folder 34, Jordan Family Papers, SCL.

21. Edna to May [Mary Jordan], September 4, 1944, Folder 36, Jordan Family Papers, SCL.

22. Telegram, J. A. Ulio to Audrey Jordan, October 10, 1944; Louise to May [Mary Jordan], October 13, 1944, both letters in Folder 41; Richard H. Jordan to Mother and Dad [Mary and Nathan Jordan, Sr.], May 6, 1945, Folder 43; all documents in the Jordan Family Papers, SCL.

23. Undated document, "Received August 23, 1945, Copied by Mother and his only Sister Audrey M. Jordan, Greer, S. C., U.S.A.," Folder 40; Major General Edward F. Witsell to Mr. and Mrs. Nathan Jordan Sr., January 6, 1948, Folder 56; all sources Jordan Family Papers, SCL.

24. Recopied letter from "Koob" to Mrs. Nathan Jordan Sr., Folder 43; Office of Special Settlement Accounts to Mary Jordan; Veterans Administration, "Contingent Beneficiary Form," both documents in Folder 47; National Service Life Insurance, "Notice of Settlement," Folder 48; "Advice of Payment of Settlement to Accompany Check," October 26, 1945, Folder 49, all of the foregoing documents in the Jordan Family Papers, SCL; J. A. Ulio to Mr. William M. McFadyen Sr., November 27, 1943; Individual Flight Record for William H. McFadyen Jr., November 1942; Inventory of Personal Property for 1st. Lt. William M. McFadyen, December 27, 1943, McFadyen Papers, UNC; Leazer Papers, VHS.

25. "Boss Crump's Son and Two Others Die in Plane Crash," May 3, 1939, *Chicago Tribune*, 1; E. H. Crump to Mrs. Mavis Mathis, November 14, 1944, Folder MA; Crump

to Home for Incurables, April 3, 1944, with a $5 donation listed in honor of Isaac Goldberg, Folder GO; all Crump sources in the Crump Papers, MPL.

26. Kennedy, *Freedom from Fear*, 712.

27. Draft Card for Harold Leazer, the Leazer Papers, VHS (the draft card is also accessible at Ancestry.com); Virginia Gold Star Honor Roll Paperwork for Harold McKnight Leazer; Missing Air Crew Report for Harold Leazer, et al.; both documents in the Leazer Papers, VHS.

28. Harold to Mother, June 11, 1944, June 25, 1944, Leazer Papers, VHS.

29. Claire Weir to Mr. and Mrs. Leazer, July 14, 1944; Dizzy to Pop [Mr. Leazer], July 23, 1944, Leazer Papers, VHS.

30. Mary Agnes Gautier Letters and Scrapbook, Box 3, LSU.

31. J. A. Ulio, Major General, to Mrs. Olin G. Dorn, Jr., January 18, 1945, Folder 10, Olin Dorn Papers, SCL.

32. Helen Morgan to Mrs. Leazer, July 24, 1944, Leazer Papers, VHS.

33. Freda Dyson to Mrs. Leazer, July 31, 1944, Leazer Papers, VHS.

34. Beryl Titus to Mrs. Leazer, July 28, 1944, Leazer Papers, VHS.

35. Telegram, C. W. Heinzel to Mr. and Mrs. Leazer, July 30, 1944; Mr. and Mrs. C. Heinzil to Mr. and Mrs. Leazer, August 14, 1944, Leazer Papers, VHS.

36. Mrs. H. A. King to Mrs. Leazer, May 21, 1945, Leazer Papers, VHS.

37. Beryl Titus to Mrs. Leazer, July 28, 1944; Telegram, CW Heinzel to Mr. and Mrs. Leazer, July 30, 1944; Mr. and Mrs. C. Heinzil to Mr. and Mrs. Leazer, August 14, 1944; Italo Damiani to Mr. and Mrs. Leazer, October 29, 1944; all sources Leazer Papers, VHS.

38. Ulio to Leazer, September 30, 1944; Johnson to Leazer, October 16, 1944; Italo Damiani to Mr. and Mrs. Leazer, October 29, 1944; Missing Air Crew Report #6434; all documents in the Leazer Papers, VHS.

39. Italo Damiani to Mr. and Mrs. Leazer, October 7, 1944, Leazer Papers, VHS.

40. Italo Damiani to Mr. and Mrs. Leazer, August 27, 1944, Leazer Papers, VHS.

41. Italo Damiani to Mr. and Mrs. Leazer, July 10, 1944, Leazer Papers, VHS.

42. Ibid.; Claire [Weir] to Mrs. Leazer, August 23, 1944, Leazer Papers, VHS.

43. Arthur Kremer's brother to Mrs. Leazer, May 18, 1945; Freda Dyson to Mrs. Leazer, May 19, 1945; Donald Johnson, Frances Volk and Italo Damiani sent Christmas cards in 1947; Mother's Day Cards, Don Johnson to Mrs. Leazer, 1946, 1951; Rev. D. M. O'Callaghan, Director, Society of the Little Flower, to Friend [Mr. and Mrs. Leazer], November 28, 1944; all documents in the Leazer Papers, VHS.

44. Titus to unknown, July 31, 1984, August 24, 1986; Leazer Papers, VHS.

45. Clipping, "Capt. W. J. Faulkner Fell to His Death War Dept. Reveals," December 29, 1944, Folder 37; Birth Certificate for William J. Faulkner Jr., Faulkner Papers; Draft Card for William J. Faulkner, Jr., Ancestry.com; "Famed Negro AAF Officer Dies in Action"; Flight Record, November 1944; Memorandum, Station Hospital Office, May 8, 1943; General Orders Number 1666, Folder 37; Marriage Certificate, May 1943, Folder 36; all of the foregoing documents in the Faulkner Papers, MSRC.

46. Kennedy, *Freedom from Fear*, 702; Moye, *Freedom Flyers*, 112.

47. Other black soldiers' families received similar treatment. See, for example, no author, "Pfc. Robinson, Former Grid Star, Is Killed in Action," *Birmingham World* (AL), March 6, 1945, 1.

48. William J. Faulkner Sr., to Major General J. A. Ulio, March 8, 1945; Bayard Johnson, Colonel, Air Corps, Commanding, to Reverend William J. Faulkner, Sr., March 31, 1945; both sources in the Faulkner Papers, MSRC.

49. J. A. Ulio, Major General, Adjutant General, March 21, 1945, Folder 61, Faulkner Papers, MSRC.

50. Lewis Jones to My dear Faulkner [William J. Faulkner Sr.], January 4, 1945, Faulkner Papers, MSRC.

51. Willie Y. Drake to Reverend and Mrs. Faulkner, July 12, 1944, Folder 45, Faulkner Papers, MSRC.

52. Fred Brownlee to William Faulkner, Wed. 14, 1944, Folder 45, Faulkner Papers, MSRC.

53. George W. Gore Jr. Grammateus, Sigma Pi Phi Fraternity to Reverend and Mrs. Faulkner, November 23, 1944, Folder 45, Faulkner Papers, MSRC.

54. Reverend S. L. Gandy to Reverend Faulkner, November 30, 1944, Folder 45; Mrs. Theresa Faulkner to Will and Bess [Faulkner], November 25, 1944, Folder 45; both sources in the Faulkner Papers, MSRC.

55. John F. Cork to Bess and Will [Faulkner], November 23, 1944, Folder 45, Faulkner Papers, MSRC.

56. Martha Harris to the Faulkners, n.d. [ca. November 1944], Folder 45, Faulkner Papers, MSRC.

57. Mrs. Margaret D. Barren to Bessabelle [Mrs. William Faulkner, Sr.], January 15, 1945, Folder 45, Faulkner Papers, MSRC.

58. James H. Lightbourns to Dean W. J. Faulkner, December 31, 1944, Faulkner Papers, MSRC.

59. Mrs. Vivian Carter to My dear Friends, December 27, 1944, Folder 45, Faulkner Papers, MSRC.

60. Margaret McCulloh to Reverend and Mrs. William J. Faulkner, ca. November 1944, Folder 45, Faulkner Papers, MSRC.

61. Ibid.

62. Mrs. Lula Fennie, "In loving memory of my son," *Birmingham World* (AL), n.d., SUSC.

63. Ruth Harper to Reverend and Mrs. Faulkner, December 24, 1944, Folder 45, Faulkner Papers, MSRC. Letter includes clipping from the Louisville (MO) *Courier Journal*.

64. Dan May to Frank M. Folsom, February 24, 1945, Daniel May Papers, TSLA; Bertram and Pansy Doyle to Reverend and Mrs. Faulkner, January 5, 1945, Folder 45, Faulkner Papers, MSRC.

65. Thelma Allison to Bess Faulkner, Wednesday [n.d. but ca. January 1945], Folder 45, Faulkner Papers, MSRC.

66. Georgia Blocker to Bess [Faulkner], January 4, 1945, Folder 45, Faulkner Papers, MSRC.

67. Reverend W. S. Ellington to Reverend and Mrs. Faulkner, December 26, 1944, Folder 45, Faulkner Papers, MSRC.

68. Reverend and Mrs. Charles L. Dickens to friends [the Faulkners], December 26, 1944; The University [Fisk] Church to Reverend and Mrs. Faulkner, December 24, 1944,

paraphrase John 14:2 [KJV], "In my Father's house are many mansions," Folder 45; both sources in the Faulkner Papers, MSRC.

69. Dr. Wyatt Aiken Smart to Dean Faulkner, Xmas Evening [ca. 1944], Folder 59, Faulkner Papers, MSRC.

70. Miss Henri Young to My Dear Friends [Reverend and Mrs. Faulkner], January 16, 1945, Folder 60, Faulkner Papers, MSRC.

71. Unknown correspondent to Mrs. Ben King Espey, n.d. [ca. April 1944], Espey Papers, TSLA.

72. Dizzy to Mother, September 4, 1944, Leazer Papers, VHS.

73. Miss Willie J. Kelley to Reverend and Mrs. Faulkner, December 26, 1944, Folder 45, Faulkner Papers, MSRC; Myrtle and Garris Thompson to friends [Mr. and Mrs. Olin Dorn Sr.], October 30, 1947, Folder 12, Olin Dorn Papers, SCL.

74. "Capt. W. J. Faulkner Fell to His Death, War Dept. Reveals," Faulkner Papers, MSRC.

75. George W. Gore, Grammateus, Sigma Phi Fraternity, to Reverend and Mrs. Faulkner, January 1, 1945, Folder 45, Faulkner Papers, MSRC.

76. Mr. and Mrs. R. A. Hundley to friends [Reverend and Mrs. Faulkner], March 2, 1945, Folder 60, Faulkner Papers, MSRC.

77. Thomas L. Cummings, Mayor, Nashville, to Reverend and Mrs. William J. Faulkner, Cummings to Faulkners, September 8, 1944, Cummings to Faulkners, November 24, 1944, all in Folder 45, Faulkner Papers, MSRC.

78. Janet Wynn to Margaret McCulloh, December 4, 1944, Folder 61, Faulkner Papers, MSRC.

79. Adeline King to Dr. Faulkner, December 24, 1944, Folder 45; Constance Rumbough, Secretary, Fellowship of Reconciliation, to Friends [Reverend and Mrs. Faulkner], November 21, 1944, Folder 59; both sources in the Faulkner Papers, MSRC.

80. Dr. Walter Stone to Dean Faulkner, November 27, 1944, Folder 59, Faulkner Papers, MSRC.

81. Hundley to Dear Friends, Faulkner Papers, MSRC.

82. Havens and Allan, Berkley, California, [Reverend and Mrs. Faulkner], n.d. [ca. January 1945], Folder 60, Faulkner Papers, MSRC.

83. Don and Theo Williams Anderson to friends [Reverend and Mrs. Faulkner], January 17, 1945, Folder 61, Faulkner Papers. MSRC.

84. Entry, August 12, 1945, Sara Jean Clark Wycott, *Diary of Sara Jean Clark Wycott* (New York: Greenwich Book Publishers, 1961), 42.

Chapter 12. Muddy Roads and Sacred Duties

1. Ed Anderson, "Unsung Hero of Wilkes County, Georgia: William James Willis, Sr.," February 2010, Private Papers of William Willis, on file with the author; William J. Willis and Dorothy S. Willis to Kristine M. McCusker and Lauren Pate, July 20, 2010, AGRC.

2. Escort paperwork for Telmer H. Knight, August 23, 1948, Folder 4, Record Group 9940, MDAH.

3. Louise to May, August 31, 1945, Folder 45, Jordan Family Papers, SCL.

4. Virginia Gold Star Honor Roll Paperwork for Wilson Edmund Tyrrel, LVA.

5. Martha Faulkner to Dad [Reverend Faulkner], June 8, 1945, Folder 65, William J. Faulkner Sr. Papers, MSRC.

6. Mary Dorn to Mr. and Mrs. Dorn Sr., March 2, 1947; Mrs. O. G. Dorn Sr. to Special Information Section, August 2, 1947, both letters in Folder 11; Colonel Charles D. Carle to Mrs. Dorn, January 21, 1948, Folder 13; all sources in the Olin Dorn Papers, SCL.

7. "Disposition of World War II Armed Forces Dead," MDAH; Mississippi Escort Paperwork, Folder 5, MDAH; James L. Prenn, Major, QMC, to Mrs. Inez Marvin, Milwaukee, November 8, 1946, Record Group 92, Office of the Quartermaster General, Box 382, NARA.

8. T. H. Metz to William Goldberg, September 21, 1948, Missing Air Crew Reports, NARA; Missing Air Crew Report #2396 for 721st Squadron, Official Website: 450th Bomb Group Memorial Association, http://www.450thbg.com/real/macr/holder/2396.shtml, accessed August 11, 2022, also at NARA.

9. Missing Air Crew Report #6434, June 8, 1948, NARA.

10. Escort paperwork for Ben C. Styart, November 17, 1948, Folder 7, MDAH; Chaplain P. G. Rasmussen to R. E. Tallant, Col. USA, Ret., January 8, 1945, Missing Air Crew Reports, NARA; William E. Bentley to American Graves Registration Command, re: Interview of Mr. Marcel Deprez, March 1, 1948, Missing Air Crew Reports, NARA; Helen Morgan to Mrs. Leazer, March 28, 1951; Yvonne Balboni to Mrs. Morgan, August 30, 1950; Yvonne Balboni to Mrs. Morgan, October 6, 1950; Alexandre Evreinoff to Madam, August 28, 1950; Helen Morgan to friends, October 17, 1950; the foregoing five sources are in the Leazer Papers, VHS.

11. Missing Air Crew Report #2396, NARA.

12. Ibid.

13. Ibid.; Jennings Titus to unknown interviewer, July 31, 1986, August 24, 1986, VHS; https://www.abmc.gov/decedent-search/volk%3Doliver, ABMC.

14. Lt. George Burchett to Mrs. Dorn Sr., September 11, 1946, Folder 11, Olin Dorn Papers, SCL.

15. Russel [*sic*] H. Herseth to Mr. Hugh L. Leazer, March 2, 1945, Leazer Papers, VHS.

16. Clipping, n.d., "Lockheed Plant Honors Pilot"; Clipping, n.d., "Local Negro Flier to be Honored Posthumously"; Clipping, n.d., "Negro Hero Given P-38 Memorial"; Martha to Mom [Mrs. Faulkner], March 30, 1945, Folder 65; all documents in the Faulkner Papers, MSRC.

17. Jamima Powell to Mr. and Mrs. Leazer, February 12, 1945, Leazer Papers, VHS.

18. R. F. Poole, President, Clemson University, to Mr. O.G. Dorn, January 18, 1945, Folder 10, Olin Dorn Papers, SCL.

19. W. J. Bullock to Mr. and Mrs. Harold Leazer and Family, February 18, 1947, Leazer Papers, VHS; Friday Nights in K-Town, http://fridaynightsink-town.weebly.com/, accessed August 11, 2022.

20. See Undated Document, "Received Aug. 23, 1945. Copied by Mother and his only Sister Audrey M. Jordan, Greer, SC. U.S.A.," Folder 40, Jordan Papers; Leazer Papers, VHS.

21. "Luther Porter Jackson," Encyclopedia Virginia / Virginia Humanities, http://www.encyclopediavirginia.org/Jackson_Luther_Porter_1892–1950#start_entry, accessed August 11, 2022; W. Edwin Hemphill, ed., *Gold Star Honor Roll of Virginians in the Second World War*, xxi.

22. Virginia Gold Star Honor Roll paperwork for James Earle Martin includes a photo of Martin, LVA.

23. Hemphill, *Gold Star Honor Roll of Virginians in the Second World War*, xix; Virginia Gold Star Honor Roll Paperwork for Gordon D. Phipps, LVA.

24. Virginia Gold Star Honor Roll Paperwork for Daniel C. Budd, LVA.

25. Hemphill, *Gold Star Honor Roll of Virginians in the Second World War*, xxx, xxxii.

26. Virginia Gold Star Honor Roll Paperwork for Lafayette N. Ford, Arthur Elzey Lassiter, Lawton Winfield, and James Edward Christian Jr., LVA; Hemphill, *Gold Star Honor Roll of Virginians in the Second World War*, 180.

27. "Disposition of World War II Armed Forces Dead," MDAH.

28. Thomas B. Larkin, Major General, The Quartermaster General, to Mr. William J. Faulkner, January 12, 1948, "In reply refer to Burial of Captain William J. Faulkner, Jr.," Folder 39 "William J. Faulkner Jr. Military Burial Materials, 1948," Faulkner Papers, MSRC.

29. Ibid.

30. Ibid. This language also appears on the American Battle Monuments Commission's online description.

31. American Overseas Military Cemeteries and Memorials, 8.

32. Virginia Gold Star Honor Roll Paperwork for Ivan Hirtzel Vredenburg, LVA.

33. James L. Press to Mr. Hugh L. Leazer, February 18, 1947; James L. Press to Mr. Hugh L. Leazer, February 18, 1947; both documents in the Leazer Papers, VHS.

34. Maurice A. Johnson, Chaplain, USAF District Chaplain's Office, Bolling Air Force Base, to Mr. and Mrs. Hugh L. Leazer, April 27, 1951; "The Funeral Service," Arlington National Cemetery; both sources in the Leazer Papers, VHS.

35. Miss Courtney Atkinson to Ola and Mr. Goode [Dorn], November 16, 1947, Folder 12, Olin Dorn Papers SCL.

36. Telegram, Val R. Spencer, Major QMC, to Olin G. Dorn, Sr., October 24, 1947, Folder 11; Bill, Shelley-Brunson Funeral Homes, January 3, 1948, Folder 13; Mobley Williams to Goode [Olin G. Dorn, Sr.], October 28, 1947, Folder 12; all sources in the Olin Dorn Papers, SCL.

37. Mississippi Escort Papers, Folder 11, Folder 12, MDAH.

38. War Department Pamphlet, No. 21–39, "Conduct of a Military Funeral," September 1948, Leazer Papers, VHS.

39. Everett C. Shroder Jr. to All Chaplains, Reserve Chaplains, National Guard Chaplains and Clergymen, October 17, 1947, Folder 11, Olin Dorn Papers, SCL; Escort paperwork for Benjamin Smith, August 16, 1948, Folder 4, MDAH; Escort paperwork for Martin Goar, June 19, 1949, Folder 13, MDAH.

40. Escort paperwork for Emmitt Gosa, June 1, 1948, Folder 13, MDAH.

41. Escort paperwork for Charlie Munn, May 25, 1948, MDAH; Escort paperwork for Henry Brannon, August 25, 1948, MDAH.

42. Richard R. Potter to Mr. Olin G. Dorn, November 5, 1947; Shroder to All Chaplains; John C. Williams, Department Commander, Department of South Carolina, Veterans of Foreign Wars, October 28, 1947, Folder 11; all documents in the Olin Dorn Papers, SCL.

43. Scrapbook, "Beloved Memories," provided by the Shelley-Brunson Funeral Home, (St. Charles, Illinois: The Reynolds Company, 1946), Folder 18, Olin Dorn Papers, SCL; "Lest We Forget," memorial book provided for the Ben Clay Espey Family in March 1950, Espey Papers, TSLA; Kristine M. McCusker, "Funeral Music and the Transformation of Southern Musical and Religious Cultures, 1935–1945."

44. Yellow sheets tucked into "Beloved Memories," Olin Dorn Papers, SCL.

45. Order Form, Florence Memorial Company, January 25, 1950, $600 for headstone for Olin Dorn's grave, Folder 13, Olin Dorn Papers, SCL.

46. Escort paperwork for Claude T. Dean, August 28, 1949, Folder 3, MDAH.

47. Escort paperwork for Wyatt B. Wood, May 26, 1948, Folder 3, MDAH.

48. Escort paperwork for Ivy V. Bradshaw, July 22, 1948, Folder 3, MDAH.

49. Escort paperwork for Willie Hopson, October 26, 1948, MDAH.

50. Escort paperwork for Benjamin J. Collum, January 5, 1949, Folder 8, MDAH.

51. Escort paperwork for Clarence Clark, June 21, 1948, Folder 3, MDAH.

52. Escort paperwork for Joseph Benson, July 23, 1948, Folder 3, MDAH.

53. Escort paperwork for James H. White, June 4, 1948, Folder 2, MDAH; Escort paperwork for Freeman Boyd, July 19, 1948, Folder 2, MDAH.

54. Escort paperwork for Harvey D. Edwards, July 1, 1948, Folder 3, MDAH.

55. Escort paperwork for John P. Morgan, August 16, 1948, Folder 4, MDAH.

56. Escort paperwork for William A. Baucum, May 24, 1948; Escort paperwork for Davis M. Beard, July 7, 1948; both in Folder 3, MDAH.

57. Escort paperwork for Isaiah McCarroll, June 25, 1948, Folder 3, MDAH

58. Escort paperwork for Johnnie M. Richardson, June 28, 1948; Escort paperwork for Willie F. Duke, July 23, 1948; Escort paperwork for Johnnie C. Bruce, May 24, 1948; Escort paperwork for Doyle Phagan, June 21, 1948; all documents in Folder 3, MDAH.

59. Escort paperwork for Jewel W. Woodall, December 21, 1948, Folder 8, MDAH.

60. Escort paperwork for Billie [*sic*] D. Jefcoat, November 29, 1948, Folder 6; Escort paperwork for Delma A. Bishop, May 28, 1948, Folder 3; Escort paperwork for Willie R. Kelly, June 9, 1948; all documents in Folder 3, MDAH.

61. Mississippi Escort Paperwork, Folder 5; Mississippi Escort Records, Folders 10–12; both sources MDAH.

62. [James McConaghie] to unknown, December 1948; James R. McConaghie, Superintendent, to Commanding Officer, Mississippi Military District, June 4, 1948; E. E. Price, District Chaplain to James R. McConaghie, June 7, 1948; all letters in Folder 5, MDAH.

63. Budd F. Sturzl to Commanding Officer, Mississippi Military District, July 1, 1948, Mississippi Escort Paperwork, MDAH.

64. Escort paperwork for L. C. Dinkins, October 20, 1948, MDAH.

65. James R. McConaghie, Superintendent, to Commanding Officer, Mississippi Military District, December 19, 1949, Escort Paperwork, MDAH.

66. Escort paperwork for John H. Ray Jr., July 5, 1949, Folder 13, MDAH.

67. Escort paperwork for James E. Pennington, October 19, 1948, Folder 6, MDAH.

68. Escort paperwork for Jessie W. Bennett, November 1, 1948, MDAH.

Epilogue

1. "Hill-Burton Free and Reduced-Cost Health Care," Health Resources & Services Administration, https://www.hrsa.gov/get-health-care/affordable/hill-burton/index.html, accessed August 11, 2022; Karen Kruse Thomas, "The Hill-Burton Act and Civil Rights: Expanding Hospital Care for Black Southerners, 1939–1960"; John Parascandola, "From MCWA to CDC—Origins of the Centers for Disease Control and Prevention."

2. Nadia Whitehead, "The U.S. Thought It was Rid of Hookworm. Wrong."

3. Emily Kumler Kaplan, "Reducing Maternal Mortality"; Roni Caryn Rabin, "Huge Racial Disparities Found in Deaths Linked to Pregnancy."

4. Sarah Kliff et al., "Closed Hospitals Leave Rural Patients 'Stranded' as Coronavirus Spreads."

5. https://www.newschannel5.com/news/cumberland-river-hospital-closes-permanently.

6. Sam Stockard, "Governor Sees End of Covid-19 State of Emergency Coming Soon."

7. Anne Case and Angus Deaton, *Deaths of Despair and the Future of Capitalism*; Gina Kolata and Sabrin Tavernise, "It's Not Just Poor White People Driving a Decline in Life Expectancy"; Paul Krugman, "America's Red State Death Trap."

Bibliography

Archival Collections and Abbreviated Titles

ABMC: American Battle Monuments Commission.

ADAH: Alabama Department of Archives and History, Montgomery, AL.

AGRC: Albert Gore Research Center, Middle Tennessee State University, Murfreesboro, TN.

ANRC: Records of the American National Red Cross, National Archives II, College Park, MD.

Avery: Avery Research Center Archives, College of Charleston, SC.

Burial Case File: Records of the Quartermaster General—Burial Case Files, RG 92, 1915–39, NM 81, E1942, HM 1997 National Archives II, College Park, MD.

BTV: Behind the Veil Oral History Project, David M. Rubinstein Rare Book and Manuscript Library, Duke University, Durham, NC.

CB: Records of the Children's Bureau, Record Group 102, National Archives II, College Park, MD.

DCW: Davidson County Wills, Tennessee State Library and Archives (TSLA), Nashville, TN.

Duke: Duke University Archives, Rare Book, Manuscript, and Special Collections Library, Durham, NC.

Emory: Stuart A. Rose Manuscript, Archives, and Rare Book Library, Emory University, Atlanta, GA.

FWP: Federal Writers' Project, Works Progress Administration, Library of Congress. https://www.loc.gov/.

GSA: Georgia State Archives, Morrow, GA.

LVA: Library of Virginia, Richmond, VA.

LSU: Louisiana State University Special Collections, Hill Memorial Library, Louisiana State University, Baton Rouge, LA.

MPL: Memphis Public Library, Memphis and Shelby County Room, Memphis, TN.

MDAH: Mississippi Department of History and Archives, Jackson, MS.
MSRC: Moorland-Spingarn Research Center, Howard University, Washington DC.
METRO: Nashville Metro Archives, Nashville Public Library, Nashville, TN.
NARA: National Archives and Records Administration, II, College Park, MD.
NARA-SE: National Archives and Records Administration, Southeast, Morrow, GA.
NCSL: Courtesy of the State Archives of North Carolina, Raleigh, NC.
Patrick County HS: Patrick County (VA) Historical Society
RCA: Rutherford County Archives, Murfreesboro, TN.
SUSC: Samford University, Special Collection, Birmingham, AL.
SCHS: South Carolina Historical Society, Charleston, SC.
SCL: South Caroliniana Library, University of South Carolina, Columbia, SC.
SBHLA: Southern Baptist Historical Library and Archives, Nashville, NC.
UNC: Southern Historical Collection, Wilson Library, The University of North Carolina, Chapel Hill, NC.
TSLA: Tennessee State Library and Archives, Nashville, TN.
TU: Tuskegee University, Special Collections, Tuskegee, AL.
UMSC: University of Memphis Library and Special Collections, Mississippi Valley Room, Memphis, TN.
VHS: Virginia Historical Society, Richmond, VA.

Oral Interviews Housed at AGRC (Other Oral Interviews Cited in Notes)

Frank Essex to Kristine M. McCusker and James H. Williams, September 10, 2008, and September 18, 2008.
Bernard R. Fielding Sr. to Kristine M. McCusker and Lauren Pate, August 2, 2010.
Jerry Gaither to Kristine M. McCusker, October 29, 2009.
Revonda Rucker to Kristine M. McCusker, October 13, 2009.
Mary Scales to Kristine M. McCusker, November 9, 2005.
John C. Scarborough III to Kristine M. McCusker and Lauren Pate, August 4, 2010.
William J. Willis and Dorothy S. Willis to Kristine M. McCusker, July 20, 2010.

Published Primary Sources

American Folklore Society. "Mortuary Customs and Beliefs of South Carolina Negroes." *Journal of American Folklore* 7, no. 27 (Oct.–Dec. 1894): 318–319.
American Overseas Military Cemeteries and Memorials. Washington, DC: The American Battle Monuments Commission, 1959.
Andress, Treeby Miller. *When I was a Little Girl: Memoirs of My Life and Family.* Edited by Thad Andress. N.p., Privately published, 2010.
Armstrong, Louis. *Satchmo: My Life in New Orleans.* New York: Da Capo Press, 1986.
Beales, LeVern. *Statistical Abstract of the United States 1939.* (Washington, DC: United States Government Printing Office, 1940).
Bethune, Mary McLeod. *Building a Better World: Essays and Selected Documents,* edited by Audrey Thomas McCluskey and Elaine M. Smith. Bloomington: Indiana University Press 1999.

Boatright, Mody C., and Donald Day, eds. *From Hell to Breakfast.* Publications of the Texas Folklore Society, no. 19 (1944): 21–28.

Bolsterli, Margaret Jones. *Born in the Delta: Reflections on the Making of a Southern White Sensibility.* Knoxville: University of Tennessee Press, 1991.

Boyd, Charles E. *Haysop: A Church, A Community, A People of Haysop Creek, Bibb County, Alabama.* Birmingham, AL: Banner Press, 1979.

Bronk, Mitchell. *Light in the Valley: Messages of Christian Hope and Consolation.* Philadelphia: The Judson Press, 1932.

Brown, James Seay. *Up Before Daylight: Life Histories from the Alabama Writers' Project, 1938–1939.* Tuscaloosa: University of Alabama Press, 1982.

Brown, Roy N. *Public Poor Relief in North Carolina.* Chapel Hill: University of North Carolina Press, 1928 (Arno Press Reprint, 1976).

Burial Ritual: Association Confederate Soldiers [sic], Tennessee Division. Nashville: Marshall and Bruce Co., 1913. TSLA.

Calderon, Erma with Leonard Ray Tell. *Erma: A Black Woman Remembers, 1912–1980.* New York: Random House, 1981.

Campbell, Marie. *Folks Do Get Born.* New York: Rinehart Publishing, 1946.

Cannon County High School. *Old'uns' Stories Told to Young'uns.* Woodbury, TN: Self-published, 2008.

Casey, Joe and Jewel, and O. B. and Joyce Wilkinson. *J. C. Moore and Sons Funeral Home Records, 1931–1966, Winchester, Tennessee.* Tullahoma, TN: Self-Published, July 1992.

Cash, W. J. *The Mind of the South.* New York: A. A. Knopf, 1941.

Chafe, William H., Raymond Gavins, and Robert Korstad. *Remembering Jim Crow: African Americans Tell About Life in the Segregated South.* New York: The New Press for the Behind the Veil Project, 2001.

Cobb, James C., ed. *The Mississippi Delta and the World: The Memoirs of David L. Cohn.* Baton Rouge: Louisiana State University Press, 1995.

Curry, Doris F. *Record of Wills Book B, Clayton County, Georgia, 1921–1940.* Riverdale: Pea Ridge Publications, n.d.

Davison, Sue Allen. *Steeples on the Riverbend: The Story of East Gadsden Baptist Church.* Tallahassee: Father and Son Publishing, 1991.

Dixon, A. C. *The Bright Side of Death.* Binghamton, NY: John Young, Publisher, 1938.

Dodd, Ruth A. "Opportunities of the Rural Public Health Nurse to Develop Child Hygiene." *Southern Medical Journal* 13 (1920): 658–662.

Dollard, John. *Caste and Class in a Southern Town.* New York: Doubleday, 1957.

Dowling, Oscar. "Some Phases of Rural Health." *New Orleans Medical and Surgical Journal* 75 (1922–1923): 424–425.

Dublin, Louis I. "The Full-Time Health Officer: His Importance in Local Health Administration and in the Advancement of Rural Hygiene." *Public Health Reports* 29, no. 1 (January 2, 1914): 13–19.

_____. "The Reporting of Disease, The Next Step in Life Conservation." *Public Health Reports* 29, no. 25 (June 19, 1914): 1611–1619.

_____. "The Improvement and Extension of the Registration Area." *Publications of the American Statistical Association* 14, no. 110 (June 1915): 578–582.

———. "The Present Status of Birth Registration in American Cities and its Relation to the Infant Mortality Rate." *Publications of the American Statistical Association* 15, no. 117 (March 1917): 533–547.

———. "Life, Death, and the Negro." *American Mercury* XII (September 1927): 42–43.

———. "The Health of the Negro." *Annals of the American Academy of Political and Social Science* 140 (November 1928): 77–85.

Dublin, Louis I., and Edwin W. Kopf. "An Experiment in the Compilation of Mortality Statistics." *Publications of the American Statistical Association* 13, no. 104 (December 1913): 639–647.

———. "The Improvement of Statistics of Cause of Death Through Supplementary Inquiries to Physicians." *Publications of the American Statistical Association* 15, no. 114 (June 1916): 175–191.

Dublin, Louis I., and Jessamine Whitney. "On the Costs of Tuberculosis." *Quarterly Publications of the American Statistical Association* 17, no. 132 (December 1920): 441–450.

Du Bois, W. E. B. *The Souls of Black Folk.* New York: Signet Classic, 1969.

Durr, Virginia Foster. *Outside the Magic Circle.* Tuscaloosa: University of Alabama Press, 1985.

Emmons, Martha. "Walk Around My Bedside." *Publications of the Texas Folk-lore Society* 13 (1937), 130–136.

Faulkner, William. *As I Lay Dying.* New York: Random House, 1957.

Federal Writers' Project of the Works Progress Administration. *Mississippi: A Guide to the Magnolia State.* New York: Hastings House Publishers, 1938.

———. *These Are Our Lives: As Told by the People and Written by Members of the Federal Writers' Project of the Works Progress Administration in North Carolina, Tennessee, and Georgia.* Chapel Hill: University of North Carolina Press, 1939.

Fields, Mamie Garvin, with Karen Fields. *Lemon Swamp and Other Places.* New York: The Free Press, 1983.

Fisker, Irving, and Eugene Lyman Fisk. *How to Live: Rules for Healthy Living Based on Modern Science. Authorized and Prepared by the Hygiene Reference Board of the Life Extension Institute, Inc.* New York: Funk and Wagnalls Co., 1916.

Frankel, Lee K. "Conservation of Life by Life Insurance Companies." The Annals of the American Academy of Political and Social Science 70 (March 1917): 77–91.

Frankel, Lee K., and Louis I. Dublin. "A Sickness Survey of North Carolina." *Public Health Reports* 31, no. 41 (October 13, 1916): 2820–2844.

Franklin, Lisa R. *Benson Funeral Home Records.* Privately Published. Georgia State Archives.

Freud, Sigmund. "Mourning and Melancholia." In *The Standard Edition of the Complete Psychological Works of Sigmund Freud,* edited by James Strachey. London: Hogarth Press, 1957.

Gebhart, John C. *Funeral Costs: What They Average; Are They Too High? Can They Be Reduced?* New York: G.P. Putnam and Sons, 1928.

The Georgia State Memorial Book, Adopted as the Official Record by the Military Dept., State of Georgia, compiled by Bert A. Boss. American Memorial Publishing Co., 1921. GSA.

Goldberger, Joseph A., G. A. Wheeler, and Edgar Sydenstricker. "A Study of the Relation of Family Income and Economic Factors to Pellagra Incidence in Seven Cotton Mill Villages of South Carolina in 1916." *Public Health Record* 35 (November 12, 1920): 2963–2701.

Gover, Mary. *Mortality Among Negroes in the United States.* Washington, DC: United States Government Printing Office, 1928.

Guzman, Jessie Parkhurst. *Negro Year Book: A Review of Events Affecting Negro Life, 1941–1946.* Tuskegee, AL: Tuskegee Institute, 1947. TU.

Hagood, Margaret Jarman. *Mothers of the South: Portraiture of the White Tenant Farm Woman.* Chapel Hill: University of North Carolina Press, 1939.

Hemphill, W. Edwin, ed. *Gold Star Honor Roll of Virginia in the Second World War.* Charlottesville: Virginia World War II History Commission, 1947.

Holcombe, Arthur N. "Report on Recent Social Trends in the United States." *The American Political Science Review* 27, no. 2 (April 1933): 222–227.

Hulett Funeral Home: Records of Funerals, Volume 1, 01 January Through 31 December 1924. Hattiesburg: South Mississippi Genealogical and Historical Society, January 1, 2004.

Johnson, Charles S. *Shadow of the Plantation.* Chicago: University of Chicago Press, 1934.

_____. *Growing Up in the Black Belt: Negro Youth in the Rural South.* New York: Schocken Books, 1941.

Johnson, James Weldon. *Along This Way.* New York: Viking Press, 1934.

_____. *The Autobiography of an Ex-Coloured Man.* New York: Alfred A. Knopf, 1979.

Jones, J. J. *If A Man Die.* New York: George H. Doran Company, 1918.

Jones, Mother (Mary G. Harris). *The Autobiography of Mother Jones.* Edited by Mary Field Parton. Chicago: Charles H. Kerr and Co., 1925. http://digital.library.upenn.edu/women/jones/autobiography/autobiography.html.

Kelly, Thomas E., and Evan B. Johnson. *The Evolution of the American Funeral Director.* New York: Traverauld Press, 1934.

Kester, John Marcus. *The Life Beyond Death.* Nashville, TN: Sunday School Board of the Southern Baptist Convention, 1930.

Kytle, Elizabeth, ed. *Willie Mae: A Poignant First-Person Account of a Black Woman's Life in the Segregated South.* Athens: University of Georgia, 1993.

Kubler-Ross, Elizabeth. *On Death and Dying.* New York: Routledge, 1969.

Le Guin, Charles A., ed. *A Home-Concealed Woman: The Diaries of Magnolia Wynn Le Guin, 1901–1913.* Athens: University of Georgia Press, 1990.

Lilienthal, David E. *The Journals of David E. Lilienthal: The TVA Years, 1939–1945.* New York: Harper and Row, 1964.

Logan, Onnie Lee. *Motherwit: An Alabama Midwife's Story.* Edited by Katherine Clark. New York: Dutton, 1989.

Lumpkin, Grace. *To Make My Bread.* Edited by Suzanne Sowinska. Urbana: University of Illinois Press, 1995.

Lumpkin, Katherine DuPre. *The Making of a Southerner.* Westport, CT: Greenwood Press, 1971.

Marsh, Helen C., and Timothy R. Marsh. *Hoover Funeral and Burial Records of Bedford County, Tennessee.* Easely: Southern Historical Press, 1989.

McDaniel, Douglass Scarborough. *Stewardship of Sorrow.* Nashville, TN: Broadman Press, 1930.

Meyer, Agnes E. *Journey Through Chaos.* New York: Harcourt, Brace and Company, 1943.

Michael, Dorothy Jean. "Grave Decoration." *Publications of the Texas Folk-lore Society* (1943): 139–136.

Miller, Caroline. *Lamb in His Bosom.* Dunwoody, GA: Norman S. Berg, 1933.

Mitchell, Margaret. *Lost Laysen.* Edited by Debra Freer. New York: Scribner, 1996.

Mitford, Jessica. *The American Way of Death.* New York: Simon and Schuster, 1963.

Murray, Pauli. *Proud Shoes: The Story of an American Family.* New York: Perennial, 1987.

_____. *Pauli Murray: The Autobiography of a Black Activist, Feminist, Lawyer, Priest, and Poet.* Knoxville: University of Tennessee Press, 1989.

Mustard, Harry S. *Cross-sections of Rural Health Progress; Report of the Commonwealth Fund Child Health Demonstration in Rutherford County, Tennessee, 1924–1928.* New York: The Commonwealth Fund, Division of Publications, 1930.

National Emergency Council. *Report on Economic Conditions of the South.* July 25, 1938.

New York Times. "National Society to Conserve Life; Life Extension Institute Formed to Teach Hygiene and Prevention of Disease." December 13, 1913. https://timesmachine.nytimes.com/timesmachine/1913/12/30/100415073.html?pageNumber=2.

Niebuhr, H. Richard. *The Social Sources of Denominationalism.* New York: Henry Holt and Company, 1929.

Official Annual: Civilian Conservation Corps, "C" District, CCC Fourth Corps Area. Baton Rouge, LA: Direct Advertising Company 1937.

Parsons, Elsie Clews. *Folk-lore of the Sea Islands.* Cambridge, MA: American Folk-lore Society, 1923.

Percy, William Alexander. *Lanterns on the Levy: Recollections of a Planter's Son.* Baton Rouge: Louisiana State University Press, 1974.

Porter, Katherine Anne. *Pale Horse, Pale Rider.* New York: Signet Classic, 1962.

Post, Emily. *Etiquette in Society, in Business, in Politics and at Home.* New York: Funk and Wagnalls, 1922.

_____. *Etiquette: The Blue Book of Social Usage.* New York: Funk and Wagnalls Company, 1945.

Powdermaker, Hortense. *After Freedom: A Cultural Study in the Deep South.* New York: Viking Press, 1939.

President's Research Committee on Social Trends. *Recent Social Trends in the United States.* New York: McGraw-Hill Book Company, Inc., 1933.

Quisenberry Funeral Home, 1931–1954. Athens, TN: McMinn County Historical Society, 2005.

Ragland, Mary Lois Sheffield. *Fisher Funeral Home Records.* N.p.: Privately Printed, 2005.

Rice, Sarah. *He Included Me: The Autobiography of Sarah Rice.* Edited by Louise Westling. Athens: University of Georgia Press, 1989.

Ritchie, Jean. *Singing Family of the Cumberlands.* Lexington: University of Kentucky Press, 1988.

Roach, Vicki B. *McPeters Funeral Records, 1916–1919.* Corinth, MS: Alcorn City Genealogy Society, n.d.

Roberts, Elizabeth. *Drums and Shadows: Survival Studies Among the Georgia Coastal Negroes.* Athens, GA: Works Projects Administration, 1940.

Rodgers, Carrie. *My Husband Jimmie Rodgers.* 2nd ed. Nashville, TN: Country Music Hall of Fame, 1995.

Russell, Sally, ed. *Roots and Ever Green: The Selected Letters of Ina Dillard Russell.* Athens: University of Georgia Press, 1999.

Schlesinger, Arthur M. *Learning How to Behave: A Historical Study of American Etiquette Books.* New York: Cooper Square Publishers, Inc., 1968.

Smith, Lillian. *Killers of the Dream.* New York: W. W. Norton, 1949.

Smith, Simon J., and Fanna K. Bee. *Canaan-Garden Spot by the Cuttacochee, 1818–1968.* Birmingham, AL: Lakeshore Press, 1971.

Stutman, Suzanne, ed. *My Other Loneliness: Letters of Thomas Wolfe and Aline Bernstein.* Chapel Hill: University of North Carolina Press, 1983.

Sulzby, James F. *Annals of the Southside Baptist Church, Birmingham, Alabama, 1886–1936.* Birmingham: Birmingham Print Company, 1947.

Sydenstricker, Edgar, and Dorothy Wiehl. "A Study of the Incidence of Disabling Sickness in a South Carolina Mill Village." *Public Health Reports* 39 (July 18, 1924): 1723–1724.

Terman, Lewis. "Social Hygiene: The Real Conservation Problem." *The North American Review* 198, no. 614 (September 1913): 404–412.

Terrill, Tom E., and Jerrold Hirsch, eds. *Such As Us: Southern Voices of the Thirties.* Chapel Hill: University of North Carolina Press, 1978.

Torrey, R. A. *Death Defeated and Defied: A Message of Comfort, Consolation and Cheer.* Los Angeles: Bible Institute of Los Angeles, 1923. SBHLA.

Twelve Southerners. *I'll Take My Stand: The South and the Agrarian Tradition.* New York: Harper, 1930.

United States Department of Commerce. *Statistical Abstract of the United States: 1929, 51st Number.* Washington, DC: United States Government Printing Office, 1929.

Voyles, Edsel F. *Pence Funeral Home Conway, Arkansas, 1916–1945.* Conway: Arkansas Research, 1989.

Wells, Ida B. *Southern Horrors: Lynch Law in all its Phases.* The New York Age, 1892.

Welty, Eudora. *One Writer's Beginnings.* Cambridge: Harvard University Press, 1984.

White, Walter. *A Man Called White: The Autobiography of Walter White.* New York: Viking, 1948.

Wilkinson, O. B., ed. *Daves Culbertson Funeral Home, 1941–1946.* Tullahoma, TN: Self-published, 1993.

Williamson, B. B., Jr. *Livingston First Baptist Church, Livingston, Alabama: 1834–1984.* Livingston: Sumter Graphics, 1984.

Wolfe, Thomas. *The Letters of Thomas Wolfe to His Mother.* Edited by C. Hugh Holman and Sue Fields Ross. Chapel Hill: University of North Carolina, 1968.

Work, Monroe N. *Negro Year Book: An Annual Encyclopedia of the Negro, 1918–1919.* Tuskegee, AL: Negro Year Book Publishing Company, Tuskegee Institute, 1919.

_____. *Negro Year Book: An Annual Encyclopedia of the Negro, 1921–1922.* Tuskegee, AL: The Negro Year Book Publishing Company, 1922.

______. *Negro Year Book: An Annual Encyclopedia of the Negro, 1925–1926*. Tuskegee, AL: Negro Year Book Publishing Company, 1925.

The WPA Guide to Tennessee. Knoxville: University of Tennessee Press, 1986 [1939].

Wright, Richard. *Black Boy: A Record of Childhood and Youth*. New York: Harper Brothers, 1945.

______. *Native Son*. New York: Perennial, 2003.

Secondary Sources

Albertson, Chris. *Bessie: Empress of the Blues*. London: Sphere Books, 1972.

Aries, Philippe. *The Hour of Our Death*. New York: Knopf, 1981.

Aronson, Louise. *Elderhood: Redefining Aging, Transforming Medicine, Reimagining Life*. New York: Bloomsbury Press, 2019.

Ball, Edward. *The Sweet Hell Inside: The Rise of an Elite Black Family in the Segregated South*. New York: Harper Perennial, 2002.

Barbeau, Arthur Edward, and Florette Henri. *The Unknown Soldiers: Black American Troops in World War I*. Philadelphia: Temple University Press, 1974.

Barry, John M. *The Great Influenza: The Story of the Deadliest Pandemic in History*. New York: Penguin Books, 2005.

Beardsley, Edward H. *A History of Neglect: Health Care for Blacks and Mill Workers in the Twentieth-Century South*. Knoxville: University of Tennessee Press, 1987.

Benson, Susan Porter. *Counter Cultures: Saleswomen, Managers, and Customers in American Department Stores, 1890–1940*. Urbana: University of Illinois Press, 1987.

Boss, Pauline. *Ambiguous Loss: Learning to Live with Unresolved Grief*. Cambridge: Harvard University Press, 1999.

Bowman, Leroy. *The American Funeral: A Study in Guilt, Extravagance, and Sublimity*. Washington, DC: Public Affairs Press, 1959.

Brackney, William H. *Baptist Life and Thought: A Source Book*. Revised edition. Valley Forge, PA: Judson Press, 1998.

Budreau, Lisa M. *Bodies of War: World War I and the Politics of Commemoration in America, 1919–1933*. New York: New York University Press, 2010.

Bundles, A'Lelia. *On Her Own Ground: The Life and Times of Madame C. J. Walker*. New York: Scribner, 2001.

Byerly, Carol R. *Fever of War: The Influenza Epidemic in the U.S. Army during World War I*. New York: New York University Press, 2005.

Case, Anne, and Angus Deaton. *Deaths of Despair and the Future of Capitalism*. Princeton: Princeton University Press, 2020.

Claridge, Laura. *Emily Post: Daughter of the Gilded Age, Mistress of American Manners*. New York: Random House Books, 2008.

Cobb, James C. *The Most Southern Place on Earth: The Mississippi Delta and the Root of Regional Identity*. New York: Oxford University Press, 1992.

Cohen, Lizabeth. *Making A New Deal: Industrial Workers in Chicago, 1919–1939*. Cambridge: Cambridge University Press, 2014.

Collingham, Lizzie. *The Taste of War: World War II and the Battle for Food*. New York: Penguin, 2011.

Cox, Karen L. *Dixie's Daughters: The United Daughters of the Confederacy and the Preservation of Confederate Culture.* Gainesville: University of Florida Press. 2003.

Crissman, James K. *Death and Dying in Central Appalachia: Changing Attitudes and Practices.* Urbana: University of Illinois Press, 1994.

Dailey, Jane, Glenda Elizabeth Gilmore, and Bryant Simon, eds. *Jumpin' Jim Crow: Southern Politics from Civil War to Civil Rights.* Princeton, NJ: Princeton University Press, 2000.

Downey, Kirsten. *The Woman Behind the New Deal: The Life of Frances Perkins, Secretary of Labor and FDR's Moral Conscience.* New York: Doubleday, 2009.

Dunn, Durwood. *Cades Cove: The Life and Death of a Southern Appalachian Community, 1818–1937.* Knoxville: University of Tennessee Press, 1988.

Edgar, Walter, ed. *The South Carolina Encyclopedia.* Columbia: University of South Carolina Press for the Humanities Council, 2006.

Farrell, James J. *Inventing the American Way of Death, 1830–1920.* Philadelphia: Temple University Press, 1980.

Faulkner, Audrey Olsen, Marsel A. Heisel, Wendell Holbrook, and Shirley Geismar, eds. *When I Was Comin' Up: An Oral History of Aged Blacks.* Hamden, CT: Archon Books, 1982.

Faust, Drew Gilpin. *This Republic of Suffering: Death and the American Civil War.* New York: Knopf, 2008.

Filene, Benjamin. *Romancing the Folk: Public Memory and American Roots Music.* Chapel Hill: University of North Carolina Press, 2000.

Flamming, Douglas. *Creating the Modern South: Millhands and Managers in Dalton, Georgia, 1884–1984.* Chapel Hill: University of North Carolina Press, 1992.

Flynt, Wayne. *Alabama Baptists: Southern Baptists in the Heart of Dixie.* Tuscaloosa: University of Alabama Press, 1998.

Friend, Craig Thompson, and Lorri Glover, eds. *Death and the American South.* Cambridge: Cambridge University Press, 2014.

Gilmore, Glenda. *Gender and Jim Crow: Women and the Politics of White Supremacy in North Carolina, 1896–1920.* Chapel Hill: University of North Carolina, 1996.

Goff, James R. *Close Harmony: A History of Southern Gospel.* Chapel Hill: University of North Carolina Press, 2002.

Grantham, Dewey. *Southern Progressivism: The Reconciliation of Progress and Tradition.* Knoxville: University of Tennessee Press, 1983.

Greene, Alison Collis. *No Depression in Heaven: The Great Depression, the New Deal, and the Transformation of Religion in the Delta.* New York: Oxford University Press, 2016.

Haberstein, Robert W., and William M. Lamers. *The History of American Funeral Directing.* 2nd edition. Milwaukee, WI: Bulfin Press, 1962.

Hair, William Ivey. *The Kingfish and His Realm: The Life and Times of Huey Long.* Baton Rouge: Louisiana State University Press, 1996.

Hall, Jacquelyn Dowd, James L. Leloudis, Robert R. Korstad, Mary Murphy, and Lu Ann Jones. *Like A Family: The Making of a Southern Cotton Mill World.* Chapel Hill: University of North Carolina Press, 2012.

Hempton, David. *Methodism: Empire of the Spirit.* New Haven: Yale University Press, 2005.

Higginbotham, Evelyn Brooks. *Righteous Discontent: The Women's Movement in the Black Baptist Church, 1880–1920.* Cambridge: Harvard University Press, 1993.

Hobsbawm, Eric, and Terence Ranger, eds. *The Invention of Tradition.* New York: Cambridge University Press, 1983.

Hochschild, Adam. *To End All Wars: A Story of Loyalty and Rebellion, 1914–1918.* Boston: Houghton Mifflin Harcourt, 2011.

Hoffschwelle, Mary. *The Rosenwald Schools of the American South.* Gainesville: University of Florida Press, 2006.

Holloway, Karla F. C. *Passed On: African American Mourning Stories.* Durham, NC: Duke University Press, 2003.

Huber, Patrick. *Linthead Stomp: The Creation of Country Music in the Piedmont South.* Chapel Hill: University of North Carolina Press, 2008.

Jordan, Terry G. *Texas Graveyards: A Cultural Legacy.* Austin: University of Texas Press, 1993.

Katznelson, Ira. *Fear Itself: The New Deal and the Origins of Our Time.* New York: Liveright Publishing Corporation, 2013.

Keister, Douglas. *Forever Dixie: A Field Guide to Southern Cemeteries and Their Residents.* Salt Lake City, UT: Gibbs Smith, 2008.

Keith, Jeanette. *Rich Man's War, Poor Man's Fight: Race, Class, and Power in the Rural South During the First World War.* Chapel Hill: University of North Carolina Press, 2004.

Kennedy, David M. *Over Here: World War I and American Society.* New York: Oxford University Press, 1980.

_____. *Freedom from Fear: The American People in Depression and War, 1929–1945.* New York: Oxford University Press, 1999.

Kraut, Alan M. *Goldberger's War: The Life and Work of a Public Health Crusader.* New York: Hill and Wang, 2004.

Kuhn, Clifford M., Harlon E. Joye, and E. Bernard West. *Living Atlanta: An Oral History of the City, 1914–1948.* Athens: Atlanta Historical Society/University of Georgia, 1990.

Laderman, Gary. *The Sacred Remains: American Attitudes Toward Death, 1779–1883.* New Haven: Yale University Press, 1996.

_____. *Rest in Peace: A Cultural History of Death and the Funeral Home in Twentieth-Century America.* New York: Oxford University Press, 2003.

Leonard, Bill J. *Baptists in America.* New York: Columbia University Press, 2005.

Link, William. *The Paradox of Southern Progressivism, 1880–1930.* Chapel Hill: University of North Carolina Press, 1992.

Marvin, Carolyn Ann. *When Old Technologies Were New: Thinking About Electrical Communication in the Late Nineteenth Century.* New York: Oxford University Press, 1990.

Mayer, Robert G. *Embalming: History, Theory, and Practice.* Norwalk, CT: Appleton and Lange, 1990.

McCusker, Kristine M. *Lonesome Cowgirls and Honky-Tonk Angels: The Women of Barn Dance Radio.* Urbana: University of Illinois Press, 2008.

McDonald, Michael J., and John Muldowny. *The TVA and the Dispossessed: The Resettlement of Population in the Norris Dam Area.* Knoxville: University of Tennessee Press, 1982.

McElvaine, Robert S., ed. *Down and Out in the Great Depression: Letters from the Forgotten Man.* Chapel Hill: University of North Carolina, 2008.

Metcalfe, Gayden, and Charlotte Hays. *Being Dead Is No Excuse: The Official Southern Ladies Guide to Hosting the Perfect Funeral.* New York: Miramax Books, 2005.

Moye, J. Todd. *Freedom Flyers: The Tuskegee Airmen of World War II.* New York: Oxford University Press, 2012.

Muncy, Robyn. *Creating a Female Dominion in American Reform, 1890–1935.* New York: Oxford University Press, 1991.

Nichols, Elaine, ed. *The Last Miles of the Way: African-American Homegoing Traditions, 1890-Present.* Columbia: South Carolina State Museum, 1989.

Ownby, Ted. *Subduing Satan: Religion, Recreation, and Manhood in the Rural South, 1865–1920.* Chapel Hill: University of North Carolina Press, 1990.

_____. *American Dreams in Mississippi: Consumers, Poverty, and Culture, 1830–1998.* Chapel Hill: University of North Carolina Press, 1999.

_____, ed. *Manners and Southern History.* Jackson: University Press of Mississippi, 2011.

Pells, Richard. *Radical Visions and American Dreams: Culture and Social Thought in the Depression Year.* Urbana: University of Illinois Press, 2004.

Roberts, Samuel Kelton, Jr. *Infectious Fear: Politics, Disease and the Health Effects of Segregation.* Chapel Hill: University of North Carolina Press, 2009.

Roll, Jarod. *Spirit of Rebellion: Labor and Religion in the New Cotton South.* Urbana: University of Illinois Press, 2010.

Rosenberg, Charles. *The Cholera Years: The United States in 1832, 1849, and 1866.* Chicago: University of Chicago, 1987.

Rosenow, Michael. *Death and Dying in the Working Class, 1865–1920.* Urbana: University of Illinois Press, 2015.

Rothman, Sheila. *Living in the Shadow of Death: Tuberculosis and the Social Experience of Illness in American History.* New York: Basic Books, 1994.

Ruggles, Jeffrey. *Photography in Virginia.* Richmond: Virginia Historical Society, 2008.

Savitt, Todd L., and James Harvey Young, eds. *Disease and Distinctiveness in the American South.* Knoxville: University of Tennessee Press, 1988.

Scott, Michelle R. *Blues Empress in Black Chattanooga: Bessie Smith and the Emerging Urban South.* Urbana: University of Illinois, 2008.

Shesol, Jeff. *Supreme Power: Franklin Delano Roosevelt Versus the Supreme Court.* New York: W. W. Norton and Company, 2011.

Sheumaker, Helen. *Love Entwined: The Curious History of Hairwork in America.* Philadelphia: University of Pennsylvania, 2007.

Sledge, Michael. *Soldier Dead: How We Recover, Identify, Bury and Honor our Military Fallen.* New York: Columbia University Press, 2004.

Smith, Susan. *Sick and Tired of Being Sick and Tired: Black Women's Health Activism in America, 1890–1950.* Philadelphia: University of Pennsylvania Press, 1995.

Smith, Suzanne E. *To Serve the Living: Funeral Directors and the African American Way of Death.* Cambridge: Harvard University Press, 2010.

Stansell, Christine. *City of Women: Sex and Class in New York, 1789–1860.* Urbana: University of Illinois Press, 1986.

Stowe, Steven M. *Doctoring the South: Southern Physicians and Everyday Medicine in the Mid-Nineteenth Century.* Chapel Hill: University of North Carolina Press, 2004.

Susie, Debra. *In the Way of Our Grandmothers: A Cultural View of Twentieth-Century Midwifery in Florida.* Athens: University of Georgia Press, 2009.

Thomas, Karen Kruse. *Deluxe Jim Crow: Civil Rights and American Health Policy, 1935–1954.* Athens: University of Georgia Press, 2011.

Tindall, George Brown. *The Emergence of the New South, 1913–1935.* Baton Rouge: Louisiana State University Press, 1967.

Vlatch, John Michael. *The Afro-American Tradition in Decorative Arts.* Cleveland: Cleveland Museum of Art, 1978.

Ward, Jason Morgan. *Hanging Bridge: Racial Violence and America's Civil Rights Century.* New York: Oxford University Press, 2016.

Weare, Walter B. *Black Business in the New South: A Social History of the North Carolina Mutual Life Insurance Company.* Durham, NC: Duke University Press, 1993.

Wiebe, Robert. *A Search for Order.* New York: Hill and Wang, 1967.

Williams, Calvernetta Beasley. *Historical Archives: The Last Century of the Millennium: The South Carolina Morticians Association, Inc., Formerly Known as The Colored Funeral Directors and Embalmers Association.* Columbia, SC: Benedict College Communications Center, 2002.

Wyatt-Brown, Bertram. The *House of Percy: Honor, Melancholy, and Imagination in a Southern Family.* New York: Oxford University Press, 1994.

Articles

Bailey, Fred Arthur. "John Trotwood Moore and the Partician [s] Cult of the New South." *Tennessee Historical Quarterly* 58, no. 1 (Spring 1999): 16–33.

Brownell, Blaine A. "Birmingham, Alabama: New South City in the 1920s." *Journal of Southern History* 38 (1972): 21–48.

_____. "A Symbol of Modernity: Attitudes toward the Automobile in Southern Cities in the 1920s." *American Quarterly* 24 (March 1972): 20–44.

_____. "The Commercial-Civic Elite and City Planning in Atlanta, Memphis, and New Orleans in the 1920s." *Journal of Southern History* 41, no. 3 (August 1975): 339–368.

Budreau, Lisa M. "The Politics of Remembrance: The Gold Star Mothers' Pilgrimage and America's Fading Memory of the Great War." *Journal of Military History* 72 (April 2008): 371–411.

Crocker, Christopher. "The Southern Way of Death." In *The Not So Solid South: Anthropological Studies in a Regional Subculture,* edited by J. Kenneth Morland. Southern Anthropological Society Proceedings, 4 (1971): 114–129.

Dye, Nancy Schrom, and Daniel Blake Smith, "Mother Love and Infant Death, 1750–1920." *Journal of American History* 73, no. 2 (1986): 329–353.

Fishback, Price V., Michael R. Haines, and Shawn Kantor. "The Impact of New Deal Programs on Black and White Infant Mortality in the South." *Explorations in Economic History* 38 (January 2001): 93–122.

Gordon, Susan L. "Home Front Tennessee: The World War II Experience." *Tennessee Historical Quarterly* 51, no. 1 (Spring 1992): 3–18.

Graham, Stacey. "The Plantation Community Cemetery: Reading Black and White Relationships in the Landscape." *Markers: Annual Journal of the Association for Gravestone Studies* XXXII (2015): 68–91.

Greene, Alison Collis. "The Faith of the 'Flotsam and Jetsam,'" *Journal of Southern Religion* 13 (2011). http://jsr.fsu.edu/issues/vol13/greene.html, Accessed March 7, 2019.

Hasson, Janet S. *Widows, Weepers and Wakes: Mourning in Middle Tennessee.* Nashville, TN: Belle Meade Plantation, 1995.

Hoffert, Sylvia. "'A Very Peculiar Sorrow': Attitudes Toward Infant Death in the Urban Northeast, 1800–1860." *American Quarterly* 39 (1987): 601–616.

Howard, Patricia Brake. "Tennessee in War and Peace: The Impact of World War II on State Economic Trends." *Tennessee Historical Quarterly* 51, no. 1 (Spring 1992): 51–71.

Jeane, D. Gregory. "The Upland South Cemetery: An American Type," *Journal of Popular Culture* 11 (1978): 159–174.

_____. "Folk Art in Rural Southern Cemeteries." *Southern Folklore* 46, no. 2 (1989): 159–174.

Johnson, Charles W. "V for Virginia: The Commonwealth Goes to War." *Virginia Magazine of History and Biography* 100, no. 3 (July 1992): 365–398.

Keith, Jeanette. "The Politics of Southern Draft Resistance, 1917–1918: Class, Race, and Conscription in the Rural South." *Journal of American History* 87, no. 4 (March 2001): 1335–1361.

Maher, Neil. "A New Deal Body Politic: Landscape, Labor, and the Civilian Conservation Corps." *Environmental History* 7, no. 3 (July 2002): 435–461.

Marks, Harry M. "Epidemiologists Explain Pellagra: Gender, Race, and Political Economy in the Work of Edgar Sydenstricker." *Journal of the History of Medicine* 58 (January 2003): 34–55.

Mathews, Donald G. "The Southern Rite of Human Sacrifice." *Journal of Southern Religion* III (2000). http://jsr.fsu.edu/mathews.htm. Accessed July 28, 2022.

McCusker, Kristine M. "Funeral Music and the Transformation of Southern Musical and Religious Cultures, 1935–1945." *American Music* 30, no. 4 (Winter 2012): 426–452.

_____. "From 'Behind the Dark Clouds, The Sun Is Shining' to 'He's Only Away': Condolence Literature and the Emergence of a Modern South, 1913–1945." In *Death and the American South,* edited by Craig Friend and Lori P. Glover. New York: Cambridge University Press, 2014, 207–228.

McDonald, Michael J., and John Muldowny, "Reburying the Dead: Disinterment and Reinterment at TVA's Norris Dam." *East Tennessee Historical Society's Publications* 47 (1975).

Parascandola, John. "From MCWA to CDC—Origins of the Centers for Disease Control and Prevention." *Public Health Reports* 111 (November/December 1996):

549–551. https://www.ncbi.nlm.nih.gov/pmc/articles/PMC1381908/pdf/pubhealthrep00045-0079.pdf. Accessed March 20, 2021.

Patterson, K. David, and Gerald F. Pyl. "The Geography and Mortality of the 1918 Influenza Pandemic." *Bulletin of the History of Medicine* 65 (Spring 1991): 4–21.

Ritterhouse, Jennifer. "The Etiquette of Race Relations in the Jim Crow South." In *Manners and Southern History,* edited by Ted Ownby. Jackson: University Press of Mississippi. 20–44.

Roediger, David. "And Die in Dixie: Funerals, Death, and Heaven in the Slave Community, 1700–1865." *Massachusetts Review* 22:1 (1981): 163–183.

Rogers, O. A. "The Elaine Race Riots of 1919." *Arkansas Historical Quarterly* 19 (Summer 1960): 142–150.

Sealander, Judith. "Curing Evils at Their Source: The Arrival of Scientific Giving." In *Charity, Philanthropy, and Civility in American History,* edited by Lawrence J. Freedman and Mark D. McGarvie. New York: Cambridge University Press, 2003, 217–240.

Seales, Chad E. "An Old Love for New Things: Southern Baptists and the Modern Technology of Indoor Baptisteries." *The Journal of Southern Religion* 13 (2011).

Shaw, Stephanie. "Using the WPA Ex-Slave Narratives to Study the Impact of the Great Depression." *Journal of Southern History* 69, no. 3 (August 2003): 623–658.

Simon, Bryant. "'New Men in Body and Soul': The Civilian Conservation Corps and the Transformation of Males and the Body Politic." In *Gender and the Southern Body Politic,* edited by Nancy Bercaw. Jackson: University Press of Mississippi, 2000, 131–154.

Sparks, Randy J. "The Southern Way of Death: The Meaning of Death in Antebellum White Evangelical Culture." *Southern Quarterly* 44, no. 1 (Fall 2006): 32–50.

Thomas, Karen Kruse. "The Hill-Burton Act and Civil Rights: Expanding Hospital Care for Black Southerners." *Journal of Southern History* 72, no. 4 (November 2006): 823–870.

Trachtenberg, Alan. "Albums of War: On Reading Civil War Photographs." *Representations* 9 (Winter 1985): 1–32.

Wilson, Charles R. "The Southern Funeral Director: Managing Death in the New South." *Georgia Historical Quarterly* 67 (Spring 1983): 49–69.

PhD Dissertations, Newspaper Articles, Paper Presentations, Microfilm Collections, Unpublished Documents, and Other Web Documents

Case, Anne, and Angus Deaton, "Mortality and Morbidity in the 21st Century," https://www.brookings.edu/wp-content/uploads/2017/08/casetextsp17bpea.pdf. Accessed July 11, 2022

Chorley, E. Clowes. "The Antecedents of the American Prayer Book." *The New American Prayer Book: Its History and Contents.* http://anglicanhistory.org/bcp/chorley1929/01.html. Accessed July 11, 2022.

Clouse, Robert A. "The Relocation and Restoration of Lucas Hill Cemetery a Historic Cemetery near the Community of Waugh Montgomery County, Alabama." Office of Archeological Research, University of Alabama, August 4, 2005, 1–60.

Couch, Dale L. "Confluence of Regional Cultures in the Savannah River Basin: Reflections of Settlement Patterns in the Decorative Arts." In *The Savannah River Valley to*

1865: Fine Arts, Architecture, and Decorative Arts, edited by Ashley Callahan. Athens: Georgia Museum of Art/University of Georgia, 2003.

Hetzel, A. M. *History and Organization of the Vital Statistics System.* Hyattsville, MD: National Center for Health Statistics, 1997. https://www.cdc.gov/nchs/data/misc/usvss.pdf. Accessed July 11, 2022.

Kaplan, Emily Kumler. "Reducing Maternal Mortality." *New York Times,* March 5, 2019. https://www.nytimes.com/2019/03/05/well/family/reducing-maternal-mortality.html.

Kliff, Sara, Jessica Silver-Greenburg, and Nicholas Kulish. "Closed Hospitals Leave Rural Patients 'Stranded' as Coronavirus Spreads." *New York Times,* April 26, 2020. https://www.nytimes.com/2020/04/26/us/hospital-closures-west-virginia-ohio.html.

Kolata, Gina, and Sabrin Tavernise. "It's Not Just Poor White People Driving a Decline in Life Expectancy." *New York Times,* November 26, 2019. https://www.nytimes.com/2019/11/26/health/life-expectancy-rate-usa.html.

Krugman, Paul. "America's Red State Death Trap." *New York Times,* December 2, 2019. https://www.nytimes.com/2019/12/02/opinion/life-expectancy-united-states.html.

Lesseig, Corey Todd. "Automobility and Social Change: Mississippi, 1909–1939." PhD dissertation, University of Mississippi, 1997.

Locker, Melissa. "Why You Should Always, Always Pull Over for A Funeral Procession," *Southern Living.* https://www.southernliving.com/culture/pull-over-funeral-procession. Accessed March 11, 2019.

Motley, Clay. "Minnie Pearl and William Faulkner: Southern Music as Part of the Literary Renaissance." Paper presented at the International Country Music Conference, Nashville, TN, May 29, 2010. Hard copy in author's possession.

Rabin, Roni Caryn. "Huge Racial Disparities Found in Deaths Linked to Pregnancy." *New York Times,* May 7, 2019. https://www.nytimes.com/2019/05/07/health/pregnancy-deaths.html.

Rosman, Katherine. "The Story of 'Team Molly,'" *New York Times,* February 21, 2021, updated April 22, 2021. https://www.nytimes.com/2021/02/21/style/team-molly.html.

Runblad, Georgeanne. "From 'Shrouding Woman' to Lady Assistant: An Analysis of Occupational Sex-Typing in the Funeral Home Industry, 1870–1920." PhD dissertation, University of Illinois, 1992.

Stockard, Sam. "Governor Sees End of Covid-19 State of Emergency Coming Soon." *Tennessee Lookout,* April 27, 2021. https://tennesseelookout.com/2021/04/27/governor-sees-end-of-covid-19-state-of-emergency-coming-soon/.

Watkins, James C. "Phase I Cultural Resources Reconnaissance of the Proposed Madison Sewer Line Realignment in Madison County, Alabama." Moundville; Office of Archaeological Research, University of Alabama. Hard copy in author's possession.

Whitehead, Nadia. "The U.S. Thought It was Rid of Hookworm. Wrong." National Public Radio, September 12, 2017. http://www.npr.org/sections/goatsandsoda/2017/09/12/550387650/the-u-s-thought-it-was-rid-of-hookworm-wrong.

Index

Page numbers in italics refer to illustrations and page numbers in bold refer to tables.

KRISTINE M. MCCUSKER is a professor of history, folklore, and ethnomusicology at Middle Tennessee State University. She is the author of *Lonesome Cowgirls and Honky-Tonk Angels: The Women of Barn Dance Radio.*

The University of Illinois Press
is a founding member of the
Association of University Presses.

University of Illinois Press
1325 South Oak Street
Champaign, IL 61820-6903
www.press.uillinois.edu